ENGLISH
GRAMMAR
BOOT CAMP

Anne Curzan, Ph.D.

THE
GREAT
COURSES®

PUBLISHED BY:

THE GREAT COURSES
Corporate Headquarters
4840 Westfields Boulevard, Suite 500
Chantilly, Virginia 20151-2299
Phone: 1-800-832-2412
Fax: 703-378-3819
www.thegreatcourses.com

ANNE CURZAN, PH.D.

Arthur F. Thurnau Professor of English
University of Michigan

A nne Curzan is Arthur F. Thurnau Professor of English at the University of Michigan. She also has faculty appointments in the Department of Linguistics and the School of Education. She received her B.A. in Linguistics with honors from Yale University and both her M.A. and Ph.D. in English Language and Literature from the University of Michigan.

In 2007, Professor Curzan received the University of Michigan's Henry Russel Award, one of the highest honors for midcareer faculty; she also has been honored at Michigan with a Faculty Recognition Award and the John Dewey Award.

Professor Curzan has published on a wide range of topics, including the history of English, language and gender, corpus linguistics, historical sociolinguistics, pedagogy, and lexicography. She is the author of *Fixing English: Prescriptivism and Language History* and *Gender Shifts in the History of English*. She is coauthor, with Michael Adams, of the textbook *How English Works: A Linguistic Introduction*, now in its third edition. She also coauthored, with Lisa Damour, *First Day to Final Grade: A Graduate Student's Guide to Teaching*, also now in its third edition. Professor Curzan's other Great Courses are *The Secret Life of Words: English*

Words and Their Origins and *How Conversation Works: 6 Lessons for Better Communication*.

Professor Curzan served as coeditor of the *Journal of English Linguistics* for nine years and is now a senior consulting editor for the journal. She has been a member of the Usage Panel of *The American Heritage Dictionary of the English Language* since 2005. Professor Curzan shares her insights on language in short videos on the website of Michigan University's College of Literature, Science, and the Arts; on the blog *Lingua Franca* for *The Chronicle of Higher Education*; and on Michigan Radio's weekly segment "That's What They Say." In her spare time, she is an avid runner and triathlete. ∎

TABLE OF CONTENTS

Introduction

Lecture Guides

Lecture 24

Supplemental Material

ENGLISH GRAMMAR BOOT CAMP

Is it *who* or *whom*? When do we use *between* instead of *among*? What is a comma splice or a misplaced modifier—and why do they matter? Is it true that you shouldn't end a sentence with a preposition? This course explores all of these well-known usage questions alongside some less well-known ones, such as whether it's legitimate to criticize the past participle *proven* or the use of *however* at the beginning of a sentence. In each case, you will get clear explanations of the terminology and judicious advice about how to handle the usage issue as a writer and as a speaker.

This course delves into the technical details of everything from pronouns to participles to passives to punctuation with a liveliness that will delight the grammar geek. You will learn why the verb *go* turns into *went* in the past tense, how "go slow" works differently from "feel bad," and whether we really should say "It is I" rather than "It is me." You will have the chance to work through the conundrum of making a possessive out of a noun that ends in *–s* and decide on the proper plural of *emoji*. The course never settles for easy answers, such as "Don't use the passive voice." One entire lecture is devoted to when passive sentences are useful and when they are ineffective, with detailed clarification of when a sentence that might look passive is not passive.

At every turn, the course tells the stories behind the rules. You will never look at a grammar checker's correction of a *which* into a *that* once you know how H.W. Fowler viewed this "rule" when he first introduced it. The rule about not splitting infinitives does not seem to go back to Latin, despite the folklore along those lines, and you'll be surprised by the power of a letter to the editor.

The pronoun *they* has been singular since before Shakespeare could use it (which he did), and it was an 18th-century woman grammarian who introduced the rule that *he* could function generically. Why did the American Dialect Society then vote singular *they* the Word of the Year for 2015? These historical facts bring usage rules to life and give you context to make informed decisions about current usage questions.

To help you make these decisions, the course pulls back the curtain on language authority and provides you an insider's view on judgments by the *American Heritage Dictionary* Usage Panel. It introduces language databases where you can explore your own questions, such as whether *based off* is replacing *based on* (the answer is not yet) and whether published academic writing starts sentences with *And* (the answer is a resounding yes).

By the end of this course, you will be able to use this knowledge of grammar to your advantage as a speaker and writer. You will have a new understanding of what makes writing "choppy"—and how to fix it. And you will see why writing a speech needs to be different from writing an essay to help your audience follow what you're saying.

Have you wondered why the Oxford comma is called the Oxford comma? Or is your concern whether you should enforce the rule about using the Oxford comma? Answers to all such questions await, framed in a way that allows you to approach grammar with meticulous care and a fun sense of exploration. ■

Lecture 1

Why Do We Care about Grammar?

"**A**ptitude is essential; but equally as important is the desire to learn." That sentence was on the usage ballot for the *American Heritage Dictionary of the English Language* (AHD) in fall 2015. All the members of the Usage Panel were asked to vote on the sentence, using these categories: acceptable, somewhat acceptable, somewhat unacceptable, or completely unacceptable. At issue: Is the phrase *equally as* redundant? Fifty-three percent of the panel deemed the sentence unacceptable. The panel tipped toward rejecting the sentence—but was still split. Blurry lines like that are what we'll discuss throughout this course.

About Usage

- The Usage Panel was created by AHD in the late 1960s to give dictionary users guidance about formal writing. The panel surveys a group of highly educated people invested in language. Today, there are about 200 members, including academics, journalists, creative writers, radio personalities, and linguists.

- Members vote on whatever grounds they choose: personal preference, favorite usage guides, data about actual usage, and so on.

- There isn't some objective measure of whether a grammatical construction is acceptable. And judgments about acceptability change over time—as we'll see in this course. This is one of the things that make studying grammar endlessly interesting.

- If you can accept and even embrace the complexity and subtlety of what "acceptable" means when it comes to usage, you can write and edit with even more nuance. It allows you to be *careful* in the best sense of that word: to care about the language and how to use it best in any given situation.

- We can master the usage rules that help us write appropriate and even beautiful prose—and we can recognize where usage guides don't agree because the language is changing or because our sensibilities are changing.

- There are bits of grammar that grammarians have paid a lot of attention to over the decades and made pronouncements about. Two examples are split infinitives and ending sentences with prepositions.

- There are also bits of grammar people haven't noticed as much. An example: Is it "have showed" or "have shown"? No one seems to care right now. Both are acceptable in formal prose. However, that is not the case for everyone with "proved" versus "proven."

An Open Mind

- This course will ask you to keep an open mind—to think about grammar in what may be a new way. That's not to say we should throw out all usage rules we've learned. The conventions of formal, edited English can be very valuable.

- Advice in usage guides, which we'll be covering in this course, helps you to write clearer, more aesthetically pleasing prose. Some rules about formal grammar can help you avoid ambiguity and capture tone and prosody on the page.

- But it's valuable to distinguish "preferable" from "correct" or "the only acceptable thing." It's worth asking questions about a usage rule that has been handed down for generations. Asking those questions and making those distinctions makes us even savvier writers and speakers: We can make deliberate, informed decisions about language we want to use in context.

- Linguists are sometimes accused of being hypocrites because they point out the very humanness of the rules that govern formal, edited English and sometimes their faulty logic, and then often follow those rules when they write books and articles.

- One way to deal with this conundrum is to avoid your pet peeves in your own writing, but resist inappropriately correcting them in the writing of others; for example, you might avoid writing the word *impactful*, but since its use is now widespread, correcting it in the work of others is harder to justify.

Some Terms

- The term *usage* means how words and phrases are used in speech and writing. This is understood broadly to cover pronunciation, word meaning, morphology, syntax, and punctuation.

- *Grammar* is typically used more narrowly in linguistics to cover morphology and syntax (not pronunciation and punctuation). However, some "grammar books" out there cover pronunciation and punctuation

- Both *grammar* and *usage* can be used descriptively to refer to what speakers and writers actually do with the language and to refer to what they should do to demonstrate "good usage" or "good grammar."

Your Inner Grammando and This Course

- The term *grammando* is a great word introduced by Lizzie Skurnick in *The New York Times Magazine*. *Grammando* means "one who constantly corrects others' linguistic mistakes." The example Skurnick gives is, "Cowed by his grammando wife, Arthur finally ceased saying 'irregardless.'"

- If you are someone with an opinionated, fairly outspoken inner grammando, this course will ask you to get in touch with that inner grammando. You can start a dialogue where the two of you can revisit usage questions your inner grammando might think are already settled.

- Why? What are the benefits of this dialogue? It will make you even more careful, with an increased sensitivity to role of context and effects of language change. It will also make you more confident that you aren't getting it wrong when you are helping others with usage

- More importantly, it allows us to understand language difference as difference, not deficit. Language is a key part of culture, and understanding the diversity in our language is an important part of understanding the diversity among speakers. We can help others master the conventions of standard, formal usage without making others feel bad about themselves or their language.

- If you are someone who feels some insecurity about your mastery of grammar, this course asks you to believe that you know more than you think you do. You "know grammar" because you are able to communicate. You may not know all the terminology or all the formal usage rules for written English, but you know a whole lot about how English grammar works.

  - The fun thing about this course is that we will unpack, analyze, and put labels on all of this knowledge that you carry around with you—and talk about the usage rules that may distinguish written English from spoken English.

  - With all of this knowledge, we can be ever more skilled speakers and writers. We'll also learn a lot of great facts about the elaborate system and kooky idiosyncrasies in English grammar.

- The next two lectures address prescriptive and descriptive approaches to grammar. Then, after a quick review of some fundamental terminology about words, phrases, and clauses, we're going to dive into the details of parts of speech and related usage rules.

- The course is loosely organized around the major parts of speech like nouns, verbs, prepositions, conjunctions, and the like. As we talk about how each part of speech works, we'll address the tricky usage issues that come up with that part of speech.

Suggested Reading

Curzan, *Fixing English*.

Gove, ed., *Webster's Third New International Dictionary of the English Language*.

Hartwell, "Grammar, Grammars, and the Teaching of Grammar."

1. How would you define *grammar*?

2. What are three of your biggest pet peeves about usage? As a mental exercise, try making the case for the acceptance of one of your peeves (e.g., using *less* for *fewer* could be seen as a streamlining of the grammar, eradicating an optional distinction without causing confusion).

Why Do We Care About Grammar?

I grew up with a mother who cared deeply about language. I was taught to answer the phone, "This is she speaking." And if, when I came home from school, I fretted, "The other kids are cooler than me," which was probably true, my mother would say, "than I," which I have to say really did not help my coolness factor at all. One of our favorite stories about my mother and grammar happened at my older sister's wedding. My younger sister was giving a toast, and in the middle of the toast she said, "For my husband and I." And my mother, from the back of the room, pipes up, "My husband and me," in the middle of the toast.

It is no wonder that I do what I do. I have been noticing the details of language ever since I was a kid, and when I found linguistics in college, I fell in love with this field. I'm fascinated by and study how the English language works and how it changes, and I'm always asking students to teach me new slang.

I'm also a meticulous copyeditor. I'm the kind of person who notices if a text says "has proved" in one place and then "has proven" in another place, or if the text isn't using commas consistently. In other words, I'm a complete geek about grammar—and I have a feeling that you're here, taking this course, because you also care a lot about language and how to use it well. You're in the right place.

So, to get things started, because we're here to geek out about grammar, let's jump into a specific usage question and see whether we can all agree about what is acceptable usage. Then we can back up and think about who we rely on—or whom we rely on—to make these kinds of calls about acceptability.

I'm going to give you a sentence and I want you to decide if there are any problems with it. You need to rate this sentence, and you have four choices. Your choices are: completely acceptable, somewhat acceptable, somewhat unacceptable, completely unacceptable. Now I do want to note that your decision here should not be about the meaning of the sentence—I don't actually care whether you agree with this sentence or not. The question is whether you think there's anything wrong or funny about the grammar. Are you ready? Here's the sentence: "Experience is equally as valuable as theory." Let me give it to you again. "Experience is equally as valuable as theory."

How did you rate that? Was it in the acceptable category or unacceptable category? Are you bothered by the redundancy of "equally as"? Do you want it to be "Experience is as valuable as theory"? Or did the sentence sound okay to you, not something you would notice as having any particular grammatical issue?

This sentence was on the usage ballot for the *American Heritage Dictionary* in fall of 2015. All the members of the Usage Panel were asked to vote on the sentence using exactly the same categories I just gave you, and with about as much instruction about what acceptability means. I'll tell you about how the Usage Panel voted in a minute, but first let me give you a second related sentence that was on the ballot. Again, I want you to vote completely acceptable, somewhat acceptable, somewhat unacceptable, or completely unacceptable.

Here's the sentence: "Aptitude is essential; but equally as important is the desire to learn." Let me give it to you again. "Aptitude is essential; but equally as important is the desire to learn." Did you find "equally as important" unacceptable? Did you want it to be "equally important"? Or did "equally as important" sound idiomatic to you, like something you might say or write?

Perhaps you're thinking right now this is not yours to decide, whether these two sentences are acceptable or not. What do the experts have to say? Well, in 1926, H. W. Fowler, the well-known grammarian, called "equally as" an "illiterate tautology"—in other words, an illiterate redundancy. Ouch! That feels like pretty strong condemnation for a sentence that perhaps some of you thought was perfectly fine.

Let's look at the usage note on this construction in the *American Heritage Dictionary of the English Language*. The editors updated the usage note after the 2015 usage ballot, and here's what it now says:

> The adverb equally is often regarded as redundant when used in combination with as, as in 'Experience is equally as valuable as theory' or 'Aptitude is essential; but equally as important is the desire to learn.' In our 2015 ballot, the example sentences above were deemed unacceptable by 64% and 53% of the Usage Panel respectively. Even among those panelists who rated the sentences as acceptable, there were several who commented that it would be preferable to avoid the redundancy for stylistic reasons. Fortunately, one can easily streamline sentences such as these, as by deleting equally from the first example and as from the second.

Interesting. Clearly this bit of usage is contested when you're getting percentages like 64 percent, 53 percent. The panel is tipping toward unacceptable, but it's a close fight, almost equally split on "equally as important." Other folks are less happy with "equally as." You'll also notice that some panelists are grappling with what is acceptable versus what they see as preferable for stylistic reasons. They're saying, "Okay, I'm willing to say it's acceptable, but I wish that you'd revise it to make it prettier." If you're thinking that this seems like a blurry line between what is acceptable and what experts prefer, you're right, and it's what we'll be talking about throughout this course.

This seems like a good moment to say that I am on the *American Heritage Dictionary* Usage Panel. I'll fill you in how I voted on those two sentences, but first let me tell you a bit more about the Usage Panel. The panel was created by *American Heritage Dictionary* in the late 1960s to give dictionary users guidance about formal writing by surveying a group of highly educated people invested in language, and that is the main criterion for being on the panel is that you are professionally engaged with language. *American Heritage*, that dictionary, was a response to the hubbub over *Webster's Third New International Dictionary*, which was published in 1961. That dictionary, which tried to be very descriptive in its approach to language, was seen by some, particularly in the United States, as too permissive—it wasn't upholding the standards of the English language.

The editors of *Webster's Third* did things like remove the usage labels, like correct and incorrect, proper and improper, as well as erroneous, and some people did not like those usage labels being gone. *Webster's Third* also wrote about "ain't" in that entry, and here I'm going to quote: "Though disapproved by many and more common in less educated speech, used orally in most parts of the U.S. by many cultivated speakers, especially in the phrase 'ain't I.'"

Now that entry on "ain't" caused an enormous amount of controversy, where people thought that there should be a stronger proscription of "ain't" than recognizing that cultivated speakers use it. As a result, suddenly *Webster's Dictionary* seemed vulnerable. *Webster's*, up to that point, was seen as the dictionary, but now the market seemed open to competitors, and *American Heritage* jumped in and said, "We will help and provide more advice and guidance on formal usage, as well as describing the language."

So they put together this Usage Panel. This panel, at this point, is about 200 people. It's academics from a range of fields, people like: Harold Bloom, Jill Lepore, Henry Louis Gates. There are journalists on it, people like Susan Stamberg. There are creative writers; here are just a few: Maxine Hong Kingston, Sherman Alexie, Rita Dove, Annie Dillard, Junot Diaz. Radio personalities: David Sedaris is on the Usage Panel, as is Garrison Keillor. There's a world-class puzzle creator on the panel; that would be Will Shortz. And until 2016, there was a Supreme Court Justice: Antonin Scalia. All in all on the panel there are about a dozen linguists, one of whom is me. I've been on there since 2005.

As you can see from that list of people, you've got a range of perspectives on this panel, a range of backgrounds, but I'll have to say mostly older, mostly non-linguist. There was actually a funny article in *The New York Times* in 2006 where they were talking about the panel, and they were talking about whether the panel could actually be hip enough the keep up with the English language. And in the article they noted that the youngest member of the panel was Anne Curzan, and the implication seemed to be that she really wasn't all that young.

Now you'll note that, of the perspectives in the group, I bring an unusual one as a linguist. This perspective is less represented, and this is one of the things that makes this course you're taking unusual. You're getting an English professor who is deeply invested in the conventions of standard, edited English, and a linguist who studies how the language works and how it changes. So you will get both the prescriptive guidance and descriptive perspective on the language side by side throughout the course.

Now, what happens when the Usage Panel is given these questions? Well, I have to say, the really unfortunate thing is that we are never all in one room at one time. I think that would be the most fun discussion if we could just debate grammar in a room, all 200 of us.

We get this ballot over e-mail and we all vote in the privacy of our home or office on whatever grounds we want to vote on. Some people vote based on personal preference; other people vote based on their favorite usage guide, which they might have in their office. Some look at data about actual usage. Now, sometimes, when I get the ballot and I read through it, I know exactly what the question is after. It could be about "they," and whether we can use it as a singular, or about the difference between "anxious" and "eager," or perhaps it's "hopefully," and whether we can use that to mean "it is hoped." But sometimes I look at the sentence and I don't know what they're after. For example, I remember a set of questions about "finalize," which it turns out was severely criticized in the 1960s as bureaucratic. It now strikes us as unexceptional.

So, how did I vote this fall on these questions about "equally as"? I got the ballot and I tried, as I always do, to read the sentences in a very open-minded way, as if I was reading something that was already published and it was just on my desk. I read these sentences, and I have to tell you, they struck me as unremarkable, not something that I would correct either as a professor or as an editor. And for those of you who felt that they were unacceptable, I hope that you have now not lost all respect for me, and think I have no standards. So let me just remind you that almost half the Usage Panel was with me on this.

But, I don't just stick with my personal preferences, or what I notice or don't notice; I want to figure out what's actually happening in the language, not just my own opinion. And I have to say, this is a really exciting moment to be able to study usage with online databases. In other words, we can now go online and use these databases for free to see what's actually happening with the language.

For example, if you go to the Google Books Ngram Viewer, you can search millions of books and see what's happening with a word or a phrase. Then there are more linguisticy databases online, including the *Corpus of Contemporary American English* and the *Corpus of Historical American English*, and I'll be relying on both in this course.

For these questions, I went to look at the *Corpus of Contemporary American English*. This corpus is over 500 million running words, which is a huge corpus, and it has 5 different registers in it. Spoken, which is based on transcripts of unscripted radio and television programs—so you have spoken, magazines, fiction, newspapers, and academic prose. You can search words and phrases and see how they compare across those different genres or what's happening over time that that database covers: 1990–2015.

I went into this corpus and search for "equally as," and I found it regularly in published prose. I found it in *The Washington Post*; I found it in the *Harvard Journal of Law and Public Policy*—in other words, places where there are clearly highly educated editors at work, and they let "equally as" got through. Now, it is more common to get something like "equally important" than it is to get "equally as important," but does that make it unacceptable to say "equally as important"? I have to say, I think no, and I voted that these sentences were acceptable.

I, too, think it's probably preferable to edit out the repetition for stylistic reasons, but, all in all, I think those sentences are perfectly acceptable in edited prose, and there are editors who are already letting it through. In other words, I'm trying to isolate the question of: Does the repetition make the sentence wrong? And my answer would be: not inherently. There's nothing inherently wrong with repetition. And you can find other examples in the language where we have no problem with repetition. Think about the expression "each and every." Well that's clearly repetitive, but we see it as usefully emphatic. Think about "terms and conditions." Also repetitive, but can do a kind of emphasis, and one could argue that "equally as" is also emphatic.

I hope that you're thinking right now that this answer I've given you about the acceptability of "equally as" does not make right and wrong sound particularly clear-cut—it's not. There isn't some objective measure of whether a grammatical construction is acceptable. Judgments about acceptability also change over time, as we're going to see throughout this course.

To me, this is one of the things that makes studying grammar endlessly interesting, and I honestly believe that if you can accept and even embrace the complexity and subtlety of what acceptable means when it comes to usage, it allows you to write and edit with even more nuance. It allows you to be careful in the best sense of that word, to care about the language and how to use it best in any given situation. We can master the usage rules that help us write appropriate prose in formal context, and even write beautiful prose, and we can recognize where the usage guides don't agree because the language is changing, or because our sensibilities are changing.

Then, there are bits of grammar people haven't noticed as much. For example, is it "have showed" or "have shown"? No one seems to care right now. Both are standard—acceptable in formal prose. That is not the case for everyone with "have proved" versus "have proven," and if you're now thinking, "Wait a minute, I'm not sure that I make any distinction there," don't worry, we'll come back to that. In the next lecture we'll think in much more detail about the grounds on which people have called some usage right and some usage wrong. Right now I'm just asking you to keep an open mind to thinking about grammar in what may be a new way.

When I say that we should keep an open mind, I'm not saying we should throw out all the usage rules we've learned. The conventions of formal, standard, edited English can be very valuable. First of all, there's just the value of standards in general. It helps that we have standard measurements so that we can all talk about inches and miles or kilometers. It helps that we have standard money. It also can help to have a standard language; it allows us to communicate across dialect differences.

It's also true that some of the advice in usage guides that governs how we write in more formal context, and that we'll be covering in this course, can help you to write clearer, more aesthetically pleasing prose. Some of the rules about formal grammar can help you avoid ambiguity and capture tone and prosody on the page in effective ways. All of this is really important and worth knowing.

But it's valuable to distinguish preferable from correct, or the only acceptable thing. It's worth asking questions about a usage rule that's been handed down for generations to see if we really do want to follow that rule anymore. Asking those questions and making those distinctions makes us even savvier writers and speakers, who are making deliberate, informed decisions about the language we want to use in context. And context is key. Being able to respond to context and adapt your language appropriately is what makes you a skilled writer.

Now linguists like me are sometimes accused of being hypocrites because we point out the very humanness of the rules that govern formal, edited English and sometimes their faulty logic, and then we often follow those rules when we ourselves write books and articles. Fair enough. But of course this is because we recognize the value of the standard like everyone else, and are aware of the expectations and judgments that may come if we don't follow them.

I'm very familiar with this conundrum, as you already know. I'm trained as a linguist and I study both how language changes and where usage rules come from, which means that you become very aware of the human foibles behind some of these rules, and I teach students all about that. At the same time, I'm an English professor whose job it is to make sure students control the conventions of formal, edited English, even the ones that aren't particularly well justified. And, as I mentioned, I'm a copy editor who cares about every comma, and who has pet peeves like everyone else.

So how do I make sense of that? How do I wear these two hats, often at the same time? The answer is that my inner grammando and I have a lot of long talks. Most of us, I think, have an inner grammando. This is a great word which was introduced by Lizzie Skurnick in *The New York Times Magazine* in 2012 in the feature called "That Should Be a Word," and she defines grammando as "one who constantly corrects others' linguistic mistakes." The example she gives is: "Cowed by his grammando wife, Arthur finally ceased saying irregardless." I have to say, I really prefer grammando to grammar Nazi, which is the other term we have for people who correct other people's grammar. If we're going to talk about Nazis, let's talk about Nazis; if we're talking about people who correct other people's grammar, let's talk about grammandos. And it also gives you the great expression "to go grammando on someone."

We have the things, each of us, that we notice and don't like—our pet peeves—and often we have very strong feelings about these bits of usage. It could be "impact" as a verb or "between you and I" or "drive slow" or "different than" or perhaps "based off" rather than "based on," and some of you are probably cringing right now, there are so many pet peeves to choose from. And we'll talk about all of those and more in this course.

What's fascinating is how strongly we can feel about these. People use words like "hate" and "drives me crazy." When we talk about grammar, it often comes to represent much more than grammar. It can be about whether education is working, about whether people care about the details anymore, about not just if language is in decline but also perhaps if culture more generally is in decline. One of the useful things about being a historian of the language is that I can see the things people hated 100

English Grammar Boot Camp 19

years ago, and 200 years ago, some of which are now standard. I'll share some of these quotes throughout the course to help us keep perspective on the usage issues that are driving us crazy today.

So what don't I like? I don't like the word "impactful"—I think it's ugly. And I prefer "a person who" to "a person that." My inner grammando and I talk about what I'm going to do with these likes and dislikes. I can choose not to use the word "impactful" in my own writing, which I do, choose not to use it. But, given how widespread the term now is in published writing, I don't have good grounds to correct it in other people's writing, and I don't.

Now, I used to correct "the person that" and change it to "the person who," but an astute graduate student pointed that I had no good grounds for doing so. As he pointed out, if you look in standard usage guides it says that it is perfectly acceptable to use "the person that" and I should've known better. As a historian of the language, I should've remembered that "the person that" has a long history in the language. So now I notice things like "the person that" but I keep my pen quiet and I don't circle it. In other words, I recognize what is my thing, and what is a point of usage that might get more widely criticized in formal writing. And if it's my thing, I keep my pen quiet. If there's a chance a student might get criticized for it, I alert them to it.

You have probably noticed that I'm using the word usage a lot, and *American Heritage Dictionary* calls the panel the Usage Panel, not the Grammar Panel. I sometimes like to call this course Grammar Boot Camp, but I'll frequently use the word usage as well. The basic definition of usage is how words and phrases are used in speech and writing. It's understood broadly as encompassing pronunciation; word meaning; morphology—in other words, the structure and form of words, including inflectional endings, a question like "Is funnest okay?" Usage also encompasses syntax—how words combine into sentences—as well as punctuation.

Grammar—that word is typically used more narrowly in linguistics to cover morphology and syntax, so not pronunciation and punctuation. But certainly you will find popular grammar books out there that cover pronunciation and punctuation. Both grammar and usage can be and are used descriptively to refer to what speakers and writers actually do with the language, and more prescriptively to refer to what speakers and writers should do with the language to demonstrate good usage or good grammar. The next two lectures will unpack this more prescriptive approach and more descriptive approach to grammar and usage in more detail.

For now, let me ask you to do a couple of things as part of being open minded, depending on how you feel about grammar. If you are someone with an opinionated, fairly outspoken inner grammando, I'm asking you to get in touch with your inner grammando and offer up a dialogue where you two can revisit usage questions your inner grammando might think are already settled and hash out how you want to handle them. I'm asking you to push pause before labeling anything right or wrong too quickly as we learn more about where these rules come from and how both the rules and the language may have changed.

Why? What are the benefits of having that dialogue with your inner grammando? It will make you even more careful, with an increased sensitivity to the role of context and effects of language change. It will also make you more confident that you aren't getting it wrong when you are helping other people with usage. More importantly, it allows us to understand language difference as difference, not deficit.

Language is a key part of culture, and understanding the diversity in our language is an important part of understanding the diversity among speakers. We can help others master the conventions of standard, formal usage without making others feel bad about themselves or about their language, which is a very worthy goal. And if you want that to be "feel badly" rather than "feel bad," stay tuned until Lecture 14.

If you are someone who feels some insecurity about your mastery of grammar, I'm asking you to believe me that you know more than you think you do, or than you give yourself credit for. You know English grammar in this really intricate way that allows you to communicate with all the speakers around you. This is the descriptive sense of grammar. You may not have every piece of terminology or all the formal usage rules for written English, but you know a whole lot about how English grammar works.

The fun thing about this course is that we will unpack, analyze, and put labels on all of this knowledge that you carry around with you, and we'll talk about the usage rules that may distinguish written English from spoken English, formal English from informal English. With all of this knowledge, we can be ever more skilled speakers and writers, and along the way you'll learn a lot of great facts about the elaborate system and the kooky idiosyncrasies in English grammar.

The structure of this course is going to work this way. As I mentioned, the next two lectures address prescriptive and descriptive approaches to grammar. Then, after a quick review of some fundamental terminology about words, phrases, and clauses, we're going to dive into the details of different parts of speech and all of the related usage issues that come with them.

I have loosely organized the course around major parts of speech like nouns, verbs, prepositions, conjunctions and the like, and as we talk about how that part of speech works, we'll address the tricky usage issues that come up with that part of speech. For example, can you leave a preposition dangling at the end of a sentence? I know you want to know the answer to that, but you're going to have to patiently wait until Lecture 18 for the answer. And if you're thinking, "Now Anne, that should be 'to wait patiently'— don't split that infinitive and put 'patiently' between 'to' and 'wait.'" If you're thinking that, then you're ready for the next lecture, because we're going to talk about where that rule about split infinitives comes from.

Prescriptivism: Grammar Shoulds and Shouldn'ts

This course has a certain viewpoint: If you speak English fluently, you know English grammar. What you may not have full control of is (1) all the terminology to describe what you know, and (2) the full set of rules that govern formal, standard English. Throughout the course, we'll be covering relevant prescriptive rules as we talk about nouns, adverbs, prepositions, and the like. In this lecture, we'll talk about the authority and history of this approach to grammar

What Grammar Means to Me

- Some writing instructors use an assignment called "What Grammar Means to Me" to learn about the baggage students may be bringing with them. One instructor got this memorable and telling response:

> When someone says the word "grammar" to me, my mind immediately flashes back to my sixth grade English teacher. She was teaching us about prepositions and our class was having trouble grasping it. The following day she brought in a Mickey Mouse figurine and a Barbie playhouse. She proceeded to place Mickey all around the house. "Mickey is BY the house, Mickey is IN the house." She has since scarred me forever by telling us that if we ever placed a preposition at the end of a sentence, Mickey would die. Grammar has terrified me ever since.

- For many people, connotations of grammar include red pens, fear, ignorance, drills, correction, and Mickey Mouse and his imminent demise. They may also think of rules like: Don't end a sentence with a preposition, don't dangle a modifier, and don't split an infinitive. These can build a sense that "I don't know English grammar."

■ This lecture will focus generally on what we will call *prescriptive grammar*: the set of rules that tell us what we should and shouldn't do in formal standard English. *Prescriptive* here means prescribing the do's and don'ts of speaking and writing formal standard English.

Split Infinitives

■ The example of split infinitives will help here. The split infinitive rule is basically: Don't put an adverb between *to* and a verb (i.e., to boldly go, to better understand). The idea is that the infinitive is a single unit and should not be split up.

■ This is one of the strongest prescriptive rules in popular understanding of grammar. However, Oxford lifted the ban in 1998, with its *New Oxford Dictionary of English*. Many style guides have also relaxed—but many editors and teachers have not.

■ Where does this rule come from? One common idea that it comes from Latin, but there is no evidence for that. Some people cite Bishop Lowth's 1762 work on grammar, but it doesn't actually address it.

■ It wasn't possible to split an infinitive until Middle English. There is evidence of split infinitives in the 14th century. For instance, the Wycliffite translation of the Bible includes: "It is good to not eat flesh and to not drink wine." By the 17th century, some writers were trying to avoid it, but there was no explicit rule.

■ Do we split infinitives today? Yes, and some sound idiomatic: to better serve; to better understand. It may also be about a weak-strong rhythm: to boldly go. Some uses are less ideal, such as when we get a lot of material between *to* and the verb: to quickly and effectively but not always consistently grade.

- So here's better advice: It is fine to split infinitives with an adverb; for clarity, one might want to avoid splitting an infinitive with a long adverbial phrase.

- Any idea about "right" and "wrong" when it comes to grammar gets complicated when we learn about the history of prescriptive rules and compare rules to the way that real speakers and writers use the language in real time. Not splitting an infinitive may be the right call for a specific piece of writing, but that doesn't make it universally "right" or how English is "supposed to" work.

The Value of Prescriptive Rules

- It is inaccurate to suggest there is no value to prescriptive rules. Contrary to what some people believe, linguists aren't saying prescriptive rules are bad and everyone should speak and write however they want all the time. However, some linguists can be overly strident in their attempt to challenge the perceived authority of prescriptive rules.

- Prescriptive rules can promote a standard, which has a real value; they can promote aesthetically pleasing kinds of prose, like parallelism; and they can promote clarity. Let's just keep perspective on their value: Be open-minded about the rules' benefits and weaknesses—and be open-minded about other ways to speak and write English, depending on audience and context.

The Scope of Prescriptive Rules

- Prescriptive grammar covers a lot of ground, much more than just syntax. Take as an example Ellie Grossman's book *The Grammatically Correct Handbook*, which touches on pronunciation, spelling as it relates to pronunciation, punctuation, lexical issues, regional differences, morphological issues, Latin plurals, past participles, syntactic issues, and stylistic issues.

- This course will cover that full range, and will usually refer to those as "usage" issues. Relevant questions are: How do we use the language? Is there guidance about how we are supposed to do something? To what extent does something affect spoken and written usage?

- The rules governing these questions are found in a loose network. Many of us were asked to purchase an academic usage guide or dictionary for an English course; examples include:

  □ Strunk and White's *Elements of Style*

  □ Joseph Williams's *Style: Lessons in Clarity and Grace*

  □ H. W. Fowler's *Dictionary of Modern English Usage*

  □ Bryan Garner's *Dictionary of American Usage*.

- Some guides hail from as far back as almost 250 years. The second half of 18th century saw a proliferation of these guides. The guides tend to focus on usage issues where there is variation in usage.

- How do they justify which usage is incorrect? We'll cover this more in future lectures, but there is a range of reasons:

  □ Etymology (a word should mean what it used to mean)

  □ Logic (language should work like math, even though it is not math)

  □ Analogy (English should work like Latin or German)

  □ Purity (English should remain true to its roots, even though it has always been influenced by other languages)

  □ Authority (great writers used the language this way)

  □ Personal taste.

- One grammarian's personal preference can get picked up as a rule in future guides. We'll see this may be the case with the rule about ending a sentence with a preposition.

- We can identify by name some of the earliest grammarians whose opinions about good usage still echo in today's guides. Some examples of influential works:

  □ Joseph Priestley's *Rudiments of English Grammar* (1761). Priestley was the chemist who isolated oxygen—and a clergyman and political theorist, who also wrote a grammar. He tried to move away from Latin models, and was interested in actual usage but still concerned with correctness.

  □ Robert Lowth's *A Short Introduction to English Grammar* (1762). Lowth's image is often framed as the "arch prescriptivist," but has been rehabilitated by Ingrid Tieken-Boon van Ostade.

  □ American lawyer Lindley Murray's *English Grammar* (1795). Murray was more prescriptive than his predecessors. This book went through 65 official editions in about 75 years. His grammar spread the idea that singular they was wrong, and one should use he instead.

  □ Richard Grant White's *Words and Their Uses: Past and Present* (1870). Many point to this as the pinnacle of prescriptivism. The author was a Shakespearean with very strong opinions about usage; for instance, he called the word donate "utterly abominable."

- These examples give us a useful perspective on guidance about usage. Things that may sound terrible to our ears may become unremarkable within a generation or two.

- This doesn't mean that we don't want to avoid usage that others strongly dislike or see as overly informal or low in some contexts.

But we can have the perspective that the judgment is not inherent to the construction—it is something that has been put on it and may change.

Fowler and Roberts

- Compared with White, we can view H. W. Fowler and his *Dictionary of Modern Usage* (1926) as a good-natured prescriptivist. The book is filled with opinions (e.g., *alright* is "not a word").

- He says it is a mistake to assume *none* can only be singular, and he categorizes the prescription against split infinitives under "fetishes" and "superstitions," mocking those who follow the prescription doggedly.

- What would Fowler have thought of Supreme Court Chief Justice John Roberts changing the oath of office when he swore in President Obama in 2008? The original oath includes the words, "I do solemnly swear that I will faithfully execute the office of

the President of the United States" Notice that *faithfully* comes between *will* and *execute*. This is not a split infinitive, but a split verb—and people who feel strongly about one often feel strongly about the other.

- Roberts's version went: "I do solemnly swear that I will execute the office of the President of the United States faithfully." That *faithfully* moved pretty far from where President Obama expected it to be. Both versions are clear and unambiguous—the concern about the verb is not a concern about clarity or even euphony (*faithfully execute* is very colloquial).

- They redid the oath and all was fine. This incident shows the power of rules to shape our sense of what is good and appropriate. It's a good reason to know and understand them—and to have enough information to make informed decisions about when we want to follow them and when we don't.

Suggested Reading

Bailey, "Talking about words: Split Infinitives."
Chapman, "The Eighteenth-Century Grammarians as Language Experts."
Crystal, *The Fight for English*.
Curzan, *Fixing English*.
Finegan, "Usage."
Grossman, *The Grammatically Correct Handbook*.
Nunberg, "The Decline of Grammar."
Ostade, *The Bishop's Grammar*.

Questions to Consider

1. When would you allow a split infinitive, and why?

2. What needs to happen for a usage rule to become inapplicable, irrelevant, or defunct? Who declares a usage rule "over"?

Lecture 2 Transcript

Prescriptivism: Grammar Shoulds and Shouldn'ts

When I teach writing, I sometimes use an assignment called "What Grammar Means to Me" so that I can learn about the baggage that students may be bringing with them when it comes to grammar. One of my colleagues started using this assignment too, and one of his students wrote a truly memorable and telling response, which I want to share with you. So here's the student's response:

> When someone says the word grammar to me, my mind immediately flashes back to my sixth grade English teacher. She was teaching us about prepositions and our class was having trouble grasping it. The following day she brought in a Mickey Mouse figurine and a playhouse. She proceeded to place Mickey all around the house. 'Mickey is by the house, Mickey is in the house.' She has since scarred me forever by telling us that if we ever placed a preposition at the end of a sentence, Mickey would die. Grammar has terrified me ever since.

Poor Mickey. What's amazing to me is how many responses like this one I can get in response to this prompt. The connotations of grammar for many are red pens, fear, ignorance, drills, correction, Mickey Mouse and his imminent demise, rules like: don't end a sentence with a preposition, or dangle a modifier, or split an infinitive. All of these rules can give you the sense that somehow you don't know English grammar.

What I want to do is put a different spin on that. If you speak English fluently, you know English grammar. What you may not have as full control of as you would like to is: one, all the terminology to describe what you know; and two, the full set of rules that govern the more formal standard English—often the written, edited version of that formal standard English.

This lecture will focus generally on what I will call prescriptive grammar, the set of rules that tell us what we should and shouldn't do in formal standard English. It is prescriptive in the sense of prescribing the dos and don'ts of speaking and writing formal English. Throughout the course, we'll be covering the relevant prescriptive rules as we talk about nouns, adverbs, prepositions, and so on. In this lecture, we'll talk more generally about the authority and history of this more prescriptive approach to grammar.

An example will help here: let's talk about split infinitives. One of my favorite stories about split infinitives also comes from a writing class. It was in the first couple of days of class, and I often ask students to tell me about the rules that they know, the rules that they learned in high school. They tell me things like "I know that I shouldn't use the first person when I write an essay for school," and one student said, "I know you shouldn't split an infinitive." And I said, "What's an infinitive?" And she said, "I'm not sure, but I know that you can't split it."

So, just to make sure that we're all on the same page, here's the rule. The rule is that we're not supposed to put an adverb, or anything that's functioning like an adverb, in between the "to" and the verb. Here are some examples of places where we have split the infinitive. "To boldly go," perhaps the most famous split infinitive out there, from Star Trek. Here's another split infinitive: "To better understand." So you can see how the "better" has come between the "to" and "understand." The idea behind the rule is that the infinitive is a single unit. It may be two words—"to" plus, for example, "understand"—but it's a single unit and it should not be split up.

The rule about splitting infinitives is one of strongest prescriptive rules in the popular understanding of grammar. When I looked online, you can find over 100,000 websites that mention or are devoted to split infinitives. There's widespread interest in, and anxiety about, split infinitives. Now, in 1998, Oxford lifted the ban on split infinitives with its *New Oxford Dictionary of English*, and many style guides have actually relaxed this rule. But interestingly, many editors and teachers have not.

Where does this rule about split infinitives come from? There's a common idea out there that the rule comes from Latin: that because in Latin you couldn't split an infinitive, in English you couldn't split an infinitive. But in fact we have no evidence that that's where it comes from. People also sometimes cite Bishop Lowth's very influential 1762 grammar of English, but that grammar, if you read it, actually doesn't address split infinitives.

So where does the rule come from? Well, before I answer that and tell you what we know, let me start by addressing when it first became possible to split an infinitive in English. This wasn't actually possible until later Middle English, so sort of the time of Chaucer, 14th century. In Old English—the time of Beowulf, up until 1050, 1100—in Old English, infinitives were one word. So an infinitive for "swim," for example, was "swimman." S-W-I-M-M-A-N—all one word, therefore it can't be split.

It's not until the 14th century or so that we start to see the "to"-plus-verb construction with regularity for the infinitive, and once that happens, you can split it. For example, in the Wycliffite translation of the Bible we get this sentence: "It is good to not eat flesh and to not drink wine." So you'll see "to not eat," "to not drink," and "not" is one of the words that often splits infinitives. By the 17th century, it looks like some writers were trying to avoid split infinitives, but from what we can tell there was actually no explicit guidance about split infinitives.

The first mention that's been found was found by Richard W. Bailey, who was a professor of English at the University of Michigan. And he found this in an 1834 anonymous letter to the editor of *New England Magazine*, and the letter writer criticizes the split infinitive because: "It is used by uneducated writers." In other words, it's used by uneducated people, therefore there's something wrong with it. Now we don't know on what basis this writer determined that it was used by uneducated writers.

Moisés Perales Escudero has found another example just after that in 1840, which is John Horne Tooke's *The Diversions of Purley*. And this book looks at the history of English, and Tooke compares English with German and its Germanic roots. And he criticizes the split infinitive on the grounds that it's not true to English's Teutonic roots, that because you couldn't have split the infinitive in earlier forms of English, you shouldn't be able to split it now.

So, do we split infinitives? The answer is yes, and sometimes it sounds more idiomatic to split the infinitive. For example, "to better serve," "to better understand." Here's another one that sounds idiomatic: "to not only say but also…" or "to just say." Those all sound quite natural to us, and they're all split. There's some chance that the desire to split an infinitive may be about the rhythm of the language, keeping it weak-strong. This is a proposal that the linguist David Crystal has put forward. He notes that if you take a split infinitive like "to boldly go," it has a nice rhythm to it: "to bold–ly go." You get that weak-strong weak-strong, as opposed to "to go boldly," which puts those two strong stresses right next to each other.

That said, some split infinitives are less ideal—for example, when we get a lot of material in between the "to" and the verb. Let me give you an example: "to quickly and effectively but not always consistently grade." As you can hear there, you've put a lot words in between "to" and "grade," and that may not be particularly effective. So here's the better advice about split infinitives: it's fine to split infinitives with an adverb. For clarity, however, one might want to avoid splitting an infinitive with a long adverbial phrase in the middle.

The key point of this example is that prescriptive rules have histories. They're made by real people often based on their preferences and/or their beliefs about how English does or how English should work. Some of the prescribed constructions, the constructions they're saying we shouldn't use, have really long histories in the language, often existing for decades if not centuries before a rule was created to say that they we should avoid that construction.

Now, none of this means that we shouldn't take prescriptive rules seriously. When we write in formal prose, we can be judged by our control over them, so it serves us well to know the rules. And sometimes, as I've said, these usage rules can make our prose less ambiguous or more aesthetically pleasing.

But as we'll talk about in this course, any idea about right and wrong when it comes to grammar gets complicated when we learn about the history of prescriptive rules, and when we compare those rules to the way that real speakers and real writers use the language in real time. Not splitting an infinitive may be the right call for a specific piece of writing, but that doesn't make it universally right, or how English is supposed to work.

As I said in the previous lecture as well, and it bears repeating, I don't want to suggest that there's no value to prescriptive rules, because that would be inaccurate. There's a belief out there that linguists, when we're asking you to think critically about prescriptive rules, are saying that prescriptive rules are bad and everyone should speak and write however they want all the time.

That is not what linguists are saying. Linguists recognize the value of a standard, but we are asking all of us to think critically about that standard. And I will say that some linguists can probably be overly strident in their attempt to challenge the perceived authority of prescriptive rules. Prescriptive rules are such a force out there that sometimes, when we're trying to poke at them, we can perhaps dismiss them too easily as silly or useless, and they are clearly not useless.

The value of prescriptive rules are many. For example, they can promote a standard, and a standard variety of a language has a real value. They can also promote aesthetically pleasing kinds of prose—for example, some rules tell us to make our constructions parallel, and that can be a very pleasing thing to do in writing and in speech. These rules can also promote clarity: they ask us to avoid ambiguity in writing because writing cannot tolerate ambiguity the way speech can. These rules can also help us use punctuation to capture prosody on the page. Let's just keep perspective on these rules' value. Let's be open-minded about their benefits and their weaknesses, and be open-minded about the other ways to speak and write English, depending on audience and context.

So what is the scope of these prescriptive rules? When you see us talk about prescriptive grammar, or you see books that address prescriptive grammar, it often covers a lot of ground, more than just syntax. Let's take as an example a book by Ellie Grossman, which was called *The Grammatically Correct Handbook*. It was published in 1997, and I became aware of it because she was interviewed on national public radio on *The Derek McGinty Show*. And I listened to her talking about these rules about how we should use the language, and people were calling in expressing their anxiety about whether they were using the language correctly. Now her book covers a lot of territory, and let me show you the range.

For example, it talks about pronunciation. Should we pronounce the word D-O-U-R as "doer" or "dour"? And her answer is "doer," although I have to say if you say, "She looked doer," not everyone will know what you mean. She also addresses the question of whether there is a "t" in the word O-F-T-E-N, and the answer is, for the last couple of hundred years, no, but the "t" is coming back in. She tells us to say "ofen." Her book also takes on spelling as it relates to pronunciation—for example, the difference between "loath" and "loathe." There's a section on punctuation, which addresses questions like, "What do you do with the apostrophe in words that end in 's'?" And I promise you that we'll talk about that in this course.

The book takes on lexical issues. For example, semantic change: can "anxious" and "eager" mean the same thing? She says no. It also addresses regional differences—for example, "bring" versus "take." Then there are morphological issues in the book—in other words, how words get inflected. This covers such topics as Latin plurals and past participles—for example, "have drunk" versus "have drank." Then there are syntactic issues in the book, the placement of prepositions, or should it be "there are books" or can you say "there's books"? Finally, there are stylistic issues covered in the book, such as is "refer back" redundant?

As you can see that's a wide range of topics, and we will cover this full range in the course. I will often refer to these as usage issues, but sometimes may call them grammar. And what I'll be covering is how do we—and by this I mean the full range of "we"—use the language? Is there guidance about how we are supposed to use the language, and to what extent does that guidance affect both spoken and written usage?

Now, where do we find these rules about usage? There is not for English an equivalent of the Académie française, which in France is supposed to govern the language and determine what is appropriate or acceptable. In the U.S. and other English-speaking countries, we rely on a much looser network of language authorities: English teachers, columnists, editors, dictionary makers.

Now I would guess that many of you were asked to purchase an academic usage guide for an English course at some point in your life. This may have been Strunk and White's *Elements of Style*, which was first published in 1959, and has gone through multiple editions since then. Perhaps you own Joseph Williams' book *Style: Lessons in Clarity and Grace*. Those two books are quite slim volumes, and they contrast with the much bigger dictionaries of usage that are available. One of the best-known ones is H. W. Fowler's *Dictionary of Modern English Usage*, which was published in 1926, and I'll come back to that. More recently, we have Bryan Garner's *Dictionary of American Usage*, first published in 1998, and has come out in new editions since then. Garner is an American lawyer, professor, and lexicographer—in other words, he's a dictionary editor—and his usage guide is one that will come up a lot in this course.

We can trace these kinds of prescriptive guides about English usage back about 250 years, back to the second half of the 18th century. This time period saw a proliferation of these guides, and I'll come back to that in a few minutes. These guides tend to focus on usage issues where there's variation in usage. After all, if we were all doing the same thing, there wouldn't be much to prescribe.

Now, how do they usually justify that what at least some us are doing in the language is wrong? This will continue to come up in future lectures, but let me just outline the range of reasons that tend to come up for why what some of us are doing is wrong. One reason is etymology, that some of these guides will say that a word should mean what it used to mean, and if we're using it in a new way, that's not so good. Another argument is based on logic. This may say that language should work, for example, like math, even though language is not math, or that it should work like some other logical system.

Another argument about usage can be based on analogy; that English should work like Latin, or like German because it's Germanic in origin. Or the argument may be based on purity; that English should return to its roots, even though I have to say as a historian of the language, what you see is that English has always been influenced by other languages. Another basis for some arguments about usage is authority: great writers use the language this way and so we should, too. And then, finally, sometimes these rules are just based on personal taste.

What's fascinating to me is that one grammarian's personal preference or taste can get picked up as a rule in future guides, and we'll see that this may be the case with the rule about ending a sentence with a preposition, as well as the rule about the difference between "less" and "fewer." We can identify by name some of the earliest grammarians whose opinions about good usage still echo in today's guides.

Now let me return to the 18th century and this dramatic rise of usage guides. What was happening in this period is that you were also seeing a dramatic rise of the middle class and of literacy in Britain and in the United States. And with the rise of the middle class and literacy, you saw a rise in demand for guidance about how to use English, because people wanted to use English in a way that would benefit them for upward mobility.

You also saw in this period a proliferation of other kinds of conduct manuals, and when you think about it, a guide on English usage is a kind of conduct manual about how you should conduct yourself in speech. There were over 1 million grammar books printed during this period at the end of the 18th century, which is for that period quite a remarkable number of books. And these books solidified the idea that there is this thing called good English, and that good English is the usage of the upper classes. Now a few of the most popular grammar books of this period, of the late 18th and 19th century, I want to think about them briefly because several of them will come up throughout the course, and looking at these books gives you a sense of the arc of prescriptive grammar over the last 250 years.

Let's start with Joseph Priestley's *Rudiments of English Grammar*, which was published in 1761. If Priestley's name is sounding familiar to you, it may be because he was the chemist who isolated oxygen. He also was a clergyman and a political theorist who also wrote about grammar. This grammar was quite influential, in particular for the ways in which Priestley tried to move away from Latin models.

It's important to realize that the earliest English grammars were highly dependent on Latin because Latin already had published grammars. So when the first grammarians tried to write a grammar for English, they turned to the model they had, and this is why some of our grammatical rules and terminology are highly dependent on Latin. So Priestley tried to move English grammars away from Latin, and it is clear that he was also quite interested in how the language was actually used. That said, when you read the grammar, you can see his pervasive concern with correctness as well.

Let's just jump forward one year to get to Robert Lowth's *A Short Introduction to English Grammar*, which was published in 1762. Lowth is often framed as the arch prescriptivist in the history of English, but he and his reputation have been rehabilitated by the linguist Ingrid Tieken-Boon van Ostade. She argues that when you read his grammar you will see that, while he certainly did propose rules, he was not as prescriptive as many people make him out to be.

As I mentioned, he is not the one who said we can't split infinitives, even though people often blame him for that. He's also often seen as the person who falsely condemned double negatives, but if we look at what he wrote, it's more complicated than that. He wrote: "Two negatives, in English, destroy one another, or are equivalent to an affirmative." Then the example he gives is: "Nor did they not perceive the evil plight in which they were." Now that construction with "nor" and "not" is a complicated one, and there is a way that one could argue that the "nor" and the "not" do counteract each other. The rule then got picked up later and generalized in ways that are trickier. It also seems that when you look at Lowth's writings, both formal and informal, he used both formal writing that would've adhered to his grammar, and more colloquial language.

Let's now turn to the American lawyer Lindley Murray and his perhaps even more influential grammar, which was called *English Grammar*, and it was published in 1795. Lindley Murray was more prescriptive than his predecessors. If we were going to find an arch prescriptivist, some linguists argued, we might need to look at him. This grammar book went through 65 official editions in about 75 years, which is a remarkable feat, and there was even a board game named after Murray called Murraymania. Lindley Murray's grammar is the grammar that spread the idea that singular "they" was wrong, and that we should use "he" instead, a rule that I'll come back to in a later lecture.

Many point to Richard Grant White's grammar, which was published in 1870 and called *Words and Their Uses: Past and Present*, as the heyday of prescriptivism. Now, Richard Grant White was a Shakespearean who had very strong opinions about usage. I read his grammar just for fun because I can't help but chuckle at some of the things that he was concerned about. I want to share a few of those with you.

For example, in his entry on "donate" he writes: "I need hardly say that this word is utterly abominable." He describes it as an ignorant back-formation from the word "donation"—which is true, that is where it was formed—and he says but we already have "give," "confer," "present," "bequeath," so we clearly don't need "donate." He also did not like the word "invest" used intransitively. In other words, he didn't think we should be able to say, "I think I shall invest." He called this a gross misuse. He condemned the compound "real estate" as a pretentious intruder from the realm of law. And White also did not like if we used the word "state" to mean "say." He said that's not true to the Latin; in the Latin it means to set forth the conditions. Clearly, he lost all of these fights.

I share these examples because I find that they give us a useful perspective on guidance about usage. Things that may sound terrible to our ears may become unremarkable within a generation or two. These complaints from Richard Grant White now seem quaint, and some of the things we're worried about in 50 or 100 years may also seem quaint. It doesn't mean that we may not want to avoid usage that others strongly dislike or see as overly informal, or low, or abominable. But we can have the perspective that the judgment is not inherent to the construction, it's something that has been put onto this bit of language, and then we will decide what we're going to do as writers and speakers. I think it's also important for those of us who serve as gatekeepers as teachers or editors to decide when we might want to allow something in more formal writing.

Compared with White, we can view H. W. Fowler and his *Dictionary of Modern Usage*, published in 1926, as a good-natured prescriptivist. His book, I have to say, is filled with opinions. For example, he describes "all right" spelled A-L-R-I-G-H-T as not a word, and he says that if you use "aggravate" to mean "annoy," that is a feminine or childish colloquialism. In addition, he describes the phrase "quite all right" as "all quite wrong." He saw that as redundant.

At the same time, Fowler says it's a mistake to assume that "none" can only be singular, such as "none of them is" versus "none of them are," and we'll talk about this. He also categorizes the prescription against split infinitives under fetishes and superstitions, mocking those who follow the prescription doggedly.

So what would Fowler have thought of Supreme Court Chief Justice John Roberts changing the oath of office when he swore in President Obama in 2008? Let's listen:

'I, Barack Hussein Obama do solemnly swear…' 'That I will execute the Office of President to the United States faithfully…' 'That I will execute…' '…the Off—faithfully the Pres—the Office of President of the United States.' '…the Office of President of the United States faithfully.'

Oh dear, what a mess. What's happened here is that Chief Justice Roberts has tried to move the "faithfully" to the end of the sentence. In the actual oath, "faithfully" comes between "will" and "execute"—I will faithfully execute. It's not a split infinitive, but it's a split verb, and people who feel strongly about split infinitives often feel strongly about split verbs as well. Roberts' version moved "faithfully" to the end: it became "solemnly swear that I will execute the Office of the President of the United States faithfully."

Now clearly this is not a question of clarity; it's completely clear what we mean wherever the word "faithfully" comes.

In the end they redid the oath and all was fine. What's interesting to me is the way in which this example shows the power of these rules to shape our sense of what is good and appropriate to the point where we might even change the language in a context that formal and solemn.

Now, there is a good reason to know these kinds of rules about things like split infinitives, and to fully understand them, as well as to have enough information to make informed decisions about when we want to follow them and when we don't. And that's exactly the aim of this course.

One key part of this knowledge is being able to put side by side prescriptive rules about usage and information about actual usage. In the next lecture, we'll turn to the rules that describe actual usage, often called descriptive grammar, so that we can decide whether to believe that two negatives really do cancel each other out in English.

Lecture 3

Descriptivism: How Grammar Really Works

This lecture starts with a look at contractions in English, not in terms of whether or not we should use them in formal writing but in terms of where contractions can and cannot happen. Then we'll move on to discuss historical underpinnings of certain rules, and how concepts like the rightness or wrongness of double negatives are somewhat fungible. We'll close with a look at other descriptive rules. The overall theme of the lecture is: If you speak and write English competently, then you actually know quite a lot about grammar, even if you don't think you do. Another theme: Nonstandard grammars aren't necessarily wrong.

Contractions

- We'll start with a straightforward and very common contraction: did + not, which can help make, "I didn't swim." Now let's coordinate that sentence to see what can happen:

  □ He swam but I didn't swim.

  □ He swam but I didn't. (This omits the main verb "swim" and leaves *didn't* stranded at end of sentence. This is not always possible.)

- Let's now look at another common contraction: I + am, as in, "I'm driving." Now let's coordinate (imagine we're talking about carpools):

  □ She's driving and I'm driving.

□ She's driving and I'm. (This doesn't work: You can't omit the main verb and leave *I'm* stranded at the end of the sentence.)

■ We couldn't strand other pronouns contracted with auxiliary verbs to end a sentence or clause:

□ Who has been to South Africa? She has. (Again, we have omitted main verb and the rest of the sentence.)

□ Who has been to South Africa? She's. (This is a no-go.)

■ This is true in a comparative sentence too, where *to be* is the main verb and not an auxiliary or helping verb: "She's taller than I'm" doesn't work.

■ No one ever taught you this; it is intuitive grammatical knowledge, learned when you were a child. You just have a sense that "She's taller than I'm" is ungrammatical, in a more fundamental way than a split infinitive. This is fundamental to your linguistic competence as a speaker of English.

Descriptive Grammar

■ Descriptive grammar is made up of this complex set of rules that allow us to make grammatical utterances. Grammatical in the descriptive sense means rule-governed, systematically constructed language delivered in a way that can be parsed by others. A rule is an established pattern of usage that speakers recognize. Descriptive grammars must be huge to capture all this knowledge compared with style guides, which capture a small percentage.

■ The most remarkable feature of grammar of human languages is that we can create an infinite number of utterances from a finite set of resources. Think about what you're doing right now: You're reading sentences you've never read before.

- Conventions are fundamental: Think of linguistic signs and grammatical rules and patterns. Those rules allow us to combine the signs in new ways.

Multiple Negations

- Ungrammatical sentences don't follow the patterns of a variety of English. Here's an example with word order. We know this is fine: A dog chased me down the street.

- We know these are not fine:

  - Dog a chased me down street the. (Determiners must come before nouns.)

  - A dog chased me the street down. (The preposition needs to come before the noun phrase.)

  - Dog me street down chased a the. (This is just a general mess.)

- What about, "We don't have nothing to hide." Is this grammatical in the descriptive sense? To answer that, let's think historically. Double negation is now considered nonstandard, but there is a long history of multiple negation in English.

- Chaucer described a knight in the General Prologue of *The Canterbury Tales*: "He *nevere* yet *no* vileynye *ne* sayde." (Translation: He never no evil thing not said à He never ever said anything vile.) Note that there are three negatives.

In Shakespeare's *As You Like It*, the character Celia asserts: "I cannot go no further."

- The system for marking negation in English was different: Some writing used *ne* rather than *not*, and it was inserted before the verb (*ne sayde*). Now we use *not* and it is inserted after the auxiliary (*cannot, has not, did not say*). Varieties of English that continue to use double negation carry on a long tradition.

- It's a myth that two negatives cancel each other out. Take, for example, the meaning of "not unhappy." We must also note that intonation matters: "We don't have none." All in all, we must consider double negation grammatical for many varieties of English. It is not formal or standard, but completely systematic and well understood by speakers of all varieties.

Multiple Grammars

- This is a good moment to make a key point about how "English grammar" works: There isn't just one. All varieties of English spoken in speech communities have systematic grammars.

- We need to talk about English grammars, as there are many varieties of English—Standard American English is just one of them. Standard American English will be the focus of much of this course, but we will often point out differences in other varieties and talk about how the standard variety has changed over time.

- Now let's return to negation, focusing on the kind with just one negative. If we step back from a negative sentence to examine what is at work, it can give you a taste of how much you know. Let's take the sentence, "It did not rain."

  □ The *not* goes after the auxiliary verb.

  □ Contraction is possible ("didn't rain").

  □ The auxiliary verb(s) come before the main verb.

- What if there is more than one auxiliary? Take as an example, "The cake has been eaten." You know that you the negative version would go as, "The cake has not been eaten," rather than, "The cake has been not eaten." A contraction is also possible, with *hasn't*.

■ That's a lot of knowledge about how to make a negative sentence that you may never have had spelled out that way before. You just learned it as a kid.

Other Descriptive Rules

■ Here are some other examples of descriptive rules:

□ Determiners come before nouns: "All her many friends" instead of, "Her all many friends."

□ An adjective will come between the determiner and the noun: "a silly song."

□ To make most nouns plural, add -s: "silly songs."

□ Prepositions precede the noun phrase: "in my head."

■ These may seem very basic and not worth spending time on, but it's powerful to remember how much we know when we know English grammar. The usage rules that we worry about are just a fraction of the universe of English grammar.

■ Being able to compare how the language works descriptively with the rules we're told to follow in formal speech and writing can help you make even more informed decisions about usage. You'll gain a new perspective on some of the rules you may have learned in school or elsewhere.

■ As an example, let's return to double negation. We've determined that historically it has been rule-governed and continues to be rule-governed and grammatical in many varieties of English.

■ But in 18th century, Bishop Lowth, in his very popular grammar, introduced the idea that negatives could cancel each other. This got extended to sentences like, "We don't have nothing to hide." They were declared illogical.

- Double negatives are now avoided in Standard American English, and in fact are often condemned as wrong or bad English. But there is nothing inherently wrong or uneducated about the construction—in fact, it used to be used in high writing.

- In fact, some people thought that the move to single negation wasn't necessarily a good thing. Here's a quote from the *London Review* (October 1, 1864) found in Fitzedward Hall's *Modern English* (1873): "The double negative has been abandoned, to the great injury of strength of expression."

- To be clear, this isn't to advocate that we all suddenly start using double negation in formal prose, or stop teaching students about the issue. We should teach students the standard use, but we shouldn't condemn the other, as this isn't well founded. This is what it means to be careful about our grammar: to be sure what we're saying is accurate and fair about how both prescriptive and descriptive grammar work.

- It is helpful for us to understand social judgment and be able to navigate it as speakers and writers; it is also intellectually interesting to see how those judgments can change over time. This perspective and background knowledge actually makes us better editors and teachers because we understand the formal written variety in the context of all the varieties of English out there. It it is a more engaging and empowering way to think about and teach grammar.

- It gives us credit for all that we already know and acknowledges all the variation that we know is out there—and that we know can function really well in context. Part of mastering the game of the formal standards is to understand how these usage rules may ask us to switch up our language from informal to formal contexts, and from speech to writing.

■ All of this can make grammar playful again, as opposed to a world of absolute rights and wrongs.

Suggested Reading

Greenbaum, *Oxford English Grammar.*
Huddleston and Pullum, *A Student Introduction to English Grammar.*
Lowth, *A Short Introduction to English Grammar.*
McWhorter, *Word on the Street.*
Ostade, "Double Negation and Eighteenth-Century English Grammars."
Pinker, *The Sense of Style.*

Questions to Consider

1. Try listing out all the things you needed to learn to create the grammatical English sentence "Jordan did not eat breakfast this morning," as opposed to the ungrammatical sentence "Jordan ate not breakfast morning this."

2. When do two negatives in a clause contradict each other—or perhaps "cancel" each other—and when do they reinforce each other?

Descriptivism: How Grammar Really Works

This lecture could be subtitled: "All the intricate things you know that you don't usually give yourself credit for knowing when you know English grammar." Let's start by thinking about contractions in English, not in terms of whether or not we should use contractions in formal writing—we'll talk about that in the next lecture—but in terms of where contractions can and cannot happen.

We'll start with a straightforward and very common contraction: "did" plus "not," as in "I didn't swim." Now let's coordinate that sentence to see what happens: "He swam but I didn't swim." Okay, straightforward enough. Let's see what happens if we take off the end of that sentence: "He swam but I didn't." Seems completely fine, and it is fine, so in that coordinated sentence you can omit the main verb "swim" and leave "didn't" stranded at end of sentence. This, I have to say, does not seem like an extraordinary fact at all, but it's not always possible in English to remove the end of the sentence—that main verb—and keep our contraction stranded there are the end of the sentence. Let me show you what I mean.

Let's look at another common contraction: "I" plus "am," as in "I'm." Here's the sentence: "I'm driving." Now let's coordinate that. Let's imagine that we we're talking about carpools, and I said, "She's driving and I'm driving." Again, completely straightforward. Let's now try to omit the second verb: "She's driving and I'm." Clearly we can't do that. You're probably sitting there saying, "Wait, she's not finished yet, she can't just end with 'I'm.'" With that, we cannot omit the main verb at the end of that clause and leave "I'm" stranded at the end of the sentence. We couldn't strand other pronouns contracted with auxiliary verbs to end a sentence or clause.

Let's try this one: "Who has traveled to South Africa? She has." Okay? There we omitted the verb, that was fine, but we did not contract the pronoun with the auxiliary verb. Let's try contracting it: "Who has traveled to South Africa? She's." Again, you're saying, "That can't work, because if I just say 'she's,' it feels like I'm not finished with that sentence." This holds true also in comparative sentences that we can't strand those contractions out there with a pronoun and an auxiliary, or a pronoun and "to be."

Let me show you one where "to be" is the main verb, not an auxiliary verb or helping verb, and again what we know is that you can't leave "I'm" stranded at the end of the sentence. Here's a version of the sentence without a contraction: "She's taller than I am." Okay, completely fine. Now let's try contracting it: "She's taller than I'm." Nope, can't do it.

Now, there are detailed explanations in linguistics for exactly why it is that we can't leave those contractions stranded at the end of a clause or sentence but we can leave "didn't" there at the end. I'm not going to get into those explanations here; my point is simply that you know this. You know when you can and can't end a clause with a contraction.

Now, no one has ever taught you that—this is intuitive grammatical knowledge, learned when you were a child. You just have a gut sense that "She's taller than I'm" is ungrammatical, and it's ungrammatical in a more fundamental way than a split infinitive is ungrammatical. And, really, this is the difference between ungrammatical in the descriptive sense—as we'll be talking about in this lecture—and dispreferred. And the split infinitive is just dispreferred in some contexts. Your knowledge that "She's taller than I'm" is ungrammatical is fundamental to your linguistic competence as a speaker of English.

As a linguist, I'm interested in the complex set of rules that allow us as speakers of English to make grammatical utterances. What I'm going to call this is our descriptive grammar. It describes our competence as speakers that allows us to string words together into utterances that make sense to other people.

So what do we know when we know a language like English? Well, we know a lot, and we know a lot at different levels of the structure of the language. For example, we have a lot of knowledge about the sounds of the language; we know which sounds to pay attention to and which sounds are not distinctive in our language. Then, of course, we have an enormous competence around words. We know the vocabulary at our disposal. We also know how those words inflect: how do verbs make past tense? How do nouns make plural?

Then there's all our competence around syntax: how can we string words together into clauses and sentences? Put on top of that all our knowledge about the discourse conventions, which allows us to be competent speakers in everyday conversation: we know how to take turns; we know how to phrase things in more polite ways and less polite ways. This is all part of our competence as speakers. And then, in a highly standardized language like English, our competence may also include all the prescriptive rules that we know, the rules that we know that allow us to write or speak in more formal contexts, and then to speak in less formal contexts.

When I use grammatical in this lecture, I'm often going to be using it in the descriptive sense. And when I use it in this sense, here's what I mean. I mean that an utterance, if it's grammatical, is rule-governed—it obeys the rules in a language that string together words in a way that will be meaningful to other speakers, that the words are inflected in ways that will be meaningful to other speakers. In other words, that the sentence or utterance is systematically constructed according to the system of the language for the order of the words, the agreement of nouns and verbs, that kind of thing. And when you have grammatical utterances that are systematically constructed, they can then be parsed by other speakers or readers if you're writing. In this sense, in the descriptive sense, a rule is actually an established pattern of usage that speakers recognize.

When linguists write descriptive grammars trying to capture all of this knowledge, these grammars are huge. It's fascinating to compare those with style guides like Strunk and White, which are so slim by comparison, and there's a reason for that. Style guides capture only a small percentage of the usage issues in a language. Style guides go after those usage issues where there's variation, where perhaps there's a change in progress, and they try to tell us what is more and less proper usage. A descriptive grammar needs to capture the whole language, both where there's variation and where we all agree on the rules of a language. In this course, we'll spend a lot of time on the prescriptive rules that we feel we're supposed to know, and we'll also compare those with the rules, the patterns, of actual usage.

The most remarkable feature of the grammar of human languages is that we can create an infinite number of utterances from a finite set of resources. This was captured eloquently by Wilhelm von Humboldt, who was a German philosopher in the late 18th and 19th century, and a linguist. He was also the brother of the famous naturalist and explorer Alexander von Humboldt, and what he said was: "Language makes infinite use of finite means."

Interestingly, at one point I was telling students this in a course at the University of Michigan, and I said, "Language—we can create an infinite number of utterances from a finite set of resources." And a student raised his hand and he said, "Well surely you do not mean infinite in the mathematical sense?" And I thought, "How else could I mean infinite?" And I do mean infinite in the mathematical sense. I mean infinite—there is no limit. And this gets to human creativity. Yes, we make new words, and that's one of the wonderful parts of human creativity with language. But here I'm talking about creativity with syntax, with grammar. I'm talking about how we can take the words we have and combine them in an infinite number of ways. This is what von Humboldt was getting at.

Think about what you're doing right now as you listen to me. You're listening to sentences you've never heard before. I've never uttered these sentences in exactly this way before, and yet—I hope—you're understanding me clearly, even though this sentence is entirely new for you. The way this works is that you and I agree on the conventions of language. We agree on what each linguistic sign means. In other words, if we take a sign like the word "skunk," well you and I all agree that that refers to a little critter that is black and white and can make a huge stink. Now, if I suddenly started using "skunk" to mean "pillow," you and I would have a problem, because now we wouldn't be able to communicate. But that's not the way human language works; there's a convention behind the signs.

And then there's convention with grammatical rules or patterns. You expect me to have my subjects in particular places, my verbs in particular places, my determiners before the nouns. And when I do that, I can combine those nouns and verbs in creative ways because they're in the right place for you, which allows you to parse the utterance.

Now how do we know that we can create an infinite number of utterances? Well, the answer is what linguists would call recursion. Recursion is the ability to embed an infinite number of elements into a grammatical structure, and once you can do this, there are no limits on how long, or how new, a sentence can be. An example's going to help here. Watch the way I'm going to embed clause inside clause in this sentence. Here comes the sentence: "My sister explained that my nephew said that his sister whispered to him that her friend had told her that her brother said that her mother said that her father said..." and I could keep putting in noun plus "said" forever. And each time I do that, the sentence is going to mean something new. "He said that she said that we said that I said..." Each time, it means a new thing.

And that's how we can say that the language is infinitely creative, because I can keep making new sentences that way. Now, of course, your brain can't actually process that sentence once I've embedded probably more than four of those clauses inside each other. Your brain says, "I give up! I can't figure out what this sentence means," but I could keep going. Now, there is a current debate in the field about whether all human languages have recursion, but it has been a standing assumption that all human languages do.

From this definition of grammar and grammatical—that is, that a language follows the rules or patterns of that language in order to communicate meaning—let's talk about what ungrammatical means. It would mean that a sentence does not follow the patterns of a variety of English. Now we already talked about the sentence "She's taller than I'm," and I think we can all agree that that feels ungrammatical.

Now here's another example with word order. We know that the following sentence is just fine: "A dog chased me down the street." Not that exciting, clearly grammatically fine. We know that this sentence is not fine: "Dog a chased me down street the." You're probably having a little trouble following that, and that's because it's ungrammatical. I said, "dog a" and "street the," but we know that determiners need to come before nouns; it needs to be "a dog" and "the street." Here's another ungrammatical version: "A dog chased me the street down." Nope, because we know that prepositions need to come before the noun phrase; it should be "down the street," not "the street down." Let me just give you one more example: "Dog me street down chased a the." Okay, so that's a total mess—it doesn't even follow subject-verb-object word order.

Those we can all agree are ungrammatical. What about the sentence: "We don't have nothing to hide." Is that grammatical in the descriptive sense? To answer that question, let's start by thinking historically. Of course, what we're talking about here is double negation, and double negation is now considered nonstandard. And I'll sometimes hear it described as illogical or wrong, which is of course different from being nonstandard, and I would argue that calling double negation illogical or wrong is not fair. Being nonstandard does not make something wrong or illogical, or at least any more illogical than some of the things we consider standard. I want to talk about this here because the history of double negation shows us that the standard can change over time, and this is a really useful perspective to have as we think about descriptive and prescriptive grammar.

All right, so double, or sometimes we call it multiple negation, because you can have more than two. This occurs when we have more than one negative marker on the clause. So that could be "not" plus "nothing," "not" plus "no one," "not" plus "never," "not" plus "no." Now, of course, many languages in the world do this. We'll just take French as one example. If you want to say "I don't know" in French, you would say "Je ne sais pas," where the "ne"—"Je ne"—is a negative, and the "pas" is also a negative. So French does double negation completely standard.

Standard American English now employs single negation. So we would say, in standard varieties of English, "We don't have anything to hide." But there is a long history of multiple negation in English. Let me give you a few examples from hundreds of years ago.

The first one comes from a document called the *Peterborough Chronicle*, which was recording the history of Britain. This entry is from 1137, and it's describing the consequences of the civil war under King Stephen. And here is the sentence; this would be early Middle English: "þe erthe ne bar nan corn." Okay, if we were to translate that directly into Modern English, it would be something like: "The earth not bore no corn." So you'll see the double negation, "not" and "no." In standard English now, we'd say, "The earth didn't bear any corn."

Here's Chaucer with some double negation. This is from the description of the knight in the "General Prologue" of the *Canterbury Tales*: "He never yet no vileynye ne sayde." Okay, so there we have "never." We also have "no" and "ne," so we in fact have triple negation. If we were to translate it directly, it would be something like: "He never no evil thing not said." Or, to translate it into Modern standard English: "He never ever said anything vile or evil." Those three negatives in there we probably should read as just emphatic. Let me give you one more historical example of double negation, this one from Shakespeare. This is from *As You Like It*, and we have Celia asserts: "I cannot go no further." A nice double negation.

The system for making negation in earlier forms of English was just different from the way it is now, so you could have double or multiple negation. You had the "ne," N-E, rather than not, and it was inserted right before the verb, so "ne bar," with the corn example, or "ne sayde"—"didn't say." We now use "not" and it is inserted after an auxiliary verb, so "cannot," "has not," did not say." Standard varieties of English no longer use double negation, but it's important to note that many varieties of English continue to use double negation, and this is carrying on a long tradition in the language.

Now there is a myth out there that two negatives cancel each other out, and I have to say that is clearly not true in these cases. If we think about something like "We don't have nothing to hide," it is clear to all of us that that does not mean "We have something to hide." Those negatives do not cancel each other out. I will hear people say, "But in math, if you multiply two negatives, you get a positive." Okay, that is true, but I have two responses to that. One is: language is not math. The second is: okay, fine, let's do math. If you have two negatives in math and you add them, what do you get? You actually get a bigger negative.

Now it is true that there are some double negatives in Modern English where the negatives do cancel each other out, or at least kind of cancel each other out. If you think about the phrase "not unhappy," well, clearly the "not" and the "un" are contradicting each other and counteracting each other, but I would also argue that "not unhappy" is not the same thing as happy. If I'm not unhappy, I'm just not unhappy; it does not mean I'm all the way to happy.

I also want to note here that there is a way we can use intonation on a double negative to make those two negatives cancel each other out. For example, "We don't have none," which would mean, "Okay, so we have some." But if I were to say it differently: "We don't have none," that means "We don't have any."

So, to answer my question of "Is double negation grammatical?" We must consider double negation grammatical for many varieties of English. It is not formal, it is not standard, but it's completely systematic, and it's well understood by speakers of all varieties: When Pink Floyd says, "We don't need no education," we all know exactly what they mean.

This is a good moment to make a key point about how English grammar works, and that is that there isn't just one English grammar. All varieties of English spoken in speech communities have systematic grammars, and they don't all stem from standard English. I think it can be tempting, because standard English is such a prominent presence, to think that all the other varieties come derived from that, but that's not actually true— the standard was just elevated for social and political reasons. We need to talk about English grammars in the plural, as there are many varieties of English; Standard American English is just one of them. Standard English will be the focus of much of this course, but I will often point out differences in other varieties and talk about how the standard variety has changed over time.

Now let's return to negation, and we'll take the kind with just one negative, the kind in Standard American English. If we step back from a negative sentence to examine what is at work—or what's at play—here, it can give you a taste of just how much you know when you know English grammar. Let's take a very simple, straightforward sentence: "It did not rain."

What do you need to know to construct that sentence in terms of the negation? Well, you need to that the "not" goes after the auxiliary verb: "It did not rain." You would not say, "It not did rain," or "Not it did rain." Then we know that we could contract it: "It didn't rain." And, of course, the auxiliary verb comes before the main verb—we say, "It didn't rain," not "It rain didn't." I know that I'm saying things that are so completely obvious to you, but in fact you did have to learn these when you were a kid.

Now, what happens if there's more than one auxiliary verb in the sentence? Take, for example, "The cake has been eaten." We have two auxiliaries: "has" and "been." Well, what you know is that the "not" goes in after the first auxiliary: "The cake has not been eaten." You would not say, "The cake has been not eaten." Or, if you did, that would be for a particular rhetorical purpose, it wouldn't be just a generic negation. And, again, you would know when you could contract. You know you can say, "The cake hasn't been eaten."

That's a lot of knowledge about how to insert "not" to make a negative sentence that you probably have never have had to spell out that way before, you just learned it when you were a kid. And, interestingly, you went through stages learning it. Kids often say things like, "No wear shoes," before they get the rule that you need an auxiliary verb plus "not."

What are other examples of descriptive rules of the language? Well, we've already covered some. Determiners come before nouns, and there is an order to those determiners, which we'll be talking about. You would say, "All her many friends," not "Her all many friends." We know that adjectives will come between the determiner and the noun, so we would say something like "a silly song," where "silly" comes between "a" and "song."

Another descriptive rule: well, to make most nouns plural, add "s"—"silly songs." And once we've made it plural, we know that we can't use "a." You can't say "a silly songs" but you could say "the silly songs." We also talked about how prepositions precede the noun phrase. We would say "in my head." And if we want to talk about the silly songs in my head, we would say "silly songs in my head" not "silly in my head songs."

I know that these rules seem very basic and not worth spending time on, but it's powerful stuff to remember how much we know when we know English grammar. The usage rules that we worry about—Is it "less" or "fewer" here? Can I split that infinitive?—are just a fraction of the universe of English grammar. What I'll show is that being able to compare how the language works descriptively with the rules we're told to follow in formal speech and writing can help you make even more informed decisions about usage, and you'll gain a new perspective on some of the rules you may have learned in school or elsewhere.

What do I mean by this new perspective? Well let's return to double negation. We've discussed that, historically, double negation has been rule-governed and continues to be rule-governed or grammatical in many varieties of English, and of course in many other languages. But in the 18th century, Bishop Lowth, in his very influential grammar, introduced the idea that negatives could cancel each other out.

Now the example he gave from *Paradise Lost* is an example where the negatives do counteract each other. The sentence was: "Nor did they not perceive the evil plight in which they were." And there you can see that the "nor" and the "not" are counteracting, at least so some extent. The issue is that that piece of advice, or that statement he made about how those two negatives cancel each other out to make a positive, got extended in later guides, and it got extended to sentences like: "We don't have nothing to hide." And then those sentences were declared illogical as if those negatives cancelled each other out.

We now avoid double negatives in Standard American English, and it's not a prestige form. And what I'm struck by is that it is, as I've said, so often condemned as wrong or bad English. But what I hope I've shown you is that there's nothing inherently wrong or uneducated about the construction. In fact, it used to be high writing. And would you believe that some people thought that the move to single negation in standard varieties of English wasn't necessarily a good thing?

There's a great quote from the *London Review*, published in 1864, and it's republished in Fitzedward Hall's book *Modern English* in 1873. And this quote laments the loss of double negation as one of the many lamentable changes in the English language. It sets up the King James Bible, published in 1611, as the high point of English usage, and since then all the changes have been for the worse. And it states: "The double negative has been abandoned, to the great injury of strength of expression."

You don't hear that complaint anymore. Or you don't never hear that in usage guides now. Now, just to be clear, I'm not advocating that we all suddenly start using double negation in formal prose—although there would be absolutely nothing wrong with that—or that we stop teaching students about the issue. It's important to teach students about the standard use, but it's equally important not to condemn the nonstandard use, as this isn't well founded.

I want you to just imagine a student, who is a speaker of a variety of English that uses double negation, coming into a classroom and being told that the two negatives in "we don't have nothing" cancel each other out. That student knows that that's not true, and suddenly, if you've said that, you're the one who loses some credibility, because that just clearly isn't true to the grammar. To recognize these different definitions of grammatical is to me what it means to be careful about our grammar, to be sure that what we're saying is accurate and fair about how both prescriptive and descriptive grammar work.

What I'm trying to do is separate out the social judgment that we put onto grammar from the grammar itself. It's helpful for us to understand that social judgment, and be able to navigate it as speakers and writers—we want to know our audience, and we don't want to distract them or annoy them. It is also intellectually interesting to see how those judgments change over time.

I would argue that this perspective and background knowledge actually make us better editors and teachers because we understand the formal written variety in the context of all the varieties of English out there. And I have to say as a teacher, I have found it a more engaging and empowering way to think about, and to teach, grammar.

It gives us credit for all that we already know, and acknowledges the variation that we know is out there: we know that some people use single negatives, some people use double negatives. And we know that both of those constructions can function really well in context. Part of mastering the game of the formal standards in writing and speech is to understand how these usage rules may ask us to switch up our language from informal to formal contexts, from speech to writing.

My hope is that all of this knowledge, this perspective, can make grammar playful again, as opposed to a world of absolute rights and absolute wrongs. We as humans love to play with language, and I don't want people to fear grammar, to have that red pen frightened feeling when they hear the word grammar. It's interesting to think about not just whether one can use double negation in formal writing at this point—most of the time no, unless for specific rhetorical purposes—but I also want to think about why standard English uses single negation when many languages and older varieties of English use double negation. That's worth talking about, that's history, that's diversity—that's really, deeply understanding English grammar.

With all of this background on different approaches to grammar, it's time to dive into the details of parts of speech. How many parts of speech did you learn there are in English? If you learned that there are eight, I'm going to add a few more. And in this lecture, we've talked a lot about the word "not." Where does that fit in, in terms of parts of speech? What about the word "um"? We'll address these questions in the next lecture.

Re Phrasing

This lecture is the last of our background lectures before we dive into the usage rules related to different parts of speech. We'll address questions like: How many parts of speech are there? How do we define them? What is the difference between a phrase and a clause? The standard parts of speech fall in this hierarchy: Words make phrases, which make clauses, which make sentences. This kind of terminology is critical for the remaining 20 lectures. Much of this will be review for many readers, but it will provide some new ways of thinking about how we define and categorize words into parts of speech, or *lexical categories.*

Distinctions and Morphs

■ Let's start by clarifying a key distinction that builds on the material from the previous two lectures: what lexical category a word belongs to versus what lexical category we think a word should belong to.

☐ A good case study is the word *impact*, which is accepted as a noun and a verb. Some people, including many who write usage guides, think it should not be a verb that means "to have an impact on."

☐ In 2001, 80 percent of the AHD Usage Panel rejected the sentence, "The court ruling will impact the education of minority students" as somewhat or completely unacceptable.

☐ Bryan Garner, in his influential *Garner's Modern American Usage*, admits that this use of *impact* as a verb has become widespread, but he also concludes that it should be avoided because we already have *affect* and *influence*.

- The word impact captures a phenomenon in Modern English that is very relevant to a discussion of lexical categories: Words can change categories—or more often, expand into new categories. Some examples:

  □ Nouns get verbed (to google)

  □ Verbs get nouned (a hire)

  □ Adjectives get verbed (to clean).

- Sometimes, people aren't happy about this when it happens. Ben Franklin wrote to Noah Webster in 1789 about several new verbs, newly created from nouns, that he didn't like: *advocate*, *notice*, and *progress*.

- In Modern English, we have very few inflectional endings; for example, regular verbs just take *–ed* to become past tense. Therefore, it's not too hard to take a noun and make it a verb (*googled*). Nouns just take *–s* to become plural and possessive. Additionally, we don't have grammatical gender. So you can take a verb like *invite* and make it a noun—and you don't have to give it a gender. If you have more than one, you have *invites*.

Lexical Categories

- This is a good moment to step back for a quick review of what lexical categories (also known as parts of speech) are available in English. While there is some basic agreement on this, not everyone agrees on the terminology or how many categories there are.

- Lexical categories can be divided into two big categories:

  □ Open class: nouns, verbs, adjectives, and adverbs. This class can take new members.

- Closed class: pronouns, determiners, auxiliary verbs, conjunctions (or coordinators and subordinators), and prepositions. This class rarely adds new members

- Some words defy these lexical categories. Examples are discourse markers, interjections, and the word *not*. Some people call *not* an adverb; some let it be its own category.

- In this lecture, we'll talk about how we define what makes a noun or a preposition or an auxiliary verb (and then we'll talk about phrases and clauses).

- In the 1970s educational show *Schoolhouse Rock*, one song advises that, "A noun is a person, place, or thing." But does this hold up? The answer is no, not entirely. Relying on what a word means (or purely "semantic" criteria) to define parts of speech is often difficult and inadequate. For instance, nouns can also be also abstract concepts (love, confusion), states of being (limbo), and actions (running).

- Linguists come at defining parts of speech from at least two other angles: how a word behaves in terms of the inflectional endings it takes and in terms of how it works in phrase or sentence.

  - Morphology covers what kinds of inflectional endings a word takes. Nouns tend to make plural with –s. Verbs tend to make past tense with –ed and present participles with –ing (walk/walked/walking). Adjectives can make comparatives with –er or more (happy/happier, beautiful/more beautiful), and so on.

  - There are some derivational endings that tend to signal what lexical category a word is in: If you see a word ending in –ize, odds are it is a verb (colonize, problematize); if you see a word ending in –ion or –ment, odds are it is a noun (realization, retirement).

- Syntax covers what slot in a phrase or clause a word can fill. This is intuitive:

  - Nouns: the _____ (cat, love, running)

  - Verbs: will _____ (swim, walk, go)

  - Adjectives: the _____ thing (happy, ridiculous)

  - Auxiliary verbs: She ____ go (will, may, might)

  - Prepositions: ____ the tree (in, up, down, around, on, to)

- We have not yet mentioned adverbs. They are tricky. There is one morphological signal: –*ly* (slowly, extremely, frankly). However, that can also signal an adjective (lovely, homely). Syntactically, adverbs appear all over the sentence and they modify all kinds of things (verbs, adjectives, and other adverbs).

Phrases, Clauses, and Sentences

- What's the difference between a phrase and a clause? Simply put: a clause is composed of a subject and a predicate. A predicate is the verb and all its accouterments. Here are two clauses, with brackets separating the subject and predicate:

  - [My sister] [took all four kids to the aquarium].

  - [I] [am tired].

- A phrase is a group of words that works together within a clause. To clarify, it can help to think intuitively about the "chunks" within a clause (or what linguists would call *constituents*). An example: <u>My sister</u> took <u>all four kids</u> <u>to the aquarium</u>.

  - *All* is more related to *four kids* than to *took*.

- Sentences work in chunks that are nested within each other, not like train cars that are just all hooked up sequentially.

- Let's unpack this straightforward sentence in terms of phrases:

  - The whole sentence is one clause, with a subject ("My sister") and a predicate ("took all four kids to the aquarium").

  - "My sister" is a noun phrase (the two words together function like a noun).

  - "All four kids" is also a noun phrase; here it is the direct object.

  - "The aquarium" is also a noun phrase, and it is nested inside another kind of phrase: a prepositional phrase ("to the aquarium"). Prepositional phrases are interesting

In the sentence, "My niece loved the fish at the aquarium," the prepositional phrase "at the aquarium" functions adjectivally to modify "fish."

because they function like adverbs and adjectives. Here the prepositional is functioning adverbially: It describes where my sister took the four kids.

■ What is the difference between a clause and a sentence?

  □ They can be the same thing when a sentence has only one clause.

  □ However, a sentence can have more than one clause: "My sister took all four kids to the aquarium, but it was inexplicably closed." These are compound or complex sentences.

Sentences and Contractions

■ Let's end this lecture with the question of what a sentence is. It seems so easy, but actually there isn't a clear answer.

  □ One definition: A sentence is a written string of words that is "complete in and of itself" that ends with a period.

  □ Typically a sentence has one or more clauses, but we can also get fragments: "Not true."

  □ In speech, how do we know where a sentence ends? Intonation is a clue, but an imperfect one. In real-time speech, we often do not speak in full sentences and we can have long run-ons.

  □ We need to accept that sentences are written products. It's not that they don't have counterparts in the spoken word, but the period is a written imposition.

  □ This highlights the difference between speech and writing, which will be a theme throughout this course. Often we are asked to follow conventions in written language that put it at odds with the way we speak. This is not a bad thing, necessarily, but it is worth noting.

- One study in the *Longman Grammar* shows that in speech we contract "do not" almost 100 percent of the time, and we contract modals like "will not" 95 percent of the time. Yet we are told that in formal writing we shouldn't do that, except perhaps for emphasis.

- That convention is changing a bit, as contractions sneak their way into more formal prose.

- Bryan Garner counters the concern that contractions make writing seem too breezy and argues that with contractions, we can gain "relaxed sincerity." But, he warns, don't contract recklessly and avoid contractions in solemn contexts.

- These are rhetorical choices: What we are trying to achieve as writers, in terms of tone and formality, matters. Again, this is a more interesting way to look at a usage rule than whether we should or shouldn't use contractions, as if there was something inherently wrong with them.

Questions to Consider

1. What is a sentence? How do we know where sentences end in spoken language?

2. If the nouns *notice* and *progress* historically got to become verbs, why shouldn't the noun *impact* also get to become a verb?

3. What part of speech or lexical category is *not*? What about *yes*?

Lecture
4 **Re Phrasing**
Transcript

I grew up in the heyday of *Schoolhouse Rock*. There were 37 of these animated educational shorts produced between 1972 and 1979, and they came with the kids' television programming on ABC—often, I will admit, as an unwelcome interruption in the Saturday morning cartoons. But, like many in my generation, I can still sing many of the lyrics of "I'm Just a Bill," and I will spare you and not sing it, but who can forget the lyrics, "Yes, I'm only a bill and I'm sitting here on Capitol Hill." Now that's one of the better-known ones along with "Three is a Magic Number" and "Conjunction Junction."

"Conjunction Junction" is part of the series *Grammar Rock*, which aired from 1973–1975, and it's really interesting to look back on these shorts now. In "Conjunction Junction" they sing about "hooking up words and phrases and clauses." Did we even know what that meant as we sang along?

This lecture is the last of our background lectures before we dive into the usage rules related to different parts of speech. In this lecture we'll address how many parts of speech are there, and how do we define them? How accurate, for example, is *Grammar Rock*'s song "A noun is a person, place, or thing"? And what is the difference between a phrase and a clause?

There's a standard hierarchy when we talk about grammar, which goes from word to phrase to clause to sentence, and we'll proceed in that order in this lecture. The kind of terminology that we're going to review in this lecture is critical for the remaining 20 lectures. Now I know that for some of you this will be review, and I would guess, and I hope, that it will provide some new ways of thinking about familiar concepts in terms of how we define and categorize words into parts of speech or lexical categories.

Before I do an overview of the lexical categories in English, or what are often known as parts of speech, let's start by clarifying a key distinction that builds on the material from the previous two lectures, and that distinction is between what lexical category a word belongs to versus what lexical category we think a word should belong to. The word that jumps to mind here is "impact," which is accepted as a noun. For example, here's a sentence with "impact" as a noun: "The court's decision will have a significant impact on university admissions." It's however not always accepted as a verb. It is a verb that means "to have an impact on," but a good number of people, including many usage guide writers, think it should not be a verb that means "to have an impact on." Now, I want to note here that usage guide writers of course wouldn't have an opinion on this if people weren't already saying it.

In 2001, which is the last time that the *American Heritage Dictionary* surveyed the Usage Panel on "impact" as a verb, 80 percent of the panel rejected the following sentence: "The court ruling will impact the education of minority students." They described it as somewhat or completely unacceptable. Now of course it's not that the members of the usage panel didn't know what that sentence meant, it was just that they didn't like it—it was dispreferred.

Bryan Garner, in his influential book *Modern American Usage*, addresses "impact" as a verb, and he admits that this use of "impact" as a verb has become widespread, but he also concludes that it should be avoided because we already have the synonyms "affect" and "influence." Now I have to say that if we were to rule out words based on the fact that they have synonyms in the language, we'd have to take a whole lot of words out of the English language, and I'm not completely persuaded that "impact" and "affect" are exactly synonymous. Garner goes on to say that, for him, the impact of using "impact" as a verb this way is too jarring. Now, of course, we need to remember there that it's jarring to him; it's clearly not jarring to the many people who use it. According to Garner and many others, you should only use "impact" as a verb if you're talking about impacted teeth.

What I want to make clear here is that "impact" is a verb at this point that means "to have an impact on." That cannot be questioned when you look at actual usage. The question then is whether we're allowed to use "impact" as a verb this way in formal writing. You can find lots of examples in formal writing, but many style guide writers still balk. Now I have to say, I'm struck by the advice that we get when we're told to avoid "impact" as a verb, and we're told we'll use "have an impact on." But sometimes these same writers are saying, "Be sure to be concise," and "have an impact on" is much wordier than just using "impact" as a verb.

The word "impact" captures a phenomenon in Modern English that is very relevant to a discussion of lexical categories—words can change categories, or, more often, expand into new categories, because they keep their former part of speech. For example, nouns get verbed: think about "to Google." Verbs get nouned: consider "a hire." Adjectives get verbed: "to clean." And sometimes people aren't happy about words changing categories like that.

Here, I find it helpful to remember Ben Franklin. And why do I want to remember Ben Franklin? Well, Ben Franklin also didn't like some words that were changing categories, particularly a few nouns that became verbs. He wrote to Noah Webster in 1789 about several new verbs that he had noticed that had been newly created from nouns. They were: "advocate," "notice," and "progress." He was writing to Webster in hopes that Webster would also criticize them. We of course now look at Franklin's concern about those three verbs as very quaint, because all three verbs are now totally standard. You can of course decide which one of these neologisms—or perhaps all of them—you don't want to use, and you can opt out, but I hope that you can see the movement of words across lexical categories as a fascinating aspect of Modern English.

How can this happen so easily in Modern English? Well, part of the answer is that in Modern English we have very few inflectional endings, as we'll talk about. For example, regular verbs just take "ed" to make past tense, so it's not too hard to take a noun and make it a verb: Google/Googled. Nouns just take "s" to make plural and possessive if they're regular nouns—again, not that hard to make "hire" a noun, and then you can have many "hires." We don't have grammatical gender in Modern English anymore, so when you create a new noun, you don't have to give it a gender—you don't have to decide is it masculine, feminine, or neuter. So you can take a verb like "invite" and make it a noun. And, as I said, it doesn't need gender, and now you can make it plural: multiple "invites."

Now I know that there are lots of folks who don't like "invite" as a noun, and I will admit that I am also not a big fan, although I am quite sure that I have used it in informal contexts. I was surprised to learn how old the noun "invite" is. I had fallen prey to the recency illusion in believing that "invite" as a noun was quite new. When you look in the *Oxford English Dictionary*, "invite" as a noun shows up as early as 1659. People were giving and accepting "invites" in the 17th century.

This grammatical flexibility in Modern English that allows words to jump around among lexical categories enhances how creative we can be. We can be playful when we do this, we can be informal; we can also be responsive to new needs: again, think about "to Google."

Okay, this seems like a good moment to step back for a quick review of what lexical categories are available in English. And while there is some basic agreement on this, not everyone agrees on the terminology or how many categories there are. Lexical categories, which are as I've said what linguists call parts of speech, can be divided into two big categories, and those big categories are open class and closed class.

Open class includes nouns, verbs, adjectives, and adverbs. We call this open class because those categories take on new members easily. We can create new nouns, create new verbs, turn a noun into a verb, an adjective into a noun—so we call those open class accepting new members.

Then you have closed class words. This includes pronouns, determiners, auxiliary verbs, conjunctions—some linguists would say coordinators and subordinators instead of conjunctions—and prepositions. We call these closed class because these categories very rarely take on new members. It's not that they never do, but we don't see new pronouns or new prepositions all that often.

Now, there are words that defy the lexical categories that I've just named. For example, discourse markers. This gets us to words like "um." Discourse markers are those little words that occur at the edges of conversation that help direct traffic in conversation, words like "well," "um," "so." We call them discourse markers, and we'll talk about them in much more detail in Lecture 21. Here, I just want to note that they are probably best considered their own lexical category. You also have interjections, like "ouch," which we probably want to deal with as their own category.

Then, what to do with the word "not"? Some will call it an adverb because it works within the verb phrase, and that's fine, but some will say it's a pretty unique—or one could say "unique" if you don't think that unique should be gradable—it's a unique word and it should be its own category in and of itself.

In the lectures to come, we'll be delving into each of these parts of speech and the various points of usage that surround them. In this lecture, I want to talk about how we define what makes a noun, or what makes a preposition, or an auxiliary verb, and then we'll talk about phrases and clauses.

So, does this *Grammar Rock* song, "A noun is a person, place, or thing," hold up? The answer is no, not entirely. Relying purely on what a word means, or what I would call semantic criteria, to define a part of speech is often difficult and inadequate. If you take nouns, it is true that that they are often persons, places, and things. But nouns are also abstract concepts: love, confusion. They're states of being, like limbo. And they are actions, such as running. And with that last one of action, we can now see that we have blurred the line between nouns and verbs if we rely only on semantic criteria. What we end up with is something like "a noun can describe an action when it does it like a noun."

You can actually see this blurriness in the *Grammar Rock* lyrics for the animated short "Verb: That's What's Happening." The song lists "to be," "to sing," "to feel," "to live," all as verbs. It's then followed by this lyric: "A verb expresses action, being, or state of being." Now obviously a noun can also express action, being, or state of being with words like "action" or "state of being." In other words, we've defined a verb with nouns. As a result, linguists will come at defining parts of speech from at least two other angles: first, how a word behaves in terms of the inflectional endings it takes; and second, how a word behaves in terms of how it works in a phrase, or clause, or sentence.

So first, what kinds of inflectional endings does a word take? This is what we would call morphology, and it's about both inflectional endings and derivational endings. Let's start with inflectional endings. Nouns tend to make plural with an "s": cat/cats. Verbs tend to make past tense with "ed" and present participles with "ing," so walk/walked/walking. Adjectives can make comparatives with "er" or with "more," so happy/happier, beautiful/more beautiful, and so on. These can be good tests to see if something is a noun, or a verb, or an adjective: does it behave this way inflectionally?

Also, there are some derivational endings that tend to signal what lexical category a word is in. For example, if you see a word ending in "ize," odds are that it's a verb—for example "colonize" or "problematize," which I know is a verb that many people don't like. If you see a word ending in "ion" or "ment," odds are that it's a noun—for example "realization" or "retirement."

So that's one way to think about what lexical category a word is in is how does it behave in terms of its inflectional endings or what do it's derivational endings signal? The second way to think about it is what slot can the word fill in a phrase or clause? And I have to say, this is a very helpful way to think about and test parts of speech. This gets us into syntax, how words are strung together into phrases and clauses, and we can see how intuitive this is.

For example, nouns tend to be able to sit after "the." So if we get "the" blank, you will tend to get a noun: "the cat," "the love," "the running" I was doing this morning. Verbs will typically be able to come in the slot after "will": "will" blank. "Will swim," "will walk," "will go."

Adjectives come between a determiner like "the" and a noun. Let's take a pretty generic noun like "thing": "the" blank "thing." We can put in adjectives: "the happy thing," "the ridiculous thing." But we couldn't put an adverb in there; we couldn't say "the slowly thing." We could say "the slow thing." Slow is the adjective, slowly is the adverb.

Auxiliary verbs; the slot they like is between a subject—here let's use the pronoun "she"—and a main verb like "go": "she" blank "go." "She will go," "she may go," "she might go"—those are all auxiliary verbs.

Prepositions come right before a noun phrase: blank "the tree." Some prepositions that could fit there: "in the tree," "up the tree," "down the tree," "around the tree," "to the tree." All prepositions.

Now some of these tests work better than others, and some parts of speech are easier to test for than others. You'll notice that I have not given you a test for adverbs, and I have to say that that is because they are very tricky. There is one morphological signal, one derivational ending, "ly," that can signal adverbs: "slowly," "extremely," "frankly," except of course when the "ly" signals that it's an adjective: "lovely," "homely." We'll talk in a later lecture about what happened in the history of English that "ly" can do both, but "ly" is now not entirely a predictable ending in terms of whether something's an adverb.

Syntactically, adverbs can appear all over the sentence, and they modify all kinds of things—verbs, adjectives, other adverbs—so it's hard to have a test where you have one slot and say adverbs fit there. Sometimes adverbs as a result are called the trashcan category.

I hope this brief survey gives you a sense of two other ways to define parts of speech other than semantically. We can look at morphology, what endings the words take; and syntax, where they show up in a phrase or clause or sentence.

Now let's turn to the difference between a phrase, a clause, and a sentence. If we return to "Conjunction Junction" we have the wonderful lyric "hooking up words and phrases and clauses." So what is the difference between a phrase and a clause? Simply put, a clause is composed of a subject and a predicate, and a predicate is the verb and all its, let's call them, accoutrements—all the objects it's coming with, maybe some prepositional phrases. Let's take a sentence as an example: "My sister took all four kids to the aquarium." That's a clause: the subject is "my sister," the predicate is "took all four kids to the aquarium." Here's a simpler sentence: "I am tired." Subject "I"; predicate "am tired." So those are clauses.

A phrase is a group of words that work together within a clause but is not a clause. To clarify, it can help to think intuitively about the chunks within a clause, or what linguists would call constituents. Let's go back to my example sentence: "My sister took all four kids to the aquarium." We know that the "all" there is more related to the "four kids" in "all four kids" than it is to "took," as in "took all." We have an intuition about that.

Sentences and clauses work in chunks, and these chunks are then nested within each other, so it's not like train cars, even though that's how "Conjunction Junction" animates the words in a sentence in that wonderful short. Instead, the words don't all line up in a row with equal relationships to each other. Rather, they nest in chunks, and then those nest within bigger structures within the sentence. Linguists often use trees as a way to capture this hierarchy where you have words being related to each other, and then they're drawn up into a larger structure.

Let's go back to my sentence about my sister and the aquarium and unpack it in terms of phrases. As I already mentioned, the whole sentence here is one clause, with a subject, "my sister," and a predicate, "took all four kids to the aquarium." "My sister" is a noun phrase—those two words function together like a noun, so you have the noun "sister" at the head, and the determiner "my." We could substitute in a proper noun like "Elizabeth" or a pronoun like "she."

"All four kids" is also a noun phrase: those three words together function like a noun. Here, it is the direct object of "took." "The aquarium" is also a noun phrase, and in this case it's nested inside another kind of phrase, which is a prepositional phrase: "to the aquarium." Prepositional phrases are interesting because they can function like adverbs and they can function like adjectives. In this sentence, the prepositional phrase "to the aquarium" is functioning adverbially: it describes where my sister took all four kids.

A very similar prepositional phrase, "at the aquarium," in a different sentence could function like an adjective. Let's imagine the sentence: "My niece loved the sharks at the aquarium." There, the prepositional phrase "at the aquarium" modifies the noun "sharks," and "the sharks at the aquarium" is one big noun phrase. So if I were to ask, "What did my niece love?" we could say "the sharks are the aquarium."

What is the difference between a clause and a sentence? Well, as I've already shown you, they can be the same thing when a sentence has only one clause. But a sentence can have more than one clause. Let's imagine, again, my sister, and here's a longer sentence: "My sister took all four kids to the aquarium, but it was inexplicably closed." There we've got two clauses connected by "but" and we have a compound sentence. When you have sentences that are more than one clause, they can be compound sentences or complex sentences, something we'll come back to in a later lecture.

Let's end this lecture with the question of what a sentence is. It seems so easy and so straightforward because we believe in sentences, but there actually isn't a clear or straightforward answer to exactly what a sentence is. I'm fascinated by this because it's such a fixture in discussions of grammar that we can assume that we understand what a sentence is.

Here's one definition of a sentence: it's a written string of words that is "complete in and of itself" and ends with a period. How happy are you with that definition? It's a little vague. What does it mean that it's complete in and of itself? The part about it ending with a period is less vague, but makes clear that this is a written item; that the sentence is written. Now, typically a sentence is one or more clauses, but we can also have fragments that we consider sentences. Think about something like: "Not true." I think many people would want to call that a sentence.

As I've been talking about, we tend to think about sentences in writing it's much clearer because you say, "Well, it ends with a period." In speech, how do we know where a sentence ends? Intonation is one clue, that often there'll be a downturn at the end of a sentence, as I did there: at the end of a sentence. But, could you know whether that downturn was a period, or was that downturn a semi-colon? Does it matter? And when you look at real speech in real time spoken by real speakers, what you see is that we often don't speak in full sentences, and we often have long run-ons where it's hard to tell exactly where this sentence is ending; there are lots of "ands" and "buts" and the like when we speak.

We need to accept that sentences are written products. It's not that they don't have counterparts in the spoken, because we clearly do speak in clauses, and we often have breaks in between clauses that seem like sentence breaks. But the period is a written imposition onto grammar that separates out sentences. This highlights the difference between speech and writing, which will be a theme throughout the course. Often we're asked to follow conventions in written language that put written language at odds with the way we speak. This isn't a bad thing necessarily, but it is a thing worth noting.

For example, one study in the *Longman Grammar* shows that in speech we contract "do" plus "not" almost 100 percent of the time. In other words, when we speak, we say "don't." And when we have something like "will" plus "not," we say "won't," "can" plus "not" "can't" about 95 percent of the time. Many of us, however, have been told that in formal writing we shouldn't contract, except maybe for emphasis. I grew up with that prescription and still tend to follow it in formal writing. But the convention is changing as contractions sneak their way into more formal prose.

Maybe you're not a fan of contractions in published prose, and if you're feeling concerned about it, maybe Bryan Garner can help in terms of how he writes about contractions in his usage guide. He counters the concern that contractions can make writing seem too breezy, and he argues that with contractions, we can gain "relaxed sincerity." And this is an important thing to think about, it's one of the things that more spoken features like contractions can do when we write. It's again a reason not to adhere too strictly to just one rule, but to think about exactly what we're trying to achieve in our writing. At the same time, Garner warns us—and it's a warning worth heeding—to not contract recklessly and to avoid contractions in solemn contexts because they wouldn't be appropriate.

What's clear here is that these are rhetorical choices. These are about what we're trying to achieve as writers in terms of tone, in terms of formality. I find this a more interesting way to look at a usage rule, such as the one about contractions, than thinking about it in terms of whether we should or shouldn't use contractions in some more absolute way, as if there was something inherently wrong with contractions.

All of this background on lexical categories, phrases, and clauses sets us up to dive into the details of these grammatical building blocks. And as we do, we'll be able to address some important usage questions. Here's one I got the other day over e-mail. The question was: "What is the plural of emoji?" Those are those little images we can use like the eggplant or the smiley face that we can use when we're texting. This person who e-mailed me said, "Is it emoji or emojis?" and how would we decide? To answer that, on we go to the next lecture to talk about nouns and all their quirky plurals, among other usage issues.

Fewer Octopuses or Less Octopi?

Lecture 5

The issue of countable versus uncountable nouns is a tricky one. Many speakers and writers don't observe the distinction, and sometimes it sounds wrong to do what is technically right. This is one of several usage issues around nouns that we're going to look at in this lecture. We'll also cover irregular plurals (like the plurals of *octopus* and *emoji*); collective nouns like *jury*; and other agreement issues, such as "*There are* a few reasons" versus "*There's* a few reasons."

Less/Fewer and Countability

- A prototypical countable noun is *pencil*, and a prototypical uncountable noun is *water*. You can count uncountable nouns with measure words, such as *drops*, *cups*, or *buckets* of water. These measure words can refer to a part (a *grain* of sand) or a container (a *bottle* of beer) or a quantity (a lot of grass). With many uncountable nouns, we can also make them countable with a shift in meaning: "A lot of beer" can become "12 beers."

- Opinions differ on when to use *less* versus *fewer*. Some use the rule of thumb that *less* can be used with both countable and uncountable nouns. This doesn't cause any issues in expressions that are unremarkable, such as, "500 words or less." However, it can be jarring in uses like, "90 percent less germs."

- Strunk's *Elements of Style* (1918) sets out the rule: "Less. Should not be misused for fewer." Less means quantity; fewer means number.

The lexicographer Bryan Garner praises supermarkets that use *fewer* instead of *less* in their express-line signs.

- But it's not that clear-cut in usage. As AHD recognizes, if you look at what feels idiomatic in American English and other varieties, you see *less* used with things we can count:

  □ Measures of time: "less than three days"

  □ Measures of amount: "less than $200"

  □ Measures of distance: "less than 100 miles"

  □ Approximations: "100 bottles, more or less"

- As writers, should we just go with what sounds right? The answer is split. With measures, time, and distance, yes—go with what sounds right. But proceed with caution in other instances.

- In 2006, only 28 percent of the AHD Usage Panel accepted the sentence, "The region needs more jobs, not less jobs." This sentence is not ambiguous or confusing, but there is still some gatekeeping with this construction.

Singular/Plural Issues

- Irregular plurals are a mixture of native English ones and borrowed ones. It can seem like a chaotic mess, but there are actually patterns that are worth sorting out. The three main categories of irregular plurals spawned from English are the *–en* plurals, the zero plurals, and the vowel changes.

- □ *–en* plurals have been dying out for some time, and are limited today to words like children, oxen, and brethren

- □ Another regular way of making plurals was a zero ending, and we still see that with *sheep* and *deer*. Interestingly, this class has expanded over time, encompassing *fish* (which used to be *fishes*). *Emoji* could be a new member of this category, and that is the plural version in Japanese.

- □ The vowel change plurals reflect a very old stage of Germanic, when there was a plural ending that caused the vowel to change. That ending has long since fallen by the wayside, but its effects remain in *goose/geese*, *man/men*, and *mouse/mice*.

- ■ Now let's look at irregularities that have come through borrowing from other languages.

  - □ One very common set of irregular plurals stems from Latin borrowings that end in *–us*, such as *syllabus*, *focus*, and *status*. Not all of these Latin *–us* words come from the same declension in Latin, so they have different plural formations in Latin, which further confuses the issue in English. And then there are a few *–us* borrowings, like *hippopotamus*, which aren't from Latin at all.

  - □ Most borrowings from Latin that end in *–us* take an *–i* plural in Latin: *focus/foci*, *stimulus/stimuli*, and *alumnus/alumni*. For all of these words, the *–i* plural is still the most common in English, but some of them are starting to get Englishified. Additionally, something like *foci* may sound too formal or even forced, even though right now it is more common in formal writing.

- ☐ Some have already become Englishified: *crocuses* not *croci*.

- ☐ *Syllabus* is a complicated case when it comes to words that take *–i* to become plural. It is borrowed from modern Latin, and it seems to stem from a scribal error that misread the Greek (it was a different word). So the Latinate plural *syllabi* is not etymologically founded, but it has taken hold. Right now, we can safely use either *syllabi* or *syllabuses*.

- ☐ Then there are *–us* borrowings from Latin that keep the *–us* in Latin. The plural of *apparatus* is *apparatus* and of *status* is *status* if we stay true to the Latin, but we haven't. Speakers for the most part use *apparatuses* and *statuses*.

- ☐ There is a third, pretty small set of *–us* words that take what looks to us like an irregular plural. Examples are *corpus/corpora* and *genus/genera*. The *Oxford English Dictionary* already includes *genuses*, but not yet *corpuses* (though it can be found in usage).

- There are two common words people often mistake for Latin borrowings. *Hippopotamus* is Greek, not Latin. It means "river horse." Many dictionaries recommend the *–es* ending (hippopotamuses), but recognize that some folks use *–i* (hippopotami). Saying or writing *hippos* is a way around this choice.

- What about *octopus*? This word is Greek. *Octopus* showed up in English in the mid-18th century; before that it was a polypus. In the late 19th century, the plural was usually *octopi*, but by the 1930s and 40s, *octopuses* became the major form.

- The takeaway here about irregular plurals is that they are idiosyncratic. Some are moving toward regular English plurals and some are not. There is not better advice than to look in standard dictionaries and usage guides when in doubt—and realize that there will be some differences of opinion. Also, Latin plurals may be read as more correct or pretentious.

- Before leaving borrowed words, let's address one big usage issue: *data*. Technically, *data* is plural, as it is plural in Latin; the singular is *datum*. But in English it has been reinterpreted as a singular mass noun. This leads to, "the data shows," as opposed to, "the data show." Both are now in common usage, with a preference for the plural in academic writing and a preference for the singular in the spoken. Regardless of which you choose, just be consistent.

Questions of Agreement

- Agreement can be a sticky issue. First, let's cover collective nouns, like *jury*, *group*, *family*, and *couple*. There are two ways to think about this: meaning and geography.

  - When it comes to meaning, ask: Are you thinking about the group as a unit or as separate individuals? Examples are "Her family is highly educated" versus "His family is all doctors."

  - Regarding geography: If you're from the US, you're likely to use the singular ("The jury is deadlocked"). If you're from U.K., you're likely to use the plural ("Arsenal are losing").

- Things can get muddy when the collective is followed by a prepositional phrase such as, "A jury of my peers is/are debating" or "A group of my friends is/are going." American grammar guides often allow some variation here based on meaning, depending on whether something like "a group" refers more to the individuals than to a unit.

- What if the noun comes after the verb? It happens in *there is/are* constructions (e.g., "There is a spider on your head.")

- At issue is the grammatical subject (the existential *there*) versus the notional subject (*a spider*). The prescriptive rule is that the notional subject governs agreement, so there's no problem in, "There is a spider on your head."

- Let's add two spiders. Could you say, "There's three spiders on your head"? We often contract to *there's*. This has become formulaic enough that the number of the following noun doesn't matter: "There's a reason for that" works, as does "There's three reasons for that."

- In formal writing, we're less likely to contract and more likely to let the following noun govern the agreement. This course's recommendation is to be careful and let the notional subject govern in formal writing. But it is fair to note that it is quite idiomatic to use "there's" with plural nouns in speech and informal writing.

Suggested Reading

Crawford, "Verb Agreement and Disagreement."
Yagoda, *When You Catch an Adjective, Kill It.*

Questions to Consider

1. What is lost and gained when *less* replaces *fewer* in a phrase like "50 percent less calories?"

2. At what point, if ever, should the word *data* be accepted as a singular mass noun (much like the noun *information*)? If lots of educated writers are using *data* as a singular noun, are they all wrong?

3. Should the plural of *computer mouse* be *computer mouses* or *computer mice*? Why?

Fewer Octopuses or Less Octopi?

As I mentioned in the first lecture, my mother cared a lot about language, and she took a largely prescriptive approach with her children's language education. As a result, I have been aware of the less/fewer distinction, that usage issue, since I was a kid because my mother would regularly point out grocery store signs that said "10 items or less" and remind me that, to be grammatically correct, the sign should say "10 items or fewer."

Why should the sign say "10 items or fewer?" This comes down to a distinction between countable and uncountable nouns. Because items can be counted, the idea is that that should take fewer. It seems straightforward but you may not be surprised to hear that it's not, both because many speakers and writers don't observe the distinction between less and fewer, and because sometimes it sounds wrong to do what we're told is technically right. This is one of the several usage issues—this less/fewer distinction—that exists around nouns, and we're going to cover these in this lecture.

Here's the outline for this lecture. We're going to start by talking about countability with nouns, which will address the less/fewer distinction. Then we'll talk about irregular plurals. Octopus? Emoji? How do those words make plural? And then finally we'll deal with collective nouns, like jury. Is that one body in the singular or 12 people in the plural? And while we're talking about words like jury, we'll deal with some other agreement issues, such as is it "There are a few reasons," or can you ever say "There's a few reasons."?

To start, let's return to the less/fewer distinction and the idea of countability. Countability is exactly what it sounds like, it's about whether we can count the noun or not, or count the thing the noun refers to. A prototypical countable noun would be pencil—you can clearly count pencils: a pencil, three pencils. A prototypical uncountable noun would be water—you can't count water, you just have water.

But there are ways in English to count uncountable nouns, and we do it with measure words. For example we can count drops of water, cups of water, buckets of water. These measure words can refer to a part of the whole of the uncountable noun, such as a grain of sand; or a container, such as a bottle of beer; or a quantity, such as a stack of hay.

With many uncountable nouns, we can also make them countable creatively with a shift in meaning. For example, if you take beer, which is generally uncountable, but you use beer to refer to a bottle of beer, it suddenly becomes countable, as in "We had two beers." You could do the same thing with love. Love in general is uncountable, but let's imagine that you've had two loves in your life—suddenly it is countable. You can do that with a lot of uncountable nouns, but perhaps the word everlasting cannot be made countable, unless of course you're referring to the flower, in which case you can count them.

But let's accept the general distinction between countable and uncountable nouns. Once you have that, you have the rule about less and fewer. Now fewer, which we're supposed to use with countable nouns, tends to mind its own business in actual usage. It is the word less that is used with both countable and uncountable nouns.

Now, there are expressions where less is used with countable nouns that are unremarkable, such as "500 words or less" or "less than 2 weeks." But then there are the expressions that many people find more jarring. For example, an advertisement that says, "You have 90 percent less germs." Or there was another ad that advertised a drink as having "50 percent less calories." For some people, that is like nails on a chalkboard.

Now, this use of less with countable nouns is not as new as you may think it is—in fact, it's not new at all. Less has been modifying countable nouns since Old English. The fact that we may think it is new is something that's known as the recency illusion. I briefly mentioned this earlier in the course as well. It refers to the idea—and this was coined by Arnold Zwicky, a linguist at Stanford, in 2005—to refer to this idea that when we notice something for the first time, something that's happening in the language, we can often assume that it is new or recent, which is why we noticed it. And then when we look into it, often it's not as new as we think it is.

So, where does this rule about less and fewer come from? It actually seems to have started as a personal preference, a personal preference that was written down in 1770 by Robert Baker in his book *Reflections on the English Language*. And I want to quote for you what he writes, because the wording is really important here. So here's Baker:

> This word less is most commonly used in speaking of a number; where I should think fewer would do better. No fewer than a hundred appears to me not only more elegant than no less than a hundred, but more strictly proper.

In other words we hear him expressing a preference of what he thinks would be more elegant, or what sounds better to him, but by the time we get to Strunk's *Elements of Style*, which he published as a single author book first in 1918, it has become a rule. This is no longer about a personal preference. In *Elements of Style*, under less, it says: "Should not be misused for fewer." And it goes on to say, "Less is for quantity; fewer is for number." This is no longer about preference; this is about right and wrong.

But it's not that clear-cut in usage. As the American Heritage Dictionary recognizes, if you look at what feels idiomatic in American English and other varieties as well, you see less used with things that we can count. For example, we like less with measures of time, even though things like days are countable—for example, "less than 3 days." We also like less with measures of amount, even when those are countable, like dollars. We will often say "less than $200." We also like less with measures of distance, even though measures like miles are countable. We'll say "less than 100 miles." In addition, the phrase "more or less" appears with count nouns all the time; that we'll say "100 cans, more or less." Finally, there's the expression "one less thing to worry about." Now things are countable, but most of us would not say "one fewer thing to worry about."

Bryan Garner, in his *Dictionary of American Usage*—the second edition, which was published in 2003—explains that less tends to go with a singular noun. In other words, when thing is singular, one thing, we'll say "one less thing."

Garner's discussion of less and fewer is interesting because he blames supermarkets for fewer's sad fate—that is, that fewer is on the decline, and Garner certainly doesn't seem happy about it. I think you know that whenever someone uses the word hegemony to refer to a word, that word is in trouble. Here's what Garner writes:

> The linguistic hegemony by which less has encroached on fewer's territory is probably now irreversible. What has clinched this development is something as mundane as the express checkout lines in supermarkets. They're typically bedecked with signs cautioning, '15 items or less.' These signs are all but ubiquitous in the United States. But the occasional more literate supermarket owner uses a different sign: '15 or fewer items.'

Now, I think one could easily argue that "15 items or less" is very idiomatic, and I am not prepared to condemn it as illiterate compared with the more literate "15 or fewer items." I'd rather go with a distinction between colloquial or idiomatic for "15 items or less" and more formal for "15 items or fewer."

So what are we to do as writers? Go with what sounds right? I would say with measures, with time, and with distance, yes, go with what sounds right. But with other constructions, such as those germs, or the calories, I would say proceed with caution.

When the Usage Panel was surveyed on this in 2006, only 28 percent of the panel accepted the sentence: "The region needs more jobs, not less jobs." Now that may feel pretty idiomatic to you—it does to me—but in writing, to use less that way may be a flag. It's not that it's ambiguous if you use less where some people would like you to use fewer, or in any way confusing, but there is still some gatekeeping with this construction.

As a side note here, perhaps this discussion has you thinking about amount versus number. The difference between amount and number is also about uncountable versus countable. And here, too, we see amount, which is for uncountable nouns—much like less—encroaching on the territory of number. So you will find, including in published writing, expressions like "the amount of people." People is plural and countable, but you'll get "the amount of people." That said, I would say be careful here—this use of amount is very colloquial and could get you judged in any kind of formal writing, probably even more than mixing up less and fewer.

The rest of this lecture is going to be about singular/plural issues also, but from a couple of different angles: countable nouns with irregular plurals, and collective nouns like jury, in terms of how to handle agreement, as well as a few other agreement issues, including "there is" versus "there are" with plural nouns.

Let's start with irregular plurals. The irregular plurals are a mixture of native English irregular plurals and borrowed ones, which come in and make the language irregular. It can seem like a chaotic mess when you get into these irregular plurals, but there are actually patterns that are worth sorting out. Let's start with the set of irregular plurals that are native forms, because these irregular forms tell us something about the history of the language.

There are three main categories of irregular plurals that go back to earlier stages in English: the "en" plurals, such as oxen; zero plurals, such as sheep; and words that take a vowel change, as in man/men. English used to have a few regular ways of making plurals. Nouns were in different categories, and each category had a different way of making plurals. One of those categories had a final "s." That's become the regular way of making plurals, but we have remnants of some of the other categories.

One of those, you created the plural by adding "an" at the end, and that has now become "en." We used to have many more of these nouns that ended with vowel plus "en," but over time they have become regular. For example, "shoen" becomes "shoes"; "eyen" becomes "eyes." All we have left in this category are "children," which is healthy; "oxen," and I'm not so sure about that, I think that that may get replaced by "oxes" because many of us don't encounter oxen that much anymore; and finally "brethren," and brethren has already specialized, so that brothers are one thing and brethren are something else.

Another regular way of making plurals in Old English was with a zero ending, and we still see that with sheep and with deer. Interestingly, this class has expanded over time as opposed to the nouns that take plural with "en," which has shrunk over time. That category has expanded to encompass, for example, fish. Fish actually used to make the plural with "s," so you had fishes, and it is still fishes if you're referring to multiple species, or if you're in the *Godfather* movie and have the unfortunate fate of sleeping with the fishes.

Occasionally, and this is fascinating to me, a borrowed word will come into the language and take a zero plural. The word moose was borrowed into English from Algonquian, and it became a zero plural in English. This raises the question for us of what should be the plural of emoji. This word is borrowed in from Japanese. It refers to those pictorial characters we can use when we text, and there has been some discussion about what the plural is. There are two possibilities: emoji, zero plural; or emojis, with the regular "s." Right now you can find both in published writing. I think the trend is going toward emojis to just make this a regular plural in English.

The vowel change plurals reflect a very old stage of Germanic. This goes back even before Old English where there was a plural ending, and that plural ending caused a vowel change earlier in the word. That ending has long since fallen off, it was gone by Old English, but its effects on the stem are still there, and we can see it in goose/geese, man/men, mouse/mice.

But mouse/mice: we now have a new meaning of mouse for all of us using computers—you have the computer mouse. What is the plural of a computer mouse? Is it computer mouses or computer mice? Many dictionaries list both as standard. Usage seems to be now favoring computer mice, and I have to say, somehow that one just cracks me up—somehow the mice are scurrying as opposed to I've gotten used to just a computer mouse.

So those are some irregular plurals than have come down from earlier stages in English. Now let's look at irregular plurals that have happened through borrowing, and this happens because English is an omnivorous language. We have borrowed words from so many languages, and those languages of course make plurals in ways that are different from English, and sometimes those different plurals come into English.

One very common set of irregular plurals stems from Latin borrowings that end in "us," such as syllabus, focus, status. Now here's the kicker with these words; that not all of these Latin words that end in "us" come from the same declension in Latin, so they have different plural formations in Latin, which further confuses the issue in English. And then there are a few words that end in "us," like hippopotamus, which aren't from Latin at all.

Let's look at the effect of all of this on English—and again, we're sorting out what otherwise can look a bit chaotic. Most borrowings from Latin that end in "us" take a plural with the final "i," so this would be focus/foci, stimulus/stimuli, alumnus/alumni. That's what happens in Latin; it's what happens in English. For all of those words I just listed, the "i" plural is still the most common in English, but some of them, and I think particularly focus, are starting to get Englishified. I think that, at this point, foci as the plural may sound too formal, or potentially even a little bit forced, even when you're writing formally.

One set of these "us" words that end in "i" have already become Englishified. For example, with a crocus we talk about crocuses, not croci. With the word alumnus there's some confusion, and I think the confusion stems from the fact that there is a feminine form. You have alumnus, which is masculine; and alumna, which is feminine. And the plural of alumnus is alumni; the plural of alumna is alumnae. That's why people are confused. If you want to get out of that, just shorten it to alum, and then the plural is alums.

Now I will be honest with you that I had long put syllabus in this category of Latin borrowings that take a final "i" to become plural. But it turns out that the history of syllabus is more complicated. It's borrowed from modern Latin, and it seems to stem from a scribal error that misread the Greek—it was actually a different word. So the Latinate plural syllabi is not etymologically founded, but it has taken hold. The *Oxford English Dictionary* has both syllabuses and syllabi as the plural of the word. In British English you'll tend to hear syllabuses; in American English syllabi. Bryan Garner thinks we are perhaps overfond of syllabi in the U.S. Right now, I think you can safely use either.

Then there are "us" borrowings from Latin that keep the "us" in Latin. There would have been a vowel change in Latin, but that gets lost, so the plural of apparatus is apparatus, and of status is status, if we stay true to the Latin, which we have not done, and for most speakers these now have become regular English plurals: apparatuses and statuses. And if you put that into Microsoft Word, the spellchecker doesn't flag them.

There's a third, pretty small set of words that end in "us" that take what looks to us like an irregular plural. This would be a word like corpus, which becomes corpora; or genus, which becomes genera. That's a pretty highly academic plural. The OED already includes genuses as the plural of genus, but it doesn't yet include corpuses, but I think if you wait, corpuses will come in, too.

So those are all Latin borrowings ending in "us." Then there are two common words people often mistake for Latin borrowings. The first is hippopotamus. Hippopotamus is Greek, not Latin: it refers to a river horse. Many dictionaries recommend a regular "es" ending to create hippopotamuses, but they also recognize that many folks use the "i": hippopotami. Again, if you're looking for a way out, shorten it to hippo and make it totally regular with hippos.

Now what about octopus? Octopus is also Greek, and it goes back to "okto"—eight—plus "pous" for foot. The stem is octopod, which means that the plural would technically be octopodes. Octopus shows up in English in the mid-18th century. Before that, we referred to this creature as a polypus. I mean, who knew how many feet it had? In the late 19th century, the plural was usually octopi, but by around the 1930s and 1940s, octopuses became the major form. Now, it's more than twice as common to say octopuses than octopi, and that is common in general works as well as biological journals. Now if we were going to be technically correct, the plural would be octopodes, but that has never gained much momentum, and I have to say that if you were to use octopodes, you might be out there on your own.

The takeaway here about irregular plurals is that they are idiosyncratic, and some of them are moving toward regular English plurals and some are not. I'm afraid that there is not better advice than to look in standard dictionaries and usage guides when you're in doubt, and realize that there will be some differences of opinion here. Also, remember that Latin plurals may sometimes be read as the most correct form, and sometimes as a slightly pretentious form.

Before leaving borrowed words, let's address one big usage issue, and that is with data. Technically, data is plural, as it is plural in Latin; the singular is datum. But in English this word, data, has been reinterpreted as a singular mass noun. As a result, you will find "the data shows" as opposed to the "the data show." You will get "this data," singular, as well as or instead of "those data." Both the singular and the plural for data are now in common usage, with a preference for the plural in academic writing, and a preference for the singular in the spoken. So given that singular data is more common in the spoken, I can tell you where I would put my money. I always put my money on the spoken. I would guess that singular data in the end will probably win.

At this point, only 34 percent of the *American Heritage Dictionary* Usage Panel still rejects data as a singular, which is interesting—you can see how the gatekeeping is changing here. The sentence the panel was given was: "Once the data is in, we can begin to analyze it." And 92 percent of the panel accept the expression "very little data" as opposed to "very few data." *American Heritage Dictionary* as a result called singular data standard. As a writer and editor myself, I simply try to be consistent: if you're going to use data as singular, do that all the time; if it's plural, do that all the time.

Data, the word, has raised one agreement issue, "data is" versus "data are," so let's run with this question of agreement. First, let's talk about collective nouns: jury, group, family, couple. There are two ways to think about this: meaning and geography.

Let's start with meaning. Are you thinking about this group as a unit or as separate individuals? It matters in terms of agreement. If you're thinking about them as a group, let's take the noun family. You could say something like "her family is highly educated." You're thinking about the family as a collective. But now let's imagine you're thinking about the family as several individuals. In that case, you could say "his family are all doctors."

Now let's talk about this in terms of geography. If you're from the U.S., you likely use the singular and say "the jury is." If you're from the U.K., you likely use plural agreement and say "the jury are." Now, some familiar collectives are singular no matter where you are in relation to the pond. One of those would be the United States, which tends always to be singular.

Now, things can get muddy when that collective noun is followed by a prepositional phrase such as "a jury of my peers." Is it "a jury of my peers is" or "a jury of my peers are"? "A group of my friends are going"? "A group of my friends is going"? American grammar guides often allow some variation here again based on meaning, depending on whether something like "a group" refers to the individuals in the group or to the unit. So let's imagine I'm talking about my group of friends, and I'm talking about them as individuals. I could say, "My group of friends are going different ways after college," because each one is going a different way.

In all of these examples about agreement that I've just given you, the noun comes before the verb: "the jury is" versus "the jury are." Now what if the noun comes after the verb? This is where things can get even trickier. This is the last tricky agreement issue we'll talk about in this lecture, and it happens with constructions that involve existential "there," as in "there is" versus "there are." Now let's imagine this sentence: "There is a spider on your head." The grammatical subject there is "there"—it's what we call existential "there." The notional subject actually comes after the verb: the notional subject is "a spider."

The prescriptive rule on this is that the notional subject, which is coming after the verb, governs agreement, so there's no problem in a sentence like "There is a spider on your head," because the notional subject is singular. But let's imagine that there are actually three spiders on your head. I could say, "There are three spiders on your head." But could I also say, "There's three spiders on your head"? You'll notice that there I've got the singular "is" with the three spiders.

What's happening here is that we often contract the existential "there" with "is" to create "there's," and this has become formulaic enough that it sometimes doesn't matter what the number of the noun following it is. So whether the notional subject is singular or plural, "there's" is already contracted and is functioning as the focuser in the sentence. So we can say "There's a reason for that," or often we'll say "There's three reasons for that." When you think about the job of "there's," really what it's doing is introducing what we call a semantically heavy bit of information. It's putting that in the second half of the sentence where speakers expect something that's semantically heavy, something that's important, and we say, "There's three spiders on your head." "There's three reasons."

In an interesting study by Bill Crawford, who's a linguist at Northern Arizona University, he found that with existential "there" constructions and plural nouns, we tend to use "there's" 50 percent of the time in speech. In other words, when we're speaking, we would say "There's three spiders on your head" half the time. And he looked at academic lectures and discovered in academic lectures we do it 45 percent of the time. We'd say things like, "There's three reasons."

The *Longman Grammar* notes that there are some analogous constructions where you get a singular and then get a notional subject that's plural. For example, "Here's your shoes" or "How's things?" Now, obviously, those expressions are more colloquial. In formal writing, we're much less likely to contract the "there" and the verb, much more likely to keep it "there is" and "there are," and more likely to let the following noun govern the agreement. My recommendation here would be to be careful and to let the notional subject govern in formal writing. But I do want to note that it is quite idiomatic to use "there's" with plural nouns in speech and informal writing.

For better or worse, we are far from finished with tricky agreement issues, and we're going to cover two more in the next lecture. Here's one of them: is it "none of the books is" or "none of the books are"? The pronoun "none" is technically singular, but the noun "books" is clearly plural. With that lead-in, let's turn to pronouns.

Between You and Your Pronouns

This lectures addresses several prominent usage issues related to pronouns. It's not accurate to say a pronoun is just a word that stands in for a noun, because pronouns can stand in for entire noun phrases. Pronouns are some of the most common words in our language. This lecture starts with a definition of our terms, then moves on to describe several categories of pronouns. Throughout, the lecture provides examples of how to use pronouns properly—and where there's wiggle room.

Personal Pronouns

- There are several categories of pronouns. We'll start with the personal pronouns, several of which are among the most common words. Examples include *I*, *you*, *it*, *he*, and *they*.

- With personal pronouns, we often hear reference to the first, second, and third person. This is about where people (or things) are relative to the discourse or text. Pronouns can stand in for the people in the discourse (with first or second person) or people or things being discussed (with third person).

Between You and I

- The first usage issue with personal pronouns we need to discuss is "between you and I" (a pet peeve for many). We need this background to understand what is happening with "between you and I," so we need to discuss the case system from Old English.

- Case is a grammatical system that distinguishes the function of a noun or pronoun in a clause. If we look at the personal pronouns, we see that most of them distinguish three cases: subject, object (direct and indirect), and possessive.

- ☐ First person: I/me/mine, we/us/ours

- ☐ Second person: you/you/yours

- ☐ Third person: he/him/his, she/her/hers, they/them/theirs, it/it/its

- In Old English, all nouns made these kinds of distinctions: subject, object, and possessive. Today, everything but possessive distinctions has dropped away. But pronouns still prop up the full historical case system.

- Given that we don't have to make this distinction anywhere else in the grammar, we can interchange pronouns when the syntax gets complicated—and it gets complicated in conjoined constructions.

  - ☐ In American English and British English, if the personal pronoun occurs by itself, you tend to consistently get *I* in subject position and *me* in object position: "I went to the store" or "My mother called me."

  - ☐ But if you create an "X-and-Y" situation with I/me, you will hear: "Me and my mom went to the store," and "My mother called my sister and I." Compare these to the standard constructions: "My mom and I went to the store," and "My mother called my sister and me."

- Conjoined constructions may not follow the same rules as single nouns. For example, while you would get accusative "me" alone, the conjoined "my sister and I" may not have to take the object case after a preposition, as in "between my sister and I". In other words, "X and I" and "me and Y" could be routinized (though not standardized) expressions.

- Interestingly, polite usage for many speakers, including highly educated ones, is "between you and I." In the long run, the distinction may well collapse. Who knows which pronoun will win?

Distinction Problems

- A collapse of singular/plural distinction in the can happen in the second person as well. We used to have *thou/thee*. This became the familiar form, but is now mostly dead (other than Quakers and old plays and novels). There are many newer plural forms: *y'all*, *you guys*, *yous*, *yous guys*, *yinz*.

- In standard English, *you* can be both singular and plural. This fact is relevant to what is known as the generic pronoun problem, which happens when we need to refer back to a noun phrase (the *antecedent*) that refers to a person whose gender is unspecified, unknown, or irrelevant. For instance: "A person at that level should not have to keep track of the hours ____ put in." (This was the sentence on the AHD usage ballot for a generic person.)

- There is also the situation where we don't know a person's gender: "We would like to think the anonymous reviewer for _____ comments."

- There is an idea out there that we don't have a singular generic pronoun for these situations, and since the late 18th century, people have been coming up with artificial ones. Some examples: *heshe*, *thon*, *e*, *hiser*, *ze*. But we do have a singular generic pronoun: *they*.

- The question is whether we're going to allow writers to use singular generic *they* in formal writing. We already use it in informal, less monitored writing.

- The push against *they* originated in the 18th century, first recorded in Anne Fisher's grammar and then picked up in Lindley Murray's wildly popular grammar at the end of 18th century.

- In the 1970s, second-wave feminism pushed against the use of *he* as the dominant pronoun. Four options arose:

  - *He or she*

  - Alternate *he* and *she*

  - Make it plural

  - Omit the pronoun.

- These are fine solutions, but why can't we also use *they*? It works well in the spoken language, and is no more ambiguous than other spoken pronouns. Luckily, if you are a writer who would like to use singular *they*, we are entering an era where this is close to becoming standard usage. We're not quite there, but we're getting close.

- There have been some artificial pronouns suggested along the way. *Ze* now has some traction as a transgender pronoun, along with *they*. These are also for those who identify outside the male/female binary.

- There is debate on college campuses about these pronouns. Overall, the pronouns are about respecting what people ask to be called and thereby creating a more inclusive, respectful space.

Interrogative Pronouns

- The collapse of case is relevant to another class of pronouns: interrogative. These are pronouns that create questions. You often see a list of five: *what*, *which*, *who*, *whom*, and *whose*. But you could argue there are three: *what*, *which*, and *who*, the last of which then has two additional mutations (*whom* and *whose*) for the object and possessive form.

- *Who/whom* is the biggest usage issue. *Who* is the subject form of the pronoun; *whom* is the object form, and it is in decline. But it has been in decline for several hundred years, so one interesting

Whom might sound appropriate in an academic context but stuffy in a social context.

question is why it hasn't died yet. It is healthiest when it comes after a preposition (examples: "to whom," "by whom"). Alone, it can look like a subject form because it appears first: "Who(m) are you calling?"

- *Whom* can sound fussy in many contexts. If you wish to avoid it in e-mails or texts, you can either rework the sentence or just use *who*: "Who did you call about getting the washing machine fixed?" Know your audience.

Indefinite Pronouns

- Indefinite pronouns pose other agreement issues, especially the pronoun *none*. An example: Should it be, "None of the books is _____" or "None of the books are _____?"

- Indefinite pronouns do not refer to a specific person or thing. They stand in for a vague or undetermined person or thing, or amount of things. Typical examples: *anyone/anybody*, *everyone/everybody*, and *someone/somebody*.

- Most are straightforward in terms of agreement with verbs: *anyone* is singular ("anyone is") and *few* is plural ("few are"). *None* is trickier, perhaps especially in a phrase where it is referring to none of a plural group of things: "None of my friends is/are."

- So, can *none* be both singular and plural? In short, yes. Over the years, sources, have varied, but now certain reputable usage guides recognize the singular or plural can be standard. Bryan Garner distinguishes between meaning of "not one" (singular) versus "not any" (plural).

This What?

- We haven't covered another category of very common pronouns, namely *this*, *that*, *these*, and *those*. These are demonstrative pronouns, which point at things inside and outside the text or discourse.

- Did you learn that you should never leave the word *this* by itself at the beginning of a sentence in formal writing? Such instruction can lead students to add nouns: "This idea means _____." This setup can in turn become clunky if it's hard to find a noun that captures exactly what *this* is referring back to.

- The good news: You can relax that stricture (if you learned it). Sometimes it is OK to leave your *this* without a noun. The key is that it needs to be clear what you're referring back to. And it is OK if, as Bryan Garner puts it, sometimes the *this* summarizes what you just wrote.

- Here's an example from Malcolm Gladwell's *Outliers*, where he's making a connection between agriculture and growing seasons, and educational reform:

  Unless a wheat- or cornfield is left fallow every few years, the soil becomes exhausted. Every winter, fields are empty. The hard labor of spring planting and fall harvesting is followed, like clockwork, by the slower pace of summer and winter. This is the logic the reformers applied to the cultivation of young minds.

- Garner's advice is worth following here: Make sure you can answer, "This what?"

Suggested Reading

Balhorn, "The Epicene Pronoun in Contemporary Newspaper Prose."
Baron, *Grammar and Gender*.
Bodine, "Androcentrism in Prescriptive Grammar."
Curzan, *Gender Shifts in the History of English*.
Newman, *Epicene Pronouns*.
Swales, "Attended and Unattended 'This' in Academic Writing."
Vuolo, "Between You and I" (*Lexicon Valley Podcast*).
Yagoda, *When You Catch an Adjective, Kill It*.

1. The second-person pronoun *you* has already lost the distinction between subject and object so that we now use *you* for both. If—and this is a big if—English were to lose the subject-object distinction in the first-person singular pronoun, do you think *I* or *me* would win? Why?

2. Studies show that many speakers use *they* as a singular generic pronoun in a sentence like "Someone left their towel on the deck chair." What are reasons for and against allowing singular generic *they* in formal writing?

Between You and Your Pronouns

One of my favorite *Calvin & Hobbes* cartoons involves pronouns. Calvin is sitting at a desk doing homework, and he says to Hobbes, "I need help on my homework. What's a pronoun?" Hobbes replies: "A noun that has lost its amateur status." There's a pause in the cartoon, and then Calvin says, "Maybe I can get a point for originality."

I love that definition. It's not going to get you very far in a grammar review, but it's wonderfully clever. Let's, however, try to do a little bit better, probably not in cleverness but at least in accuracy. So, before we address several prominent usage issues related to pronouns, let's define our terms.

If we take the word pronoun, we can see that it's created from "pro" plus "noun," which suggests that a pronoun is a word that's standing in for a noun. That's kind of accurate but not entirely accurate, because in fact what a pronoun does is it stands in for a noun phrase. Sometimes that will be just a noun. For example, "Spinach is good for you." We could then substitute in "it" for "spinach," it's just a noun: "It is good for you." But pronouns often are substituting in for a longer noun phrase. For example, "The book that I just finished is great." And then we could substitute in "it" for "the book that I just finished." "It is great."

Now pronouns are some of the most common words in the language, along with articles and prepositions. One study of the most common words in spoken British English found "the" and "and" at the top of the list, the pronoun "I" was in 3rd, then "you" at 6th, "that" at 7th—and "that" I have to say is a little complicated because it's both a determiner and a pronoun—"it" came in at 9th, "this" at 13th, and "he" at 17th.

English Grammar Boot Camp   105

In the corpus of contemporary of American English, the most common words once again put "the," "be," and "and" at the top of the list, "it" comes in at 10th, "I" is in 11th, "that" at 12th, "you" at 14th, "he" at 15th, "this" at 20th, and "they" at 21st. You can see how important function words are to the language and how often we use them. Pronouns are central to the function words.

Now there are several categories of pronouns, and we're going to start with the personal pronouns, several of which figured in these lists of the most common words, pronouns such as I, you, it, he, and they. And I can't give you a particularly good explanation of why we talk about "he" more than "she" other than a cultural one. I will leave it to you to make your own decisions about what's happening there.

With the personal pronouns, we often hear reference to first person, second person, and third person, and I thought I'd quickly review those. Those terms are about where people are with respect to the discourse or the text. Let me explain. The pronouns can stand in for the person who is doing the talking, that would be the first person, I or we. It can also be for the other person in the discourse, the person that the speaker's talking to. That would be the second person, which would be you. Then you have the third person, which is the people or things that we are talking about, that are being discussed. That would be he, she, it, and they. Because personal pronouns are so common in the language, they tend to be quite stable over time, but English has a couple of notable exceptions.

The first of these exceptions is the pronouns they, them, and their. These pronouns are borrowed into Old English from Old Norse in the Old English period. It speaks to the intense language contact that was happening between Old Norse speakers and Old English speakers after the Viking invasions in the 8th and 9th centuries. It is highly unusual to borrow pronouns this way, but English did, and there's some chance that those "th" forms— they, them, and their—were providing a useful distinction in the language. It's not that Old English didn't have pronouns for the third person plural, it did, but they started with "h," as does the third person singular "he," so the "th" pronouns introduced a useful distinction.

Let me now turn to the second exception of a pronoun that suddenly appears in English, and that would be the pronoun "she." The origins of "she" are in fact unclear. Old English did have a word for "she," it was "heo," spelled H-E-O. "She" first appears in 1154 in the north of England. Again, it may have been that "she" provided a useful distinction; it was more different from "he."

Now the first usage issue with personal pronouns that we need to discuss is "between you and I," and I say need to discuss because this is a pet peeve for many people. And since we're already talking about Old English, let's talk about the case system, because we need this background to understand what's happening with "between you and I." After we talk about "between you and I," we'll talk about the singular generic pronoun question, then we'll talk about "who" and "whom," then indefinite pronouns like "none," and finally the question of how we use the pronoun "this" in academic writing. I know that's a lot, but there are a lot of usage issues around pronouns.

Okay, so back to case. Case is a grammatical system that distinguishes the function of a noun or a pronoun based on its function in a clause or in a sentence. If we look at the personal pronouns, we can see that most of them distinguish three cases: subject; object, be that direct or indirect or the object of a preposition; and possessive. For example, in the first person singular we have subject "I," object "me," possessive "mine." In the plural: we, us, ours. If we do the third person we see very similar distinctions. For example, in the masculine, subject "he," object "him," possessive "his." In the feminine, subject "she," object "her," possessive "hers."

Let's now do third person plural: they, them, theirs. If we do the neuter in the singular with "it," we see we only have two distinctions instead of three. We have subject "it," object "it," possessive "its." Finally, let's look at the second person. We have subject "you," object "you," possessive "yours."

Again, you'll notice that there's no distinction between the subject and object—this has collapsed over time. There used to be a distinction in English. It was subject "ye," and object "you." In older forms of English, you would get something like "Ye are fantastical" versus "I beseech you."

But even by the time of Shakespeare, you see Shakespeare mixing up his "yes" and "yous" and now we have "you" for subject and "you" for object.

Now, in Old English, all nouns made these kinds of distinctions between subject, object, and possessive. And within the object category, there were also distinctions between direct object and indirect objects and sometimes objects of prepositions. Now all we have left with nouns is the possessive "s," and the pronouns are the ones that still prop up the historical case system.

But here's the thing. Given that we don't have to make this distinction between subject and object anywhere else in the grammar, we can sometimes get a little mixed up with our pronouns, and we can interchange subject and object pronouns when the syntax gets complicated, and it gets complicated in conjoined constructions such as x and y—think "between you and I."

Now in most varieties of English around the world, and that includes American and British English, but it's not true of all varieties, if the personal pronoun appears by itself, you tend to consistently get "I" in subject position and "me" in object position. In other words you'll get things like "I went to the store." "My mother called me." But if you create an x and y situation with "I" and "me" you will hear some variations. You will hear things like "Me and my mom went to the store," and "My mother called my sister and I." This would be as opposed to the standard construction, "My mom and I went to the store," or "My mother called my sister and me." What's happening here?

The first thing that I want to say is that this is not new. Here's an example from Shakespeare's *Othello*: "Yes, you have seen Cassio, and she together." And here's another example from *The Merchant of Venice*: "All debts are cleared between you and I." These may sound strikingly modern to you if you think that "between you and I" is just a modern thing.

Patricia O'Conner, who wrote the entertaining grammar *Woe is I*, has examples of constructions like "between you and I" back into the Middle English period, and she's found criticism of the construction back to the

18th century. So it's not new, even though many people think it is, but that doesn't answer the question about what is happening here, and I'm going to focus particularly on the construction "between you and I."

It is possible that conjoined constructions of the x and y variety may not follow the same rules as single pronouns. So, while you would get an accusative "me" alone, the conjoined "my sister and I" may not have to take the object case after, say, a preposition. So you would say "for me," but perhaps it's possible to just say "for my sister and I." In other words, the phrase "x and I" could become a routinized expression; it becomes fixed. And that way it doesn't matter if it's the subject or the object: "My sister and I went" for "my sister and I."

I think that we want that preposition in "for my sister and me" or "my sister and I" to function distributively. It's like math where it would distribute to both the x and the y, so you would get "for me," "for my sister," so "for my sister and me." But it looks like maybe it doesn't. For lots of speakers, it is "for my sister and I." Now to say that these expressions, these conjoined expressions, are routinized, and to explain how they might happen, is not the same as saying that they are standard. We still would need to say that standard usage is "between you and me."

But interestingly, at this point, I think we may need to say that polite usage, or perhaps hyper-polite usage for many speakers, including highly educated ones, is "between you and I." I tend to go with the standard form, "between you and me," as opposed to the hyper-polite, or some might call it hypercorrect form, and it is always safe to go with "between you and me," especially in edited prose. In the long run, I'm not sure what will happen here. There is some chance, if we think in the way distant future, that the distinction between subject and object pronouns might collapse all the way through the system. If you think that sounds like a terrible fate, just remember that the distinction between subject and object has already collapsed for the pronoun "you" and we all survived.

While we're on personal pronouns and collapsing distinctions, let's talk about another collapse in the second person pronouns that we have managed to survive. This is the collapse of the distinction between the singular and the plural in the second person. We used to make a distinction here, we had singular "thou" and "thee," and plural "ye" and "you." Thou became the familiar form and now it's mostly dead, other than for Quakers and some old plays and novels.

Now it is true that we have created some new plural second person pronouns to recreate this distinction, although in standard varieties "you" can function both as a singular and a plural. But new plural forms include things like "y'all," "you guys," "yous," "yous guys," "yinz"—if you live in Pittsburgh. And there are reports that in some parts of Texas, "y'all" has become singular and the new plural is "all y'all." In standard English, though, "you" can function as both a singular and a plural, and it's worth noting that we continue to use the verb "are" both when it's singular and plural.

This fact about "you" is relevant to what is known as the generic pronoun problem. This problem arises when we need to refer back to a noun phrase, what's called the antecedent, a noun phrase that refers to a person whose gender is unspecified, unknown, or irrelevant. Let me give you an example to show you what I'm talking about. Here's a sentence: "A person at that level should not have to keep track of the hours mmm put in." Should not have to keep track of the hours he puts in, she puts in, he or she puts in, they put in. This sentence was the sentence on the *American Heritage Dictionary* usage ballot when they were asking us what pronoun we thought was acceptable for a generic person, a person of unspecified gender.

Now there's also the situation where we don't know the person's gender. This would be something like "We would like to thank the anonymous reviewer for mmm comments." His comments, her comments, their comments, his or her comments. So we have these situations where we have someone who is a person who's truly unspecified gender or we just don't know the gender, or perhaps we just don't want to tell you.

Now there's an idea out there that we don't have a singular generic pronoun for these situations, and since the 19th century, people have been coming up with some artificial ones to solve the problem. They've come up with pronouns such as "heshe," spelled as one word; "thon"; "e," just lowercase e; "hiser"; and "ze." Now, none of these have caught on; it's very hard to introduce an artificial pronoun into the language. But here's what I would say about this. We do have a singular generic pronoun, and that pronoun is "they."

We've been using "they" as a singular in these situations where we have a person of unspecified gender, unknown gender, irrelevant gender, for several hundred years. If you search the Internet for Jane Austen and singular "they" you can find a website with all the examples where she used singular "they" in her writing. You can find examples back into Middle English. Shakespeare does it, and almost all of us use singular "they" today, at least in speech.

Now one of the arguments I'll hear is that "they" cannot be singular, and what I'm going to say is that's actually not an interesting argument to have. "They" is singular. If you look at usage, "they" is singular. I can say to you something like, "I was talking to a friend of mine, and they said that it's a terrible movie." I was talking to "a" friend and "they" said—"they" is clearly singular. If you're perhaps thinking, "But a pronoun can't be singular and plural at the same time," please remember what we just talked about with the pronoun "you" where it is singular and plural at the same time, and continues to use plural agreement with the verb, for example "are."

So the real question is whether we're going to allow writers to use singular generic "they" in formal writing. Many of us already use it in informal, less monitored writing, and almost all of the studies show usage in speech. So why wouldn't we allow it?

The rule that tells us that we should not use singular "they" in writing, but that instead we should use singular generic "he," originates in the 18th century. It was first recorded in Anne Fisher's grammar, and then it was picked up in Lindley Murray's wildly popular grammar at the end of 18th century. So, for about 200 years, we lived with the rule that we should use generic "he," as in "A person at that level should not have to record his time."

In the 1970s, with second wave feminism, we started to get some pushback against generic "he," and over time it was successfully replaced with four different options for what we could do in this situation where we need a generic singular pronoun. The first option was use "he" or "she," and that's fine, although it can get a little bulky if you need to use a lot of those, if you have a string of them in a row: he or she, his or her, and he or she. It just gets a little bulky.

Another solution is to alternate "he" or "she" by sentence or by paragraph. Again, this is okay, but I have to say, as a reader, I can find it a little discombobulating if an unknown person's gender appears to be changing before my very eyes. A third option is to make the whole sentence plural, and then you can just use "they" as a plural pronoun. The fourth option is omit the pronoun entirely; rewrite the sentence so you don't need a pronoun.

These are all perfectly fine solutions, but I'm still left with the question of why not also allow us to use singular "they" in writing? It works well in the spoken language. It's a proven solution with centuries of usage behind it. It's no more ambiguous than other pronouns. Sure, sometimes in a sentence a pronoun can be ambiguous, but this is true of "he," "she," and "they," and if you have an ambiguous pronoun, rewrite the sentence.

As you can probably tell, I am a big fan of singular "they," but I also know my audience, and I know not everyone agrees with me on this. My solution right now is to footnote my first use of singular "they," and in the footnote I explain why I'm using this as a singular generic pronoun. And I'll continue to do this until singular "they" this becomes fully acceptable. And I do think this is happening. Some interesting things have been afoot.

In 2015, *The Washington Post* redid its style guidelines to say that writers could use "they" as a singular generic, as well as to refer to individuals who identify outside the male/female binary. The *American Heritage Dictionary* Usage Panel shows decreasing opposition to singular "they"; at this point it's almost a 50/50 split on a sentence like the one about "the person at that level." And, with an indefinite pronoun such as "If anyone calls, tell them I can't come to the phone," more than half the panel accepted the sentence.

Now I recognize that it may still strike your eye as wrong in writing to use singular "they," but I would guess that even you use singular "they" in your speech sometimes. And if you are a writer who would like to use singular "they" in your writing as a generic pronoun, I would say we're entering an era where this is close to becoming standard usage. We're not quite there yet, but we're close.

As I mentioned, there have been some artificial pronouns suggested along the way and "ze" has now gotten some traction as a transgender pronoun along with "they." It is also sometimes used, both "ze" and "they," for individuals who identify outside the male/female binary. There is a debate going on right now on college campuses about whether, for example, on class enrollment forms, you should allow students to specify their pronoun of choice—what is their preferred pronoun.

I've been asked about this recently in terms of what do I think, and I have to say for me this comes down to an issue of respect. If people have a pronoun that they prefer, and they ask you to use that pronoun, it is a signal of respect to use the pronoun that people prefer, and as a result we create a more inclusive, respectful space.

The collapse of case is relevant to another class of pronouns: this would be the interrogative pronouns. These are the pronouns that create questions. Often see this as a list of five—what, which, who, whom, and whose—but I think you could argue that there are only three pronouns here: what, which, who. And "who" then has the additional forms for the object and the possessive "whom" and "whose."

Let's focus on who/whom, because this is the biggest usage issue we have here. "Who" is the subject form of the pronoun asking for information about people; "whom" is the object form, and it is in the decline. But it's actually been in decline for several hundred years, so one interesting question is why hasn't it died yet? It is healthiest, "whom" is healthiest, when it comes after a preposition, things like "to whom" or "by whom." Alone, when it appears in a question, it can look like a subject form because it appears first, and I think that's often why we see "who."

For example, here's a question where we have the subject form: "Who is calling you?" Who is the subject. Now let's look at one where "whom" is the object: "Whom are you calling?" But that question word, the interrogative pronoun, is still at the beginning of the sentence. If we rearrange it to put "whom" as object, you can see you have "You are calling whom?" But the way we make questions, "whom" bumps up to the front, "Whom are you calling?" and many of us will say, "Who are you calling."

While I will adhere to the prescriptive notion of when to use whom in my most formal writing, I find that at this point whom can sound a little fussy in many contexts. I tend to avoid whom in my e-mails or text messages, either by reworking the sentence so that I don't need who or whom at all, or just by using who. For example, I would probably e-mail "Who did you call about getting the washing machine fixed?" even though some part of me knows it should be whom. You need to know your audience and what you're trying to get across.

So far, a lot of the usage issues with pronouns that we've talked about are about a pronoun expanding its function in the system, which is really another way of looking at collapsing distinctions. Subject forms are taking on object functions; plural pronouns are taking on singular functions. We hit on agreement briefly with singular generic "they," as to whether "they" can refer back to a singular antecedent. Now generic "they" can also come up a lot with indefinite pronouns like "everyone" because "everyone" is semantically plural. "Everyone should bring their receipts on Monday."

So let's talk about indefinite pronouns because they pose other agreement issues, especially the pronoun "none." Let me return to the example from the end of the previous lecture: "None of the books is/none of the books are." Indefinite pronouns as a class do not refer to a specific person or thing: they stand in for a vague or undetermined person or thing, or amount of things. You can see this when you look at examples of indefinite pronouns, things like: anyone/anybody, everyone, someone/somebody, anything, everything, either, few, many—these are all indefinite pronouns.

Most of these indefinite pronouns are straightforward in terms of agreement with verbs: anyone is singular "anyone is"; few is plural "few are." None is trickier, perhaps especially in a phrase where it is referring to none of a plural group of things. For example, "None of my friends is/none of my friends are." We often will do both of those depending on context, and think about a sentence like "Some of my friends are coming to visit this weekend, but none are getting here before Friday." We could say "none is getting her before Friday" but I think it sounds much more colloquial to say "none are getting here before Friday." So can none be both singular and plural? I'm going to ruin the punch line and say yes.

We are often taught that none must be singular, and I was taught that, although our gut may want a plural verb here. And the rule itself seems to be bogus, and I will admit that I'm guilty of correcting student papers and making none singular when they have tried to make it plural.

Lindley Murray put this rule in his 1795 grammar, and he first noted none's etymology, but he did this after saying none is used in both numbers, both singular and plural. And what Murray said about its etymology wasn't entirely accurate because he said it was only singular in Old English, but in fact in Old English it has both singular and plural forms. That said, Murray noted that there was good authority for using none in the plural.

The shame is that somewhere this got lost. By the late 19th century this had become a hard-and-fast rule about none as a singular, and this still appears in some style guides. Luckily, other reputable usage guides recognize the singular and plural function of none and say that both the singular and plural can be standard. Bryan Garner distinguishes usefully between the meaning of none as "not one," where you should use the singular, and the meaning of none to mean "not any," and there you would use the plural. I would say in conclusion that you are in good company if you use that as your guide.

As we near the close of this lecture, let's review which pronouns we've covered: personal pronouns, interrogative pronouns, and indefinite pronouns. We haven't covered another category of very common pronouns, namely this, that, these, and those. These are called demonstrative pronouns. They're pronouns that point at things either inside the text or discourse, or outside the text or discourse, and I want to address one usage issue related to "this" that comes up with academic writing.

Did you learn that you should never leave a "this" by itself at the beginning of a sentence in formal writing? I did, and so I found that I was always trying to add a noun to refer back to whatever I was talking about: "This idea, this reason, this point, this concept." And I have to say, this could get clunky—and notice what I just did there with "this"—and sometimes when I was trying to do it it was hard to figure out what noun captured exactly what I was referring back to. Was it a hypothesis, or a conjecture, or an assertion?

Now the difference we're talking about here is "this" as a stand-alone pronoun and "this" as a determiner modifying a noun. The good news here: you can relax that stricture if you learned it. Sometimes it is okay to leave your "this" unattended—that is, without a noun next to it. The key is that it needs to be clear what you're referring back to. And it is okay, as Bryan Garner puts it, if sometimes the "this" summarizes what I've just said.

Let's look at one example from my bookshelf. I pulled down Malcolm Gladwell's book *Outliers*. He's making a connection between agriculture and growing seasons, and educational reform. Here's what he writes:

> Unless a wheat or cornfield is left fallow every few years, the soil becomes exhausted. Every winter, fields are empty. The hard labor of spring planting and fall harvesting is followed, like clockwork, by the slower pace of summer and winter. This is the logic the reformers applied to the cultivation of young minds.

Notice what Gladwell did there—he used "this" to refer back to everything he was saying about agriculture and the growing seasons. We knew exactly what he was talking about.

There's an interesting study by John Swales, who's retired from the University of Michigan, about what happens with "this" in academic writing, and he looked at "this" every time it appeared at the beginning of a sentence in academic writing and found that a full one-third of those were unattended. In other words, you cannot say that published writers don't use unattended "this"—they use it about a third of the time. I would say that Bryan Garner's advice is worth following here: just make sure that you can answer the question, "This what?"

The word "that" is even more complicated: it can be a demonstrative pronoun, a determiner, and a relative pronoun. The Microsoft grammar checker asks us to think about the relative pronoun every time it puts a green squiggly line under a "that" or a "which," identifying it as somehow misused. Relative pronouns, and what's going on with the grammar checker, are complicated enough that they merit their own lecture, and so that is what we will do.

Lecture

7   Which Hunting

The Microsoft Word grammar checker has strong feelings about the difference between *that* and *which* as relative pronouns—and it expresses those feelings in green squiggly lines under our words. Informal polling suggests that a good number of writers aren't sure what the problem is but change the *that* into a *which* or the *which* into a *that* until the grammar checker has been appeased. This lecture's aim is to give a better sense of what is going on with those words.

Relative Clauses

- Let's look at an example that the grammar checker in Microsoft Word 2010 would flag: "I have a great dress which you can borrow." The checker wants *that* here because it is a restrictive relative clause. The checker would allow *which* in a sentence with a nonrestrictive relative clause, such as: "I bought a great dress, which happened to be on sale."

- A relative clause modifies a noun or noun phrase: "the dress <u>that I just bought</u>" or "the man <u>who wouldn't stop talking to me on the airplane</u>." The relative clause is introduced by a relative pronoun that stands in for the noun being modified. Relative pronouns include *that*, *which*, *who*, *whom*, *whoever*, *whomever*, and *whose*.

- Two more examples:

    □ "I had lunch with a friend <u>who just returned from China</u>." *Who* stands in for *friend*.

- "Alex recently ran into our old roommate, <u>who now lives in Hong Kong</u>." *Who* subs in for *our old roommate*.

- These examples captured the restrictive/nonrestrictive distinction. In restrictive clauses, the clause narrows the set to specify who/what you're referring to. In nonrestrictive clauses, the clause adds information about the noun but does not restrict the set.

  - "... <u>who just returned from China</u>" restricts from a large set of friends to one friend.

  - "... our old roommate, <u>who now lives in Hong Kong</u>" simply adds information about the roommate's whereabouts. We already understood who the old roommate was. Also note that the clause occurred after a comma.

- Clearly, *who* can be both restrictive and nonrestrictive. The distinction becomes relevant with *that* and *which*. There's a rule that says we should use *that* for restrictives and *which* for nonrestrictives, as well as a comma for the latter, which captures the pause typical of speech.

That/Which

- Let's look at two examples with *that/which*:

  - "I have the keys to the car that is in the driveway." (There are multiple cars and I'm specifying which one I have keys for—as opposed to one in the garage and one in the street.)

  - "I have the keys to the car, which is in the driveway." (There is only one car, and I'm just letting you know where it's parked)

- This rule is an attempt to create complementary distribution where it may never have existed. For most speakers, *that* applies only to restrictive clauses. They tend not to use it after a comma for nonrestrictives. But a good number of us can use *which* for both: "I have the keys to the car which is in the driveway."

- If we use *which* only for nonrestrictives, then there is no overlap. The prescription goes back to H.W. Fowler's *The King's English* (1908):

  > This confusion is to be regretted; for although no distinction can be authoritatively drawn between the two relatives, an obvious one presents itself.

- He goes on to say that *that* should be the defining/restrictive relative and *who/which* the nondefining/nonrestrictive. He then adds: "'Who' or 'which' should not be used in defining clauses except when custom, euphony, or convenience is decidedly against the use of 'that.'"

- In other words, Fowler is presenting an idealized distinction between *that* and *which*—and allowing exceptions only for euphony or convenience. Fowler is also recommending *that* as the restrictive pronoun with animate and inanimate nouns, and then *who* and *which* for nonrestrictive uses.

- Most guides now allow *who* to be restrictive and nonrestrictive. (Fowler wasn't letting *who* be restrictive—just *that*.)

The Debate Continues

- Fowler returned to that/which in his influential *A Dictionary of Modern English Usage* (2nd edition). He clarifies his preference for complementary distribution and yet shows his awareness that actual usage and his preferred order do not necessarily align. He starts by acknowledging that grammarians have less influence on usage than they may realize, but that it's hard to resist having preferences about what would be best usage.

- He then notes:

  > The relations between *that*, *who*, and *which* have come to us from our forefathers as an odd jumble, and plainly show that the language has not been neatly constructed by a master

builder who could create each part to do the exact work required of it, neither overlapped nor overlapping.

■ So he accepts the jumble, but he goes on to say it doesn't mean we couldn't, at least theoretically, do better. The jumble that Fowler describes gets lost in Strunk and White's version of "the rule" in *Elements of Style*. They make a clear distinction: *That* is restrictive; *which* is nonrestrictive.

■ But they then note there are exceptions, such as this sentence from the Bible: "Let us now go even unto Bethlehem, and see this thing which is come to pass." However, the exception for euphony or convenience doesn't seem to be an option for most of us. In the end, they tell us to go *which*-hunting to improve our work.

■ The *Associated Press Stylebook* makes no exceptions to the restrictive/nonrestrictive rule. Bryan Garner's *A Dictionary of English Usage* (1998) has strong words on the subject, seeming to say that if you follow this rule, you are detailed-oriented as a writer and care about niceties.

■ AHD usage guidelines take a more tempered tone: *Which* with restrictive relative clauses is common and may be preferable if there is a *that* in the antecedent noun phrase: "We want to assign only that material which will be most helpful."

Zero Relatives

■ Let's now talk about a couple of other features of relative clauses: clauses introduced by a *zero relative*, and pied-piping, which involves moving the preposition that is connected to the relative pronoun up to the front of the relative clause. Both zero relatives and pied-piping involve relative clauses with a relative pronoun in an object position.

■ In zero relative clauses, the relative pronoun doesn't appear at all. An example: "I can't remember the name of the person whom I met last night" versus "I can't remember the name of the person I met last night." The latter contains a zero relative clause, missing *whom*.

- This can only happen when the relative pronoun functions as the object in the relative clause. For example, take, "the book that I just finished," where the relative clause is "that I just finished."

  - If we put the relative pronoun where it would be as the object in the clause, we would get: "I just finished that [book]." But it doesn't get to stay in the object position.

  - The object relative pronoun gets fronted to the beginning of the relative clause, up next to the noun it modifiers: "the book [I just finished that]" turns into "the book that I just finished." Then you can delete the *that*: "the book I just finished."

- When the relative pronoun is the subject of the relative clause, it is already up in the front. Let's take the sentence, "I saw my friend who lives in Beijing." *Who* is in subject position, already at the head of the relative clause. We cannot omit the relative pronoun when it is the subject: "I saw my friend ~~who~~ lives in Beijing" doesn't work.

- But when it is an object relative pronoun, we can omit: "I can't remember the name of the person ~~whom~~ I met last night" works because it is still easy to parse. The noun *person* is followed by another noun, *I*, so we know that we have hit a relative clause.

Pied-Piping

- Pied-piping sometimes happens when the relative pronoun is the object of a preposition in the relative clause. An example: "I am wondering whom I should send the RSVP to." The *whom* gets fronted; the question is what happens to that preposition at the end.

- Grammatically, it can stay there at the end of the sentence (we'll come back to the rule about that in Lecture 18). Or we can front it:

"I'm wondering to whom I should send the RSVP." This is called pied-piping because it is following the relative pronoun just like the children following the Pied Piper.

- What happens when we're not using a *whom* but a *that* as the object of the preposition? Consider this sentence: "She read the book that I referred to." If we decide to pied-pipe the preposition, the *that* must turn into a *which*: "She read the book to which I referred." Why? Because. Because English syntax is full of little idiosyncrasies made to seem normal through usage.

Animate Beings

- Here's another oddity with relative pronouns: As a general rule, we restrict *who* and *whom* to animate beings. But there is an exception. We have an odd gap in the language for how to handle possessive relative pronouns for inanimate objects.

- An example will help here: "I returned the computer whose hard drive is broken." Another example: "The car whose horn is blaring is driving me crazy." We can use *that's* there—"The car that's horn is blaring"—but *whose* is also accepted as standard.

- Where do animals fall in terms of the animate/inanimate line? A general rule can be to use *that* when we're talking about animals in general, but *who* when talking about a specific animal.

You could say, "The cat that ate a canary might get sick," or, "Our cat Emily, who ate a canary, might get sick."

Suggested Reading

Fowler and Fowler, *The King's English*.

Questions to Consider

1. Have you ever wondered where the rules in the grammar checker in your word processing program come from? If you haven't, why haven't you asked that question?

2. When you refer to animals, do you use *which/that* or *who*? What do you make of that?

Which Hunting

7

Transcript

The Microsoft Word grammar checker has very strong feelings about the difference between "that" and "which" as relative pronouns, and it expresses those feelings in the green squiggly lines under our "whichs" and "thats." My informal polling of friends and coworkers at the university suggests that a good number of writers aren't entirely sure what the problem is with their "whichs" and "thats," but they change the "that" into a "which" or more often the "which" into a "that" until the grammar checker has been appeased. I would like everyone to have a better sense of what is going on here with those green squiggly lines.

Let's look at an example that the grammar checker in Microsoft Word 2010 would flag. Here's the sentence: "I have a great dress which you can borrow." The grammar checker wants a "that" here because it is a restrictive relative clause. It would allow "which" in a sentence with a nonrestrictive relative clause, such as: "I bought a great dress, which happened to be on sale."

Now let's back up: what is a relative clause? A relative clause is a clause that modifies a noun or a noun phrase, and in English it comes after that noun or noun phrase. So, for example: "the dress that I just bought"; "the man who wouldn't stop talking to me on the airplane." The relative clause is introduced by a relative pronoun that stands in for the noun being modified. The relative pronouns include: that, which, who, whom, whoever, whomever, and whose.

Let me give you two more examples of sentences that have relative clauses in them. Here's one: "I had lunch with a friend who just returned from China." Here you can see that the "who" subs in for "a friend": a friend "who

English Grammar Boot Camp   125

just returned from China." And "who just returned from China" modifies "a friend." Here's another sentence: "Alex recently ran into our old roommate, who now lives in Hong Kong." Here, we can see that the "who" subs in for "our old roommate" within the relative clause, and "who now lives in Hong Kong" all modifies "our old roommate."

In the two examples I've just given you, I have captured the restrictive/ nonrestrictive distinction again, and let me define those terms and then go back to the examples. A restrictive relative clause is a relative clause that narrows the set—it restricts the set—to specify who or what I'm referring to in the sentence. A nonrestrictive relative clause is a relative clause that adds additional information about the noun or noun phrase I'm referring back to, but the information I'm providing in the relative clause does not restrict the set, it's just additional information. With those definitions, let's go back to the two examples.

"I had lunch with a friend who just returned from China." Now clearly I have many, many friends—of course I do—and what I'm trying to do here is restrict which friend I just had lunch with. I had lunch with "a friend who just returned from China." So "who just returned from China" is a restrictive relative clause because it specifies the friend that I am talking about here.

Let's look at the second sentence: "Alex recently ran into our old roommate, who now lives in Hong Kong." Here, we need to imagine that there's just one roommate, and we all know who this roommate is. In that case, the relative clause "who now lives in Hong Kong" is just additional information that I'm providing about this roommate. It's already understood who the roommate is, and the nonrestrictive clause just adds information about the roommate's whereabouts. It's interesting to note here that what we do in the written language as well is that with nonrestrictives, "who now lives in Honk Kong," we put a comma right before it, and that comma captures the pause that we would use in the spoken language.

So let's look at two examples with restrictive and nonrestrictive clauses with "that" and "which." Here's the first one: "I have the keys to the car that is in the driveway." Now for this to work we need to imagine a scenario in which I have multiple cars—I don't actually have multiple cars but let's imagine

I have multiple cars—and I'm specifying which car I'm talking about. I'm talking about the car that is in the driveway, that's the car I have the keys for, as opposed to the car that's in the garage or the car that's on the street.

Here's another sentence: "I have the keys to the car, which is in the driveway." In this scenario, there's only one car. You and I all know what car it is, and I'm just letting you know where the car is parked. The car happens to be in the driveway.

This rule about "that" and "which," where "that" is supposed to be used in restrictive relative clauses and "which" is supposed to be used in nonrestrictive relative clauses is an attempt to create complementary distribution where it may never have existed. For most speakers "that" applies only to restrictive relative clauses. "That" sort of behaves itself, stays within that territory, and we tend not to use it after a comma for nonrestrictives, so "that" restrictives we tend not to use it for nonrestrictives.

But a good number of us can use "which" for both. We can use it for nonrestrictives, which is what the rule tells us to do, but we can also use it for restrictive relative clauses. For example, many of us can say: "I have the keys to the car which is in the driveway." And in that sentence, it's when I'm trying to specify that it's the car which is in the driveway, not the car which is in the garage or the car which is in the street. And you'll hear that there I used "which" in all three of those restrictive relative clauses. If you can get us to use "which" only for nonrestrictives, and that's a big if, then there is no overlap—it's a very neat picture.

The prescription about when to use "that" and when to use "which" in relative clauses can be traced back to H. W. Fowler's *The King's English*, published in 1908. But what you're going to notice is that it doesn't start as a clear-cut rule. Here's Fowler in 1908:

> This confusion—and he's talking about the confusion between that and which—this confusion is to be regretted; for although no distinction can be authoritatively drawn between the two relatives, an obvious one presents itself.

I love that quote. He recognizes that there is not a clear-cut distinction, but he says, "I can find one." He goes on to say that "that" should be used in defining restrictive relatives and "who" or "which" in non-defining or nonrestrictive relatives. He then adds: "'Who' or 'which' should not be used in defining clauses except when custom, euphony, or convenience is decidedly against the use of 'that.'"

So we're starting to get the rule here about when to use "that" and when to use "which" or "who," but Fowler is presenting it as an idealized distinction, as one that does not match reality, and allowing for exceptions based on euphony or convenience. Now you may have noticed something else here that I want to note, which is that Fowler here is recommending "that" as the restrictive pronoun both for animates and inanimates, and then he recommends "who" and "which" for nonrestrictives.

As you already know, I used to have a peeve about people using "that" with animates, as in "the student that" or "the person that," and it's interesting to me to see Fowler prescribing "that" in those instances. As I mentioned before, I have no good grounds for my peeve, given the long history of "that," referring back to animate antecedents, and I have stopped marking it in student papers.

It's also worth noting that most guides would now allow "who" to be used in restrictives—as you noted, Fowler puts "that" in restrictives for animates and inanimates. Now we would use "who" for restrictives with animates and for nonrestrictives with animates.

Fowler returns to the that/which distinction in his influential grammar *A Dictionary of Modern English Usage*. He clarifies his preference—and notice what I'm saying here, his preference—for complementary distribution, and yet he shows his awareness that actual usage and his preferred order of things do not necessarily align. He starts by acknowledging that grammarians have less influence on usage than they may realize, and I think that that's worth noting. And he goes on to say that even though he realizes they may not have influence, it can be hard to resist having preferences about what would be the best usage. He then notes:

The relations between that, who, and which have come to us from our forefathers as an odd jumble, and plainly show that the language has not been neatly constructed by a master builder who could create each part to do the exact work required of it, neither overlapped nor overlapping.

So Fowler accepts the jumble, but he says it doesn't mean that we couldn't, at least theoretically, do better. He explains:

If writers would agree to regard that as the defining relative pronoun, and which as the non-defining, there would be much gain both in lucidity and in ease. Some there are who follow this principle now; but it would be idle to pretend that it is the practice either of most or of the best writers.

So Fowler recognizes that good usage as practiced by the best writers does not always follow the rule that he is proposing.

The jumble that Fowler describes gets lost in Strunk and White's version of the rule. When they write about this in *Elements of Style*, they make a very clear distinction. They say "that" is restrictive and "which" is nonrestrictive. But they do then note that there are exceptions, such as this sentence from the Bible: "Let us now go even unto Bethlehem, and see this thing which is come to pass." "This thing which is come to pass." We see the "which" there in a restrictive relative clause.

But I have to say that the exception that Strunk and White seem to allow—again based on euphony, perhaps convenience—doesn't seem to be an option for most of us, because in the end they tell us to go which-hunting, to go look for all our "whichs" and change the ones that need to be changed to "that" to improve our work. We find similarly definitive advice in lots of other places. The *Associated Press Stylebook*, for example, makes no exceptions to the restrictive and nonrestrictive rule.

Bryan Garner's *A Dictionary of English Usage*, the first edition published in 1998, is worth quoting in full on this, and this is a pretty long quote, but it's a really interesting one. So here's Garner:

You'll encounter two schools of thought on this point. First are those who don't care about any distinction between these words, who think that which is more formal than that, and who point to many historical examples of copious whiches. They say that modern usage is a muddle. Second are those who insist that both words have useful functions that ought to be separated, and who observe the distinction rigorously in their own writing. They view departures from this distinction as mistakes. Before reading any further, you ought to know something more about these two groups: those in the first probably don't write very well; those in the second just might.

So that was Garner on "that" and "which," and I have to say that is pretty strong language about people who use "that" and "which" interchangeably in restrictive clauses to suggest that those folks may not be good writers, whereas the folks who observe the distinction are. The idea seems to be that if you follow this rule about "that" and "which," you are detailed-oriented as a writer and care about the niceties. I'm not sure that is fair given the history of the jumble. It may mean if you're observing that distinction that you have a good editor who's in there fixing things for you.

Now the *American Heritage Dictionary* usage note on this takes a more tempered tone. The editors note that "which" with restrictive relative clauses is common, and they note that it may be preferable if there is a "that" in the antecedent noun phrase. Let me show you what I mean and you'll hear why you might want to use a "which" here. Here's the sentence: "We want to assign only that material which will be most helpful." "We want to assign only that material which will be most helpful." So it's a restrictive clause but we use "which." Let's see what happens if we use "that." "We only want to assign that material that will be most helpful." You get those two "thats" very close to each other—may not sound so good.

Now the Microsoft Word grammar checker—let's return to the grammar checker—suggests with that green squiggly line that you are making an error if you use "which" in a restrictive relative clause. If you look it up in the grammar checker, you will see that this issue of "that" and "which" is put into the category of style errors and it's called a questionable use of "that" and "which." But I have to say that I think when people see the green squiggly line, that does not suggest that this is questionable. It suggests that, if you're using "which" in a restrictive relative clause, you've made a mistake. After this discussion, I hope that you now have a more complicated picture about what's going on with that green squiggly line, and about this so-called rule about "that" and "which."

Let's now talk about a couple of other features of relative clauses. The first that I want to talk about is clauses introduced by a zero relative, and the second one that I want to talk about is something called pied-piping, which involves moving the preposition that's connected to the relative pronoun up to the front of the relative clause. I've grouped these two constructions together because both zero relatives and pied-piping involve relative clauses with a relative pronoun in object position. Okay, I know that this is going to get nitty-gritty here, but it's why you're here, so let me explain each of these in turn.

Let's start with zero relatives. In these relative clauses, the relative pronoun does not appear at all. Let me show you what I mean. Let's take the sentence "Let me lend you the book that I just finished." "Let me lend you the book that I just finished." Well in that sentence we can omit the relative pronoun and get "Let me lend you the book I just finished." See, that "that" is gone—it's just gone. "Let me lend you the book I just finished."

Let me give you another example. First we'll do it with the relative pronoun. "I can't remember the name of the person whom I met last night." "I can't remember the name of the person whom I met last night." But we could just get rid of that "whom." "I can't remember the name of the person I met last night." The "whom" is gone.

Now, this zero relative, where we omit the relative pronoun, can only happen when the relative pronoun functions as the object of the relative clause. Let me show you what is happening in these relative clauses. Let's take the first example I gave you about lending "the book that I just finished," where the relative clause here is "that I just finished."

If we put the relative pronoun "that" back into where it would be as the object of the relative clause, we would get: "I just finished that." Book, right? "I just finished that." But the relative pronoun doesn't get to stay in object position in the relative clause. The object relative pronoun gets fronted up to the beginning of the relative clause, up next to the noun that it modifies. So we get a relative clause, we get "the book," and then the relative clause—again, I'm going to keep "that" in object position—"the book I just finished that." But then we move the "that" up and we get "The book that I just finished." So, yes, as you may have noticed, the object pronoun there in the relative clause gets moved up in front of the subject "that I just finished." And once you've done that, you can delete the "that." "The book I just finished."

Let's review that again by looking at the other sentence. The sentence was: "I can't remember the name of the person whom I met last night." Again, let's put the relative pronoun back into object position in the relative clause. If we do that, we would take "whom I met last night" and turn it into "I met whom last night," because "whom" I've put into that object position. But, again, "whom" doesn't get to stay there in the relative clause; it gets fronted in the relative clause. And so "the person I met whom last night," the "whom" gets fronted and we get "the person whom I met last night." Once "whom" is up there, you can delete it, and you can get "the person I met last night."

Now, when the relative pronoun is the subject of the relative clause, it's already up there in the front of the relative clause. Let me show you what I mean; let's take another sentence: "I saw my friend who lives in Beijing." "I saw my friend who lives in Beijing." Here we've got "my friend who lives in Beijing." "Who lives in Beijing" is the relative clause, and "who" is in subject position: "who" lives in Beijing. Given that it's already at the head of the relative clause, it doesn't have to get fronted—it has nowhere to go. And when that relative pronoun is in subject position, we cannot omit it; we cannot have a zero relative.

So, again, let's look at that sentence: "I saw my friend who lives in Beijing." Just try omitting the "who" and see what happens. "I saw my friend lives in Beijing." It just doesn't work. "I saw my friend lives in Beijing." But when that relative pronoun is in object position, when it's an object relative pronoun, we can omit it.

Go back to my sentence: ""I can't remember the name of the person I met last night." Now it's probably possible to omit that relative pronoun in object position because it's still easy to parse the sentence. The noun "person" is followed by another noun: "the person I met last night." So your brain knows that some new grammatical structure is starting right now, okay? So you're getting one noun next to another: "the person I met last night," and so we can omit the relative. But when it's in subject position, our brain clearly struggles somehow. Remember the sentence "I saw my friend lives in Beijing." And part of that may be that when you get "my friend lives in Beijing" it seems like we've started another clause right there, and it's fairly difficult to process.

The option of deleting the relative pronoun in these constructions, I have to say, is really convenient when you're dealing with "who" and "whom." You may have noticed that in my example sentence, I was talking about the person, I can't remember their name—I can't remember the name of the person "whom" I met last night. Now I have to say, in colloquial speech, that's not what I would say. I would say, "I can't remember the name of the person who I met last night," but some people would think that I don't know my "whos" from my "whoms." And the easy thing is just to omit the relative pronoun entirely; it gets you out of the conundrum, and just say, "I can't remember the name of the person I met last night." And you don't have to deal with "who" or "whom," and as we've talked about before, that "whom" can sound very formal, if not sometimes even a little pretentious.

So, just as a quick review with "who" and "whom." You would, at least in theory, always get a "whom" when the relative pronoun functions as the object in the relative clause. It then gets bumped up to the front of the relative clause, which makes it harder to recognize as the object, because once it's up front it sort of looks like a subject.

Let me show you what I mean. Here's a sentence: "She's the colleague whom we recommended for the award." That "whom" has gotten bumped up to the front of the relative clause. It would be very tempting to say instead, even though the "whom" is technically correct: "She's the colleague who we recommended for the award." And as I said, you can avoid the whole issue by saying: "She's the colleague we recommended for the award."

Let's now turn to pied-piping. This is what happens when the relative pronoun is the object of a preposition in the relative clause, and it also happens in nominal clauses. Let me give you an example: "I am wondering whom I should send the RSVP to." "I am wondering whom I should send the RSVP to." Or "I'm wondering to whom I should send the RSVP." If we undo this, we get "I'm wondering I should send the RSVP to whom." "I'm wondering"—and then if we take the clause and put the "whom" back with its preposition—"I should send the RSVP to whom." But that "whom" gets fronted, so then the question is what happens to that preposition?

Grammatically, it can stay there at the end of the sentence. We'll come back to the rule about whether or not you can strand those at the end of a sentence in Lecture 18, but if we're thinking descriptively, the preposition can stay at the end of the sentence. Or we can front it, too. This is what's called pied piping, because the preposition is following the relevant pronoun up to the front of the relevant clause, just like the children were following the Pied Piper. And I absolutely love this term to describe this phenomenon.

Now pied-piping can feel very formal when you say "To whom should I send the RSVP?" as opposed to "Who should I send the RSVP to?" Now here's an oddity of English syntax, and I just can't resist telling you about this. This is what happens when we are not using a "whom" but we're using a "that" as the object of the preposition. Consider this sentence: "She read the book that I referred to." "She read the book that I referred to." If we decide to pied-pipe that preposition, the "that" must turn into a "which." "She read the book to which I referred." "She read the book to which I referred."

So you would have that, "She read the book that I referred to," but front the "to" and suddenly "that" becomes a "which." Why? Because English syntax is full of idiosyncrasies like that. This seems completely normal to us, and you may never have thought about it, but it also I think confirms that the that/which distinction is a bit of a muddle.

While we're talking about oddities, here's another one with relative pronouns. As a general rule, we restrict "who" and "whom" to animate beings. Can we then say "who" is only used for animates? No. There is an exception. We have this odd gap in the language for how to handle possessive relative pronouns for inanimate objects.

An example will help here. Here's an example sentence: "I returned the computer whose hard drive is broken." "I returned the computer whose hard drive is broken." Suddenly we've got a "whose" referring back to the computer. Or here's another one: "The car whose horn is blaring is driving me crazy." "The car whose horn." We can use "that"—"The car that's horn is blaring"—but "whose" is also accepted as completely standard, and I have to say it often sounds better than "of which," if you can even use "of which" in some of those sentences at all.

Where do animals fall into this inanimate/animate distinction with "who" versus "that" and "which"? Let's end with that question. I don't actually think this is about a grammatical rule at all, I think this is more about how you feel about the animals in question. I did a search of the *Corpus of Contemporary American English* on this, and I searched for "the dog that" versus "the dog who," and "the dog that" was more than twice as common as "the dog who." I got the same thing when I searched for cats and elephants and turtles.

We tend to use "that" when we're talking about animals in general: "The cat that ate the canary." We're more likely to use "who" when we're talking about a specific animal, perhaps a specific cat about whom we have strong personal feelings.

And since we're speaking of pets, I'm going to start the next lecture on determiners by sharing a pet peeve of mine, a peeve of historic proportions, so to speak. Okay, so that was a very bad play on the word pet to transition to the next lecture, but I have given you a historic hint about my pet peeve.

Lecture

8   A(n) Historical Issue

It grates on some people when others say "an historical novel" or "an historic event." *A* and *an* are indefinite articles used with countable nouns (like historical novels or historic events). This lecture aims to unravel the rules surrounding those articles, answering questions like: Which one goes best before words like *historical*? Then the lecture moves on to cover determiners more generally as a lexical class. We'll close with a look at some capitalization issues.

A versus *An*

- When it comes to *a* and *an*, the general rule is *a* before consonants and *an* before vowels. Examples are "a cat" and "an elephant." Exceptions exist, though: Take "a unicorn," where the *u* is pronounced like a *y*, which is a consonant.

- What happens with the words *history* and *historical*? Over time, the /h/ sound has become more likely to be pronounced at the beginning (moving the word from *'istoric* to *historic* in practice). Today, the *Associated Press Stylebook* and *Chicago Manual of Style* both recommend *a historic(al)*.

- The site *Grammarist* calls *an historic* "an unnecessary affectation." Maeve Maddox, on dailywritingtips.com, quotes comment sections on this. There is much vitriol, including: "When people use 'an historical' on NPR, it's because [they're] snooty."

- It is useful to step back and remember that we're just talking about the presence or absence of one consonant: *a* versus *an*. This shows how loaded even the smallest language choices can become. They can get you judged as snooty in some cases and illiterate in others.

Determiners

- *A/an,* as indefinite articles, both fall in the broader category of determiners. Determiners are the little words that introduce nouns to create noun phrases. We'll focus on three things: the highly intuitive rules that govern their ordering, the agreement issues with the word *either,* and some regional differences in usage.

- The category of determiners is bigger than many people realize, and there isn't a lot of agreement about how to categorize them. Let's look at just one way we can subdivide the set. Here's one version with seven major categories, forming the acronym Pi and IQ.

  □ Possessives (my, her, their, our)

  □ Interrogatives (which, what, whatever)

  □ Articles (a, an, the)

  □ Numbers (cardinal and ordinal: one/two and first/second)

  □ Demonstratives (this, that, these, those)

  □ Indefinites (any, each, other, another)

  □ Quantifiers (many, some, several, most)

- We can also subdivide this set into three categories based on the order in which they occur in a noun phrase: predeterminers, central determiners, and postdeterminers. Those terms are just about order.

- Two examples are, "The first several pages" or "all my many quirks." We wouldn't say, "the several first pages" or "my all many quirks." How do we know this? This is the kind of intuitive knowledge that makes up a lot of "descriptive grammar."

- Let's go through how the determiners sort into these three categories based on the order in which they appear in the noun phrase.

  □ Predeterminers include terms like *all/both*, multiplying expressions, and fractions.

  □ Central determiners include definite and indefinite articles, possessives, and demonstratives.

  □ Postdeterminers include cardinal and ordinal numbers; general ordinals (like *next* and last); and quantifiers (like *many* and *some*).

Adjectives and Pronouns versus Determiners

- How are determiners different from adjectives and pronouns? We'll start with adjectives. Adjectives are an open class (we can add new ones) and determiners are a closed class (we don't get new ones very often at all).

- Adjectives can occur before a noun and then out in the predicate (e.g., "the friendly cat" and "the cat is friendly"). Determiners only appear before the noun: "the cat" and not "cat is the."

- Adjectives will consistently fall between the determiners and the noun: "All our friendly cats, not "all friendly our cats." Additionally, adjectives can be modified by an intensifier like *very*: "very friendly." And adjectives usually make comparatives: "more friendly."

- Let's now look at determiners compared with pronouns. Many of the words that function as determiners can also function as pronouns. The key is whether the word is standing alone in the place of a noun, as opposed to modifying a noun.

- Take the example of *many*. Consider the difference between "Many clichés have some wisdom in them," and in a conversation about clichés, "Many have some wisdom in them." In the latter sentence, *Many* stands in for *clichés*, but in the former, it modifies *clichés*.

- *The*, *a*, and *an* cannot be pronouns.

Regional Variation

- Now that we have defined determiners and how they work within the noun phrase, let's look at some regional variation.

- If we're speaking generically, in British English someone is "in hospital," but in American English they're "in the hospital."

- Note that Americans "go to prison" and "go to college"—which is different from going to "the prison" or "the school" to visit.

Capitalization

- To close this lecture, let's look at a capitalization issue that can come up when we think about determiners: capitalization of nouns like *president*.

  - If we're talking about a president in general, clearly it's not capitalized. And when we refer to the current president—so if it were 1978, we'd say President Carter—it is clearly capitalized.

  - But what about when you refer to "the president/President" of the U.S.? In this case, you mean the current president, but you don't say President [Name].

- Note that capitalization has been a moving target in the history of English; our current rules are relatively recent and still to some extent in flux.

- In the Renaissance, there was a good amount of variation in terms of nouns that might get capitalized in the middle of a sentence, sometimes for emphasis.

- By the 17th century, it was settling down: A word would be capitalized at the beginning of a sentence, in proper names, the word *I*, and in important nouns like titles and personified nouns (such as Virtue).

- The 18th century witnessed increased use of capitalization for nouns deemed important and for things like fields (such as Rhetoric). Ben Franklin was quite fond of this practice, and it appears in the Constitution and Declaration of Independence.

- In the second half of the 18th century, grammarians clamped down on this use of capital letters for nouns of special note. Grammarians started to claim that it "disfigures" one's writing to use capitals for all nouns. Capitalizing for emphasis started to be proscribed in 19th century.

18th-Century Capitalization

"No Person except a natural born Citizen, or a Citizen of the United States, at the time of the Adoption of this Constitution, shall be eligible to the Office of President" — the U.S. Constitution

"...we mutually pledge to each other our Lives, our Fortunes, and our sacred Honor." —the Declaration of Independence

- Today, capitalization is mostly restricted to the start of a sentence, proper names, and titles when they occur with the person's name.

- According to the *Chicago Manual of Style*, we are not to capitalize titles even when the referent is specific (so we'd say "Dean Munson," but "the dean"). The exception is in cases of directly addressing someone, in which case it would be "Mr. President," or "Senator."

- But you will certainly see capitalization of "the Dean" or "the President," which can be read as an attempt to be formal and polite. This drives some people crazy, but there isn't an intuitive logic to using "President Roosevelt" and "the president" when we're talking about the same person.

- Bryan Garner points out the contradiction of "Stone Age" (capitalized) versus "space age." He does provide leeway for capitalizing for "some rhetorical purpose," although he asks us to minimize capitalization

- Another capitalization issues that might trip you up: You have to figure out whether *the* is part of a newspaper title: *The New York Times* versus the *Los Angeles Times*.

- In 2016, the Associated Press decided to stop capitalizing *Internet* and *Web*, saying most viewed them as generic. But there has been some criticism of the *Associated Press Stylebook* for *internet*. As one *Slate* writer put it, "It's one place as proper and unique as Saturn. And it's utterly reasonable to capitalize this realm's name." In the end, a style manual will be key.

- Now for a historical note on why we capitalize *I*. It used to be *ic*, but lost the *c* by the 12th century. By the late 1300s, the letter/pronoun was becoming taller. It has been pretty consistently capitalized in written standard English ever since

- Why *I* is now capitalized is one of those mysteries of the language, and can strike non-English speakers as odd. They may also find it odd that *English* is capitalized in English, as not all languages consider the names of languages to be proper nouns.

Suggested Reading

Maddox, "A Historic vs. An Historic."

Question to Consider

1. Rules about capitalization in English have fluctuated over the past few centuries. If we're referring to the current elected leader of the United States, would you advocate writing "the president" or "the President?"

A(n) Historical Issue

It's been a few lectures since I confessed to a usage peeve, so this seemed like a good time. Here's one: it grates on me just a little bit when people say "an historical novel" or "an historic event." Now, if these people are h-droppers—and that's actually a technical linguistic term, h-dropping or h-droppers, people who drop the "h" at the beginning of a word—if these people are h-droppers, and are h-droppers with the word "historical" and say 'istorical, it doesn't bother me at all. They would say "an 'istorical novel." But if these folks pronounce that initial "h" in historical, it sounds odd and maybe even affected to me to say "an historical." I hear it all over the university, and I notice it every time.

What's going on here? "A" and "an" are indefinite articles used with countable nouns like "historical novels" and "historic events." The rule is that you put "a" before consonants and "an" before vowels—that is something we all learned at a young age: "a cat," "an elephant." So why would we say "a unicorn"? I once put this on a final exam in one of my classes and I got fascinating responses to this, including: "It is a unicorn because unicorns are mythical beings and they defy the rules of English grammar."

It's a great answer, but it's not actually the answer to this question. We say "a unicorn" because, although unicorn is spelled with an initial vowel, if you listen to how we pronounce it, it is pronounced with a "yuh" at the beginning, "yuh-nicorn," and "yuh" is a consonant. This also explains why we say "an hour," because hour is spelled with an initial "h" but pronounced with an initial vowel.

So what's going on with the words "history" and "historical"? Well, you'll notice in those two words the stress shift: "history," stress on the first syllable; "historical," stress on the second syllable. Because the stress is on the first syllable in history, it's more likely that the "h" will be pronounced in history. For people who drop the "h," they may be more likely to drop it in "historical," although they can drop it in both, but many of use pronounce the "h" in both "history" and "historical."

This issue of "a historical" versus "an historical" has been addressed in usage guides, and you might be surprised what the guides say about this, because high usage from what I can tell at the university, in the academy, is often "an historical."

Here's H. W. Fowler in his *Dictionary of Modern English Usage* from 1926. He notes that the "h" is now usually pronounced in words like "historical," which, as he notes, starts with an unaccented syllable. It has not always been the case that that "h" was consistently pronounced, but Fowler says now it is, and then he writes: "Now that the h in such words is pronounced the distinction has become pedantic, and a historical should be said and written."

The *AP* stylebook and the *Chicago Manual of Style* both recommend "a historic" and "a historical." When did this shift? When did we start saying "a historical" rather than "an historical"? From what I can tell, "a historical" starts to be used regularly in the early 19th century. By 1900, "a" and "an"— "a historical" and "an historical"—are used with about equal frequency in writing. It's in the late 1930s, early 1940s, when we see what I'll call the crossover, when we start to see "a historical" become more common than "an historical." At this point, if you search the Google Books Ngram Viewer, you will find that "a historical" is more than twice as common as "an historical."

The site *Grammarist*, that website, calls "an historic" an "unnecessary affectation," and Maeve Maddox, on the website *dailywritingtips.com*, she looks at comment sections online and notes that there is a lot of vitriol about this question, including this quote: "When people use 'an historical' on NPR, it is because they're snooty."

As you know, I'm one of the people who notice this, and I find it a little bit exaggerated, but I also try to check myself and not be too judgmental about it. I think it is very useful to step back and remember that in the end all we're talking about here is the presence, or absence, of one consonant: "a" versus "an." What we see here is how loaded even the smallest language choices can become. They can get you judged as snooty, or in other cases, as uneducated or illiterate. Remember the harsh language we talked about with "less" on grocery store signs. With that introduction about "a" and "an," let's talk about determiners more generally as a lexical class.

"A" and "an," as indefinite articles, both fall in the broader category of determiners, and determiners will be the focus of the rest of this lecture. Determiners often don't get that much attention, but here in this course, everything gets attention. Determiners are the little words that introduce nouns to create noun phrases. In this lecture, we'll focus on three things: the highly intuitive rules that govern the ordering of determiners; then, some regional differences in usage; and finally, at the end of the lecture, we'll talk about some issues of capitalization in noun phrases that include determiners—for example, "the president" versus "President Lincoln."

The category of determiners is bigger than many people realize, and there isn't a lot of agreement about how to categorize them. Let's think about this as a set of little words and look at just one way we can subdivide the set. Here's one version with seven major categories. I've created an acronym for this: PI AND IQ. You may be able to do better but that's what I came up with. So, PI AND IQ.

The P is for possessives. These are determiners like my, her, their, our. I, interrogatives: which, what, whatever. A, articles: a, an, the. N, numbers. These would be the cardinal and the ordinal numbers, so things like one and two, as well as first and second. D, demonstratives: this, that, these, those. I, indefinites: any, each, other, another. Q, quantifiers: many, some, several, most.

But I have to say, we can categorize them this way, and that's helpful, but it doesn't strike me as the most interesting thing to think about with all these different kinds of determiners.

We can also subdivide this set into three categories based on the order in which they occur in a noun phrase: predeterminers, central determiners, postdeterminers. And those terms are really about the order in which they occur. Predeterminers happen before central determiners, postdeterminers happen after central determiners. It is true that the central determiners have some of the most common determiners, like "a," "an," and "the."

Now thinking about determiners this way, in terms of the order, is interesting to me because it captures the rules we don't get credit for knowing. We've talked about this before with some usage issues, and it really comes into play here, because I would guess many of you have never thought about the order in which these determiners have to occur.

Let me give you two examples: "the first several pages"; "all my many quirks." We wouldn't say "the several first pages." We just wouldn't, we would say "the first several pages." We also wouldn't say "my all many quirks." We would say "all my many quirks." How do we know this?

It's the kind of intuitive knowledge that makes up a lot of descriptive grammar, and I want to note that there has been over the years some prescription on this—not a lot, but some—that now won't feel very intuitive at all. John McWhorter has noted that in the late 1800s, there was an argument that it should be "the two first people" not "the first two people," unless of course you were referring to the first pair of people who arrived, in which case you could say "the first two people" because those two people came together, but otherwise you would say "the two first people." Now, clearly the prescriptivists who were fighting that fight did not win.

Let's now go through how the determiners sort into these categories of predeterminer, central determiner, and postdeterminer, and this is again based on the order in which they appear in the noun phrase.

So predeterminers, the ones that will come first, would include things like "all" and "both," multiplying expressions and fractions—so words like "twice" or "half." These predeterminers don't tend to co-occur; you'll tend to get only one of them. Then you get the central determiners. This includes definite and indefinite articles, so "a," "and," and "the"; possessives; and demonstratives. Then you have postdeterminers. This can include the cardinal and the ordinal numbers, general ordinals like "next" and "last," as well as quantifiers: "many" or "some." Now these postdeterminers can co-occur. For example, we can say "the next few meetings" but we would not say "the few next meetings." Why? Because.

Let's pause for a moment here to clarify how determiners are different from adjectives as well as from pronouns. As we've talked about before, adjectives are open class: we can add new adjectives somewhat at will. Determiners are closed class; they're function words, and we don't tend to get new ones very often at all.

Adjectives can occur before a noun. They also can occur out in the predicate. As an example: "the friendly cat." So they're friendly—the adjective occurs before the noun. I don't know why I'm talking about friendly cats, but I am, and I'm going to keep going. So we have "the friendly cat": "friendly" before the noun. We can also say "the cat is friendly." There, the adjective has moved out into the predicate. But determiners only appear before the noun within the noun phrase, so we get "the cat" and not "cat is the."

Adjectives will consistently fall between the determiners and the noun, so we would have "all our cats"—we only have two determiners, "all our cats." If we put in an adjective, we get "all our friendly cats." We would not have "all friendly our cats." It just doesn't work that way. Adjectives can also be modified by intensifiers such as "very"—"very friendly." We would not say "very the."

Adjectives usually take comparatives and superlatives, so we could say "more friendly" or "friendlier," but we can't say "more the" or "the-er." You can now see why sometimes people take the word "few" and categorize it as an adjective, because you can say "very few" and "fewer," but you'll also see "few" categorized as a determiner. So that's the difference between determiners and adjectives. Let's now look at determiners compared with pronouns.

Many of the words that function as determiners can also function as pronouns. The key here is whether the word is standing alone in place of a noun phrase, as opposed to modifying a noun. To look at this, let's start with "many." It's the difference between the sentence: "Many clichés have some wisdom in them." In that sentence, "many" is a determiner: "Many clichés have some wisdom in them." But let's imagine we're having a conversation about clichés, and I say, "Many have some wisdom in them." There, "many" is a pronoun because it's standing on its own to substitute for the noun phrase: "Many have some wisdom in them."

Let's take another example. I say, "I read a few good books this summer." There, "few" is a determiner. "I read a few good books this summer." But let's imagine that you ask me, "Did you read any good books?" And I say, "I read a few this summer." There, "few" is a noun substituting in for the noun phrase.

The possessives—as we think about determiners versus pronouns—the possessives change form, so the determiner, for example, is "my." The pronoun is "mine," because "mine" can stand alone: "Mine is blue." "Our" becomes "ours." "Your" as a determiner becomes "yours" as a pronoun. Her/hers, their/theirs. The only ones that don't change are the determiners that already end in "s": "his" remains "his" and "its" remains "its." As a result, if we say "my friend," with the determiner "my," it becomes "a friend of mine" with the pronoun "mine" in what is a double possessive: "a friend of mine," with "of" and "mine." We'll come back to that in Lecture 23 when we talk about possessives and apostrophes. It is worth noting here that the determiners "the," "a," and "an" cannot be made pronouns.

So now we have defined determiners and how they work within the noun phrase. Let's look briefly at a few cases of regional variation, one of which is well known to Americans, and one of which might not be. Let's start with an American/British distinction. If we're speaking generically, in British English, one goes "to hospital" or one is "in hospital." In American English, one goes "to the hospital" or is "in the hospital," even though it's not a specific hospital, it's just a generic hospital.

And there are people who say, "Why do we have this distinction? Why do the Brits say 'in hospital' and we say 'in the hospital' here in the United States?" I don't have a great answer to that, but it is worth noting that Americans in other places speak about things generically without the determiner "the." For example, Americans go "to church" not "to the church" generically. Americans go "to prison" and "to college." It's the difference between going "to prison" or "to college" in general, to anyone, versus going "to the prison" to visit. There, we have a specific prison in mind we're going to visit. We're going "to the school" to visit, as opposed to going "to school" in general.

Now here's another regional distinction that you may not be aware of. I wasn't aware of it until I moved to the state of Michigan. I moved to Michigan when I was in graduate school, and the first few weeks of graduate school my fellow graduate students would sometimes talk about going "to the bar." They would say, "Tonight we'll go to the bar," and I have to say I felt pretty left out, because it seemed to me that they had all agreed on some bar, and they all knew what bar they were going to. And so they were going "to the bar," the one they all knew about, and somehow nobody had told me about what bar it was—poor me. But what I learned was that in Michigan, going "to the bar" is generic. It's what I would say as going to "a" bar. But in Michigan you go to the bar—who knows where you're going, you'll decide that later.

Now we may not all agree in the end on "a bar" versus "the bar," but we can all agree that the bar there is not capitalized, unless there's a bar called The Bar, with a capital T and a capital B, and that's just confusing.

To close this lecture, let's look at a capitalization issue that can come up when we think about determiners. This is the capitalization of nouns like "president." If we're talking about a president in general, it's clearly not capitalized, and when we refer to the current president, it is capitalized. So, for example, let's imagine it's 1978. We would say "President Carter" with a capital P, and obviously Carter is capitalized. But what about when you refer to the president of the United States—and there, is it "the president" lowercase P or "the President" capital P if we're talking about the current president. We're not naming that president by name but we all know who we're talking about. So we don't say "President Carter," we just say "the president." Capitalized or not? I have to say, this is one of those usage issues that comes up a lot and people send me queries about it.

To answer this about current rules for capitalization, I need to note that capitalization has been a moving target in the history of English. Our current rules about when to capitalize and when not to capitalize are relatively recent and, to some extent, still in flux, so let me go back in time a little bit. In the Renaissance, we find a good amount of variation in terms of which nouns might get capitalized and which might not, and this can happen in the middle of a sentence. Sometimes nouns get capitalized just for emphasis.

By the 17th century, capitalization was settling down so that a word, for example, would always be capitalized at the beginning of a sentence. That was not always a given, I have to note. Words would be capitalized in proper names, in the word "I," and in important nouns like titles and personified nouns. This is a period of time where nouns like virtue were often capitalized.

The 18th century witnessed an increased use of capitalization, and in this case it was for nouns that were deemed important, for things like fields of study—for example, Rhetoric. Ben Franklin was actually quite fond of this practice of capitalizing nouns, and you can see it in the Constitution and in the Declaration of Independence. Let me show you what I mean.

Here's an excerpt from the U.S. Constitution: "No" capital N "Person" capital P "except a natural born Citizen," capital C "or a Citizen" capital C "of the United States," United States is capitalized "at the time of the Adoption" capital A "of this Constitution," capital C "shall be eligible to the Office" capital O "of President" capital P. Now, if that were getting rewritten today, a lot of those nouns would not be capitalized, but in the Constitution they are.

Here's an excerpt from the Declaration of Independence: "We mutually pledge to each other our Lives," capital L "our Fortunes," capital F "and our sacred Honor" capital H. When we see texts that have these kinds of patterns of capitalization, I think we just recognize them as older, but I'm not sure we always connect them to the ongoing concerns about capitalization.

In the second half of the 18th century, grammarians started to clamp down on this use of capital letters for nouns of special note. These grammarians would claim things like "this sort of capitalization disfigures one's writing," and capitalization for emphasis actually started to be explicitly proscribed in the 19th century. So it went from being a preference—"this can disfigure your writing"—to being a proscription: "don't do it."

So, at this point, capitalization is mostly restricted to the start of a sentence, proper names, and titles when they occur with the person's name—we go back to "President Carter" with a capital P. According to the *Chicago Manual of Style*, we are not to capitalize titles even when the referent is specific. So, for example, it would be Dean Munson, with a capital D, but "the dean," lowercase D, even if I'm talking about Dean Munson. That is unless it is direct address, in which case I would use a capital: "Mr. President" or "Ms. President," with a capital P, or "Senator" with a capital S.

But you will certainly see capitalization of "the Dean" or "the President," which I read as an attempt to be formal or to be polite, in recognition of the importance of that position. In some ways I think about it as capitalization as respect. I know that this practice drives some people crazy, but I have to say there isn't a clear, intuitive logic, at least to me, that when we're talking about President Roosevelt, for example, we would say "President Roosevelt" with a capital P but then use a lowercase P with "the president" when we're talking about the same person.

Bryan Garner, in his usage guide, points out some other contradictions that we struggle with as we try to figure out capitalization practices. For example, he points out Stone Age is a capital S and a capital A, but space age is all lowercase. And Garner provides some leeway for capitalizing, saying that sometimes capitalization can work well for a particular rhetorical purpose, but he does ask us to minimize our capitalization, to use it only when we have a specific rhetorical purpose in mind.

Now other capitalization issues that might trip you up—for example, you have to figure out whether the "the" in a newspaper title is actually part of the title. For *The New York Times*, the "the" is part of the title and it is capitalized, but for the *Los Angeles Times*, it's not part of the title and it is not capitalized.

In 2016, it made headlines when the *Associated Press* changed its stylebook and decided to stop capitalizing internet and web. The AP, when they made the announcement, said that most people viewed both of these nouns them as generic, and I have to say that many of us had stopped capitalizing internet and web a while ago. But when these headlines came out, there was widespread criticism of the stylebook for the lowercase letter in internet. For example, there was an article in *Slate* that said, "There's only one Internet and it should be capitalized."

In the end, I have to say, a style manual is going to be key here, that you're going to need to figure out, if you're working on a formal piece of writing, what does that style manual say about what needs to be capitalized and what shouldn't be. And I myself am quite interested in what's happening in informal writing, in texting, and on the internet—no capital letter there for me on the internet—where you see some folks returning to capitalization for emphasis. And I think that that's an interesting turn back in time to use capitalization for emphasis in these informal writing spaces, and you see in these spaces that people are using lowercase "i."

And since we're talking about the pronoun "I," let me try to answer the question of why do we capitalize the pronoun "I"? Okay, but here's the problem—I can't give you a very good answer to this question.

Here's the history. This pronoun used to be spelled I-C. It was pronounced "each," and it lost that final consonant by about the 12th century to become just "E" which eventually was pronounced "I." By the late 1300s or so, the letter that represented this pronoun started to become taller. Now we don't know exactly why it started to get taller. One is maybe people just thought it didn't look good as a lowercase letter—it was an aesthetic issue. It could also be that they were trying to distinguish the pronoun "I" from a shorthand "i" that was shortened from "in" or from "if." But, in any case, that "i" got taller and became a capital letter, and it has been pretty consistently capitalized in written standard English ever since.

Now, why the "I" is capitalized is one of those mysteries of the language that we don't have a great answer to, and can strike non-English speakers as odd. And those speakers may also find it odd that "English" is capitalized in English, as not all languages consider the names of languages to be proper nouns. In French, "je," which is the pronoun for "I," is lowercase J, and languages like "anglais" for English and "francais" for French are not capitalized.

In German, in contrast, all nouns are capitalized. The formal "you"—Sie—is capitalized, but the pronoun for "I" is not capitalized. In addition, in German, adjectives for nationalities like American or German: not capitalized. In English they are. Different strokes of the pen for different folks who speak and write different languages.

In this lecture on determiners, the question of how determiners compare with adjectives has come up. So let's talk about adjectives in detail in the next lecture, rounding out our discussion of the many key components of the noun phrase, and then we'll turn to the complicated tangle of the verb phrase.

Lecture

9 | Funnest Lecture Ever

This lecture covers adjectives, starting with the fuss around the terms *fun*, *funner*, and *funnest*. Next the lecture turns to a general discussion of comparatives and superlatives. We'll talk about those, along with double comparatives, and then turn to an odd set of adjectives that mean different things depending on where they appear in the sentence. At the end of the lecture, we'll talk about how to handle noun phrases where the adjective, oddly, shows up after the noun.

A Fun Question

- Let's start with a recent question from the ballot for the AHD Usage Panel. It is about the word *fun*. Panelists received five sentences and had to rate each one on a four-point scale: completely acceptable, somewhat acceptable, somewhat unacceptable, or completely unacceptable. Here are the first three, innocuous-seeming sentences:

  □ That party was really fun.

  □ That party was so fun.

  □ We went to a fun party.

- What's the point of asking about those sentences? Why would anyone be concerned about them? The answer lies in the history of the word *fun*. The word is only relatively recently an adjective. It showed up as a noun in the early 1700s.

- It's hard to know exactly when it started being used as an adjective. It isn't until the 1950s that it showed up with any regularity. Interestingly, the *Oxford English Dictionary* has not yet recorded *fun* as an adjective. The dictionary has it as a noun.

- Younger speakers at this point see the adjective *fun* as standard; there are some lingering concerns but they are dwindling. Bryan Garner, however, argues that *fun* as an adjective "remains casual at best."

- Back to the usage ballot. The last two sentences in the *fun* entry were:

  □ That party was funner than I expected.

  □ That was the funnest party I've been to this year.

- If you're cringing right now, you're not alone. But let's take a closer look to see if *funner* and *funnest* are really wrong. This look takes us back to the newness of the adjective.

- As a noun, *fun* takes *more*: "more fun." This is why, right now, *fun* often still takes *more* even when it is an adjective. But lots of other one-syllable adjectives make the comparative and superlative in

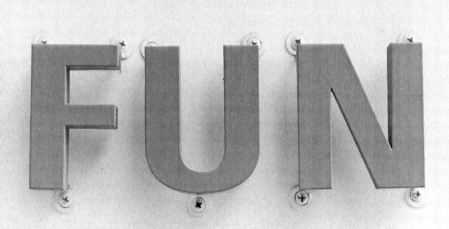

a different way: tall/taller/tallest, wide/wider/widest, smart/smarter/smartest, blue/bluer/bluest.

■ Kids, when they learn the word *fun*, make it behave like other one-syllable adjectives until corrected. But a shift is underway: Students have a much stronger negative reaction to *funner* than to *funnest*. This course's prediction is that kids will win out in the long term. Some advice for now: Beware of *funner*.

Comparatives and Superlatives

■ The usage question about *fun/funner/funnest* makes for a good introduction to a lecture on adjectives because one of the characteristic features of adjectives is that they create comparatives and superlatives.

■ One-syllable adjectives typically take *–er* and *–est* to form comparatives and superlatives. These inflectional endings are the oldest way to create comparatives and superlatives. English used to rely much more heavily on inflectional endings than it does now. The historical antecedents of *–er* and *–est* were the default in Old English. The use of *more* and *most* is newer; it spread slowly through 14th century and peaked in the late medieval period.

■ Then an unpredictable thing happened: By the Renaissance, inflected forms with *–er* and *–est* began reasserting themselves. The history of English generally involves the loss of inflections, but speakers are unpredictable.

■ Now we have had something of a division of function. Generally, *–er* and *–est* are used for shorter (and more frequent) adjectives made up of one or two syllables. *More* and *most* are used for longer (and less frequent) adjectives. Those are typically three syllables or more, but it can occur with two-syllable adjectives as well. Two-syllable adjectives can go either way.

■ What is going on with those two-syllable adjectives? It's not a total free-for-all. One study suggests that when the adjective precedes the noun, it favors the *–er/–est* ending; for example, "the coolest school ever." When the adjective is out in the predicate, it favors *more* or *most*: "Sam was a little more cool."

■ We also know that the sound of the final syllable in an adjective or the suffix at the end of an adjective can have an impact.

    □ The ending *–y* prefers *–er/–est*: Happy becomes happiest; easy becomes easiest.

    □ The ending *–ful* tends to take *more* or *most*: more hopeful; most cheerful.

■ Studies of comparatives and superlatives in contemporary spoken English will turn up a not insignificant number of double forms, usually with two-syllable adjectives, such as *more wealthier* and *most deadliest*. These are now severely criticized.

Historical Uses

■ Let's look at historical figures that we deem to be very literate who used double comparatives and superlatives. Here are some examples from Shakespeare:

    □ In *Measure for Measure*: "To some more fitter place"

    □ In *King Lear*: "To take the basest, and most poorest shape"

    □ In *King Lear*: "Harbour more craft, and more corrupter ends"

■ Interestingly, these have all sorted out in different ways. *Fit* usually takes *–er* or *–est*, but *more/most fit* is not uncommon. *Corrupt* now almost categorically takes *more* or *most*. *Poor* overwhelming uses *–er* or *–est*.

■ Of course, there are some adjectives that at least theoretically can't take comparative and superlative forms because their meanings do not allow for comparison: *unique*, *equal*, *perfect*, and *pregnant*, for example. In reality, all four of these do show up with comparatives sometimes

- *More perfect* is perhaps the most famous in the U.S. The phrase "a more perfect Union" appears in the Preamble to the Constitution. Is this wrong? Patricia O'Conner and Stewart Kellerman provide a useful defense on their blog *Grammarphobia*. They argue that *more perfect* is capturing the process of striving toward perfection rather than surpassing it.

- The issue with *unique* is different; here, we are getting a change in meaning. The word spawned from the Latin *unicus*, meaning "single, sole, alone of its kind."

  □ It came into English via French, appearing in the early 17th century and meaning "one of a kind."

  □ But by the mid-18th century there were already examples where it meant "remarkable" or "unusual." Lots of people still don't like this, but it's not new.

  □ Nevertheless, we probably want to be careful with *more unique* in formal writing: When the AHD Usage Panel was surveyed in 2004, 66 percent of the panelists disapproved of "Her designs are quite unique." But this was down from 80 percent in 1988.

  □ Editors of the AHD point out some very rhetorically effective uses of comparative *unique*, such as this sentence from Martin Luther King Jr.: "I am in the rather unique position of being the son, the grandson, and the great-grandson of preachers."

Two-Syllable Adjectives

- Let's now return to two-syllable adjectives, and whether they appear in attributive or predicative positions. An attributive adjective appears right before the noun: "coolest school." A predicative one appears after a linking verb like *was*: "Sam was more cool."

■ There are a few adjectives that typically if not exclusively appear only in the attributive or predicative position. The adjectives *former* and *latter* appear only attributively: "the former point." The adjectives *awake* and *asleep* typically appear only predicatively: "The student is asleep."

■ But we can imagine contexts, especially where we are setting up a contrast, where adjectives like *awake* and *asleep* could be used attributively: "Look at that student over there. No, not the awake one, the asleep one."

■ Another set of adjectives mean different things when they are used attributively and predicatively. Let's take the adjective *late* as an example: "His wife is late" has a much different meaning from "his late wife."

■ The adjective *sheer* also changes: "The curtains are sheer" contrasts sharply with "That is sheer stupidity." In "sheer stupidity," *sheer* is doing a kind of intensifying work.

Post-Noun Adjectives

■ We have a few phrases where the adjective appears after the noun, usually because they have been borrowed from French. *Attorney general* may be the most common, but we also have the *solicitor general*, *postmaster general*, *surgeon general*, and the like. Other examples include *poet laureate* and *professor emeritus/emerita*.

■ These are often official titles and part of government or law (e.g., *heir apparent*, *court martial*). They are mostly left over from post–Norman Conquest England, when French and Latin were the languages of court, law, and nobility.

■ The usage issue is how to make them plural. Let's take *attorney general*, which means "the attorney with the most general jurisdiction."

The plural should be *attorneys general*. The same system applies for *poets laureate, surgeons general*, and *heirs apparent*.

■ What about *court martial*? *Courts martial* appears in writing, but you can find *court martials* in speech. There is probably some confusion here with the completely different but similar-sounding *court marshal*, which refers to a judicial officer who provides security and handles other processes in a court.

■ In sum, if you find yourself writing about attorneys general or poets laureate or courts martial, remember that they are quirky in their Frenchness, check your intuitions about where the adjective is in the compound, and put that –*s* on the first word—not the second.

Suggested Reading

D'Arcy, "Functional Partitioning and Possible Limits on Variability."

O'Conner and Kellerman, *Grammarphobia: Grammar, Etymology, Usage, and More*, http://www.grammarphobia.com/.

Yagoda, *When You Catch an Adjective, Kill It*.

Question to Consider

1. Try spelling out your objections to *funner* and *funnest*, and don't settle for "It doesn't sound right." What is actually wrong with these words?

2. Can the word *unique* mean "one of a kind" and "very unusual" at the same time? Why or why not? Could any potential confusion be resolved?

Funnest Lecture Ever

Lecture

9

Let's start this lecture on adjectives with another recent question from the usage ballot for the *American Heritage Dictionary* Usage Panel. This question was on the ballot that I received in fall of 2015. The question is about the word fun. Now, as you know, when we get the ballot and we get these questions, we're given sentences and asked to rate them in one of four categories: completely acceptable, somewhat acceptable, somewhat unacceptable, completely unacceptable. In this case, with the word fun, there were five sentences that we were asked to rate.

The first three sentences under fun are ones that I marked as completely acceptable, and I would guess that many, if not most, of you do not have concerns about these sentences either, or at least not very serious concerns. In fact, when I give you these sentences, you may even be wondering why they're on the usage ballot at all. So here are the sentences: "The party was really fun." Let me say that again. "The party was really fun." How are you going to rate that one? Here's the second one: "That party was so fun." "That party was so fun." And here's the third one: "We went to a fun party." "We went to a fun party."

Why would anyone be concerned about these sentences? Now, maybe you're feeling a little concern, but when I survey people, they say, "I don't know, all those sentences seem fine to me. Maybe the 'so fun' is a little colloquial, I might not use it in formal writing, but all the sentences seem grammatical." The answer to what might be wrong, or what people might be concerned about, lies in the history of the word fun.

The word fun is only relatively recently an adjective. It shows up in English as a noun in the early 1700s, and it's hard to know exactly when it started

English Grammar Boot Camp   161

being used as an adjective. I have found examples of very fun—and once you can get very fun, you know fun is working as an adjective—I found those as early as 1910, but it isn't until the middle of the 20th century, the 1950s or so, that you can find fun as an adjective with any regularity.

Now, interestingly, when I went to the *Oxford English Dictionary* to see what they were recording in terms of the noun and the adjective use, the entry for fun has not yet been updated to include the adjective—the entry only has fun as a noun. But then again, that entry was first published in 1898 and hasn't yet been fully revised.

It's relatively easy to understand how the noun fun got reinterpreted into the adjective fun. Let's imagine a sentence like: "The party was fun." That would've been said early in the life of fun, with fun as a noun. So "The party was fun" would be like saying "The party was chaos." But if children in particular are hearing sentences like "The party was fun," it's very easy to reinterpret fun, in that case, as an adjective. We could say, "The party was great." "The party was terrible." "The party was fun." Fun sure looks like an adjective there, and kids when they hear it might reinterpret it as an adjective, and sure enough they did.

Now, as someone who teaches younger speakers of the language on a regular basis, I asked them about these sentences with fun, and at this point younger speakers see the adjective fun as completely standard. There are some lingering concerns from people who may have lived through some of the transition between fun as a noun and fun as an adjective, but I think that those concerns are dwindling.

I was actually struck when I looked at Bryan Garner's usage guide and his entry on fun when he argues that fun as an adjective "remains casual at best." I'm not sure that's entirely true. It may be that in formal writing we aren't always talking about fun things, that the context in which we use the adjective fun may often be informal, but I'm not sure that the word itself is completely casual.

Back to the usage ballot, and now let's look at the last two sentences in the entry on fun. Here's the first of those sentences: "That party was funner than I expected." Remember, you get to rate this as unacceptable to acceptable. "That party was funner than I expected." And the here's the last sentence: "That was the funnest party I've been to this year." "That was the funnest party I've been to this year."

If you are cringing right now, especially about "funner," you are not alone. "Funner" and "funnest" can elicit very strong reactions. I have actually been in auditoriums where people have booed when I have said the word "funner." But let's take a closer look to see if "funner" and "funnest" are really wrong. What's wrong with them? And this takes us back to the newness of the adjective.

As a noun, the word fun takes "more" and "most." You would say "more water," because water is a noun, and you would also say "more fun."—"We had more fun," with fun as a noun. And this is why, right now, fun as an adjective often still takes "more." It sounds more correct to people because, in its life as a noun, it took "more."

But let's think about other one-syllable adjectives in English and how they make the comparative and superlative. Let's take an adjective like tall. We make the comparative: taller. We make the superlative: tallest. Let's take wide: wide/wider/widest, smart/smarter/smartest, blue/bluer/bluest, fun/funner/funnest. I know you're cringing, but you can see the pattern that what's happening here is that kids, when they learn the language and they learn that fun is an adjective, they try to make it behave like other one-syllable adjectives. That is a completely natural thing for kids to do as they're learning the language and looking for patterns. So they will say "funner" and "funnest" until they are corrected by some adult or an older child who says, "No, no, it's not funner, it's more fun," and then they will record that as an exception.

Now I think we may be watching a shift in attitudes here. Students at the University of Michigan have a much stronger reaction to "funner" than they do to "funnest." With "funner," when I have tried out that sentence from the usage ballot, they say, "Ugh! Funner is terrible. That sentence is unacceptable." When I give them the sentence with "funnest" they say, "Eh. It's not great but I might actually say it. That one doesn't strike my ear as terrible." And I do wonder if the iPod advertisement that describes the iPod as the "funnest iPod ever," and there are big billboards that say, "The funnest iPod ever," might help "funnest" gain traction.

What is my prediction for the long term? My prediction for the long term is that the kids will win. This is what often happens with language change, that the kids who are trying to make fun behave like other one-syllable adjectives will, in the long run, be the people who change the language. And in the long run, we'll probably see "funner" and "funnest." I would guess that "funnest" will come in first, given that people right now don't seem to have as strong a reaction that "funnest" is wrong, and then "funner" may scoot in on "funnest's" coattails. My advice for now would be beware of "funner" and probably beware of "funnest," too. Certainly not something you're going to want to use in writing of any formal kind, and you may get judged.

That said, I do want to just step back here and think about why the word "funner" elicits such strong reactions. People will say, "It sounds terrible." But think about the word "runner," which is completely standard. There's nothing about the sound of "funner" that's terrible, it's just that our ears have somehow been tuned to hear it as wrong.

I decided to use this usage question about "fun," "funner," and "funnest" as our introduction to a lecture on adjectives, because one of the characteristic features of adjectives is that they can create comparatives and superlatives. We'll talk about that issue, along with double comparatives, and then we'll turn to an odd set of adjectives that mean different things depending on where they appear in the sentence. At the very end of this lecture, we'll talk about how to handle noun phrases where the adjective, oddly, shows up after the noun—for example, "attorney general."

We'll start with comparatives and superlatives. As I mentioned, one-syllable adjectives typically take a final "er" or "est" to form the comparative and superlative: tall, taller, tallest. These inflectional endings, "er" and "est," are the oldest way to create comparatives and superlatives in the English language. English as a language used to rely much more heavily on inflectional endings than it does now, and the historical antecedents of "er" and "est" as endings were the default comparative and superlative endings in Old English. The use of "more" and "most" is newer. It occurs to some extent in Old English and it spread slowly through the 14th century and peaks in usage in late Middle English.

Then, in the history of English, something unpredictable happens. By the Renaissance, we see the inflected forms with "er" and "est" reasserting themselves. It looked like "more" and "most" were going to win, and then suddenly those er/est forms come back into the picture. So when you look at the history of English, this is fascinating, because the history of English is generally about the loss of inflections. We've lost an enormous number of inflectional endings over the course of the last 1,000 years. But speakers are unpredictable, and around the Renaissance we see a resurgence of the er/est forms.

Now we have had something of a division of function where "er" and "est" are used for shorter and sometimes more frequent adjectives, those with one and two syllables: tall/taller/tallest, happy/happier/happiest. "More" and "most" are used for longer adjectives, and sometimes these are less frequent, adjectives with three syllables or more: beautiful/more beautiful/most beautiful. We don't say "beautifuler" or "beautifulest." You can use "more" and "most" with two-syllable adjectives as well. So, as you've seen, those two-syllable adjectives can go either way. They can take er/est or "more" and "most."

With one-syllable adjectives, the comparative and superlative with "er" and "est" occurs as high as 96 percent of the time. And with that statistic, again I want you to think about fun. This is one of the reasons why fun may very well start to take "funner" and "funnest" as its standard forms.

There are some less common one-syllable adjectives that will often take "more" and "most"—think about the adjective "apt." We will often say "more apt" or "most apt" as opposed to "apter" and "aptest." With three-syllable adjectives, it's pretty much always "more" and "most."

So what's going on with those two-syllable adjectives? Sometimes it can feel like a free-for-all, but it's actually not a total free-for-all in terms of how those two-syllable adjectives will pattern.

Let me tell you briefly about a study by Alexandra D'Arcy, who's at the University of Victoria, who did a study of New Zealand English, and her study suggests that when one- and two-syllable adjectives precede the noun, it favors the er/est ending. So, for example, "the coolest school ever," as opposed to "the most cool school ever." When the adjective, that two-syllable adjective, is out in the predicate, it tends to favor "more" and "most." "Sam was a little more cool," as opposed to "Sam was a little cooler." Now clearly you could do either there; this is about tendencies.

We also know that the sound of the final syllable of those two-syllable adjectives can be part of the pattern of what they will do to make a comparative or superlative. For example, adjectives that end in "y" often prefer "er" and "est," so happy/happier, easy/easiest, wealthy/wealthier/wealthiest. Adjectives that end in "ful," F-U-L, tend to take "more" and "most." We would say "more hopeful" and "most cheerful," not "hopefuler" or "cheerfulest." At least as a general rule that's not what we'd say. The adjective "mature" tends to take "more" and "most"—"more mature." "Simple," that adjective prefers "er" and "est." In other words, there are some patterns with two-syllable adjectives.

Studies of comparatives and superlatives in contemporary spoken English will turn up a not insignificant number of double forms—and notice what I did with that double negative there: a "not insignificant" number of double forms—and these are usually with two-syllable adjectives. What do I mean by double form? I mean something like "more wealthier" or "most deadliest." These kinds of double forms can now be pretty severely judged. When Alexandra D'Arcy did her study, she found them about a little over 7 percent of the time. As I said, these forms are now severely criticized, including sometimes they are called illiterate. But, of course, I'm going to turn to the history of the language.

Here I go, telling you that, once again, if you look at the history of the language, you're going to see that you can find those double forms. These historical figures that we now deem to be very literate sometimes used double comparatives and double superlatives. These double forms used to be, as far as we can tell, more common in Middle English and early

Modern English, and as I noted, they're not entirely uncommon today. Here are some examples from Shakespeare.

Let's start with *Measure for Measure*: "To some more fitter place." There it is: "more fitter." Here's one from *King Lear*: "To take the basest and most poorest shape." "Most poorest." And here's another one from *King Lear*: "Harbour more craft, and more corrupter ends."

Now, interestingly, the three adjectives in those examples from Shakespeare have all sorted out in different ways in Modern English. Corrupt now almost categorically, or at least very often, takes "more" and "most," so more corrupt/most corrupt. Poor, as a one-syllable adjective, tends to take "er" and "est": poorer/poorest. Fit: the "er" and "est" ending is more common, fitter/fittest, but "more fit" and "most fit" are fair from uncommon as we talk about our fitness levels.

When I did a search of this in the *Corpus of Contemporary American English*, it looked like the er/est, the inflected forms of fit, were about two-and-a-half times more common than "more fit" and "most fit."

Of course, there are some adjectives that, at least theoretically, can't take comparative and superlative forms because their meanings do not allow for comparison. I'm talking about adjectives like unique, equal, perfect, pregnant. But you will notice that I said at least theoretically. In fact, all four of these adjectives do show up with comparatives and superlatives if you look at actual usage.

This creates a usage issue: should we allow it? Well, let's look at perfect and unique to start. "More perfect" is perhaps the most famous in the U.S. given the phrasing "a more perfect Union" in the Preamble to the Constitution. So here's the Preamble of the Constitution, the relevant passage: "We the People of the United States, in Order to form a more perfect Union, establish Justice, insure domestic Tranquility, provide for the common defense, promote the general Welfare." Is this wrong? Is "more perfect Union" wrong?

Patricia O'Conner and Stewart Kellerman provide a useful defense of the phrase on their blog *Grammarphobia*. They argue there that the phrase "more perfect" is capturing the process of striving toward perfection, so that we are trying to get closer to this ideal of perfect. It's not that we're more than perfect; it's the striving toward the ideal.

Now the issue with unique is different—here we are getting a change in meaning. The word unique goes back to Latin; it goes back to unicus, which means single, sole, alone of its kind, and that goes back Latin unus: one. The word unique comes into English via French. It appears in the early 17th century, and it means one of a kind—you can see that root of one there. But by the mid-18th century, there are already examples where unique means remarkable or unusual.

Now, lots of people still don't like this. I do want to note that some people think it's brand new, that we just started using unique to mean remarkable. It's not that new, and I do understand the concern that it doesn't match where unique comes from. But this kind of semantic weakening is actually not that unusual in the language. If you take a verb like "quell"—"cwell"—it used to mean "kill," and now it has weakened in meaning.

All of that said, with history and what's happened to unique, it is probably still the case that you should be careful with "more unique" in formal writing. When the *American Heritage Dictionary* Usage Panel was surveyed about unique in 2004, 66 percent of the Usage Panel still disapproved of the sentence: "Her designs are quite unique." And it can't be "quite unique" if unique can't be compared. If it's one of a kind, it's one of a kind. But that 66 percent is down from 80 percent who disapproved of that sentence in 1988.

The editors of the *American Heritage Dictionary* point out that there also can be some very rhetorically effective uses of comparative unique, such as this sentence from Martin Luther King Jr: "I am in the rather unique position of being the son, the grandson, and the great-grandson of preachers." I'm not saying that you need to use unique comparatively, and it's probably still worth alerting students and others to this issue, but it is helpful to know that criticism of "more unique" is not indisputable. And if you're sitting there thinking about how is one "more pregnant," here's an example: "As I became more pregnant, I found that I craved ice cream more." So it does seem like pregnant you shouldn't be able to compare, but in fact, over those nine months, you can compare how pregnant you are.

Let's now return to the distinction that I brought up earlier with the position of adjectives, which is whether they appear in attributive position, before the noun, or in predicative position out in the predicate. The examples I gave you were "coolest school" and "Sam was a little more cool."

So the attributive position, just to review, is when the adjective happens right before the noun, "coolest school," and predicative position is when it occurs in the predicate after a linking verb like "was": "Sam was a little more cool." Most adjectives behave pretty similarly in both places, although we talked about whether those two-syllable adjectives might favor er/est or more/most depending on where they appear in the sentence.

That said, there are a few adjectives that typically, if not exclusively, appear only in attributive or only in predicative position. The adjectives former and latter appear only attributively: "the former point." We don't say "the point is former." The adjectives awake and asleep typically appear only predicatively: "the student is asleep." We don't tend to say "the asleep student," but we can imagine a context in which you and I are looking at an auditorium of students, and I'm trying to point one out, and I say, "Oh, look at that student. No, no, not the awake one, the asleep one." And there we see asleep in attributive position.

Another set of adjectives mean different things when they are used attributively and predicatively. This is one of those idiosyncrasies in English. Let's take the adjective late as an example. If we put it in predicative position, we get something like "his wife is late." Okay, so the traffic was bad. Compare that to "his late wife." Now, suddenly, his wife is no longer alive. So you can see late means differently depending on where it appears. The adjective sheer also changes meaning depending on where it appears in a sentence. We could say, "The curtains are sheer." That's about the material of the curtains. There, we see sheer out in the predicate. That is quite different from a sentence like "That is sheer stupidity," where we see sheer in attributive position, and now this is no longer about fabric.

In "sheer stupidity," sheer is doing a kind of intensifying work, and there are a couple of other adjectives that can work similarly when they appear in attributive position. For example, "someone can be perfect" but they can also be "a perfect idiot," in which case they're probably not perfect. Of course, "a perfect child" is perfect, or at least trying to be perfect, so what we see here is that there's some ambiguity when perfect appears in the attributive position. "A perfect child," there we have perfect meaning without flaw. "A perfect idiot," we have perfect meaning that this idiot corresponds to the prototype of idiots.

In all of the examples of attributive adjectives I've talked about in this lecture, the adjective has appeared before the noun. But we have a few phrases in English where the adjective appears after the noun, usually because these compounds have been borrowed from French. Attorney general may be the most common of these, but we also have the solicitor general, the postmaster general, the surgeon general, and similar expressions. Then there is the poet laureate, and professor emeritus or professor emerita.

You'll notice that these are often official titles, sometimes part of government or law, for example heir apparent and court martial. These phrases, these compounds, are mostly leftover from the Norman Conquest and, really, post-Norman Conquest England when French and Latin were the languages of court, law, and nobility. And we see a lot of French borrowings coming into English in these areas of the vocabulary including that noun-plus-adjective construction which is typical of French.

The usage issue is how do you make these nouns plural? Let's take attorney general. This is the attorney with the most general jurisdiction, so the plural, at least in theory, should be attorneys general, and that's how it usually is in writing in American English, but in British English you can find attorney-generals. The same is true for making the plural of poets laureate, surgeons general, and heirs apparent.

What about court martial? This is an ad hoc military court that tries people accused of violating military law. You will typically in writing find courts martial where the noun takes the plural, but you can also find court martials in speech. There may be come confusion here with between court martial, spelled M-A-R-T-I-A-L, and court marshal with M-A-R-S-H-A-L, and the court marshal—S-H-A-L—is the judicial officer who provides security and handles other processes in a court, and that would be court marshals.

In sum, if you find yourself writing about attorneys general or poets laureate or courts martial, remember that these nouns are quirky in their Frenchness. Check your intuitions about where the adjective is in that compound, and put the "s" on the first word, not the second.

In this lecture, we've talked about a few quirky things about adjectives, including ones that mean different things depending on where they are in the sentence. In the next lecture, we will turn to verbs, a lexical category that has some fascinating irregularities. For example, have you ever asked yourself why the past tense of "go" is "went"? It's such a common verb that we can learn it as children without ever considering just how odd it is. This course is our chance to step back and understand these aspects of English grammar in just this kind of detail.

Lecture

10 Going, Going, Went

This lecture is about the simple past tense form and past participles, as well as about some idiosyncrasies in English verbs. We'll start by clarifying the past tense versus past participles. We'll look at questions like: Why is *went* the past tense of *go*? What's happening with the phrase *have went*? The lecture also looks at the process of regularization of verbs, as well as what happens when irregularities come up. We'll close with a look at usage issues like *proved* versus *proven*.

Past Tense and Past Participles

- How do you create the past tense of a verb? It can seem like such a straightforward question with a simple answer: Add an *–ed*. Except for all the verbs where you don't do that.

  □ The simple answer is true for the majority of verbs: *talked*, *walked*, *played*, *dined*, *stayed*, etc.

  □ But consider verbs with vowel changes: *sing/sang*, *drink/drank*, *swing/swung*, *hold/held*, *run/ran*, and so on.

- Old English had two classes of regular verbs: weak (which take *–ed*) and strong (which take a vowel change). Over time, many strong became weak. For example, *swell*'s past-tense version went from *swoll* to *swelled*. The verb *shine* is still undergoing the change now, from *shone* to *shined*. Now, strong verbs are considered "irregular." But they still have a pattern: *sing* becomes *sang*, *swim* becomes *swam*, and *drink* becomes *drank*.

- The past participle is formed differently for the two different classes of verbs. The past participle is the form used in perfect aspect (e.g., *have talked*) and the passive voice (e.g., *was written*).

  □ To form a past participle with regular verbs, add *–ed*. This means the past tense and the past participle are the same.

  □ With irregular verbs, often a vowel changes. *Sung*, the past participle of *sing/sang*, is an example. And sometimes *–en* is added: *Written* is the past participle of *write/wrote*.

Have Went

- So, what's going on with *have went*? Why do people say, "It seems to have *went* well" instead of "It seems to have *gone* well?" Think about all those regular verbs where past tense is the same as the past participle.

- With irregular verbs, the past tense and past participle are typically different: we *drank*/we *have drunk*. But there can be an understandable tendency to regularize the verbs to make past tense and past participle identical, like regular verbs: we *have went* or we *have drank*.

- Will *have went* and *have drank* win because they are more regular? It's hard to know: They could, but language can maintain irregularities for a long time, especially with common words like *go*, *drink*, and *run*.

Irregularities

- While regularization can be a powerful force, sometimes we create new irregularities: Consider *dive/dove* and *sneak/snuck*. *Snuck* is an Americanism. Bryan Garner still describes *snuck* as nonstandard—even though he notes that it appears almost as often as *sneaked* in modern print materials.

- To show the kinds of irregularities we can maintain without even noticing it, let's consider the verb *to be*.

- ☐ Present: am, is, are

- ☐ Past: was, were

- ☐ Past participle: been

- ☐ Present participle: being

- ☐ Infinitive: be

- ■ What a mess! Three different stems came together over time: *b–*, *w–*, and vowels. The present tense also has more forms than any other verb: First-person singular (*am*), third-person singular (*is*), and plural (*are*).

- ■ Other verbs just have two present-tense forms: the base form and the third-person singular. But in some dialects, there is only the base form: *she walk* and *he go*. This is nonstandard but totally logical and the completion of a longstanding change in the language of losing verb inflections. We used to have *–est* as in *thou sayest* and *–en* as in *they sayen*.

Present Participles and Lie/Lay

- ■ At this point in the lecture, we have covered four of the five forms of every verb: the base form (example: *talk*), the third-person singular (*talks*), the past tense (*talked*), and the past participle (*talked*). The fifth is the present participle, which takes the base word plus *–ing*; for example, *talking* or *writing*.

- ■ Even the most confusing verbs are regular in the present participle, like *lie/lay*. But what is going on with those verbs? They're frequently misused. Garner says they spawn "one of the most widely known of all usage errors." When should we use *lie/ lay/have lain* versus *lay/laid/have laid*?

- ■ In Old English, there were some intransitive strong verbs, like *lie,* that had related *–ed* verbs that could be used transitively (or causatively). In other words, a verb like *lie* had a related verb that meant to cause something to lie down—i.e., to lay it down.

- This is why the past tense *lay* (which is intransitive) looks identical to the base for the transitive verb *lay* (whose past tense is then *laid*). Speakers and writers have been confusing them for over 500 years.

- "Lay myself down to sleep" works because *myself* is the object: People lay objects down. But someone can also *lie down* on a bed to sleep.

- Do you *lie low* or *lay low* when you are hiding out? The answer is both. Garner describes *lay low* as "loose," but he recognizes it as common—and quotes William Safire, among others, using the past-tense "I laid low."

Grammatical Information

- Now that we have all these forms, we can talk about all the grammatical information they carry within a sentence, such as tense and aspect.

- The three tenses are typically present, past, and future. But some linguists will say the tenses are actually past and non-past. "The plane lands at 5:00 pm" would be non-past. Of course, we do express the future, but not with an inflectional ending. Take, for example, *will* and *gonna*. We'll come back to auxiliary verbs in the next lecture.

- *Aspect* refers to how we view an event with respect to time (versus when it occurred in time). Progressive and perfect are the two most well-known aspects.

  - Progressive describes actions in progress at the moment we are talking about them. An example: "Her husband is cooking right now."

- ☐ Perfect describes an action in the past and its relation to another moment in time.

    - Present perfect covers an action that began in the past and is still happening or relevant now: "I have run five miles." Present perfect can also suggest that something happened recently: "I have started running."

    - Past perfect covers an action that began in the past and ended before another moment in the past: "I had run five miles when my shoe fell off."

- For fun, we can combine the perfect and the progressive, as in, "I have been running for two hours." This started in the past and in progress now.

- Standard English does not have a way to express habitual aspect through the verb form, but African American English (one of the systematic dialects of American English) does. *Be* serves as a habitual verb: "She be running these days." Standard English does this primarily with adverbials, like *usually* or *all the time*.

- Habitual *be* is seen as nonstandard variation, but there is a system there—it's just different from Standard American English. Note that Standard American English has variations of its own, like *swelled/swollen*.

Proved versus Proven

- When it comes to *proved* versus *proven*, the latter has been criticized in the past. The verb was borrowed from French and was regular, but then developed *proven*, which originates in past participle of Scottish English *preve*.

- When *proven* was newer, it met with resistance, to say the least. Richard Grant White, in *Words and Their Uses, Past and Present*, wrote in 1876:

[*Proven*], which is frequently used now by lawyers and journalists, should, perhaps, be ranked among words that are not words. ... *Proved* is the past participle of the verb *to prove*, and should be used by all who wish to speak English.

■ Garner weighed in: "*Proved* has long been the preferred past participle of *prove*. But *proven* often ill-advisedly appears."

■ But many of us use *proven* as a past participle, as in this sentence from the *Journal of International Affairs*: "The above mentioned measures have been implemented half-heartedly and for the most part have proven to be ineffective." This is a useful reminder that views on what is good and bad usage change over time. *Proven* is now unremarkable for many if not most of us.

Suggested Reading

Green, *African American English*.

Questions to Consider

1. Why might speakers introduce new irregular past tense forms into the language, such as *dove* and *snuck*?

2. Would you say/write "have proved" or "have proven"? Would you consider both of them standard usage? If so, why is this variation in standard usage OK?

Going, Going, Went

Transcript

Two women walk into a bar. One asks the other, "How did your interview go today?" The other answers, "It seems to have went well."

Are you cringing? Did that sentence make you wince? Were you expecting a normal walks-into-a-bar joke and then I threw a grammatical pet peeve in there? Or did you not notice? Were you ready for the punch line of the joke? What I said in the joke, what the second woman said, was "seems to have went well" versus "seems to have gone well."

I looked online to see if people were feeling concerned about this construction "have went" and what I found is that there's a lot of correction out there about this, including some criticism that "have went," someone said, "there's no such phrase."

But of course there is such a phrase, which is why people are writing about it online. They're writing about other people saying things like "we should have went." Now, in these comments online, there are some far-fetched explanations where people are throwing out language about the subjunctive and particles to explain why other people are saying things like "have went," but we don't need that terminology to explain this particular feature. This is about the simple past tense form and the past participle, as well as about some idiosyncrasies in English verbs. When you think about it, as I asked at the end of the last lecture, why is the past tense of the verb go "went"? Why would a "g" turn into a "w"?

That's my teaser, and we'll come back to that, to answer the question about "go" and "went," as well as what's going on with "have went," in a few minutes. But let's start by clarifying past tense versus past participle.

How do you create the past tense of a verb? It can seem like such a straightforward question, not even worth asking, but it is worth asking. You add a final "ed" except for all the verbs where you don't do that. Adding the "ed," that ending is true for the majority of verbs: talked, walked, played, dined, stayed out late. But then there are verbs that make the past tense through an internal vowel change. Think about "sing" and the past tense "sang," "drink" past tense "drank," swing/swung, hold/held, run/ran, help/holp—oh wait, no, not that one. But it actually used to be help/holp.

In Old English, if we go back 1,000 years, there were two classes of regular verbs. You had what were called weak verbs, and those ended in what has become in Modern English "ed." And then there were strong verbs that made the past tense through an internal vowel change, and if you're trying to make sense of why some were called weak and some were called strong, please don't try to do that, they're just the labels on those categories. And what you're going to see is that the weak verbs actually won.

Over time many strong verbs, the ones that took an internal vowel change to make past tense, became weak; started taking a final "ed." For example, "help" moved from past tense "holp" to "helped." "Swell," the past tense used to be "swoll" became "swelled." "Step," the past tense was "stop" became "stepped." "Shine" is still undergoing this change. It still has the past tense "shone" but you are often also hearing the past tense "shined."

So, as lots of strong verbs became weak verbs, the remaining strong verbs came to be seen as just irregular verbs. But when you look at those irregular verbs, you can actually see patterns. Look at the vowel pattern in sing/sang, swim/swam, drink/drank. You can see that those all belong to the same class in some earlier period of English.

And then there are some completely irregular verbs such as "go." The past tense of "go" used to be "gan," which makes more sense, but that past tense was replaced by the past tense of "wend"—"went." Now, "wend" had to get a new past tense, and it took "wended," because "go" took the past tense "went." We call this a suppletive verb where a verb takes a form from another verb.

The past participle of verbs is formed differently for those two different classes of verbs. This is why it's helpful to know about the history of strong and weak verbs. The past participle is the form that we use in the perfect aspect, and the perfect aspect is when we have the auxiliary "has" or "have" plus the past participle, so has talked/have talked. The past participle is also used in passive constructions, for example "was written."

How do we form the past participle? Well, with regular verbs we form the past participle with "ed," so the past tense is exactly the same as the past participle. "I talked": past tense. "I have talked": past participle. With irregular verbs, there's often a vowel change in the past participle form, and sometimes a final "en." So here are ones where you just get a vowel change: "sing," past tense: "sang," past participle: "sung." "Swim," past tense: "swam," past participle: "swum." But then there are ones where you get that vowel change and the final "en." "Write," past tense: "wrote," past participle: "written." Give/gave/given.

If we return to the verb "swell," we can actually see competing past participles. "Swell" was a strong verb, so it was "swell," "swoll" for the past tense, "swollen." The past tense has now become regular, so we get "swell," "swelled," and then the past participle can be regular "swelled" or irregular, looking back to its past, and be "swollen." The verb "go" keeps that initial "g" in the past participle, so we get "go" as the infinitive, "went" as the past tense, "gone" as the past participle.

Now let's return to "have went." Think about all those regular verbs where the past tense is exactly the same as the past participle: we walked/we have walked. With irregular verbs, the past tense and the past participle are typically different: we drank yesterday/we have drunk, we went/we have gone. Now, there can be an understandable tendency to regularize those irregular verbs, at least to the point where you make the past tense and the past participle identical, just the way that regular verbs work. If you do that, you get "go," the past tense "went," and then you would keep that past tense as the past participle and have "have went." "Drink," past tense: "drank," and then if you want to keep the past tense as the past participle, "have drank."

Will "have went" and "have drank" win because they are more regular? It's hard to know, but they might not. Languages can maintain a lot of irregularities for a long time, especially with common words like go, drink, and run. This use of the past tense for the past participle with "have went, have drank" is also widely seen as nonstandard, and so whether we're suddenly going to get a change in attitudes and those will be seen as standard, we should stay tuned. Hard to know, but they could remain nonstandard for a long time.

And while regularization, as we've seen there with folks who say "have went," can be a powerful force, sometimes we create new irregularities in the language. For example, dive/dove, sneak/snuck, maybe drag/drug? Let me explain. The verb "dive": what is your past tense of "dive"? Do you say "I dove into the pool" or "I dived into the pool"? Right now, both are seen as standard, and "dove" might be winning. If you think historically, though, the past tense of "dive" historically was "dived." It was a regular verb, and then we introduced this irregular form, "dove," and it seems to be taking over. It probably comes through analogy with drive/drove: dive/dove.

What about "sneak"? Well, this new past tense "snuck" is an Americanism. Bryan Garner, in his book *Modern American Usage*, still describes "snuck" as nonstandard—the historical past tense is "sneaked." And Garner describes it as nonstandard, even though he notes that "snuck" appears almost as often as "sneaked" in modern print materials, which raises the interesting question of how common "snuck" has to be before it gets called standard. The *American Heritage* Usage Panel is willing to call it more standard. In 2008, 75 percent of the panel accepted "snuck" as the past tense of "sneak," which interestingly is up from 33 percent accepting it just 20 years before.

What about drag/drug? Well, "drug" is not nearly as widespread as a past tense of "drag," but it made for a great teaching moment in my own career. I was at one point talking about sneak/snuck and how we've created this irregularity, and one student raised his hand and he said, "You know, the other day I heard somebody use 'drug' as the past tense of 'drag.'" And I, being quite interested in this, turned to the rest of the class, and I say, "How many of you are drug users?" And as soon as I heard it come out of my mouth, I thought, "Oh that's not what I meant to say." And I said, "Don't answer that, don't answer that." So I don't know how many of them have "drug" as the past tense of "drag." But in any case, the irregular new past tense "dove," as well as "snuck," are becoming standard—they're becoming standard irregular past tenses.

And to show you the kinds of irregularities we can maintain without even noticing, let's consider the verb "to be." The present tense of "to be": I am/ he, she, it is/they are. Past: was/were—okay, now we have a "w" where before we started with vowels. Past participle: "been"—okay, now we have a "b." Present participle: "being." The infinitive: "be." Okay, that's a mess. What's happening here is that we actually have three different stems that came together over time into one verb. We have the "b" stem; we see that in "be" and "being." We have the "w" stem: was/were. And the vowel stem, which you see in things like: am/is/are. The present tense of the verb "to be" also has more forms than any other verb. You have first person singular "am," third person singular "is," and plural "are."

Other verbs just have two present tense forms: the base form, which we sometimes call the infinitive form; and the third person singular form, which ends in "s," at least in standard varieties of English. In some dialects, there's just one present tense form. It's exactly the same as the base form or the infinitive form, so you have "she walk" and "he go." Something like "she walk" is, right now, considered nonstandard, but it's arguably completely logical and the completion of a long-standing change in the language of losing verb inflections.

In English we used to have many more inflections on verbs. For example, we had a final "est" as in "thou sayest," and a final "en" as in "they sayen." All of those endings have fallen off except for the final "s" in the third person singular. When you think about that third person singular "s," it is redundant. There's no vital information lost if you say "she walk" rather than "she walks," because the way Modern English works now, the subject "she" is always going to come before the verb, so you know it's third person singular. You don't actually need the "s." Of course, there's a lot of redundancy in grammar, it can be helpful, but I'm just pointing out that we don't actually need that "s."

At this point in the lecture, we have covered four of the five forms of every verb. You have the base form, sometimes called the infinitive form, such as talk, sing, go, be. You have the third person singular: talks, writes, or talk, write in nonstandard varieties. Past tense form: talked, wrote. And the past participle: talked, written.

The fifth form is the present participle, and that is made through the base of the verb plus "ing": talking, writing. This form is the most regular form in English—it doesn't matter whether this is a regular verb or an irregular verb. Even the most confusing verbs are regular in the present participle, confusing verbs like "lie" and "lay."

What is going on with these verbs? Bryan Garner calls lie and lay "one of the most widely known of all usage errors," and I have to say, maybe you are one of the lucky people who does not have to pause to think about whether it should be "lie" or "lay" or "laid" or "lain." I'm not; I have to pause. We have two verbs here: "lie," past tense "lay," present participle "lain"— "have lain." Then we have "lay," past tense "laid," and then "have laid" for the past participle.

Let me explain why this is so confusing. In Old English, there were some intransitive strong verbs, verbs that don't take an object, like "lie," that had a related weak form, an "ed" verb, that could be used transitively, or causatively, that could have an object. In other words, a verb like "lie" had a related verb that meant to cause something to lie down, and that verb was created from the past tense of "lie." So you have "lie" as the infinitive, and then "to lay it down," where you have that causative verb. This is why the past tense of "lay"—lie/lay, which is intransitive—looks identical to the base of the transitive verb "lay," whose past tense is "laid."

Speakers and writers have been confusing these two verbs for over 500 years. You have "lie down" but then "lay myself down to sleep," and it becomes "lay" because "myself" is now the object. Now, do you "lie low" or "lay low" when you're hiding out? I realized recently that I could do both, that I would often say "I'm laying low." Bryan Garner describes "lay low" as loose, but he recognizes that it is common, and he actually quotes William Safire, the language pundit who wrote for *The New York Times Sunday*

Magazine for years, he quotes him among others as using the past tense "I laid low" in published writing.

There's some chance that our confusion about "lie low" versus "lay low" is influenced by the fact that something like a virus can "lay you low." So this is a pair of verbs that can confuse even the most grammatically confident of writers, or at least make them pause.

Now that we have all these forms, we can talk about the grammatical information that they carry within a sentence, such as tense and aspect. I'm going to spend some time here because some of this terminology, such as perfect and progressive, will come up again in future lectures. And the way we pack information into verb phrases is fascinating.

All right, let's start with tense: present, past, future—or maybe not. Some linguists will say that English has past and nonpast. For example, so they will say we don't have future because we don't have a future tense that is inflected, we only inflect the past with "ed" or with that vowel change. You can use the present to describe the future—for example, "the plane lands at 5 pm." Of course, we do express the future, but as I said not with inflectional endings. We use auxiliary verbs, such as "will" or less formally "gonna," and we'll come back to auxiliary verbs in the next lecture.

Let's now turn to aspect. We're going to talk about two categories here: progressive and perfect. Aspect is about how we view an event with respect to time versus when it occurred in time, which is about tense. All right, we'll start with the progressive. The progressive is used to describe actions that are in progress at the moment we are talking about them. So if we're talking about right now, I could say, for example, "Her husband is cooking right now," because we're in this moment, and that is happening right now—it's in progress. Let's imagine we're talking about a past moment and I want to describe what was in progress at that moment. I would say, "Her husband was cooking when she got home." "When she got home" is that moment in time and "her husband was cooking" is what was in progress at that moment. You'll see here that all aspect has tense. I gave you an example in the present tense and an example in the past tense.

The perfect is a little trickier to explain, but here we go. The perfect describes an action in the past and its relation to another moment in time. Let's start with the present perfect. The present perfect describes an action that began in the past and is still happening or is still relevant now. Examples will help here. "I have run five miles." That's the present perfect, and we use it because I started running at some point earlier, but it is still relevant now: I have run five miles at this moment. Or another example: "I have read half the book." So I started at some moment in the past, it's still relevant in the present. "I have fallen in love." I fell in love in some moment in the past, and all indications are that I'm still in love.

The past perfect describes an action that began in the past and ended before another moment in the past. All right, again let me give you an example. "I had run five miles when my shoe fell off." So I had run those five miles until this other moment in the past. That other moment in the past is when my shoe fell off. Another example: "I had read half the book when I decided it wasn't worth finishing," which does happen to me sometimes. I had read half the book I started in the past, and then I read it up to this other moment in the past, which is when I decided it wasn't worth finishing. The present perfect can suggest also that something happened recently. For example, I say "I have started running." This suggests that I started sometime in the recent past and it is still relevant today.

For fun, just for fun, we can combine the perfect and the progressive, as in "I have been running for two hours." This action started in the past and is in progress now. And let's unpack this phrase to show the remarkable amount of information you need to know to construct this completely mundane verb phrase. "I have been running." Okay, the perfect here involves "have" plus the past participle. The progressive involves "be" plus the present participle. In "have been running" the perfect comes first, so we get the "have" first, and then we get the progressive, we get the "be." So we start with "have" and then we get the "be" for progressive. Now, "have" needs a past participle, so the "be" form becomes the past participle form because it's affected by "have"—"have been." Then the "be" needs the present participle, so it makes a present participle out of "running"—"have been running." That's a lot of information to know to create this phrase that you create all the time.

Standard English does not have a way to express habitual aspect through the verb form itself, but African-American English, one of the systematic dialects of American English, does have habitual aspect captured through what linguists call habitual "be." For example, in African-American English, a clause like "she be running" would be to express a habitual action, like "she be running these days." This is something she's doing habitually. Another example: "He be joking around all the time." So that "be" there suggests that this is something that happens habitually.

When people who are not speakers of African-American English try to create sentences in African-American English, they will often get this use of "be" wrong because they don't realize the grammar behind it, that the "be" marks habitual aspect. Standard English marks the habitual primarily through adverbials such as "usually" or "all the time."

Habitual "be" is seen as nonstandard variation, as is the past tense "drug," the phrase "have went," and "it go down that way," where you don't have the "s" on the third person singular. But what I hope I've shown you is that there is a system here, there's a grammatical system at play here. It's different from Standard American English, but there's a system. And it's not that there's no variation in standard English. We already saw this with "has swelled" and "has swollen" and let's look at another example.

Let's look at the past participles of the verb "prove." Many of us, myself included, have both "proved" and "proven" available. Are both of those standard for you? They are for me, and I think I don't even notice whether I'm using "proved" or "proven," but it hasn't always been the case that both have been considered standard. "Proven" was criticized in the past when it came into common use. The verb "prove" is borrowed from French and it came in as a regular verb: prove/proved/past participle proved. But then it developed the past participle "proven." "Proven" seems to originate in the past participle of the Scottish English form "preve," spelled P-R-E-V-E, on analogy probably with cleave/cloven, weave/woven, prove/proven.

When "proven" was newer, it met with resistance, to say the least. Here's Richard Grant White in his book *Words and Their Uses, Past and Present*, published in 1876. He writes of "proven":

> Proven, which is frequently used now by lawyers and journalists, should, perhaps, be ranked among words that are not words. Proved is the past participle of the verb to prove, and should be used by all who wish to speak English.

Wow. Who knew that proven wasn't even a word. Bryan Garner addresses it in his usage guide as well. He writes: "Proved has long been the preferred past participle of prove. But proven often ill-advisedly appears." For all of us who are part of the "often there" who are using "proven," we may not realize that it was ill advised. Now the use of "proven" is accepted in some legal contexts—for example, "innocent until proven guilty" and "not proven." The *Associated Press* stylebook also tells us not to use "proven" as a past participle, to use "proven" only as an adjective, as in "a proven remedy."

But, of course, many of us do use "proven" as a past participle, and here's an example from an academic journal, the *Journal of International Affairs*, just to show how easy it is to find these in standard, edited prose: "The above mentioned measures have been implemented half-heartedly and for the most part have proven to be ineffective." Many standard dictionaries list both past participles, "proved" and "proven," as standard. All in all, I find this a useful reminder that views on what is good and bad usage change over time, and "proven" is now unremarkable for many if not most of us.

There are a few other irregular past participles that are now typically adjectives, for example "shaven" and "mown," M-O-W-N. Now I have to say my students, however, believe that "mown" is not a word at all, they just look at me like I'm crazy when I say "mown." Both "shave" and "mow" were strong verbs in Old English, so they were verbs that made past tense through a vowel change, and that means that they made a past participle with the final "en." Over time, both "shave" and "mow" have developed regular "ed" past tenses and past participles, "shaved" and "mowed"—it's part of that regularization. As a result, we have something like "he has shaved" but "he is clean shaven." "They have moved the lawn" and "it is a freshly mown lawn." Or maybe it's a freshly mowed lawn if you also believe that "mown" is not a word.

It is tempting to think that the same pattern must hold for the verb "sew" and its two past participles "sewed"—and here I'm talking about "sew" S-E-W—its past participles "sewed" and "sewn." I have sewed/I have sewn, both of which are now seen as standard past participles for the verb "sew." But "sew"—S-E-W—started as a weak verb. It started as what we now consider a regular verb with a past tense with "ed" and a past participle with "ed," so past participle "sewed." By Middle English, "sew" had developed the irregular past participle "sewn" probably through analogy with "sow"— S-O-W—and its past participle "sown." As a result, now we have "have sewed" and "have sewn," and "have sewn" is actually now significantly more common than "have sewed."

The example of "sew" is a good reminder that in the verb system, like other places in the language, there can be a pressure to regularize, but new idiosyncrasies are introduced into the system all the time. In this lecture, we've talked about strong and weak verbs, and how there has been some movement back and forth over time.

In the next lecture, we'll look at another way to categorize verbs. This time we'll categorize them based on how they function in a sentence, specifically whether or not the verb can take an object or not take an object. And if it can take an object, how many objects can it take?

Object Lessons

Lecture

11

We'll spend this lecture thinking about how we categorize verbs based on how they function in the sentence. Specifically, we'll ask: Do they take an object, or two, or none? There are a surprising number of usage issues linked to this categorization of verbs, including the "It is me" versus "It is I" conundrum. We'll start with linking verbs, and then we'll move on to the transitive versus intransitive distinction, including some usage questions. The lecture closes with some less known types of verbs.

It Is Me?

- A common conundrum is the question: Do we say "It is me" or "It is I"? The traditional rule for this construction sets out "It is I" as the correct form. The basis for the correction is that *to be* is a linking verb, which equates the subject with the predicate noun phrase or adjective phrase that follows it, for example, "Anne is a grammar geek."

- Semantically, the linking verb equates the subject noun phrase and the noun or adjective phrase in the predicate. But what happens grammatically? The subject is in the nominative case, which means that if it is a pronoun it will be *I*, *we*, *he*, *she*, *they*, or *you*.

- Does the predicate noun also need to be in the nominative? Some prescription on this question says yes, so we'd get "It is I" and "It is she speaking." But it sounds very odd to most of us to say, "It is we" instead of "It's us." Here's another awkward sentence: "I asked who called yesterday, and it was he."

- The good news: Many usage guides now say that both "It is me" and "It is I" are acceptable. It is, rather than an issue of grammaticality, an issue of formality.

Good or Well?

- *To be* is far and away the most common linking verb—because it is the most common verb. There is a well-known usage issue around its linking status: When someone asks, "How are you?" are you *good* or are you *well*?

- Some people learn to say, "I am well" but not "I am good." But this prescription does not hold up under scrutiny. Given that *to be* is a linking verb, in the clause "I am _____," we should expect an adjective (like *terrible* or *tired*).

- *Well* is both an adjective and an adverb, and this is part of where things get confused. *Well* is the adverb form of *good*: "I'm a good cook" can also be stated as "I cook well." But *well* is also an adjective in reference to health.

- *Good* is generally an adjective: "the good food." But in some nonstandard varieties of English, it is also an adverb: "He runs good." This is a fairly stigmatized construction.

- One theory is that concerns about *good* as an adverb have bled over to encourage a sense that there is something wrong with "I am good," but there, *good* is serving as an adjective, just as it is in "I feel good." So in reality, we can say either, depending on what we mean. Also consider formality.

Bad or Badly?

- *Feel* is another linking verb, and it raises a usage question of its own: When something unfortunate happens and you are feeling sympathy for someone, are you feeling *bad* or *badly*?

- The confusion stems from this: *Feel* can be a transitive verb ("I felt the cold tile under my feet"); an intransitive verb ("I can feel!"); and a linking verb ("I feel ducky").

- *Bad* is an adjective and *badly* is an adverb. We would use *bad* after any other linking verb: "That seems bad." And we would use *badly* after an intransitive verb: "I failed badly." At least in theory, one can feel bad or feel badly, but it seems the latter doesn't come up often.

- There is, technically, a meaning difference between *I feel badly* and *I feel bad*. If you feel badly, the idea is that you have a bad sense of feel; if you feel bad, you have a bad feeling. Technically, then, you feel bad for someone else's misfortune—although that sounds overly informal or even wrong to many speakers.

- It looks like confusion has led to anxiety about what is correct. That has led to some hypercorrection. In the end we may need to rethink what is technically correct (*feel badly* may become standard).

Objects

- With all other verbs in English (sometimes referred to as *action verbs*), we talk about their relationship to objects. Can they take an object or not? If so, can they take one object or two?

- It's actually a mistake to think of these as categories of verbs. It's more accurate to think about it as how a verb behaves in a sentence, as many verbs can appear both with and without objects. For example, take the verb *read*: It can take no object, one object, or two objects.

  - No object: "I read" or "I read every day." Here, *read* is intransitive.

  - One object: "I read the newspaper." Here, *read* is monotransitive, or just transitive.

  - Two objects: "I read my grandmother the newspaper." Here, *read* is ditransitive.

- Intransitive verbs don't take objects and transitive ones take at least one. Even verbs we typically think of as intransitive can often be made transitive. For example: "I walk" can become "I walk the dog."

- Sometimes this is controversial, as in the case of whether *grow* can be transitive outside of agriculture. Take, for example, this sentence: "One of our key strategies is to grow our business by increasing the number of clients." In 1992, 80 percent of the AHD Usage Panel rejected it; in 2014, 60 percent accepted it.

Word Order

- To talk in more detail about transitivity, let's step back and talk briefly about word order in English. The subject/object relationship is determined pretty much entirely by word order at this point.

☐ With ditransitive verbs, the direct and indirect object always appear in the same order. Here's an example: "I sent her my tennis racket." There, the subject (*I*) occurs before the verb (*sent*), which occurs before the indirect object (*her*), which occurs before the direct object (*tennis racket*). The indirect object covers to or for whom the action was done. The direct object is the recipient of the action.

☐ In Modern English, the order will always be (1) subject, (2) verb, (3) indirect object, and (4) direct object: "(1) My friend (2) made (3) me a (4) birthday cake." Note that the indirect object can always be bumped to the end with *to/for*: "I sent my tennis racket to her."

Other Subsets

■ Complex transitive verbs look like they have two objects, but they function differently from ditransitive verbs. Take this example: "We elected Morgan president of the class." *Morgan* is the object and then *president of the class* is being equated with Morgan.

■ *President of the class* here would be called an object complement. It completes the predicate and refers to the object. It could also be called an object predicative. There can also be an adjective there: "My brother called me crazy."

■ Another subset of verbs always appear with a prepositional phrase as their complement. Let's take the verb *depend*. It can be intransitive ("It depends"), but if we want to specify what it depends on, we have to use *on*: "It depends on the weather," not, "It depends the weather."

■ The verb *listen* works much the same way. We can listen intransitively. If we want to specify the object, we have to add *to*: "We listened to music." Technically, these verbs don't take a direct object; they take a prepositional phrase.

- A final subset of verbs look like verbs that require prepositional phrases, but they work differently. These are phrasal verbs; they're composed of a main verb and a particle (or sometimes two). A particle is a word that fulfills a grammatical function but doesn't fall into a traditional lexical category. Examples of particles include *call up*, *ask out*, *look up*, and *come down with*.

- One might think it was a verb plus a preposition, but you can test and tell the difference. Let's look at the difference between these two sentences:

  □ "Mary looked up the hill."

  □ "Mary looked up my phone number."

- In "Mary looked up the hill," *up the hill* is a prepositional phrase expressing where Mary looked. It functions as a unit.

- In "Mary looked up my phone number," *looked up* is a unit. You can move the object to create, "Mary looked my phone number up" or "Mary looked it up." But you can't do "Up my phone number is where Mary looked," because *up my phone number* is not a prepositional phrase.

- In these cases, you have a phrasal verb with a direct object. And these verbs will come back when we talk about the well-known rule about whether you can end a sentence with a preposition— because sometimes it is not a preposition.

Question to Consider

1. At this point English follows fairly strict subject-verb-object word order. Can you come up with examples where the object comes first?

Object Lessons

I started the previous lecture on verbs with a joke, or at least the start of a joke, and for some inexplicable reason I got inspired to start this lecture on verbs with a joke as well. Let's start with a knock-knock joke that I made up just for this occasion: "Knock, knock." "Who's there?" "It's me." "No, it's I." "No, it's not you, it's me." "No, it's not me, it's I." "Are you having an identity crisis?"

Okay, so it's a bad knock-knock joke, but the correction it captures is a familiar one. We are just trying to self-identify, that we're the ones on the phone or at the door, and we face this grammatical conundrum: Do we say "It is me" or "It is I"? I grew up being corrected on this, being told that I should say, "It is I," and the traditional rule for this construction sets out that "It is I" is the correct form.

The basis for this correction is that the verb "to be" is a linking verb, and as a linking verb it equates, so to speak, the subject with the predicate noun phrase or the predicate adjective phrase that comes after to be. If we say something like, "Anne is a grammar geek," we are equating Anne and grammar geek. If we say, "Anne's grammar jokes are weak," we are equating Anne's grammar jokes with the adjective weak. So, semantically, the linking verb equates the subject noun phrase and the noun phrase or adjective phrase that's in the predicate.

But what happens grammatically? The subject of the sentence is in the nominative case, which means that, if it's a pronoun, it will be one of these pronouns: I, we, he, she, it, they, you. Does that mean that the predicate noun, the noun after the verb "to be," also needs to be in the nominative case? Does it need to match the subject? Some prescription on this question says yes, and if you say yes, then it needs to be "It is I" or "It is she speaking."

But it can sound odd to most of us to say something like "It is we. It is we at the door," instead of "It's us." And here's a pretty awkward sentence: "I asked who called yesterday, and it was he." Our gut may want to say "It was him" or "It's me," and I can put your mind at ease here, many usage guides now say that both "It is me" and "It is I" are acceptable. It is, rather than an issue of grammaticality, often an issue of formality.

Are you still not feeling completely comfortable with "It's me"? Let me just point out that other languages show that the predicate noun, the noun coming after "to be," does not need to be in the nominative case. For example, in French you would say "C'est moi," which is the equivalent of "It is me." And Joseph Priestley brought this up in the 1700s in his grammar as part of his defense—and this is in the 1700s—of the phrase "It's me." Both constructions, "It's me" and "It's I," have been in educated use for several centuries.

We'll spend this lecture thinking about how we categorize verbs based on how they function in the sentence. Specifically, do they take an object, or two, or none, like a linking verb? There are a surprising number of usage issues linked to this categorization of verbs, including the "It is me" "It is I" conundrum. We'll start with linking verbs, and then will talk about the transitive/intransitive distinction with verbs, including some usage questions such as whether the verb "grow" can function transitively. For example, can you "grow" a business?

Back to linking verbs. The verb "to be" is by far and away the most common linking verb, probably because it is the most common verb in the English language. And there is another well-known usage issue around the linking verb "be," and the question: "Are you good or are you well?" It is such a simple question: "How are you?" And it's simple if we answer with just one word: fine, okay, good, exhausted, fantastic, ducky. I'm trying to bring ducky back as a response to "How are you?" We'll see if I can succeed. In any case, if we just say one word, we're fine. But if we say, "I am __." we are told that things get more complicated. I learned growing up that I should say, "I am well." I should not say, "I am good." I was told, "It's not about your moral goodness, Anne. It's not about whether you are a good person. It is about whether you are well." But is it?

When I say "I am well," I am, at least in my own head, referring to my health, my state of wellness. But what if I want to answer the question more generally about my overall state of being? If I want to say that I'm in a good place, that my life is generally free of troubles, why can't I say "I'm good" in the same way that I could say "I feel good" or "the food is good"? You can. This prescription about "I'm well" instead of "I'm good" does not hold up under scrutiny, and let me explain why.

Given that "to be" is a linking verb in the clause "I am __." we should expect an adjective there: terrible, tired. The word "well" is both an adjective and an adverb, and I think this is where things get confused. "Well" is the adverb form of "good," so if you were to say, "I am a good cook,"—there you have "good" as an adjective—and you wanted to put an adverb in, you would say, "I cook well," at least in standard varieties of English. But "well" is also an adjective in reference to health. "I am well. I am feeling well." "Good" is generally an adjective. For example, "The food is good, the good food." But in some nonstandard varieties of English it is also an adverb, so that you could say something like "He runs good. He cooks good." This is a fairly stigmatized construction.

My guess is that concerns about "good" as an adverb and things like "he runs good" have bled over to encourage a sense that there's something wrong with "I am good." But in that sentence, "I am good," good is serving as an adjective. It is just like saying "I feel good." So, in fact, we can say either, depending on what we mean. And I would add that I do think there is a formality distinction. I will sometimes hear people, when they're bumping it up a little bit, say "I am well."

Some other common linking verbs in addition to "to be" are "to become," "to appear," "to seem," "to feel," and the verb "feel" raises another usage question. When something unfortunate happens and you are feeling sympathy for someone else, are you feeling "bad" for that person or are you feeling "badly" for that person? Here's where I think the confusion stems from in this case. "Feel" can function in different ways. It can be a transitive verb—in other words, it can take an object: "I felt the cold tile under my feet." "Feel" can also be an intransitive verb. Imagine that I had lost feeling in my hand, and now I have gotten the feeling back in my hand, and I say, "I can feel!" because I'm so excited. And then "feel" can be a linking verb in a sentence like "I feel great" or "I feel ducky."

The difference then between "bad" and "badly" is the difference between an adjective and an adverb. So we would use the adjective "bad" after any other linking verb, for example "That seems bad." And we would use the adverb "badly" after an intransitive verb, for example "I failed badly." And I think that is on my mind because clearly I'm still worried about that bad knock-knock joke I started this lecture with.

At least in theory one could feel "bad" or feel "badly" depending on what you mean, although I have to say the latter seems like it wouldn't come up too much, and let me explain. There is, technically, a meaning difference between "I feel badly" and "I feel bad." If you "feel badly," the idea is—or at least so the story goes—that you have a bad sense of feel. In other words, you're trying to feel things but you're having trouble feeling them and you feel badly. If you "feel bad," then you have a bad feeling. So technically, you feel bad for someone else's misfortune, although I think that that can sound at this point overly informal or even wrong to some speakers to say "I feel bad that that happened to you." People think, "Oh, I'm not sure that's right."

What seems to be happening here is that confusion has led to anxiety about what is correct, and that has led to some hypercorrection, in this case toward "badly," and in the end we may need to rethink what is technically correct. In other words, "feel badly" to mean "feel bad" may become standard.

With all other verbs in English sometimes referred to as action verbs, we talk about their relationship to objects. Can they take an object or not? And if they can take an object, do they take one object or two? It's actually a mistake to think of these as categories of verbs. I think it's more accurate to think about it as how a verb behaves in a sentence, because many verbs can appear both with and without objects—sometimes with one object, sometimes with two—and you see this in dictionary entries. If you look up a verb, you'll often see a definition for the verb intransitive and the verb transitive, showing that many verbs can do both.

For example, let's take the verb "read." It can take no object, one object, or two objects. Here's a sentence with no object: "I read" or "I read every day," because "every day" there is functioning adverbially. With no object, we call that an intransitive verb. "Read" can also take one object: "I read the newspaper." We would call that a monotransitive verb, taking one—mono—object. Sometime you will also just see that referred to as transitive. Then "read" can take two objects. For example: "I read my grandmother the newspaper." There, the verb is ditransitive, it takes two objects, and we'll come back to the issue of which is the direct object there and which is the indirect object.

Right now, the key is that intransitive verbs don't have objects and transitive ones take at least one. Even verbs we typically think of as intransitive can often be put in a sentence to be made transitive. For example, take the verb "walk." We would often say, "I walk. I walk around the park. I walk around the house. I walk to school." All of those are intransitive. But we can make it transitive—for example, "I walk the dog." And we can even make it ditransitive with two objects: "I walked him the bike."

Sometimes this question of whether a verb can be transitive or intransitive is controversial—for example, whether "grow" can be transitive outside of agriculture. Everyone agrees that you're allowed to grow crops, but are you allowed to grow your business? What do you think of this sentence? "One of our key strategies is to grow our business by increasing the number of clients." This exact sentence was given to the *American Heritage* Usage Panel in 1992 and 80 percent of the Usage Panel rejected it. It was given to the Usage Panel again in 2014 and 60 percent accepted it, which is a pretty striking change. In other words, it looks like "grow" as a transitive verb in the context of, for example, business is becoming accepted as more standard.

Conversely, there have sometimes been transitive verbs, verbs that take an object, that people felt shouldn't become intransitive. For example,

Richard Grant White in his book *Words and Their Uses, Past and Present*, published in 1876, had this to say about the verb "leave."

> This verb is very commonly ill used by being left without an object. Thus: Jones left this morning; I shall leave this evening. Left what? shall leave what? Not the morning or the evening, but home, town, or country. When this verb is used, the mention of the place referred to is absolutely necessary. To wind up a story with, 'Then he left,' is as bad as to say, then he sloped – worse, for sloped is recognized slang.

So there's Richard Grant White feeling cranky about using "leave" as an intransitive verb. Of course, now it seems completely unremarkable to do that. "We all left. We all left the building." To end a novel with "Then he left."? I mean, maybe it would be a sad ending to a novel, but there'd be nothing ungrammatical about it.

To talk in more detail about transitivity, let's step back and talk briefly about word order in English. At this point in Modern English, we have quite rigid word order. Subject and object are determined pretty much purely though word order. The subject comes before the verb; the object comes after the verb. As we've talked about, this was not always the case in English.

Old English had a case system where nouns took inflectional endings that marked their grammatical function. Were they the subject? The direct object? The indirect object? When you have those kinds of inflectional endings you can have more flexible word order. If the direct object comes before the verb, you still know it's the direct object because it's carrying that ending. As we lost those inflectional endings, we developed more rigid word order, so we have subject-verb-object. Now, only the pronouns still carry case—for example, "I"-subject "me"-object—but they still need to obey the rigid word order we have of Modern English.

So now, in Modern English, as many people will say, "The dog bites the man" is not news, because we know the "dog" is the subject there, but "The man bites the dog" is news. Occasionally you'll see subject-verb-object word order get mixed up. For example, in the song "The Little Drummer

Boy" we get the object fronted. The lyrics "Come they told me / A newborn king to see." Obviously we need to do that for the rhyme, as opposed to saying "To see a newborn king." But this kind of word order is rare and can sometimes feel a little bit stilted.

Let me show you an example of what I mean by fairly rigid word order in Modern English. With ditransitive verbs, the verbs that take two objects, the direct and indirect object always appear in the same order. Now, just to clarify the difference, the indirect object is "to whom" or "for whom" the action of the verb was done. The direct object is "what" or "who" was the recipient of the action. In Modern English, a sentence with two objects will always be subject-verb-indirect object-direct object. Let me give you a couple of examples. "I sent her my tennis racket." I sent "her"—indirect object, the person to whom I sent the racket—my "tennis racket"—my tennis racket being the direct object. Here's another example: "My friend made me a birthday cake." So "me"—the indirect object, because my friend made the cake for me—a "birthday cake" is the direct object, what my friend made.

You can test which is the indirect object in an interesting way now in Modern English. The indirect object can always get bumped out to the end of the sentence with the preposition "to" or "for." Let's go back to the sentence: "I sent her my tennis racket." We can take the "her," bump it out, and add a "to." "I sent my tennis racket to her." Or the birthday cake; we had "My friend made me a birthday cake." You can take that indirect object "me," bump it out: "My friend made a birthday cake for me."

As a historical side note here, now in most standard varieties of English we cannot use the word order subject-verb-direct object-indirect object, something like "I sent my tennis racket her." But that has not always been true in English. In Old English—and remember that Old English had more flexible word order—you could get both verb-indirect object-direct object, for example "send you money," and verb-direct object-indirect object: "send money you."

The verb-direct object-indirect object "send money you" becomes unusual in Middle English, at least with two nouns. But if you have two pronouns, it continues to be used with things like "send it you." And it in fact remains something of a norm to be able to say things like "send it you" through the Renaissance. Some 18th-century grammars of English even recommend these constructions, like "show it him," "show them me." And while standard varieties of English no longer allow this, or at least don't typically allow verb-direct object-indirect object, other dialects of English still do.

I scatter these historical facts throughout as reminders that standard usage changes, and now what used to be standard, in this case, can feel almost ungrammatical if you're a speaker of a dialect that no longer allows that. To summarize where we are, we've covered linking verbs, and then verbs that function intransitively, monotransitively, and ditransitively. It seems like we should be done, but there is one remaining funny little class of verbs, and sometimes my students will ask "Can we just ignore those verbs?" But of course we're not going to ignore those verbs.

These verbs are called complex transitive verbs. It can look like they have two objects, but they function differently from ditransitive verbs. Let me give you an example, and then I'll explain how they function differently. Here's the example: "We elected Morgan president of the class." "We elected Morgan president of the class." "Morgan" is the object, and then "president of the class" is being equated with "Morgan." You can imagine an equal sign between "Morgan" and "president." "We elected Morgan president of the class." Here, "president of the class" would be called an object complement, and complement here means a phrase that is completing the predicate. And sometimes you'll hear this called an object complement or an object predicative.

You can also get an adjective with these complex transitive verbs. For example, "My brother called me crazy." Again, think about that equal sign: "me" equals "crazy," because "my brother" called "me" crazy. A few of the more common verbs that function in this way as complex transitives are elect, call, name, consider, find, prove, keep—think about the expression "Keep it real."

Okay, I know I said there was one remaining class of verbs to talk about, and that was the complex transitive verbs, but in fact, even with that additional category, we haven't covered the whole set of verbs. There's another subset of verbs that always appear with a prepositional phrase as their complement—in other words, again, it's that complement as what's completing the predicate. Let's think about the verb "depend." The verb "depend" can be intransitive—for example, "It depends." But if we want to specify what it depends on, we have to use "on" the way I just did there with "what it depends on." For example, "It depends on the weather." We cannot say "It depends the weather."

The verb "listen" works much the same way. We can "listen" intransitively; we just "listen." Then, if we want to specify the object, we have to add "to": "We listened to music." So technically these verbs like "listen" and "depend" don't take a direct object, they take a prepositional phrase as their complement.

And I'm still not finished, but I promise that this is the last subset of verbs. These verbs look like verbs that require prepositional phrases but they work differently. I'm going to call these phrasal verbs—you'll sometimes hear them called multipart verbs. They are verbs composed of a main verb and what linguists will call a particle. Now this particle looks like a preposition but it's not, and the word particle is—you're going to see it's a little bit of a cop out here in terms of what we're referring to—a particle is a word that fulfills a grammatical function in the language but doesn't fall into the traditional lexical categories.

Let me give you some examples of phrasal verbs: call up, ask out, look up, blow up, break up, break out, cheer up, come down with—there you can see a phrasal verb with two particles—find out, fill out. You can see with those examples why you might think it was a verb plus a preposition, because those particles look like prepositions, but you can test and tell the difference. Let me show you what I mean.

Let's look at the difference between these two sentences. "Maya looked up the hill." "Maya looked up my phone number." Obviously they mean different things, and they work differently grammatically, and I think this is fascinating the way you can test to see how they function differently.

Let's start with "Maya looked up the hill." In that sentence, "up the hill" is a prepositional phrase expressing where Maya looked, and it functions as a unit because it's a prepositional phrase. You can tell it's a unit because, for example, you can substitute in another adverb there. "Maya looked there." Or we could move "up the hill" around in the sentence. "Up the hill is where Maya looked." Where did Maya look? "Up the hill."

Now let's look at the sentence "Maya looked up my phone number." Here, "looked up" is a phrasal verb. It's a little unit in and of itself, and we can tell when we start to try to move things around in the sentence. You're going to see that, in this case, "my phone number" works as a unit, it's the direct object, and it doesn't work with "up" the way "up the hill" worked. If I were to ask "What did Maya look up?" where "look up" gets to stay together, we would say, "My phone number." We can move the object "my phone number," that noun phrase, around. "Maya looked my phone number up." And then we could substitute in "it" there: "Maya looked it up." You couldn't do that with "the hill." If Maya was "looking up the hill," she wasn't "looking it up."

But, and with the "Maya looked up my phone number," what you can't do is "Up my phone number is where Maya looked." No. That's because "up my phone number" is not a prepositional phrase here. "Look up" is a phrasal verb; "my phone number" is the object of the phrasal verb "look up."

So in these cases you have a phrasal verb with a direct object, and these verbs, these phrasal verbs, will come back when we talk about the well-known rule about whether you can end a sentence with a preposition. And they're going to come back up because sometimes that word at the end of a sentence is not a preposition.

Shall we talk about that now? No, we shall not. I will hold off until we talk about prepositions in Lectures 17 and 18. Instead, we'll talk in the next lecture about "shall" and other auxiliary verbs, including why my saying "we shall not" may have sounded overly formal to you and perhaps even a little stilted.

Perhaps the best-known usage rule involving auxiliary (or helping) verbs is the distinction between—or the lack of distinction—between *can* and *may*. This lecture covers that issue, as well as many other sticking points that we run into when using auxiliary verbs. We'll spend a deal of time on the verb *will*. The issue of combining auxiliary verbs will also get attention, and we'll close with a look at the word *ain't*.

Can and May

- There is a traditional rule that *may* is about permission and *can* is about ability. So, for example, a student *can* leave a class whenever they want to; the issue is whether they *may* leave (with permission from the instructor).

- Historically, *can* has been used to express permission for almost 200 years—so these two auxiliary verbs overlap in the realm of permission. Note that we don't use *may* for ability.

- There are times when all of us want to use *can* for permission. Specifically in a contracted negative construction, we prefer *can't* to *mayn't* when we're talking about permission: "Can't I come?" works much better than "Mayn't I come?"

- For some speakers, *can* versus *may* is a formality distinction regarding permission. However, as of 2009, 37 percent of the AHD Usage Panel rejects *can* when used for permission, specifically in the question, "Can I take another week to submit the application?" Rejection is falling, but that is still over a third of the Usage Panel.

At a play, you might hear the formal instruction, "Audience members *may* take photographs," or the more informal, "Yes, you *can* take a photo."

- A side note: Both *can* and *may* express possibility for the future: "It may get crazy in here!" or "It can snow in Michigan in May." The usage issue we've been talking about here is not about possibility, but about permission versus ability.

Auxiliary Verbs

- *Can* and *may* are two of nine modal auxiliary verbs, or modals, in English. The other seven are *may*, *might*, *must*, *could*, *shall*, *should*, *will*, and *would*. Modal auxiliaries express ability, necessity, obligation, or permission. This is referred to as deontic modality. They can also express assessment of reality or likelihood, which is called epistemic modality.

- For example, deontic *must* is about obligation or necessity: "I must finish this essay." Epistemic *must* is an evaluation of reality: "It must have fallen below freezing last night."

- In addition to the nine modal auxiliaries, there are three auxiliary verbs, known as primary auxiliaries, that are not modals: *be*, *have*, and *do*. All auxiliaries appear before the main verb and require a main verb, except in cases of elision.

Modals

■ Modals work differently from other verbs in that they do not inflect: There is no *–s* or past tense *–ed*. "She *mights*" or "They *musted*" don't happen. There is also no *–ing* ("*Coulding*" never occurs) and no past participle ("He has *shalled*" doesn't happen either).

■ Modals have no infinitive form, and the main verb after them appears in the base or infinitive form: It's "can go," not "can goes." We can see the effect of inserting a modal on our understanding of whether something is possible or likely or allowed. Take these examples:

   □ I play ping-pong.

   □ I can play ping-pong. (Someone has asked if I know how or permission.)

   □ I might play ping-pong. (This is a possibility in the future.)

   □ I would play ping-pong. (This is a possibility, perhaps if something else happens.)

   □ I must play ping-pong. (Two interpretations: I need to do this for whatever reason, or this must be true—e.g., you found photos of me playing last week.)

■ The auxiliary modal *will* also has two meanings, the most common of which is future tense. It can also express epistemic modality of something we think is likely to happen or want to happen. Think about the two different interpretations of this sentence:

   □ I will play ping-pong. (This is a simple statement of future action.)

- I will play ping-pong! (This expresses determination to learn this sport.)

- In standard varieties of English, you get only one modal per verb phrase, but in some varieties of Southern American English, you can get double modals or multiple modals.

  - Examples include *might could*, *might should*, *may can*, and *useta could*. In a sentence, someone might say, "I might should send a contribution."

  - It's not impossible to put two modals next to each other in English. It doesn't typically occur in standard English, but it occurs in other varieties.

Primaries

- The three primary auxiliary verbs do much heavy lifting. Two of them (*be* and *have*) express aspect and voice for verbs, and auxiliary *do* has become all wrapped up in how we ask questions and express negation.

- The three primary auxiliaries do inflect within the verb phrase; for example: "I am talking," "she has listened," and "he does exercise." In talking about these three auxiliaries, let's start with *be*, *have*, and aspect.

  - The progressive aspect takes *be*: "I am playing ping-pong" and "I was playing ping-pong."

  - The perfect aspect takes *have*: "I have played ping-pong" and "I had played ping-pong."

- The auxiliary *be* also plays a role in creating passive voice. This takes *be* plus a past participle: "The ping-pong paddle was stolen."

- Then there is auxiliary *do*, which has dramatically increased its functions in English grammar since the Renaissance. *Do* has long been used in declarative sentences: "He does exercise." At this point it typically expresses emphasis: "I do care about the fate of porcupines, I do!"

- Since the Renaissance, *do* has become a standard part of how we make negative statements and questions: "I like dark chocolate" becomes "I do not like dark chocolate." But we don't need *do* if there is another auxiliary there, modal or primary: "Ashley was not playing video games earlier."

- We also don't need *do* if the main verb is *to be*: "Video games are not a good distraction."

- The auxiliary *do* is now a key part of how we make yes/no questions. During the Renaissance and earlier, you could flip the main verb and subject to make a question: "Know you the address?"

- Now, if there is no other auxiliary present and the main verb is anything other than to be, we insert *do* and move it to the front: "Do you know the address?" Again, if there is another auxiliary verb there, we don't need *do*: "Was Ashley playing video games earlier?"

Changes

- Two modals are in serious decline. The first, which won't surprise you, is *shall*. While we're talking about *shall*, let's address a usage issue.

  □ There is a rule out there about *shall* and *will*. For those who know it, the idea is that one expresses future and one obligation, and it varies by person. In first person, *shall* expresses the future and *will* expresses obligation.

  □ The supposed rule continues: In the second and third person, *will* expresses future and *shall* expresses obligation. Has this ever been true? Not as far as we know. It was imposed by prescriptivists trying to create a logical system where there has never been one. But you can find it in Strunk and White's work. (For Americans, *shall* is more formal, sometimes used to express official, legal obligation. Lawyers can care a lot about this.)

- The other modal in decline may surprise you: It's *must*. *Must* has been in decline for much of the 20th century. But this is only the deontic *must*—the one that expresses obligation or necessity.

- On reflection, *must* often sounds too strong: "I must run errands tonight after work" comes off as an overstatement. We'd usually say something more like, "I hafta run errands tonight after work."

- This example points to the rise of a new set of auxiliary verbs that are emerging, sometimes called semi-modals or emerging modals. They include *hafta* and *gonna*. Those aren't standardized spellings, but they are how we say them. In fact, *gonna* and *going to* now mean different things: "I'm gonna run errands" versus "I am going to run errands."

- We still recognize these are informal and don't write them in formal prose, but their rise in American English is dramatic. These significant changes in the modal system are happening without a lot of fanfare or stigmatization (other than informality).

Ain't

- Before we finish this lecture on auxiliary verbs, we need to talk about *ain't*. This must be the most notorious auxiliary verb out there. Dictionaries tend to treat it as nonstandard, and some people claim it isn't a word.

- What is wrong with *ain't*? Mostly it is that style guides tell us there is something wrong with it. In the 18th century, a whole set of contractions were condemned: *shouldn't, can't, won't,* and *ain't*. All of these have redeemed themselves—they're seen as informal, but not ignorant—except *ain't*.

- One key point: Almost all speakers of English use *ain't* sometimes. Some speakers use it routinely as part of their grammar. Some use it for emphasis or in stock expressions— "Ain't gonna happen"—to create an unpretentious or folksy tone.

- But the stigma is pretty strong when it is used as part of daily speech. An example: When he was at the University of Michigan, football coach Rich Rodriguez caught heat from a university regent for using *ain't* in a speech in front of fans.

- If think about it, "ain't I?" seems more systematic than "aren't I?" Why do we accept "aren't I?" as standard when we do not accept "I aren't?" This is one of the many examples of the ways in which what is considered standard is not necessarily more logical than other possibilities.

- Defending the logic of *ain't* this way is not an assertion that *ain't* is standard usage—it clearly isn't. The linguistic defense is meant instead to ask us to think critically about the arguments we make about standard and nonstandard usage, especially if we find ourselves making claims that one thing is more logical than another.

Suggested Reading

Skinner, *The Story of Ain't*.

Questions to Consider

1. Consider these two sentences: "I must run errands after work" and "I have to run errands after work." What differences in connotation do you see between the two sentences?

2. What is actually wrong with the auxiliary verb *ain't*? The word is in standard dictionaries, so the answer cannot be "*Ain't* ain't in the dictionary."

Lecture 12 Shall We?
Transcript

Perhaps the best known usage rule involving auxiliary verbs, which are sometimes known as helping verbs, is the distinction between—or the lack of distinction between—"can" and "may." There is a traditional rule that "may" is about permission and "can" is about ability.

So, for example, my students "can" leave class any time they want to, at least in theory. Given the expectations at the university, however, and the expectations on my syllabus, they "may" leave when I end class for the day or they "may" leave early if they've let me know ahead of time. What they are physically able to do—what they "can" do, which is get up and leave—and what societal expectations and my syllabus allow them to do, what they "may" do, are different. And I've sometimes used this example with my students in class, and I'm waiting for the day that then some students just get up and head for the door, even if it's just as a joke. It has yet to happen.

With respect to this "can" versus "may" distinction, there are also stories circulating out there about elementary school students who ask the teacher, "Can I go to the bathroom?" And the teacher makes them sit there until they get their auxiliary verbs straightened out and ask, "May I go the bathroom?" And I have to say, that just seems mean, because of course we know exactly what that kid means when they say, "Can I go to the bathroom?" And I say, "Let them go."

I thought we'd start this lecture with "can" and "may" because they provide a useful example for talking about actual usage of auxiliary verbs, and the history of actual usage versus attitudes about what is right and what is wrong in terms of how we use these auxiliary verbs. Historically, the auxiliary verb "can" has been used to express permission for about 200 years, so these two auxiliary verbs, "can" and "may," have overlapped in the realm of permission for quite a while. We don't tend to use "may" to talk about ability, we only use "can" for that.

Then there are times when all of us want to use "can" to refer to permission, specifically in a contracted negative construction, especially a question. Let me show you what I mean about how we prefer "can't" in those constructions as opposed to "mayn't" when we're talking about permission. Let's imagine that your friends were all invited to the opening party for a new hip bowling alley, because those things happen, and you ask your friends, "Can't I come?" which seems like a very colloquial question compared with "Mayn't I come?" or "May I not come?"

To give you another example, let's imagine—not that this would ever happen—that I'm negotiating with the lifeguard who's trying to kick me out of the pool in order to put in that cleaning machine, and I say, "Can't I swim just a couple more laps?" It sounds much more colloquial, again, than "Mayn't I swim just a couple more laps?"

For some speakers, the "can" versus "may" distinction is really a formality distinction about permission. Let's imagine again that you're at a play and there are those formal instructions over the loudspeaker, and the instructions are: "Audience members may take photos during the performance." "Audience members may take photos,"—you're allowed. But I'm at the play and I wasn't paying attention, and I turn to the usher and I say, "So are photos allowed?" And the usher says, "Yeah, you can take photos." There we're seeing that formality distinction around permission.

But here's an important thing to know, and here I feel like I should have this "This is a usage warning, usage warning!" A reasonable percentage of the *American Heritage Dictionary* Usage Panel rejects "can" used for permission, specifically the panel was asked to think about the question "Can I take another week to submit the application?" "Can I take another week to submit the application?" It's a pretty colloquial question. And yet 37 percent of the panel still rejected that in 2009. That's what I said, a reasonable percentage—37 percent. That's still one in three people on the Usage Panel rejecting that. It is falling, but clearly there's the percentage of people who don't approve, but there's clearly still some resistance. I have to say, it's not something I'm especially attuned to, this difference between "can" and "may," and it is very common in speech, but it is something to watch for in formal writing.

As a side note here, both "can" and "may" can express possibility for the future. I could say, "It may get crazy in here," which is about possibility, or I can say, "It can snow in Michigan in May," which is true and I find it really annoying. The usage issue that I've been talking about here in the first part of this lecture is not about possibility though, as I was talking about with those two sentences right there, but about permission versus ability.

"Can" and "may" are two of nine modal auxiliary verbs, sometimes just called modals, in English. They are: "can," "could," "may," "might," "must," "shall," "should," "will," "would." Or, at least, we say there are nine— traditionally, there are nine. As we'll talk about later in the lecture, we could add a couple more. Now modal auxiliaries express ability, necessity, obligation, or permission. The ones that do that we say express deontic modality, or are deontic modals. And then some of them assess the reality of something, or the likelihood of something, and we call those epistemic modals that express epistemic modality.

You can see the difference between deontic modality and epistemic modality in the two meanings of the auxiliary verb "must." Deontic "must" is about obligation or necessity: "I must finish this essay. I must. This is about obligation." And then there's epistemic "must," which is an evaluation of reality. This would happen in a sentence like—let's imagine I walk out of my house and I see frost on the grass, and I say, "It must have fallen below freezing last night. It must have. That must be the reality."

In addition to the nine modal auxiliaries, there are three other auxiliary verbs that are called primary auxiliaries. Now these are not modals, and they include "be," "have," and "do." All of the auxiliaries, the primaries and the modals, appear before the main verb, and they require a main verb. The times that they appear at the end of a sentence without a main verb, it's because the main verb has been elided—it's been omitted. Let me show you what I mean. If I were to ask, "Will you go?" and you said, "I will," there's an understood main verb there: "I will go." If someone asked, "Can we do that?" "Yes, we can." Again, the main verb has just been elided. "Yes, we can do that."

Let's proceed by first talking about modals, and then we'll talk about the other auxiliaries, and finally the intricate ways in which they interact with each other. This is another example of how much grammar you know without having to think about it. Modals work differently from other verbs in that they do not inflect. What that means is that there is no third person singular present tense "s" on modals—we wouldn't say "she mights"— and there's not past tense "ed"—they "musted." There's also no "ing"—we wouldn't say "coulding"—and there's no past participle—we wouldn't say "he has shalled" or "he has shallen."

Historically, in Germanic, "might," "could," "should," and "would" were the past tense forms of "may," "can," "shall," and "will," but then all of them became modals, so it's no longer the case that they are present and past tense, except sometimes for "can." Let me give you an example. Think about if I said, "Now you can't see the lake from here, but when I was a kid, you could." There we still see a present/past tense distinction.

Modals, unlike the regular verbs, also have no infinitive form. We don't say "to must" or "to shall." The main verb that appears after the auxiliary verb appears in its base form or its infinitive form, so we say "can go" and not "can goes" or "can going" or "can gone."

We can see the effect of inserting a modal on our understanding of whether something is possible or likely or allowed in the following sentences. Let's start with the base sentence: "I play ping-pong." Now we start adding some modals. "I can play ping-pong." I would probably say this if someone asked me, for example, do I know how to play ping-pong? And I say, "Yeah, I can play ping-pong." Or if they want to know whether I will play ping-pong with them tonight, and I say, "Yeah, I can play ping-pong tonight."

I could add a different modal. "I might play ping-pong." This is about possibility in the future. "I might play ping-pong tonight, I might not." A different modal: "I would play ping-pong." This is clearly about possibility.

"Perhaps I will play ping-pong if something else happens. If that happens, I would play ping-pong." "I must play ping-pong." There are two possible interpretations here. One is about obligation, that "I must play ping-pong." Who knows what reason there is that I must play ping-pong, but I must for my own mental health. Or let's imagine—and this would be the epistemic "must"—that you found some photos of me playing ping-pong, and then I say, "Well then, clearly I must play ping-pong. That must be the reality."

The auxiliary modal "will" also has two meanings, the most common of which is future tense. But "will" can also express epistemic modality of something we think is likely to happen or we want to have happen. Think about the two different interpretations of this sentence—I'm back to ping-pong. "I will play ping-pong." Here it is just a simple statement of future action. I will play ping-pong at some moment in the future." And then, and here I'm going to do it with slightly different intonation, "I will play ping-pong!" This is to express my determination to learn this sport.

In standard varieties of English you get only one modal per verb phrase, but in some varieties of Southern American English you can get what are called double modals or multiple modals. If you are someone who can say "might could," you know exactly what these are. These double modals are as I said used most frequently in the South, and they include things like "might could," "might should," "may can," "useta could." These double modals often occur in face-to-face interactions as a kind of politeness. For many speakers they will reduce the face threat, and I talk about face threats as a speech act where we're worried that this might insult someone, we're worried that it's not what they want to hear and we're trying to be polite here. If you're a speaker who can use double modals, you can say something like "I might should send a contribution." Or "I might could help contribute to that."

So it's not that it's not possible to put two modals next to each other "in English." It doesn't typically occur in standard English, but it occurs in other varieties.

Okay, that's modal auxiliaries, and they do a lot of work in the language, but the three primary auxiliaries do even more heavy lifting in the language, given that two of them, "be" and "have," express aspect and voice for verbs, and auxiliary "do" has gotten all wrapped up in how we ask questions and how we express negation.

The three primary auxiliaries do inflect within the verb phrase. For example, and here we'll use "to be": "I am talking," or, with have, "She has listened." "He does exercise." There you see "do" inflecting. In talking about these three auxiliaries, let's start with "be" and "have" and talk about aspect. This will be some review from the previous lecture, and then we'll talk about "do."

As a review, we have the progressive aspect in English, and this takes the auxiliary verb "be" in a sentence like "I am playing ping-pong." Or "I was playing ping-pong." The perfect aspect uses the auxiliary verb "have." "I have played ping-pong. I had played ping-pong." As I mentioned in Lecture 10, in African-American English, habitual aspect is expressed with invariant "be," as in "She be jogging early in the morning."

Auxiliary "be" also plays a role in creating passive voice. Passive voice in English takes "be" plus the past participle. An example would be "The ping-pong paddle was stolen." So now it's hard for me to play ping-pong. Sometimes students confuse passive and progressive, I think probably because both of them take "be" as an auxiliary verb, and in an attempt to avoid the passive, given that they've been told to do that, they sometimes remove the progressives as well. We'll return to the passive in much more detail in the next lecture.

Then there is auxiliary "do," which has dramatically increased its functions in English grammar since the Renaissance. "Do," as an auxiliary, has long been used in declarative sentences: "He does exercise." And at this point it typically expresses emphasis. Let me give you an example: "I do care about the fate of porcupines, I do!" Very emphatic about those porcupines. Since the Renaissance, "do" has also become a key part—and now a standard part—of how we make negative statements and questions. Let me show you what I mean.

Consider how we make negative statements. A basic negative statement adds "not." If we take the sentence "I like dark chocolate," and we make it negative, we get "I do not like dark chocolate." But you'll notice that when I made that negative, I didn't just add "not," I also added a form of "do." "I do not like dark chocolate." That "do," its only function is to hold the not. That's what it does, it is just there so the "not" can come right after it and often contract with it.

In the Renaissance and earlier in English, you could just add the "not." "I like not dark chocolate." Not that they were talking about dark chocolate in the Renaissance necessarily but you get my point. Or I could quote Iago from *Othello*: "I like not that." Or from Shakespeare's *Richard III*: "He sends you not to murder me for this."

We call this phenomenon where "do" starts to be inserted for negatives the rise of periphrastic do. Periphrastic do is also sometimes called dummy do, which I think is a great expression, and it's called dummy do because it is a dummy form. The "do" does not carry any meaning, it is just performing a grammatical function to hold the negative particle "not." This example of the rise of dummy do does I think help show that English, when it's changing, is not always streamlining. I know there are people who like to think that, over time, English is streamlining, but what we've done with negation has made it much more complicated.

Now, we don't need dummy do all of the time. We don't need the auxiliary "do" if there's another auxiliary verb there, be that a modal or a primary auxiliary. Let me give you an example sentence: "Ashley was playing video games earlier." There, because we have the auxiliary verb "was," we can put the "not" in right after that. "Ashley was not playing video games earlier." Here's another sentence with an auxiliary: "My sister can always make me laugh." Again, we can just put the "not" after the auxiliary "can." "My sister can't always make me laugh."

We also don't need dummy do if the main verb of the sentence is "to be," and I have to say that when you study English you learn that "to be" is often an exception if you have a rule. Here's an example sentence: "Video games are a good distraction." And now we want to make that negative, we can actually just put the "not" after the main verb "are." "Video games are not a good distraction."

Auxiliary "do," that same periphrastic or dummy do, is also now a key part of how we make yes/no questions. These are questions that just require yes or no as an answer. In the Renaissance and earlier in English, you could simply flip the main verb and the subject to make a question. It was a very straightforward way to make a question. For example, "Know you the address?" Let me give you an actual example from the history of English. Here's one from *Romeo and Juliet*: "How cam'st thou hither?"

Now, in Modern English, if there is no other auxiliary verb present and the main verb is anything other than "to be," we need to insert "do" and then we move that auxiliary "do" up to the front: "How did you come hither?" "Do you know the address?" So we can't say "Know you the address?" We put in the "do," we bump it up to the front, in front of the subject: "Do you know the address?"

Now, again, as was true with negation, if there's another auxiliary verb there, you don't need to add "do." We could say, "Was Ashley playing video games earlier?" where we take the auxiliary verb "was," switch it with the subject, and we get "Was Ashley playing?" Or "Can your sister always make you laugh?" We started with "your sister can," we flip the subject noun phrase and the auxiliary: "Can your sister always make you laugh?" And if the main verb is "to be," we can also still just reverse the verb and the subject: "Are video games a good distraction?"

I want to take a quick moment here to distinguish auxiliary "be," "have," and "do" from the main verbs "be," "have," and "do," just to make sure that that's clarified. It would be the difference between "I am going," where the "am" is the auxiliary verb and "go" is the main verb, versus "I am nice," where "am" is the main verb. Or "She has read the book," where "has" is the auxiliary verb, "read" is the main verb, compared with "She has lots of books," where "have" is the main verb. An example with "do": "He does lift weights," where "do" is an auxiliary, versus "He does chores around the house," where do is the main verb.

You can just for fun combine the auxiliary and main verb of each together. For example, "I am being nice!" I am, auxiliary "be," being, main verb "be," nice. "She has had pets before." "He did do the chores."

A remarkably complicated thing happens in English when we start to combine auxiliary verbs together. We talked about this briefly in the previous lecture, without the modals, and it's worth reviewing again both because of the intricacy of the grammar and because of the impressive fact that if you learned English as your native language, you learned to do this with no explicit instruction.

Each auxiliary verb specifies the form of the verb that comes after it, and it turns out whether that's the main verb or another auxiliary verb. A modal is combined with an infinitive. "Be," as an auxiliary, is combined with the present participle in "ing" form. "Have" is combined with a past participle in "en" or "ed" form. "Do" is combined with an infinitive form.

When we start to put multiple auxiliaries together, each one will specify the form of the next one in the string, be that an auxiliary that comes next or the main verb. An example will help here. Let's start with "Our dear friend might date a celebrity. Our dear friend might date a celebrity." "Might" requires an infinitive, so we get "might date," "date" in its infinitive form. Now we add another auxiliary. "Our dear friend might be dating a celebrity." Might be dating. So "might," as we talked about, requires an infinitive, so we get "might" and then "be" in the infinitive form. "Be" requires an "ing" form, so "date" now becomes "dating." Might be dating.

Let's keep going. "Our dear friend might have been dating a celebrity." "Might" again requires the infinitive, so we get "have." "Have" needs a past participle form, so we get "been." "Be" wants that "ing," so we get "dating." Might have been dating.

I mentioned already a couple of changes that have happened in auxiliary verbs in the history of English. We have, for example, that "could" and "should" used to be past tenses of "can" and "shall." Periphrastic do emerged in the history of English. Then there are some changes happening around us right now with auxiliary verbs declining and getting added.

There are two modals that are in serious decline. The first, which probably won't surprise you, is "shall." If you search Google Books using the Ngram Viewer, it shows about an 80 percent drop in the use of "shall" over the past 200 years. The *Corpus of Historical American English*, which allows you to search written material over the last 200 years, shows an even more dramatic decline in "shall." "Shall" is preserved in phrases like "Shall we?" but I think that for many of us, if you answer that with "We shall," it sounds a little bit like a joke, and you can hear what I did with my voice right there, "We shall," because it isn't very colloquial for me to say "We shall."

While we're talking about "shall," let's address a usage issue that maybe you've heard of, but I would guess that at least most of you probably don't follow. There is a rule out there about "shall" versus "will." For those of you who know it, the idea is that one expresses future and one expresses obligation, and it varies by person. In the first person, "I" or "we," "shall" expresses future and "will" expresses obligation. In second and third person, "will" expresses future and "shall" expresses obligation.

Has this ever been true? Well, as far as we can tell, it's never been that neat. It seems to be more true in British English than in American English, but there's some chance that, for the prescriptivists who are now trying to enforce this rule, they're trying to create a logical system where there may never have been a system that was quite this logical. You can however still find this rule in a usage guide like Strunk and White's *Elements of Style*. I think for most Americans, "shall" is more formal, sometimes used to express in a formal setting what you "shall" do, perhaps as obligation. And in legal settings, "shall" still can be used to express a formal, legal obligation. Lawyers often care about the difference between "will" and "shall."

The other modal in decline may surprise you, at least at first, and this is the modal "must." "Must" has been in decline for much of the 20th century. Actually, it's not "must" in general; it's only deontic "must," the one that expresses obligation or necessity. Once you reflect on it, I think you might agree that "must" now can feel awfully strong. If I were to say, "I must run errands tonight after work. I must run errands." I think many of us would more typically say instead, "I hafta run errands tonight after work. I hafta run errands."

This example of "I hafta run errands" points to the rise of a new set of auxiliary verbs that are emerging, sometimes called semi-modals or emerging modals. That's what we're calling them until we decide they've made it into the modal category. These include "hafta" and "gonna." If we didn't have such a standardized spelling system, they would be spelled H-A-F-T-A, "hafta," and G-O-N-N-A, "gonna," as that is how we say them. And in fact, "gonna" and "going to" now mean different things, and stick with me here because I'm sure I'm right. Let's say I say, "I'm gonna run errands. I'm gonna run errands." There it's functioning as a modal about what I need to do. Compare this with "I am going to run errands. I am going to run errands." I think for most of us that would mean "I'm on my way out the door, maybe I'm getting in the car, maybe I'm on foot, I'm going to run errands, I'll see ya later, I'm outta here."

We still recognize that these modals like "hafta" and "gonna" are informal and we don't tend to write them in formal prose, but their rise in American English is dramatic. And I would keep an eye on the other modal "sposta." "I'm sposta go." Which, again, if we didn't have such standardized spelling, we would spell S-P-O-S-T-A.

These significant changes I've been talking about here in the modal system are happening without a lot of fanfare or stigmatization, which is interesting to me. They may be considered more informal, "hafta" and "gonna," but I think most people don't consider them wrong.

Before we finish this lecture on auxiliary verbs, we need to talk about "ain't." This must be the most notorious auxiliary verb out there. Dictionaries tend to treat it as nonstandard; some people claim it isn't a word. As you may recall, *Webster's Third New International Dictionary*, published in the early 1960s, got into trouble, or at least was controversial, for the way it handled "ain't," saying that many speakers use it, and not labeling it as nonstandard. Now what is wrong with "ain't?" I have to say that mostly what's wrong with it is that style guides tell us there's something wrong with it.

In the 18th century, there was a whole set of contractions that were condemned, including "shouldn't," "can't," "won't," and "ain't." All of these other contractions have redeemed themselves. They may be seen as informal, but they're not seen as ignorant, except for "ain't."

Now one key point here is that almost all speakers of English use "ain't" at least some of the time. Some speakers use it routinely as part of their grammar. They use it for "am not," "is not," "are not," "has not," "have not," and in some cases "do not" and "does not." Some speakers use it for emphasis or perhaps in stock expressions like "ain't gonna happen." Sometimes people will use it to create an unpretentious tone. But the stigma on "ain't" is still pretty strong when it's used as a part of one's daily speech.

Let me give you an example of how the stigma around "ain't" can play out. This is an example from the news. It was in an article in *USA Today* by Christine Brennan in 2011, and it was about the former University of Michigan football coach Rich Rodriguez, sometimes known as Rich Rod. Rich Rod was leaving the University of Michigan. He'd come to Michigan from West Virginia. The article starts by talking about how Rich Rod never really fit in at Michigan, and then it goes on to talk about how he gave this speech, and a university regent got upset after the speech about his language. A staffer came to tell Rich Rod that somebody was upset about his language, and here I quote from the article: "As Rodriguez frantically racked his brain to recall what he might have said, the staffer sheepishly offered up the offending word: Rodriguez had said 'ain't.'"

Some people say the problem with "ain't" is that it's not transparent. "Ain't" comes from "amn't"—"am not." And over time, as it becomes "ain't," it—yes—it's less transparent. But won't, which comes from "will not," is equally not transparent and it is not condemned as being wrong or ignorant. Some people say, "I don't like the sound of ain't." And my response is, "How do you feel about the words paint and faint?" And often they say, "Oh, well those are fine." And I say, "Then why isn't ain't fine?"

And if you think about it, "ain't I?" seems more systematic than "aren't I?" Why do we accept "aren't I?" as standard when we do not accept "I aren't." I point this out as one of the many examples of the ways in which what is considered standard is not necessarily more logical than the other possibilities.

Defending the logic of "ain't" this way is not an assertion that "ain't" is standard usage—it clearly isn't. My linguistic defense of "ain't" is meant instead to ask us to think critically about the arguments we make about what is standard and nonstandard usage, especially if we find ourselves making claims that one thing is more logical than another.

This lecture on auxiliaries has set us up to spend the next lecture looking specifically at passive sentences, which use auxiliary "be" and a past participle, and passives raise a host of questions about what is okay and what is not okay in formal writing.

Passive Voice Was Corrected

Lecture 13

In 2009, *The Chronicle of Higher Education* published an essay called "50 Years of Stupid Grammar Advice," written by Geoff Pullum, a linguist at the University of Edinburgh. Pullum is not known for pulling his punches, especially when it comes to Strunk and White's *The Elements of Style*. The essay was published a day after the 50th anniversary of that book. As the title makes clear, it was far from celebratory. Central to Pullum's case is the treatment of the passive voice in Strunk and White. This entire lecture focuses on the passive voice, starting with Strunk and White.

Active Voice

- In *The Elements of Style*, Strunk and White give us the following advice:

  > The active voice is usually more direct and vigorous than the passive. … This rule does not, of course, mean that the writer should entirely discard the passive voice, which is frequently convenient and sometimes necessary. … The habitual use of the active voice, however, makes for forcible writing.

- The leeway in this advice is important: The passive is sometimes convenient or necessary. As we'll talk about, the passive is also highly conventionalized in scientific writing and other kinds of academic prose.

- Where Strunk and White run into trouble is that their examples potentially could confuse people about what is passive and what is not. They provide four example sentences, and only one of them is actually passive. They introduce the sentences by saying they show "how a transitive verb in the active voice can improve a sentence." Therefore, they have two topics in this advice: transitive verbs and active voice. But given that the whole section is about active voice, the transitive verb part can get lost.

- Here are the sentences:

    1. There were a great number of dead leaves lying on the ground.

    2. At dawn the crowing of a rooster could be heard.

    3. The reason that he left college was that his health became impaired.

    4. It was not long before she was very sorry that she had said what she had.

- Only number 2 is passive: "At dawn the crowing of the rooster could be heard." We can see one of the ways the passive voice can create stylistic stumbles: We don't know who is doing the hearing. The passive here has inserted an unknown agent who is hearing the rooster, as opposed to just letting the rooster crow at dawn.

Defining Passivity

- The active voice has a subject (the agent) acting upon an object. In the passive voice, the object gets fronted; the verb takes an auxiliary *be* and a past participle; and the subject can gain the word *by* (and becomes optional).

    □ Active voice: "Big Bird tickled Cookie Monster."

    □ Passive voice: "Cookie Monster was tickled by Big Bird."

- The point is that the recipient of the action becomes the subject, and the agent moves to end and becomes optional. The optionality of agent is very helpful when we don't want to take responsibility: "Mistakes were made."

■ It's also helpful when we don't know who was responsible: "My car was side-swiped in the parking lot."

To Be

■ What is happening in the other Strunk and White sentences if it is not the passive? What we're seeing in all of these is the unnecessary insertion of *to be*, which weakens the clout of the verb and often adds extra words to the sentence. Let's review each sentence in turn.

1. There were a great number of dead leaves lying on the ground.

■ This is just a *to be* sentence, and the *be* became necessary when we added the introductory *there*. One cleaner version of the same sentence would be, "Dead leaves covered the ground."

■ Next up:

3. The reason that he left college was that his health became impaired.

■ This raises much of the same issue as number 1. "The reason that X is Y" introduces a *to be* verb. It is worth looking at whether, in context, we can just use a *because* construction instead: "He left college because his health became impaired." This causes a shift in emphasis, from why he left college to the fact that he left.

■ Finally:

4. It was not long before she was very sorry that she had said what she had.

■ "It was not long" could be become "soon" or "quickly," but it is going to depend on what the writer wants to emphasize. "It was not long before she did X" is not exactly the same rhetorically as "She quickly did X."

- "She was very sorry" could become "She regretted." This is really a word choice issue that involves verbs.

- "... she had said what she had" could probably become "she said what she did" or "she regretted her words." We need a little more context.

- Putting all four of these sentences under pro-active-voice advice becomes potentially confusing, particularly in terms of equating all uses of *to be* as a main verb with the passive voice. That is Geoff Pullum's concern.

Better Advice

- Better advice about the passive voice is to consider whether a passive construction is the most rhetorically effective choice. There are several reasons why it might be the best choice rhetorically.

- The passive voice sometimes helps us maintain continuity between sentences. Consider these examples against each other:

  □ "I have a new favorite mug. It was given to me by graduate students in the English and Education program."

  □ "I have a new favorite mug. Graduate students gave it to me."

- The passive voice is gone in the second example, but there is a rough jump between the sentences.

- Sometimes we don't know the agent, as mentioned earlier, and the passive is really helpful here. Think about some of the terrible news we hear, where reporters need to be careful not to assume agents before we know: "Two people were shot last night."

- Then there is scientific writing. The passive voice has become more conventionalized in this register than in many others. Think about the description of an experiment. Researchers are doing all the actions: taking the sample, putting it in a petri dish, adding whatever they're adding, and so on.

  - If we told it like a story, there would be people involved: "We took the sample and put it in the petri dish." But that no longer sounds all that scientific.

  - Let's try instead: "The sample was placed in the petri dish and water was added." Now the human agents are invisible or at least very marginalized. The specimens take center stage and its sounds more objective.

- There are a few other passive phrases common in academic writing beyond scientific writing that don't typically get edited out as ineffective passives. Examples include "It could be argued" and "Other relevant factors must be considered."

  - "It could be argued" is a way we introduce counterarguments as part of defending our own claims. Others may have argued these or they may be hypothetical, but it doesn't actually matter who has argued them.

  - "[X] must be considered" can be a solution to the abstract *we* in academic writing. Take the sentence, "We must consider other relevant factors." Who is we? The author(s)? The author and the readers? All researchers in the field?

- Pick your poison with the passive or the abstract *we*: Both of them present stylistic issues.

She Got Cheated

- Let's talk about a passive variant that doesn't use *be* but instead uses *get*: "My car got side-swiped in the parking lot." This setup feels much more colloquial. It's not something we are going to do in formal writing.

- In addition to being more colloquial, *get* passives may also carry two other differences in connotation.

    1. They can reflect the responsibility of the grammatical subject: "Mario got fired" blames Mario more than "Mario was fired."

    2. They can reflect the attitude of the speaker toward the event, expressing adversity or sympathy: "My car got hit" expresses adversity. "She got cheated" expresses sympathy.

- *Get* passives are older than you might guess. They first popped up in the mid- to late 17th century, although they were only sporadic until the late 18th century.

Passive Progressives

- The 19th century witnessed the rise of the passive progressive in English. A passive progressive is a passive that is in progress, for example, "The house is being built." This is now totally unremarkable, but people hated it when it came into the language. Here is George P. Marsh in *Lectures on the English Language* (1863):

    > ... the clumsy and unidiomatic continuing present of the passive voice, which, originating not in the sound common sense of the people, but in the brain of some grammatical pretender, has widely spread, and threatens to establish itself as another solecism in addition to the many which our syntax already presents. The phrase 'the house *is being built*,' for 'the house *is building*,' is an awkward neologism, ... an attempt at the artificial improvement of the language in a point which needed no amendment.

- David Booth's 1830 work, *An Analytical Dictionary of the English Language*, argued, "For some time past, 'the bridge is *being built*,' 'the tunnel is *being excavated*,' and other expressions of a like kind, have pained the eye and stunned the ear." (This was not in the 1805 edition.)

- Before this construction arose, did people really say things like, "The house is building?" The answer is yes.

  □ Jane Austen wrote in the novel *Northanger Abbey*: "The clock struck ten while the trunks were carrying down."

  □ Samuel Richardson wrote in the 1753 novel *Sir Charles Grandison*: "Tea was preparing. Sir Charles took his own seat next Lord L—, whom he set in to talk of Scotland."

"The tea was preparing" now sounds funny to us, while "the tea is being prepared" sounded funny to people in the 19th century.

Suggested Reading

Collins, "*Get*-passives in English."

Fleisher, "The Origin of Passive *Get*."

Pullum, "50 Years of Stupid Grammar Advice."

Questions to Consider

1. When do you find passive constructions helpful in your writing? When do you find them ineffective in your own writing or in other people's writing?

2. Consider these two sentences: "My cousin was fired" and "My cousin got fired." Is there a subtle difference in meaning for you? If so, what is the difference?

Passive Voice Was Corrected

In 2009, *The Chronicle of Higher Education* published an essay called "50 Years of Stupid Grammar Advice." The article was written by Geoff Pullum, who's a linguist at the University of Edinburgh; he's also an active blogger for Language Log—and if you haven't already checked it out I encourage you to do so—as well as for the equally terrific blog Lingua Franca for *The Chronical of Higher Education*. And I should disclose here that I also blog for Lingua Franca.

Geoff is not known for pulling his punches, especially when it comes to Strunk and White's *Elements of Style*. The essay that Jeff wrote was published a day after the 50th anniversary of that book. It was first published on April 16, 1959, and as the title of his essay makes clear, his article was far from celebratory. Geoff concedes that some of the style advice in Stunk and White is fine, if not especially revolutionary. Advice like be clear; yes, always a good idea, and omit needless words. Of course, the question is always figuring out which ones are needless.

Jeff's concern is what he considers to be bad grammar advice, and grammar and style are not always clearly distinguished in Strunk and White. Central to Jeff's case is the treatment of the passive voice in Strunk and White. This entire lecture will focus on the passive voice, and Strunk and White seems like a good place to start. So let's dive in.

The relevant section in Elements of Style is called use active voice, and it's going to become important that it is about using the active voice, not about not using the passive voice. So it's called use the active voice, and then Strunk and White give us the following advice, and here I'll quote.

The active voice is usually more direct and vigorous than the passive. This rule does not, of course, mean that the writer should entirely discard the passive voice, which is frequently convenient and sometimes necessary. The habitual use of the active voice, however, makes for forcible writing.

So that's Strunk and White on the passive. And I have to say that the leeway in this advice is really important: the passive is sometimes convenient or necessary; and as we'll talk about, the passive is also highly conventionalized in scientific writing and some other kinds of academic prose.

Where Strunk and White run into trouble is that their examples potentially could confuse people about what is passive and what is not. Strunk and White provide four example sentences, and only one of them is actually passive, as I'll show you. Now Strunk and White introduce the sentences by saying they show, and here I'll quote "how a transitive verb in the active voice can improve a sentence." So really Strunk and White have two things going on here in this advice—transitive verbs and active voice, but given that the whole section is called use active voice and is about active voice, the transitive verb part can get lost.

Let me give you the four sentences that are in Strunk and White in this section about using the active voice. First—There were a great number of dead leaves lying on the ground. Second—At dawn the crowing of a rooster could be heard. Third—The reason that he left college was that his health became impaired. Fourth—It was not long before she was very sorry that she had said what she had.

As I'm sure many of you caught, only the second sentence is passive, "At dawn, the crowing of the rooster could be heard." And we can see one of the ways in that sentence that the passive can create what I call stylistic stumbles; we don't know who in that sentence is doing the hearing. The passive in this sentence has inserted some odd unknown agent who is hearing the rooster, as opposed to just saying, "The rooster crowed at dawn," and then we just assume that whoever heard it heard it.

So let's pause and just make sure we're all on the same page about what the passive is. Let's start with an active sentence. Here you get subject, verb, object where the subject is the agent, the person or thing doing the verb, and then the object is the thing or person who or which is acted upon. Passive, that object—and in English in can actually be a direct object or an indirect object—gets fronted in the sentence. Then the verb is transformed to take an auxiliary 'be' and then the main verb is put into the past participle. The subject is moved to the end, and you put a 'by' in front of it to create a prepositional phrase. That prepositional phrase 'by' plus subject also becomes optional.

An example. The active—Big Bird tickled Cookie Monster. We turn in into the passive—Cookie Monster was tickled by Big Bird. And I have to just explain here why these sentences came to mind. When I was an undergraduate, I worked in a language lab where we were studying how early kids learned the passive voice. And these were the sentences we were using and kids were looking at monitors with a Cookie Monster and a Big Bird and we were trying to see when they started understanding passive voice.

So to keep going with my passive voice examples. You can take a passive construction and add aspect, for example, let's add the progressive to our sentence about Big Bird and Cookie Monster. Here's the active—Big Bird is tickling Cookie Monster, and then to make it passive—Cookie Monster is being tickled by Big Bird. The point is that the recipient of the action becomes the subject and the agent moves to end and becomes optional.

The optionality of the agent is very helpful when we don't want to take responsibility for an action. Think about the famous statement "Mistakes were made," by someone who remains unnamed. We could take a more quotatiate example at home where you say, "The red shirt was put in with the whites in that load of laundry." The red shirt was put in with the whites; no one is taking responsibility for that red shirt getting in there. The fact that we can leave out the agent in a passive is also helpful when we don't know who's responsible.

Think about a sentence like, "My car was side-swiped in the parking lot," I don't know who sideswiped it. If I wanted to make it active, I would have to say something like, "Someone sideswiped my car in the parking lot," or more likely I would probably say, "Some turkey sideswiped my car in the parking lot." But it is an unidentified someone or turkey.

You can also think about a sentence like, "He was murdered." We don't know who murdered him. If you wanted to make that active, you would have to say something like, "Someone murdered him," with that indefinite pronoun as your subject.

Going back then to Strunk and White. what is happening in these other Strunk and White sentences if it's not the passive? What we're seeing in all of these sentences is the insertion of 'to be' as a main verb where you don't need it, where it probably weakens the clout of the verb and often adds extra words to the sentence.

Let's review each sentence in turn.

Number one, "There were a great number of dead leaves lying on the ground." This is just a pretty straight forward 'to be' sentence, and the 'be' became necessary when we added the introductory 'there.' The 'there' we often call existential there, "There were a great number of leaves lying on the ground." So now we have two verbs in this sentence. We have the 'were' in 'there were,' and then we have the verbs 'lying on the ground'. These kinds of 'there' constructions are quite frequent in speech, but in writing, they're worth watching as 'there were,' which focuses our attention on what's about to come, also arguably adds extra words; maybe call them needless words. You can see why Strunk and White don't like this sentence.

Is there a way that we can we make 'lie' or some other descriptive verb the main verb in the sentence? For example, "Dead leaves covered the ground." You'll notice that in that rewrite I also got rid of 'a great number' because the verb 'covers' to me captures that there are a great number of leaves.

Let's now look at sentence number three from Strunk and White "The reason that he left college was that his health became impaired." This sentence raises much of the same issue as the first sentence. The phrasing that "The reason that X is Y" introduces 'to be' as the main verb, and it is worth looking at whether, in context, we can just use a because-construction instead. Can we say, "He left college because his health became impaired?" Now you'll notice that in those two sentences there is a shift in emphasis, and that's why I said you'd want to make sure you were rewriting this in context. It is really about whether we're emphasizing that he left college or why he left college. Let's imagine that I am talking to someone who thinks that he—whoever he is—just quit college, and I want to emphasize that there was a reason, and so I say, "No, the reason that he left college is..." You can see how in context that wording works.

Now the fourth sentence in Strunk and White, "It was not long before she was very sorry that she had said what she had." OK, there is a lot going on in this sentence—more than we probably need, I think. "It was not long," well that could become 'soon' or 'quickly,' but again I'm going to say that that will depend on what the writer wants to emphasize. If we say, "It was not long before she did X" that's not exactly the same rhetorically or semantically as "She quickly did X." Then we have the phrasing "she was very sorry" which could become "she regretted" really that's a word choice issue that depends what verb you choose. Then we have the last part, "she had said what she had," which could probably become "she said what she did" or "she regretted her words." We need a little more context to rewrite that sentence.

You can now see why putting all four of these sentences under the advice "Use active voice" becomes potentially confusing, particularly in terms of equating all uses of 'to be' as a main verb with the passive voice. And that is Geoff Pullum's concern. I don't think the concern is unfounded given what I have seen in classrooms at all levels, where sentences like number one, and three, and four where you have 'to be' as a main verb are getting identified as passives. As I've talked about, all of these sentences could probably benefit from some revision, but not because they are all in the passive voice.

It is good advice to look at each time we use the verb 'to be' as a main verb in our writing that we go back look at those, and see if there is some more dynamic or evocative verb that we could use instead. That may simultaneously change the syntax of the sentence, sometimes in good ways. So that advice about be careful about those 'to be' verbs is worth heeding. It's not that there is anything grammatically wrong with 'be' as a main verb, but stylistically you may be able to do better, at least some of the time; you may be able to avoid repetition in part it's because we use 'be' as a main verb in speech and so it can get into our writing as a very frequent main verb. And getting it out of there so that you don't have too many sentences with 'to be' as a main verb is good, it can also be good in terms of concision. As I showed you in rewriting some of those sentences when you took out the 'to be' verb the sentence sometimes tightens up.

So what is better advice about the passive? Here's what I would say. In every instance, consider whether a passive construction is the most rhetorically effective choice. I'm not just being wishy-washy here; there are several reasons why it might be the best choice rhetorically, why you might want to use the passive, and I'm going to outline those reasons here. Before I do, let's look at some of the passives you probably should rewrite because they are not rhetorically effective. Here's the kind of sentence that I have to say I do see in student writing fairly often. I think sometimes the passive gets in there because students are trying to be more formal and somehow the passive feels more formal.

Here are two sentences, the second one is passive. "The exam began. The shuffling of paper was heard in the room." Again, like the rooster sentence we this odd, unnamed hearer who has suddenly been introduced into the picture, who's hearing the shuffling. We could change the sentence to something like "The shuffling of paper filled the room."

Here's another example of a sentence in the passive that is not great. "A more streamlined process was envisioned by the committee." That sentence is probably better if we left the committee be the subject, "The committee envisioned a more streamlined process." But I am going to say that it depends on exactly where that sentence is in a paragraph and what it's trying to do. Let me explain.

There are times where to maintain continuity from sentence to sentence; the passive helps us. To show you what I mean here, I'm going to talk about the opening two sentences of a blog post that I wrote a few months ago. The first sentence of the blog post was "I have a new favorite mug," which is true. Then my second sentence was, "It was given to me by graduate students in the English and Education program." You'll notice that that second sentence is passive. I could have said, "I have a new favorite mug. Graduate students in the English and Education program gave it to me." But you'll notice that when I take that second sentence and put it into the active, there is suddenly a jump. I was talking about the mug, and now I'm talking about the graduate students who gave it to me. In the passive I'm talking about the mug, "I have a new favorite mug. It was given to me," and we get that continuity across sentences. So that's one reason the passive voice may be more rhetorically effective.

Sometimes, as we've talked about, we don't know the agent, and the passive is very helpful here. Think about some of the terrible news we hear, where reporters need to be careful not to assume agents before we know who the agents are. An example like "Two people were shot last night," or "The store was set on fire sometime early this morning." You need passive constructions there.

Then there is scientific writing. Scientific writing tends to follow a set of unique conventions in terms of how articles are structured overall. For example, you have a methods sections, a results section, and then a discussions section, and the passive has become more and more conventionalized in this register of scientific writing than in many others.

Let's think about the description of an experiment. When you think about an experiment, in fact, researchers are doing most of the actions. They're taking the sample, they're putting it in a petri dish, they're adding whatever they're adding, and so on. If we told the experiment like a story, there would be a lot of people involved. We'd be saying things like, "We took the sample, and we put it in the petri dish, and then we added this to it." But, certainly, at this point that no longer sounds all that scientific to us, that sounds more like a story.

Instead, let's try making it sound more scientific. "The sample was placed in the petri dish, and then X was added to the sample." Clearly, there were human agents putting things in that petri dish and adding things to it, but they disappeared from the grammar. The human agents are invisible or at least very marginalized. The specimens themselves take center stage in that description, which is important. In science, we often do want people to focus on what the experiment was about, not the people who were doing it. And so the passive can help there. The passive 'an' also make this scientific experiment sound more objective, more scientific; that can be a really good thing. But it is important for us to remember that it can also hide or at least obscure from view, make marginal those human decisions in an experiment, and perhaps the bias that can happen with an experiment, and the uncertainty that is part of humans doing experiments.

Here is a great example of the passive voice in scientific writing from the *Journal of Experimental Biology*. It's from an article called "Biomechanical control of vocal plasticity in the echolocating bat." Yes, we're going to talk about bats. "Six individuals of adult *Phyllostomus discolor*—3 males and 3 females—were tested in an echo- and sound-attenuated acoustic chamber." Okay, so they were tested, clearly by people, but the people are not part of the grammar. Let me continue with the passage. "During the experiment, two bats were tested simultaneously, with bats held individually in pyramidal mesh cages." So now the bats are being held again by humans, but they're just being held. Onward. "Bats were assigned to the same pairs throughout the experiment...Sound recording and noise playback were synchronized through an audio interface...Bat vocalizations were continuously sampled at 192 kHz." We can see they're being sampled; somebody is sampling them, but we're not told who, and the excerpt ends with, and they're talking about specific "these data were saved to hard disc." Obviously, there's a person doing that saving, but we just know that the data were saved.

This passage now strikes us as just typical scientific writing, "those vocalizations were continuously sampled," "the data were saved," the bats were tested." But as I noted, scientific writing doesn't have to happen this way. There are some rhetorical reasons it's happening, it allows us to focus on the bats and what's happening to the bats. It also doesn't allow us necessarily or doesn't help us imagine the humans who are holding the bats.

Scientific writing has not always worked that way. To show you what I mean I'm going to give you a passage from the 18th century. This is a passage from the Physiologist John Hunter from a work in 1775. I'm pulling this excerpt from work by Dwight Atkinson, who's been looking at the history of scientific writing. You'll see that Hunter is using some passive, very object-centered language at the beginning of his passage, but then the language shifts. Here's the passage. "The first experiment was made on two carp." Right, so you see the passive, "The experiment was made on two carp." And now I will continue with Hunter,

> They were put into a glass vessel with common river water, and the vessel put into freezing mixture; the water did not freeze fast enough; and therefore, to make it freeze sooner, we put in as much cooled snow as to make the whole thick. The snow round the carp melted; we put in more fresh snow, which melted also; and this was repeated several times, till we grew tired.

I love this passage because it's so wonderfully human. You can imagine the people taking the snow and packing it around the carp until they get tired. We probably would not let a student now write up a lab report this way, but it is important to remember that the conventions of scientific writing are something that we've all come to agree on over time. You see Hunter, who had this mixture of the more passive object-centered language along with this much more narrative language where we can see him and his fellow experimenters experimenting with the carp.

There are a few other passive phrases that are now commonplaces in academic writing beyond scientific writing that don't typically get edited out as ineffective passives. These would be passives like "It could be argued" or "Other relevant factors must be considered."

"It could be argued" is a way we introduce counterarguments into our writing as part of defending our own claims. These arguments may have been argued by others, or they may be hypothetical, but it doesn't actually matter who argued them. We need to get them into our writing as part of constructing our own argument and addressing possible counterarguments.

With "X must be considered" it can be a solution to what I call the abstract 'we' problem in academic writing. If you were going to make this active, you'd probably need to say something like "We must consider other relevant factors." And my question is, "Who is we?" The authors? The author and the readers? All researchers in the field? All researchers in the field and the readers?

So here I would say pick your poison with you can use the passive and say, "These things must be considered," or you can use the abstract 'we,' "We must consider them." Both of those options present some stylistic issues.

While we're talking about the passive, let's talk about a variant that doesn't use 'be' but instead uses 'get.' For example, "My car got sideswiped in the parking lot" or "she got arrested" These 'get' passives feel I think for most of us much more colloquial—not something we are going to write in formal settings. We wouldn't tend to say "The test tube got warmed to 100 degrees," we would say "It was warmed."

In addition to being more colloquial, "get" passives may also mean slightly differently from 'be' passives. They may carry a difference in connotation. It could be about the responsibility of the grammatical subject. For example, "Mario got fired." I think for many of us that means something slightly different from "Mario was fired," at least in terms of connotations. "Mario got fired," I think Mario has to take a little more responsibility for getting fired. It's like, "Mario got himself fired."

The 'get' passive may also reflect the attitude of the speaker toward the event, perhaps expressing adversity or benefit. For example, "My car got hit." And I think that that is my own sense of adversity that my car got hit. Or, let's say I'm trying to express sympathy for someone. "She got cheated," that expresses my sympathy for her.

'Get' passives, which can still feel quite colloquial are older than you might guess. They're first attested in mid- to late-17th century, although they're only sporadic in that period. And it's really not until late 18th century that they take off. So the get passive is in place in the grammar before another change starts to take place, and we'll end the lecture with this change.

The 19th century witnessed the rise of the passive progressive in English. What is that? It is the passive that is in progress, so it is a sentence like "The house is being built." Now this sentence is completely mundane now, but people hated it when it came into the language in the 19th century.

Here is George P. Marsh in *Lectures on the English Language* published in 1863, and he's talking about this new passive progressive, which he describes this way:

> The clumsy and unidiomatic continuing present of the passive voice, which, originating not in the sound common sense of the people, but in the brain of some grammatical pretender, has widely spread and threatens to establish itself as another solecism in addition to the many which our syntax already presents. The phrase The house is being built," for "the house is building," is an awkward neologism, an attempt at the artificial improvement of the language in a point which needed no amendment.

I think this criticism can seem so funny to us now because a sentence like "The house is being built" doesn't even seem worthy of notice let alone criticism. But criticism it got. Here is David Booth in *An Analytical Dictionary of the English Language*, which was published in 1830, so a few decades earlier. And he writes, "For some time past, 'the bridge is being built,' 'the tunnel is being excavated,' and other expressions of a like kind, have pained the eye and stunned the ear." What interesting here is that in an earlier edition of that book published in 1805 he doesn't mention the passive progressive. Clearly, it wasn't in such wide circulation that it was on his radar.

Richard Grant White also addressed the passive progressive in 1869. He described it as the worst of, and here I quote him, "those intruders in language ... which, about 70 or 80 years ago, began to affront the eye, torment the ear, and assault the common sense of the speaker of plain and idiomatic English." But Richard Grant White had to admit in the end that the passive progressive, and here again I'll quote, "seems to many persons to be of established respectability."

Now it is of course completely respectable now to use the passive progressive, in fact, we think it sounds a little odd not to use it and to say, "The house is building" instead of "The house is being built."

Did people really say "the house is building" as a passive? Yes, they did. Let me give you an example from Jane Austen's *Northanger Abbey*, which you may or may not have noticed if you've read the novel. "The clock struck ten while the trunks were carrying down." This is not how we now say that. We would say, "While the trunks were being carried down." Here's a second example, this one's from Samuel Richardson's novel, *Sir Charles Grandison*, published in 1753, and this example is cited in a very nice discussion of the passive progressive on the blog Grammarphobia. Here are the two sentences. "Tea was preparing. Sir Charles took his own seat next Lord L. whom he set into talk of Scotland." "Tea was preparing."

This way of doing the passive progressive, the bags were carrying down, tea was preparing now sounds funny to us, while the tea is being prepared sounded funny to people in the 19th century.

All of this is a good reminder of how grammar changes over time as well as how what is considered standard and abominable, an assault to the eye and ear, can also change over time. Speaking of which, does it affront your ear when you hear Apple's slogan "Think Different"? If so, you are not alone, and the next lecture is for you.

Only Adverbs

Lecture 14

Two well-known company slogans have raised some grammatical hackles based on their use, or non-use, of adverbs. Subway has long used the slogan "Eat Fresh," and in 1997 Apple rolled out "Think different." Do we have grammatical problems here? This question is where we'll start our lecture on adverbs. Then we'll move on to consider other adverb topics, including intensifiers, tricky adverbs like *hopefully*, and flat adverbs.

Eat Fresh

- "Eat Fresh" sounds like "eat right," but "right" can clearly be an adverb as well as an adjective. This leaves us with the question of whether *fresh* can be an adverb. It's usually an adjective: "The fish are fresh."

- But *fresh* can be an adverb: "The bread is baked fresh every day." However, "Eat Fresh" works differently from "Baked Fresh" would. In the latter, *fresh* means recently.

- Is "Eat Fresh" a shortening of "eat fresh food?" Is this a nonstandard meaning of the adverb? In the end, we know what it means, and it has done its work: We notice the language.

Think Different

- Apple's "Think different" is another case. With standard grammar, the phrase would be "think differently"—but this could have a different meaning, too. It boils down to thinking in different ways versus think about different things.

- *Different* can be an adverb: "Carol didn't know different until Eleanor told her." So, in Apple's slogan, is *different* an adjective or adverb? Are we to think about different kinds of computers or think differently about computers? This ad didn't win an Emmy for nothing—the ambiguity works.

- The ambiguity is possible because English has words that can be both adjectives and adverbs without changing form. We'll come back to those "flat" adverbs.

Defining Adverbs

- Adverbs are difficult to pin down and define. Merriam-Webster's stab at it is this: "a word that describes a verb, an adjective, another adverb, or a sentence and that is often used to show time, manner, place, or degree."

- Unlike adjectives, which modify nouns, adverbs modify a whole range of things.

  - Modifying verbs: go *quickly*, protest *peacefully*.

  - Modifying adjectives: *incredibly* nice, *very* happy.

  - Modifying adverbs: *really* stupidly, *ridiculously* slowly.

  - Modifying a clause/sentence: *Frankly*, this situation with adverbs is a mess.

Only Some Confusion

- The adverb *only* sometimes causes confusion. For example, some would nitpick "Anne only gave me two dollars" as having a different meaning from "Anne gave me only two dollars." Bryan Garner called *only* "perhaps the most frequently misplaced word in English." But if it happens so frequently, is it really misplaced?

- Garner is echoing a long-standing concern. Concern about *only* goes way back, as early as Bishop Lowth in 1763, who went after

"I only spoke three words" instead of "I spoke only three words."

☐ Why the objection? If the focus is that it was just three words, then *only* should come before *three words*.

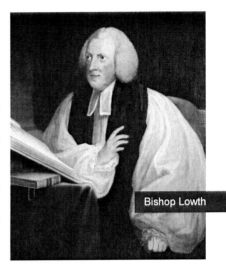

Bishop Lowth

☐ If the focus is what you spoke (instead of wrote), then *only* should come before *spoke*.

☐ If the focus is on you speaking (instead of others), then *only* can also come before *spoke*.

■ In speech, intonation would address much of this. Some later grammarians called Lowth hypercritical on this. English likes the *only* before the verb.

■ Do you have a problem with the following two sentences, the first written by James Thurber and the second by Samuel Johnson?

☐ "We feel very badly about your only having one turkey."

☐ "Every other author may aspire to praise; the lexicographer can only hope to escape reproach."

■ They really aren't confusing, so are we quibbling over too fine a point? *Merriam-Webster's Dictionary of English Usage*, which provides those two sentences, points out that in edited prose, the *only* does tend to appear before the phrase it modifies (something writers and editors are paying attention to).

- Here's Thurber again: "Indeed, we spent so little time in bed most of us had only one child." Is it worth editing for this? Maybe, at least some of the time. Here's an example from editors of the AHD: "Dictators respect only force; they are not moved by words" versus "Dictators only respect force; they do not worship it."

- Let's be clear that this is about disambiguating sentences that require it. In sum, the issue with *only* stems from the flexibility many adverbs show in terms of sentence placement—but not all of them show it.

Intensifiers

- Intensifiers (a subset of adverbs) are less flexible: They appear before adjectives and adverbs. Examples include *very* happy, *really* fast, and *truly* superb.

- Some attention recently came to the rise of *super* as an intensifier. The *Corpus of Contemporary American English* showed it was five times more frequent in 2010–2012 than in 1990–1994. "Super fast" is faster than "really fast," but as *super* does this work more frequently, it will weaken.

- New, slangier forms in American English include *hella* cool, *uber* cool, and *wicked* cool. British English has its own slangy intensifiers: *flipping*, *chuffing*, *dead*, *blooming*, and the mildly expletive *bloody*.

- In formal writing, it is worth looking at all intensifiers and seeing if you need them:

  □ "This finding is quite remarkable" can just be "This finding is remarkable."

  □ "The very dramatic decrease" can be "The dramatic decrease."

- But this does not make the case that one should omit all adverbs. Some work to boost our claims, such as *clearly*, *surely*, and *obviously*. Equally importantly, adverbs can hedge our claims: Take *perhaps*, *possibly*, and *arguably* as examples.

Hopefully

- Let's discuss one other controversial adverb: *hopefully* as a sentence adverb. In the first couple of decades of the 20th century, the adverb *hopefully* started to be used to mean "I hope/we hope/it is hoped that ...." Speakers could say, "She smiled hopefully" and "Hopefully it won't snow tomorrow."

- The sentence adverb use of *hopefully* gained in popularity. But in the 1960s, prescriptive commentators noticed this new use and condemned it, calling it overly ambiguous. Speakers have continued to use it prolifically as a sentence adverb, but starting in the 1960s, the sentence adverb use dropped precipitously in edited prose.

- The AHD Usage Panel has been asked about this regularly. For a time, the panel was getting more prescriptive about it: In the 1969 survey, 44 percent of the panel accepted the new usage of *hopefully* in "Hopefully, the treaty will be ratified." But in 1999, only 34 percent accepted it.

- Now the tide has turned: In 2012, 63 percent accepted that sentence. Furthermore, 89 percent accepted *mercifully* as a sentence adverb: "Mercifully, the play was brief."

- Given how common the sentence adverb use of *hopefully* is in speech, it seems that whatever ambiguity there is, it is an ambiguity that speakers can tolerate. Human language is often ambiguous.

Flat Adverbs

- To end this lecture, let's come back full circle to flat adverbs. These are adverbs that have the same form as their adjective counterparts (examples: *fast*, *up*, *down*, and *soon*). For instance, take "I am a fast eater" and "I eat fast."

- One of the common markers of adverbs is the suffix *–ly*, which we can add to an adjective to make an adverb: *quick* becomes *quickly*.

- There are also a few adjectives that have that *–ly* ending, such as *homely* and *comely*. The suffix *–ly* has come to be used to form adverbs, which leaves an adjective like *friendly* in an awkward position: What is the adverb form? *Friendlily*? In a *friendly* way?

- There are, though, many adverbs with no distinctive *–ly* marking, such as *soon*, *up*, *down*, *fast*, *hard*, *tight*, and *slow*.

  - You might question whether *slow* is an adverb, since we have *slowly*. There is some controversy over "drive slow," but historically there is no problem here.

  - There used to be a lot of flat adverbs in English because we used to mark adverbs with final *–e*. When that dropped off, *slow* was an adjective and an adverb. Shakespeare, in *A Midsummer Night's Dream*, wrote: "But oh, me thinks, how slow / This old Moone wanes."

- What about "drive safe?" Historically, the adverb here has been *safely*. But why not let *safe* be a flat adverb? Merriam-Webster recognizes this, but the AHD and OED do not.

- What about "play nice?" *Nice* historically has been an adverb, although now it would be considered nonstandard in sentences like "He sings really nice." Again, Merriam-Webster recognizes *nice* as an adverb; the AHD does not.

- Some flat adverbs mean something different from the *–ly* form; for example, take "work hard" versus "hardly work."

- In some cases, the flat adverb will feel more informal or more playful, but that doesn't make it ungrammatical. Remember: Flat adverbs have been around for centuries. They can make us think when they are used in creatively ambiguous ways, as in "Think different."

Suggested Reading

Tagliamonte and Roberts, "So Weird; So Cool; So Innovative."
Yagoda, *When You Catch an Adjective, Kill It.*

Questions to Consider

1. Would you be willing to consider both *drive slowly* and *drive slow* standard usage? Why or why not?

2. In what way is the sentence "Hopefully it won't rain tomorrow" ambiguous? Is it an ambiguity that you can manage as a listener or reader?

Lecture 14 | Only Adverbs

Two well-known company slogans have raised some grammatical hackles based on their use, or non-use, of adverbs. This seemed like a good place to start our lecture on adverbs. What are the slogans? Subway restaurant has long used the slogan "Eat Fresh," and in 1997 Apple rolled out "Think Different." Do we have grammatical problems here?

Let's start with "Eat Fresh." Sounds a lot like eat right, but right can clearly be an adverb as well as an adjective. We talk about the right choice, adjective; this fits right, adverb. Eat fresh also sounds like eat well, but well clearly established as an adverb. This leaves us with the question of whether fresh can also be an adverb. Fresh is usually an adjective, we talk about fresh flowers, the fish are fresh. But fresh can be an adverb. For example, "The bread is baked fresh every day." We could also there say "The bread is baked freshly every day," but fresh there is pretty clearly an adverb.

So what about eat fresh? Well, eat fresh works differently from baked fresh. Baked fresh means baked recently, but that's clearly not what fresh means in eat fresh. Perhaps eat fresh is just a shortening of eat fresh food, or perhaps it's a nonstandard meaning of the adverb fresh, where eat fresh means that you eat fresh things. We know what it means, even if we're not quite sure how the grammar is working. And the point is that that means the slogan has done its work, we notice the language, and here we are talking about it.

Let's talk about "Think different," the Apple slogan. Standard grammar arguably would be think differently, but this also means differently. Think differently means think in different ways versus think about different things? We do have expressions like think big, and there big is functioning as an adverb, think in big ways, maybe also about big things. We also get the expression talk big where the adverb big means boastfully. Now different can be an adverb. *The American Heritage Dictionary* has the example, "Carol didn't know different until Elinor told her," where different is clearly an adverb. So in think different is different an adjective or an adverb? Is it asking us to think about different kinds of computers or to think differently about computers? Now I have to say; this ad didn't win an Emmy for nothing—the ambiguity is brilliant.

There's an interesting article from a 2011 issue of *Forbes* by Rob Siltanen, who was a creative director and managing partner at the ad agency that came up with "Think different," and he was part of the team that was involved in the process. He tells us that "Think different" was based on "Think IBM" and then it was paired with different-thinking people like Einstein and Gandhi. The ambiguity of think different is possible because English has words that can be both adjectives and adverbs without changing form; words like big and fast, and we'll come back to those as flat adverbs when we talk about flat adverbs. For now, I think we just recognize that "Think different" is a brilliant play on the ambiguity between adjectives and adverbs in English when words don't change form.

This seems like a good moment to try to define an adverb—except that there is never a good moment to define an adverb. As I mentioned before, adverbs are sometimes described as the trashcan category of English grammar that we're putting in apples, oranges, and grapefruits and calling them all adverbs. Here is Merriam-Webster defining an adverb—a word that describes a verb, an adjective, another adverb, or a sentence and that is often used to show time, manner, place, or degree. In other words, unlike adjectives which consistently modify nouns, adverbs modify a whole range of things.

They can modify verbs, for example, go quickly, protest peacefully. They can modify adjectives—incredibly nice, very happy. There you're seeing those intensifiers like very. Intensifiers are considered adverbs. Adverbs can modify other adverbs—really stupidly, ridiculously slowly. And then adverbs can modify entire clauses or sentence, for example frankly, this situation with adverbs is a mess.

As you can see, it is hard to pin down adverbs in terms of what they modify; they're equally hard to pin down in terms of where they appear in the clause or sentence. When they're modifying a verb, for example, they can move around. Let me give you an example. She wrote the email quickly—there the adverb is at the end. She quickly wrote the email—now the adverb has moved between the subject and the verb. Quickly she wrote the email–Now it's right at the beginning of the sentence. The one that we probably can't do is she wrote quickly the email.

Let look at what happens when the adverb is modifying the entire clause. One again we're going to see a lot of flexibility about where this can go. Frankly, this situation is a mess—there that adverb is at the front. This situation, frankly, is a mess—now we put it after the subject, before the verb. This situation is, frankly, a mess—now it's come between the verb and the predicate noun. And finally, this situation is a mess, frankly—now we put it all the way at the end of the sentence. The only thing we can't do here is break up "this situation" and put frankly right into the middle of that because that's a noun phrase. And we can't put it right in that middle of "a mess."

Most of the time this flexibility with adverbs in terms of where they can go in a sentence is not an issue, but then there's the adverb only and where it's supposed to go. Let me give you an example. You ask to borrow some money for coffee, and I give you two dollars. You are disgruntled and say, "Anne only gave me two dollars." Have you made an error? Some would say that what you should have said is, "Anne gave me only two dollars," versus "Anne only gave me two dollars; she loaned me ten dollars." You can see what the only is modifying. Do you care or does this seem overly nit-picky to you? Bryan Garner in *Modern American Usage* calls this issue with only "perhaps the most frequently misplaced word in English." When you hear that, you should ask, "If it happens so frequently, is it really misplaced?" But Garner is echoing a long-standing concern about only.

And before I continue with only, I just want to pause here to remind you of why I'm talking so often about particular style guides, like Brian Garners *Modern American Usage*, Strunk and White's *Element of Styles*, H.W. Fowler's *Book on Usage*. I've decided to focus on these because they are very influential, well-established usage guides. They're the kinds of guides that we often go to, to look for advice. I could choose from a whole range of grammars, and I expect that many of you are using a range of them. I picked some of the better-known ones so that we can look at what they say and evaluate the kinds of advice that we're finding in these usage guides. That we can think about that advice from the perspective, I'm offering in this course of what are being prescribed, what are we being told to do compared with actual usage and decide what we want to do as writers. Now back to only.

As I said, Garner is echoing a concern about only, and this concern goes way back, as early as Bishop Lowth in 1763. And Lowth went after the sentence, "I only spoke three words," an equivalent of that sentence. "I only spoke three words," instead of "I spoke only three words" Now, what's the objection here? The objection is that it is arguably ambiguous if we apply strict logic to the sentence. If the focus is that it was just three words that I spoke, then only should come before three words, "I spoke only three words." If the focus is what you spoke versus what for example what you wrote, then only should come before spoke, "I only spoke three words." If the focus is on you speaking versus others, then only can also come before spoke, for example, "I only spoke three words." In speech, intonation would address much of this issue, but in writing the argument is that we need to be much more careful about the placement of that only and that's a fair argument to make.

Some later grammarians called Lowth hypercritical on only. They noted that English likes to put only before the verb. Fowler himself defends misplaced only in the sentence "The man only died a week ago." If we were trying to apply that logic, we would say "The man died only a week ago." But if we say, "The man only died a week ago," we know that those mean the same thing.

Let's think about only as we encounter it in published prose, and see if you would notice the placement of only in the following two sentences? Here's the first one, "We feel very badly about your only having one turkey." "You're only having one turkey," instead of "You're having only one turkey." This comes from James Thurber. Here's the second one. "Every other author may aspire to praise; the lexicographer can only hope to escape reproach," that's Samuel Johnson. And if we're following the logic here you would say, not "only hope to escape" but "hope only to escape." Now, clearly these sentences aren't confusing, so are we quibbling over too fine a point of usage?

This issue is addressed in the *Merriam-Webster Dictionary of English Usage*, which I highly recommend as a resource. It's a great place to find historical information about points of usage that you're interested in. So Merriam-Webster, which provides those two sentences I just gave you, points out that in fact when you look at edited prose, the sentences I gave you are actually a little bit exceptional. The only does tend to appear before the phrase it modifies; it does appear to be something that writers and perhaps their editors are paying attention to. Here's Thurber again with the only in the "correct" place. "Indeed, we spent so little time in bed that most of us had only one child."

Is it worth editing for this? Should you be watching your onlys? I would say maybe, at least some of the time. It's probably a good practice. Here's an example, where it does matter where the only goes. And this example comes from editors of the *American Heritage Dictionary*. "Dictators respect only force; they are not moved by words." So there we see dictators respect only force; only puts the focus on force and then we can contract that with they're not moved by words. Now see what happens when we move the only. "Dictators only respect force; they do not worship it." Dictators only respect force puts the focus on respect, they do not worship it. That's a place where the placement of the only matters.

But let's be clear that here, this is about disambiguating sentences that require it often where only is in the sentence does not create that kind of confusion. In sum, the issue with only really stems from the flexibility many adverbs show in terms of sentence placement—but not all of them are that flexible.

That takes us to intensifiers, which are a subset of adverbs and they are much less flexible about where they can appear. They appear right before adjectives and adverbs. There are words like very, really, truly; so when we say things like very happy, really fast, truly superb, so egregiously. Very and really are perhaps the most generic intensifiers right now, and the most common ones. But the most common ones change over time.

Sali Tagliamonte and Chris Roberts at the University of Toronto have done a study of intensifiers, and they show a layered history of these, where you have intensifiers coming in and replacing other intensifiers. They start with well as an intensifier, which his then replaced by full as an intensifier, which is then replaced by right as an intensifier in a phrase like right welcome. They are replaced by pretty as an intensifier. We now use pretty as a hedge, not an intensifier, and the then pretty by the 16th century is replaced by very. Since then really has come to prominence and so now we have really and very up there as two very common intensifiers. And I think for many of us very feels probably a little more formal, really a little less formal. But not as informal as so. And so is now overtaking really in terms of its frequency as an intensifier.

I was interviewed about this for an article in a newspaper, and to prepare for the interview, I went into the Corpus of Contemporary American English to see what was going on with super as an intensifier. I searched for super plus adjective and super plus adverb, and I found that super used this way five times more frequent in 2010–2012 than it was from 1990–1994. So in 20 years, super has gained enormously in frequency. And I do think that at least for some of us super fast is faster than really fast because superfast is super fast. And that super is now—and probably part of it is because it's new—able to do this kind of intensifying work with a little more intensity. That said, as super does this work more frequently, it probably will weaken and stop functioning as an intensifier that adds more impact than something like really.

There are also new and slangier forms of intensifiers in American English; this would include things like hella, hella cool, uber cool, wicked cool. In British English you get slangy intensifiers such as flipping, chuffing, dead, blooming, bloody. And it is important for Americans to remember that bloody remains an expletive, perhaps now a more mild expletive in British English. For Americans, it can seem like a harmless word.

In formal writing, it is worth looking at all of your intensifiers and seeing if you need them. Let's take a sentence like, "This finding is quite remarkable." You could just take out that intensifier quite and write "This finding is remarkable." Or take the phrase the very dramatic decrease.

Take out that very, just make it the dramatic decrease. And there is a way actually without this intensifier that dramatic gets to just do its work, the dramatic decrease because dramatic is already pretty dramatic.

But I want to know here that my advice to look at your intensifiers and see where you need them and often take them out does not make the case that one should omit all adverbs. And I do see that advice sometimes about writing that you should take out all your adverbs. Adverbs do important work, and many of them are worth saving. For example, some adverbs work to boost our claims when we say for example, clearly, surely, obviously. Equally importantly, some adverbs can hedge our claims; thinks like perhaps, possibly, arguably. Why are these important? These are important because part of academic writing is negotiating our commitments to our arguments. We're letting people know whether we're quite confident that this is true or whether this is an assertion and we need some contingencies here. We're also letting people know our stance in terms of our assessment of other people's claims, and whether or not they are valid.

I think that when I talk with students sometimes about strong arguments I realize that they interpret that to mean that this should be an argument that has no hedges, that makes strong claims and doesn't allow for exceptions, doesn't allow for uncertainty. And what we know actually is that in the academy—in academic writing—strong arguments are sophisticated in terms of where they boost their claims, where there is certainty, and where they hedge their claims, where they make space for counterarguments, for readers to disagree or raise questions, for additional evidence.

Let's now talk about one other controversial adverb, and this is hopefully as a sentence adverb. In the first couple of decades of the 20th century, the adverb hopefully started to be used to mean I hope, we hope, it is hoped, in addition to its original meaning full of hope. So as a result, speakers could say, "She smiled hopefully" as in she was full of hope, and they could say "Hopefully, it won't snow tomorrow." The sentence adverb use of hopefully as in "Hopefully, it won't snow tomorrow," which captures our general hope, gained in popularity throughout the 20th century. What happened is that in the 1960s then, as hopefully gained in popularity prescriptive commentators noticed. And when they noticed this new use they started to condemn it, calling it overly ambiguous. They said, "We don't know who's hoping." They also said if you get a sentence like "Hopefully she opened the gift," that could be the that she is opening it full of hope or that we hope she opened it. Now, speakers have continued to use hopefully as a sentence adverb prolifically, but starting in the 1960s, the sentence adverb dropped precipitously out of edited prose.

I did a search of *TIME* magazine, of the Time Magazine Corpus, which you can find online, and you can search all off *TIME* magazine from when it started in the 1920s. And when I searched on hopefully you see a dramatic increase across the first half of the 20th century as it takes on the sentence adverb function because the sentence adverb function is useful. And then suddenly, starting in the 1960s it drops out of use in *TIME* magazine, and I believe that it's because the editors started noticing it and they were told to edit it out. It doesn't fall out completely because, of course, you still get hopefully in quoted text because people were still saying it.

The *American Heritage Dictionary* Usage Panel has been asked about this sentence adverb use of hopefully regularly over the years, and here is the interesting thing. For a while, the panel was getting more prescriptive about it. In the 1969 survey, 44 percent of the panel accepted the new use of hopefully in "Hopefully, the treaty will be ratified;" but in 1999 only 34 percent accepted it, in other words, the panel was getting crankier about this. But now the tide has turned; when the panel was asked again in 2012, 63 percent accepted that sentence "Hopefully, the treaty will be ratified," and I will say I was one of those people who accepted it. And 89 percent accepted mercifully as a sentence adverb, as in "Mercifully, the play was brief."

And mercifully raises a key point. There are many other sentence adverbs in English that are fully accepted—mercifully, fortunately, briefly, frankly, which I used in some sentences earlier in this lecture. And given how common the sentence adverb use of hopefully is in speech, it seems that whatever ambiguity there is, it is an ambiguity that speakers can accept, that we can work with. And it's important to realize that human languages are often ambiguous, and it often serves us well. At least in speech where we can clarify if something goes awry. It is true that in writing we sometimes have to be careful because we're not there to clarify if there is ambiguity.

With hopefully, the ambiguity may even be helpful. Think about the sentence, "Hopefully, it won't snow tomorrow." I actually don't want to specify who is hoping. I mean it's probably me, it's probably you, but it's really sort of bigger than us, it's a general hope; we're all hoping, "Hopefully, it won't snow tomorrow." And this use of hopefully is coming to be accepted. You saw it with the Usage Panel, and in April 2012, the *Associate Press Stylebook* changed its stance and said that writers could now use hopefully to mean it is hoped, or we hope. What I found interesting is the fact that the AP Stylebook made this decision made headlines. We are really interested in grammar.

To end this lecture, let's come back full circle to those flat adverbs. Those adverbs that have the same form as their adjective counterparts. These would be words like fast, up, down, soon. You can say for example, "I am a fast eater," fast is an adjective, "I eat fast," fast is an adverb. And we would not say "I eat fastly." Fast does not like that -ly ending there.

But one of the common markers of adverbs is that suffix –ly, which we can add to an adjective to make an adverb, at least some of the time—quick becomes quickly, beautiful becomes beautifully.

But, there are also a few adjectives that have that –ly ending—homely, comely, manly, friendly, and there is a historical reason for this. The historical source of modern –ly had an adjective and adverb form. It goes back to what would be spelled in old English -lic, pronounced lic—that would be the adjective form; and -lice with the final –e was the adverb form. Because one of the ways that old English distinguished adverbs was that final -e. Now over time -lic or -lice lost the final -c and it also lost the final -e and it turned into -ly, which is how we have some -ly adjectives as well as some -ly adverbs. The suffix –ly now is used productively to make adverbs, such as quick becoming quickly, but we have these remnants of its earlier use also to make adjectives. The fact that -ly remains in some of these adjectives can sometimes put us in an awkward spot, particularly with an adjective like friendly. What is the adverb form of friendly? "I greeted her friendlily." "I greeted her in a friendly way." I think to me this gap in the language is such an interesting one because we use the word friendly on a very regular basis, and we clearly need to talk about things we do in a friendly way, how are we missing an adverb from there, other than friendlily, which I think some of us think sounds a little funny. There are, though, many adverbs with no distinctive –ly marking, such as soon, up, down, fast, hard, tight, slow.

Wait, wait, wait, you say: did Ann just say that slow is an adverb? But there is slowly. There is some controversy over a phrase like "drive slow," but historically there is actually no problem here, and I think that perhaps something like "Go slow" sounds better? There used to be a lot of flat adverbs in English because as I mentioned earlier, English used to mark adverbs with final –e and when the final -e dropped off in the history of English, those adverbs and adjectives looked the same way.

Here is an example of a flat adverb, in this case slow, from Shakespeare's *Midsummer Night's Dream*, "But oh, me thinks, how slow this old Moone wanes." How slow this old moon wanes, it's not how slowly.

What about drive safe? This is one of those expressions that people bring up as one of the ones that they really don't like. Historically the adverb here has been safely, drive safely. But why not let safe be a flat adverb? *Merriam-Webster* already recognizes it as an adverb; the *American Heritage Dictionary* and the *Oxford English Dictionary* do not yet. For me, I have to say there is actually a difference between drive safe and drive safely. For example, if I have people over to my home for a dinner party, and they're leaving my home, and I want to wish them well I will say, "Drive safe." It feels friendlier to me. If I say, "Drive safely," it feels like I'm part of a campaign to make sure that people are safe on the roads.

What about the expression play nice? Nice historically has been an adverb, although now that would be a nonstandard use of nice. For example, in "He sings really nice." So historically that would have been more standard than it is now. *Merriam-Webster* recognizes nice as an adverb, *American Heritage Dictionary* does not, and this came up for me in a question and answer session at a talk that I gave at the Ann Arbor City Club. At the City Club, there is a sign during the Bridge Club meetings that says "play nice." Play works in kind of a funny way. We could also say "play dirty" and "play clean" the latter, where clean is working as an adverb is recognized in the

American Heritage Dictionary, the former, "play dirty," is not recognized yet. But there is precedence for saying something like "play nice.

Some flat adverbs mean something different from the –ly form. Think about "work hard" versus "hardly work." Clearly, those mean different things. Or the expression we sometimes say at night, "sleep tight." There tight is functioning as an adverb, and it means soundly, "sleep soundly," versus could we even say "sleep tightly?" But we could use tightly to say "lock it up tightly," or "lock it up tight."

In sum, in some cases, the flat adverb will feel more informal or more playful, but that doesn't necessarily make it ungrammatical. Remember that flat adverbs have been around for centuries. And they can make us sometimes think that in creative ways they can allow us to do things like "Eat fresh," "Think different." And I love that part of human language that we can play with is something an adjective or is it an adverb and how does it make us think or think differently about the language

So is that a wrap on adverbs for this lecture? Absolutely. OK, maybe not quite yet because check out that use of absolutely to mean yes. Definitely, can do the same thing. These are intensifiers that have taken on this positive connotation of agreement to become synonymous with yes. Think how rude it would be if you'd use absolutely to mean no. Now, is yes an adverb? Oy. That's a hard question. Yes, yes is an adverb and it's other things too, which we'll come back to in Lecture 21 when we talk about the grammar of conversation.

Before we get there, we'll talk about conjunctions in the next lecture and how different speech and writing can be when it comes to these connecting words.

No Ifs, Ands, or Buts

The Microsoft Word grammar checker is arguably the most powerful prescriptive force in the world. It is on roughly 90 percent of word processing programs and it is on by default. Writers are much more likely to encounter the rules in that grammar checker than any usage guide. And when it puts a green squiggly line under something, it makes you wonder: What's wrong with that? Frequently, it targets words such as *and*, *like*, and *but*—the subject of this lecture. We'll review coordinating conjunctions and coordinators; subordinating conjunctions/subordinators; and then talk about the dramatic differences between speech and writing.

And

- The grammar checker underlines *And* at the beginning of a sentence. This is a tipoff that there might be some problems with the rules in the grammar checker, because this rule simply isn't a rule. It is a myth. *Merriam-Webster's Dictionary of English Usage* summarizes:

  > Everybody agrees that it's all right to begin a sentence with *and*, and nearly everybody admits to having been taught at some past time that the practice was wrong. Most of us think the prohibition goes back to our early school days. ... [T]he prohibition is probably meant to correct the tendency of children to string together independent clauses or simple declarative sentences with *and*s.

- There's a reason kids have a tendency to use a lot of *and*'s (it's the way we talk). As writers, they need to learn in less colloquial ways. But first, let's think about the power of the MS Word grammar checker putting green squiggly lines under sentence-initial *And* and *But*. It sure makes it seem like there is something wrong with them.

- The software's explanation is that it is informal to start a sentence that way: "Although sentences beginning with 'and,' 'but,' 'or,' or 'plus' may be used informally, use the suggested replacement for a more formal or traditional tone." But not everyone makes a distinction between informal and wrong, and these aren't even strictly informal: You can find sentence-initial *And* and *But* all over academic writing, in literature, and in the Bible: "And God said, 'Let there be light.'"

- In informal polls, a good number of people revise their prose until the green squiggly line goes away, so this myth suddenly takes on new power.

Coordinators and Subordinators

■ This lecture will typically use the terminology *coordinator* and *subordinator*, but there is not unanimity in the linguistics community about terminology. Geoff Pullum and his co-author Rodney Huddleston have argued that we are getting the terminology wrong in their book the *Cambridge Grammar of the English Language*.

■ They argue that we should think about many words that are typically called *subordinating conjunctions* as prepositions. But you will continue to encounter the terms *coordinator* and *subordinator*, as well as *coordinating* and *subordinating conjunction*, in most usage guides, grammar books, and dictionaries, so this lecture will use that categorization.

Coordinators

■ Coordinators (or coordinating conjunctions) like *and* and *but* join two units of equal status, for instance, two nouns or noun phrases. *And* is a prototypical coordinator and can coordinate words, phrases, and clauses. Examples are below.

    □ Words: "apples and oranges"; "cease and desist"; "safe and sound."

    □ Phrases: "the young and the restless"; "reading books and writing essays."

    □ Clauses: "My phone rang, and I jumped."

■ Some coordinators can also take more than two. The key point overall is that the coordinator occurs between the coordinates: "My phone rang and I jumped," not "And I jumped, my phone rang."

■ The coordinator *or* can do all the things *and* can do: It can connect words, phrases, and clauses, and coordinate more than two items. In contrast, *but* can't do all of that. It does less well with words and phrases: "I bought apples but oranges" doesn't work, although we can say, "I bought apples but not oranges."

- These more prototypical coordinators also can't co-occur: "He loves chocolate and but it keeps him up at night" doesn't work. However, you can make *and* and *or* co-occur with a slash: "He should eat chocolate earlier in the day and/or eat less chocolate."

- *So* and *yet* are sometimes called marginal coordinators. *So* can't typically connect words or phrases—only clauses. We can say, "They were late, so they parked illegally right in front," but not "They were late so frantic." That said, *so* can connect verb phrases: "They were late, so drove fast." *So* and *yet* can also combine with *and*: "They were late, and yet they stopped to get coffee on the way."

The Word *Plus*

- Some controversy surrounds the word *plus*. Let's start with the well-known mathematical expression "two plus two equals four." The *–s* in *equals* suggests that "two plus two" is singular. Some interpret this to mean *plus* is a preposition, so "plus two" is a prepositional phrase, which allows "two plus two" to be singular.

- This is different from how *and* works in identical constructions: "Two and two are four." *Plus* can also feel like a preposition in a sentence like this: "All school-aged children, plus an accompanying adult, can get in for free."

- The editors of the AHD reject the idea that *plus* is a preposition. They call *plus* here a conjunction and simply state that convention means that "two plus two" is treated as a singular.

- Another controversy: Can you use *plus* to coordinate clauses or even to begin a sentence?

  □ Using it to coordinate clauses is out there, but sounds informal, as in this example from *Esquire*: "The next woman, the forty-three-year-old, already has two kids, plus she's recovering from thyroid cancer."

□   *Plus* can also start a sentence, but not all critics like it. Its use is on the rise, though. In 2009, 67 percent of the AHD Usage Panel accepted the example, "He has a lot of personal charm. Plus, he knows what he's doing."

Subordinating Conjunctions

■   Subordinating conjunctions connect clauses. In the process, they subordinate one to the other such that it can no longer stand alone but depends on the main clause. The prototypical example is *if*: "If it snows tomorrow, we probably won't run." We can reverse the clauses: "We probably won't run if it snows tomorrow." But "If it snows tomorrow" can't stand on its own.

■   Note that fragments that begin with a subordinator are possible for rhetorical effect. For instance: "Researchers say we might be able to stave off climate change with a 40 percent reduction in global emissions. Unless the unexpected happens." This short fragment can add emphasis.

■   Common subordinating conjunctions include *although*, *because*, *while*, *when*, *after*, *before*, *since*, *unless*, *as if*, *in order that*, and *as soon as*.

■   Most subordinating conjunctions are not controversial, but *because* and *like* have raised some hackles.

□   The first concern: Can you begin a sentence with *because*? Yes, but if you start with *because*, you need to remember to add the independent clause.

□   The second concern about *because* regards the use of "the reason is because" rather than "the reason is that." It is redundant, and is largely edited out of more formal writing, but you can still find it.

Like a Cigarette Should

- The word *like* as a subordinating conjunction or subordinator has also caused controversy. The best example is this text from a Winston cigarette ad in the 1950s and 1960s: "Winston tastes good, like a cigarette should."

- Newspapers, magazines, and usage guides wanted *like* only to be a preposition. But *like* as a conjunction seems to go back to the 14th century. It shows up in Shakespeare and later Charles Dickens, George Eliot, John Keats, and Emily Bronte.

- Criticism started as early as the 18th century. Noah Webster called the sentence "He thinks like you do" an "improper and vulgar" expression. By the 20th century, the consensus position was that it was wrong to use *like* to mean "as if" or "as."

- In the end, what do we make of the Winston cigarette ad? It did its job. It had people talking. If you want to use *like* as a subordinator, it's your decision. You're in good company if you decide to do so.

- Is it OK to use *like* as a preposition? Yes, but some people seem to be scared of it because of the criticism of *like* as a subordinating conjunction. *Like* as a preposition expresses similarity: "Dave, like many other Ann Arborites, own a Prius." It also can be used synonymously with *such as*: "Our friend's daughter wants to go to a smaller school like Oberlin."

Slash

- The word *slash* has begun to emerge as a new coordinator between clauses. Here's an example in oral communication: "I really love that hot dog place on Liberty Street slash can we go there tomorrow?"

- It can express what one should do versus what one is going to do: "I'm going to go home and work on my paper slash take a nap."

- It can also mean "following up on that." Here's an example from Twitter: "When is your next tour slash will you be making any pitstops in Dallas and/or OKC?"

- Why write it out instead of using the symbol? As one teenager explained in a comment on a blog post regarding *slash*, the main reason for *slash* over / is "for it to be seen clearly and read as 'slash' instead of 'or.' The two words now have a completely different meaning and function, even though they are both expressed using the same symbol."

- This is linguistic innovation under our very noses, and it's innovation of the most interesting kind: It involves a function word.

Suggested Reading

Curzan, *Fixing English*.
Yagoda, *When You Catch an Adjective, Kill It*.

Questions to Consider

1. Did you learn not to start a sentence with *And* or *But*? What reasons were you given, and how well do you think those reasons hold up?

2. Should *like* be able to function like a subordinator in a sentence such as "She ate like she hadn't seen food in days?" Why or why not?

Lecture 15   No Ifs, Ands, or Buts

Transcript

A few years ago, I became very interested in, some might even say obsessed with, the Microsoft Word grammar checker. I started asking, "Where do these rules come from?" And I couldn't get a clear answer. Why does this matter? It matters because the Microsoft Word grammar checker is arguably the most powerful prescriptive force in the world—and I'm going to make that argument. Think about it. It is on something like 90 percent of the word processing programs out there in the world, and it is on by default. You have to know to turn it off to make it go away.

People are much more likely to encounter the rules that are in the Microsoft Word grammar checker than they are to encounter the rules in any particular printed usage guide such as Strunk and White or Brian Garner's *Modern American Usage*. It's so easy. The rules are right there on your computer as you type. You don't even have to stand up and go to your bookshelf to get a book. And when the grammar checker puts a green squiggly line under something, it can make any of us wonder, "What's wrong with that? And maybe I should change it."

I talked about the grammar checker already in the lecture on relative clauses, and I'm returning to it here in this lecture on conjunctions for a reason. What is that reason? I first got interested in the grammar checker because it underlines And at the beginning of a sentence. What is up with that? It tipped me off that there might be some problems with the rules in the grammar checker. This is because this rule—this rule about not starting a sentence with And simply isn't a rule. It's a myth. Or, as H. W. Fowler put it early in the 20th century: "It is a 'faintly lingering superstition.'" It's a myth or a superstition that is perpetuated by English teachers and other language mavens who are enforcing rules that, in this case, you can't find in any typical usage guide.

The *Merriam-Webster's Dictionary of English Usage* summarizes the situation with And at the beginning of a sentence this way, and here I quote:

> Everybody agrees that it's all right to begin a sentence with And, and nearly everybody admits to having been taught at some past that the practice was wrong. Most of us think the prohibition goes back to our early school days. The prohibition is probably meant to correct the tendency of children to string together independent clauses or simple declarative sentences with Ands.

I appreciate that explanation from *Merriam-Webster*. I think that it is probably true—there's a reason that kids have a tendency to use a lot of Ands in their writing, and that's because we use a lot of Ands when we talk. As writers, children need to learn to write in less colloquial ways, but that doesn't mean that one cannot start a sentence with And. But before we continue with this rule about And, let's think about the power of the Microsoft Word grammar checker putting green squiggly lines under sentence-initial And or But. It sure makes it seem like there's something wrong with putting And or But there.

If you pull up the pop-up box in Microsoft Word 10 when it underlines, for example, a sentence-initial And—you can get an explanation. And what it says is that to use And this way is informal. And they go on to say, "Although sentences beginning with 'and,' 'but,' 'or,' or 'plus' may be used informally, use the suggested replacement for a more formal or traditional tone." The box—the little box in Microsoft Word then suggests that you replace Plus with something like In addition or Moreover; and suggests you replace But with Nevertheless or However.

But I'm not sure that everyone makes a distinction between informal and wrong. I'm also not convinced that everyone reads the explanation in the little box. I'm also not convinced that sentence-initial And is informal. You can find sentence-initial And and sentence-initial But and Or all over academic writing, It's in literature. It's also in the Bible. Think about, "And God said, 'Let there be light.'" That's in the English translation.

In informal polls that I've done, a good number of people tell me that they revise their prose until the green squiggly line in their document goes away. And what that means is that this myth about sentence-initial And and But and Or suddenly takes on new power.

In this lecture, we'll review coordinating conjunctions, which are sometimes called coordinators, and subordinating conjunctions or subordinators, and then talk about some usage issues such as Plus—what's going on there—Because, and Like. At the end of the lecture, I'll show you some new evidence for what the word Slash is doing—evidence that suggests that Slash is becoming a coordinator between clauses.

In this lecture, I'll typically use the terminology coordinator and subordinator, and I want to note that there is not unanimity in the linguistics community about terminology. Geoff Pullum, who I mentioned in the lecture on passive voice, and his co-author Rodney Huddleston, who wrote the *Cambridge Grammar of the English Language* have argued that we are getting the terminology wrong around coordinators and subordinators. They argue that we should think about many words that are typically called subordinating conjunctions, or subordinators, as prepositions—an argument that I will return to in lecture 17. It's a really provocative and important argument. I also recognize that you will continue to encounter the terms coordinator and subordinator, as well as coordinating and subordinating conjunction, in most usage guides, grammar books, and dictionaries. So I will use that categorization in this lecture.

Let's start with coordinators or coordinating conjunctions such as And and But. Coordinating conjunctions, coordinators, join two units of equal status. That could be two nouns, two noun phrases, two full clauses, and the like. One mnemonic that you may know to help you remember your coordinators is FANBOYS. It's and acronym, and it stands for For, And, Nor, But, Or, Yet, So. Where does that acronym come from? Brett Reynolds wrote an interesting article in TESL—Teaching English as a Second Language—*TESL Canada Journal.* And what he found is that acronym seemed to come from a 1951 grammar book and in the end, it may not be that helpful—not everyone accepts For, Yet and So as coordinators

Let's start with a more typical coordinator—that would be And—some people would call it a prototypical coordinator. And "and" can coordinate words, phrases, and clauses. Let's just quickly look at examples of that.

Words—an expression like apples and oranges, cease and desist, safe and sound. And connecting phrases: the young and the restless, reading books and writing essays. And then, of course, And can connect clauses. For example, "My phone rang, and I jumped." In relation to clauses, it's important to know that And always occurs initially in the second clause: My phone rang, and I jumped. You cannot move the And around. You cannot say, "My phone rang, I jumped and."

Some coordinators can also take more than two coordinates. The examples I have given you have all included just two. If it takes more than two, it's something like X, Y, and Z. And if you're wondering if there should be a comma after Y, in X, Y, and Z just hang on—we'll get there in Lecture 22.

The key point here is that coordinators occur between the coordinates. As I said, And, has to occur right between: "My phone rang, and I jumped." Cannot be moved. And the whole second clause can't be moved. You cannot say, "And I jumped, my phone rang." The And has to come between the clauses. The fact that you can't say, "And I jumped, my phone rang," becomes important when we talk about subordinators. The coordinator Or can do all the things that And can do. It can connect words, phrases, and clauses. It can also coordinate more than two items.

In contrast, the coordinator But can't do all of that. It can conjoin clauses. For example, She ordered a smoothie, but she doesn't like bananas. But "but" does less well-coordinating words and phrases. For example, "I bought apples but oranges." I think most of us would say that that doesn't feel entirely grammatical. That said, we can say, "I bought apples but not oranges," And I think all of us could probably also say, "I saw one doctor but three nurses."

But also typically takes only two coordinates. That said, I'm not sure it's impossible to say the following: She ran, showered, but didn't eat breakfast. I don't know, maybe she didn't have breakfast because they only had bananas, and she doesn't like bananas.

These more prototypical coordinators also cannot co-occur. In other words, we cannot say something like the following: He loves chocolate and but it keeps him up at night. You got to choose—you either get And or you get But. Unless, of course, you put a slash in between something like And/Or. For example, "He should eat chocolate earlier in the day and/or eat less chocolate."

Given all of this, what about So and Yet? So and Yet are sometimes called marginal coordinators. And here's why—So, for instance, can't typically connect words or phrases. It only does clauses. We can say, "They were late, so they parked illegally right in front." But we cannot say, "They were late so frantic." That doesn't work. That said, I think we might all agree that So can connect verb phrases. See if you think this is okay: They were late, so they drove fast. For me, that seems pretty acceptable.

So can also combine with And. And remember that But and And cannot combine. But And and So can combine. For example, "She decided she wanted to get a Ph.D., and so she started doing research on Ph.D. programs in linguistics." Yet can also combine with And. Here's a sentence: They were late, and yet they stopped to get coffee on the way.

With that set up about coordinators, let's talk about the controversy surrounding the word Plus. Let's start with the well-known mathematical expression: two plus two equals four. Two plus two equals four. The –s in equals suggests that two plus two, as a unit, is singular—two plus two equals. Some interpret this fact to mean that Plus in this expression is a preposition. So plus two is a prepositional phrase, which allows two plus two to be singular.

This is different from how And works in an identical construction. Think about: two and two are four. That's what we would say, "Two and two are four," whereas, "Two plus two is four."

Plus—so there we see the argument of Plus as a preposition—can also feel like a preposition in a sentence like this one: All school-aged children, plus an accompanying adult, can get in for free. However, the editors of the *American Heritage Dictionary* reject this idea that Plus is a preposition and call Plus in these constructions a conjunction—what I'm calling a coordinator. And they simply state that convention means that two plus two is treated as a singular.

X plus Y can also be singular outside of math. For example, "My love of sports plus my interest in marketing makes it a perfect job for me." That said, I think all of us could probably also make that plural. We could have a plural verb: My love of sports plus my interest in marketing make it a perfect job for me.

While we're here, it's also worth noting that X and Y can be singular if it's thought of as a notionally singular unit. For example, I could say, "Peanut butter and jelly is an excellent combination." Peanut butter and jelly—X and Y—is. That said, this isn't even the most controversial issue about the word Plus. Here's the controversial part: Can you use Plus to coordinate clauses or even to begin a sentence?

Let's start with the use of Plus to coordinate clauses. It is out there, but it's much less common than Plus followed by a noun phrase—and it remains quite informal. When I searched for it in the *Corpus of Contemporary American English*, it's harder to find in newspapers and academic prose than it is in speech, but you can find it. Here's an example from the magazine Astronomy: "It made for a great start to the conference, plus I really enjoyed seeing some old friends."

Or here's an example from *Esquire*: "The next woman, the forty-three-year-old, already has two kids, plus she's recovering from thyroid cancer."

If plus can coordinate clauses, can it also start a sentence the way that And can? The answer is yes it can, but not all critics like it. The *Corpus of Contemporary American English* shows it on the rise at the beginning of a sentence. I discovered it's about four times more common from 2010–15 than in 1990–94. It's favored in magazines, which I think probably captures its informality. And given that, I was expecting the *American Heritage Dictionary* Usage Panel to be critical of Plus at the beginning of a sentence, but I was surprised. The majority of the panel accepts it.

In our 2009 survey, 67 percent of the panel accepted this example: He has a lot of personal charm. Plus, he knows what he's doing. Sixty-three percent accepted an example expressing a negative judgment. Here's the sentence: We were a terrible team. Plus, we had bad uniforms. My guess is that we will see this use of Plus increasing in ever more formal genres.

With all that said about coordinators, let's turn to subordinators or subordinating conjunctions. Subordinators connect clauses and in the process, they subordinate one clause to the other clause such that the subordinated clause can no longer stand alone but depends on the main clause. This is why you'll hear the terminology independent clause and dependent clause because the subordinator makes the clause it's independent on the independent clause.

A prototypical example of a subordinator is would be If. And here's a sentence with If in it: If it snows tomorrow, we probably won't run. We could reverse those two clauses, unlike what we could do with coordinators. If we reverse them we would get: We probably won't run if it snows tomorrow. And the dependent clause here cannot stand-alone. If I just said, "If it snows tomorrow," then you would be waiting for me to be finished to finish that sentence because it's clear that it's dependent—something is still coming.

One time it could stand-alone is, for example, in response to a question. If we had the question, "Will you all skip running tomorrow," we could say, "If it snows." With this example of "If it snows tomorrow," let me quickly address the question of fragments that begin with a subordinator. It is certainly possible to have these kinds of fragments for rhetorical effect. And let me give you a passage where you can see that happening: "So researchers say we might be able to stave off climate change with a 40 percent reduction in global emissions. Unless the unexpected happens." You can see how isolating that dependent clause, "Unless the unexpected happens," can create a focus on that information. And that can be rhetorically effective. It can add emphasis.

Common subordinating conjunctions or subordinators include: although, because, while, when, after, before, since, unless, as if, in order that, as soon as. Most subordinators are not controversial, but Because and Like have raised some hackles. Let's take them in that order.

There are two concerns about Because, and we're going to start with this one: Can you begin a sentence with because? The answer is yes. This idea that you can't may once again come from writing instruction at earlier ages, where we're trying to help younger writers avoid fragments. If you start with Because, there's some chance you might not remember to put that independent clause in later, and thereby, end up with a fragment.

You can, however, find introductory Because all over academic writing. Here's just one example from the academic journal *Politics and the Life Sciences*. This is from 2014. And here I'm going to quote:

> Because Nietzsche is one of the few thinkers to so openly and comprehensively question the very basis of conventional morality, and because Nietzsche also proposed and elaborated such a distinctive solution to the problems from conventional morality, I will refer extensively to his writings on this topic.

You'll notice there that we actually have two introductory Becauses. Note also the split infinitive in that passage. Did you catch it? It was right at the beginning: "Nietzsche is one of the few thinkers to so openly and comprehensively question…"

The second concern about Because is about the phrase: "the reason is because" rather than "the reason is that." Okay, fair enough—it is redundant to say, "the reason is because." It reminds me of our discussion in the very first lecture about "equally as."

But as I have noted before, we do accept other redundancies in standard formal prose. The editors of the *American Heritage Dictionary* in their usage note point out that people don't seem to be bothered by this similar redundancy. And here I'll quote, "The last time I ate red meat was when,"

"The last time," "Then." That's arguably redundant. That said, "the reason is because" is largely edited out of more formal writing, although you can find it.

When I searched for it, I found this in the *Michigan Law Review* from 1998: "If regulatory competition is desirable, the reason is because, without it, the U.S. would require too much disclosure, not too little."

Now let's talk about like as a subordinating conjunction or a subordinator, and to talk about this, we have to go back in time to a very controversial Winston cigarette ad in the 1950s and 1960s. Here's the ad: "Winston tastes good like a cigarette should." This ad was criticized in newspapers and magazines and usage guides. It was criticized by people who wanted Like only to be a preposition. From that time, there's a terrific quote from *The New Yorker*, which is quoted in the *Merriam-Webster Dictionary of English Usage*. And here's the quote:

> We hope Sir Winston Churchill, impeccable, old-school grammarian that he is, hasn't chanced to hear American radio or television commercials recently. It would pain him dreadfully, we're sure, to listen to the obnoxious and ubiquitous couplet 'Winston tastes good, like a cigarette should.' That pesky 'like' is a problem for us Americans to solve, we guess, and anyway, Sir Winston has his own problems.

But Winston Churchill was known to use Like this way. The *Longman Grammar of Spoken and Written English*, which by the way, is a terrific resource. That book quotes one of Churchill's wartime letters, in which he's talking about special committees. And here's what he writes: "We are overrun by them like the Australians were by rabbits." There you'll see that Like as a subordinator.

Like as a subordinator seems to go back to the 14th century, and while it wasn't common in earlier years, it does show up in Shakespeare and later in Dickens, George Eliot, Keats, Emily Bronte, as well as many others. This use of Like starts to be criticized as early as the 18th century, including Noah Webster who called the sentence "He thinks like you do," improper and vulgar.

Criticism rises in the 19th century and as Ward Gilman, who's the editor of the *Merriam-Webster Dictionary of English Usage* explains, the criticism was consolidated in the 20th century to come to a consensus position that it was just plain wrong to use Like to mean As if or As.

Of course, if you look at literature we admire, you can find Like used as a subordinator a lot. Here are just two examples—these are quoted in the *Merriam-Webster Dictionary of English Usage*. The first is from Carl Sandburg in "Smoke and Steel" published in 1920: "I can go hungry again like I have gone hungry before." And here's T. S. Eliot from "Sweeney Agonistes" in 1932: "… you wake like someone hit you on the head."

In the end, what do we make of the Winston cigarette ad? I have to say, at some lever, it did its job because it had people talking. Think about our discussion of "Think Different" and "Eat Fresh." Do you want to use Like as a subordinator? In the end, that is going to be your decision, but I have to say that you're in good company if you decide that you want to do so.

Is it okay to use Like as a preposition? Yes, definitely, but some people seem to be scared of Like as a preposition because of the criticism of Like as a subordinator. Like as a preposition can express similarity. For example, "Dave, like many other Ann Arborites, owns a Prius."

Like as a preposition can also be used synonymously with Such As. Here's an example, "Our friend's daughter wants to go to a smaller school like Oberlin." You can see there the potential ambiguity the Like there could mean Such As: "… a smaller school such as Oberlin." Or it could be used to express similarity, "… a smaller school similar to Oberlin."

I want to end this lecture with an exciting development in the language: the potential emergence of a new coordinator between clauses. And this may have happened as early as 2005. Here's the story of how I learned about this new coordinator.

When I teach my course on the history of English, I have students teach me new slang. They have to teach me two new slang words each day before I will start class. This was about three months into the term, and one of my students said, "Do you know what we're doing with the word Slash?" And I said, "I have no idea. What are you doing with the word Slash?" And here's the example sentence she gave me about: "I really love that hot dog place on Liberty Street. Slash can we go there tomorrow?"

And I've got to tell you then in that, "I really love that hot dog place on Liberty Street period," slash, written out as a word, "Slash can we go there tomorrow?" I looked at her and said, "I cannot do that," and I turned to the class and I said, "Can other people in here use Slash that way?" And more than half the students said, "Oh absolutely." Now students are never allowed to use phones in my class, but I made an exception and said, "Okay, pull out your phones and show me some text messages where you use Slash this way." And they did. The next class, I came back for more examples because I was so interested in what was happening here. My students thought I was a little crazy. They said, "Why is this so interesting?"

But let me show you what's fascinating here. You can find what is the more traditional use of Slash that I can do. For example: run Slash walk—in other words, this is a combination of running and walking. So you can run Slash walk. Or I could say, "He is my friend slash mentor." Those two descriptions refer to the same thing. That's the more traditional use of Slash.

But here are some of the newer uses. One way that the students that I talked to were using Slash was to distinguish between "what I should do," versus "what I am going to do." Here's an example, "I'm going to go home and work on my paper/take a nap." Or if you want what you might want versus reality. And here's one of my favorite examples from Twitter, "It was fate slash you stalked him."

Slash can also be used now to mean something like "following up on that" or "While we're on that topic, here's another thing..." I did a study searching for these on Twitter, and here are a couple examples that I found:

"When is your next tour slash will you be making any pit stops in Dallas or Oklahoma City?"

Here's another one: "Why are cycling shoes so expensive slash why do I have to buy the clips separately?" As I said, this is written out as Slash. It can come after a comma. It can come after a period, or there can be no punctuation around it—it can just be a coordinator in between the two clauses.

I ended up writing a blog post on this new use of Slash, which attracted a lot of attention out there on the Internet. And I have to say, the thing that make me happiest about that was that I could go back to class and tell the students, "Look, other people are interested," which gave me some credibility because otherwise, they thought I was crazy to think that this was such a cool development in the language.

Now, why would they be writing out Slash? It seems inefficient. Well, here's one answer that was posted in response to my blog post, and it was posted by someone named, Sunshine. Sunshine writes:

> As a teen who uses slash in oral communication and written e-communication, I would say the main reason I spell the word out is in order for it to be seen clearly and read as Slash instead of Or. The two words now have a completely different meaning and function, even though they are both expressed using the same symbol.

I love this informal comment from Sunshine because it captures Sunshine's very clear sense that this use of Slash is different from what we might mean by the symbol. This is a linguistic innovation right under our very noses—and one of the most interesting kind because it involves a function word.

You'll notice that I have not talked about However in this lecture, and that is because I am not categorizing However as a coordinator, but instead as a conjunctive adverb. Or at least maybe I am. So let's turn to However in the next lecture as we think about conjunctive adverbs.

Lecture
16   **However to Use *However***

W hen a writer is struggling to get an idea onto the page, sometimes people will recommend, "Just say it out loud and write that down" or "Just write it like you would say it." That advice might help you get the idea out of your head initially, but in any formal register of writing, we should not write the way we speak. We are expected to use different vocabulary and different syntactic structures. One key example: Certain conjunctive adverbs are used much more heavily writing, especially in formal writing. Those are the focus of this lecture.

Therefore, Thus, and So On

- According to the *Corpus of Contemporary American English*, *therefore* is far and away most common in academic writing. It occurs five times more often in academic writing than magazines and speech, and ten times more than it appears in newspapers or fiction.

- *Thus* is an even more extreme case. It's more than 30 times more common in academic writing than speech. In speech, we're more likely to say something like *so* than we are to say *thus* or *therefore*. We might even just use *and* to show a consequence: "Rosie didn't get enough sleep the night before and she didn't do well on the final exam."

- We show more reliance on coordinators in speech than many conjunctive adverbs. *Consequently* is 25 times more common in academic writing than speech. Newspapers don't like it as much. There, it's only twice as common as it is in speech.

- *Moreover* is 40 times more frequent in academic writing than speech. Even less academic-sounding conjunctive adverbs (or adverbials—phrases that function as adverbs) are more written than spoken. *In addition* is more than twice as common in newspapers and magazines than in speech. In academic writing, we seem to love it: It's more than seven times more common in academic writing than in speech.

- Some conjunctive adverbs pattern the other way. Two examples are *anyway* and *then*. So we do have some colloquial conjunctive adverbs.

Defining Conjunctive Adverbs

- The most basic definition of conjunctive adverbs is that they are adverbs that conjoin two clauses. The clauses remain independent. They may be separate sentences or joined by a semi-colon. Take this example from *The Atlantic* (2015): "I feel depressed; therefore, my marriage is not working out" could instead be "I feel depressed. Therefore, my marriage is not working out."

- But a conjunctive adverb is different from a coordinator because it can move. A coordinator has to appear exactly between the two clauses, joining them from that medial position: "I feel depressed; and my marriage is not working out."

- The conjunctive adverb can appear in the same place as *and*, but it can also move in the second clause:

  - "I feel depressed; therefore, my marriage is not working out."

  - "I feel depressed; my marriage, therefore, is not working out."

  - "I feel depressed. My marriage is, therefore, not working out."

Uses of Conjunctive Adverbs

■ Why do we get such a range of conjunctive adverbs in writing? They have many uses:

☐ They can show with some specificity how two clauses are connected (versus the informal *and* and *but*).

☐ They can add to previous information (*furthermore*, *in addition*, *moreover*).

☐ They can contrast (*notwithstanding*, *nonetheless*, *nevertheless*, *in contrast*).

☐ They can illustrate (*for example*, *for instance*).

☐ They can summarize (*in short*, *in sum*).

☐ They can show sequence in time or logic (*consequently*, *therefore*, *thus*).

☐ They can emphasize (*certainly*, *indeed*).

Usage Issues

■ Let's now turn to some usage issues with conjunctive adverbs. We'll start with *however* given how many problems this causes writers. However is one of the most common conjunctive adverbs in writing. Interestingly, it is on the decline overall in writing.

■ Students often want *however* to behave like *but* and just put a comma before it rather than a semicolon. This doesn't happen to only students, either. The *Harvard Review*, for instance, announced the following on its submissions webpage: "Writers at all stages of their careers are invited to apply, however, we can only publish a very small fraction of the material we receive."

■ Usage guides would tell you that you need a semicolon before *however*, because *however* is a conjunctive adverb, not a coordinator. That would make the *Harvard Review* example: "Writers at all stages of their careers are invited to apply; however, we can only publish a very small fraction of the material we receive."

■ The question is: Can *however* be a coordinator? If enough people think it is, and treat it like it is, can it become one? Fundamentally, *however* continues to act like a conjunctive adverb because it can move around within the clause. For example: "We can publish, however, only a very small fraction of the material we receive."

■ Another consideration: Does *however* tend to occur more often initially, which would make it look and act more like a coordinator? Research using the *Corpus of Contemporary American English* and *Corpus of Historical American English* shows that clause-initial *however* has risen dramatically over the past 150 years. In other words, it has become more and more common to start a sentence with *however*.

■ As *however* becomes more and more common at the beginning of a sentence, it looks more like a coordinator. That could help explain why so many people treat *however* as a coordinator. We are left with the question of whether we can accept that *however* might be working as both a conjunctive adverb and a coordinator.

■ There is a history of prescription against using however at the beginning of the sentence. But this restriction is fading: Editors aren't editing *however* from the starts of sentences.

■ As the restriction on clause-initial *however* fades, usage guides strictly police the use of semicolons before *however* when used to connect two clauses within one sentence.

Introducing Importance

- Let's now turn to how you should introduce a sentence that you want to signal is more important than what precedes it. Should you begin, "More important," or "More importantly?"

- "Even more important" and "Even more importantly" both express the writer's stance toward the assertion. The writer believes it is more important.

- *Merriam-Webster's Dictionary of English Usage* traces debate over *more important* vs. *more importantly* back to 1968 with some commentators condemning the adverbial phrase and others, including William Safire, concluding that both were acceptable.

- *More importantly* rose dramatically from 1960. In 2000, it passed *more important* in Google Books. We're seeing exactly the same thing happen with *more notable* versus *more notably* (the latter is now more common). *More strikingly* is on the rise, although *more striking* remains more common.

Firstly and Thusly

- There is one conjunctive adverb that some argue shouldn't even be a word: *firstly*. It has long been subject of debate. In the 19th century, it was getting criticized openly. H.W. Fowler, in the early 20th century, as part of his defense of *firstly*, quoted Thomas De Quincey, who wrote, "I detest your ridiculous and most pedantic neologism of firstly."

- Thomas Lounsbury wrote about the debate about *firstly* in *Harper's* in 1905. He quoted the English poet and writer Walter Savage Landor as saying, "Firstly is not English." However, he also pointed out that letter writers such as Lady Mary Mortley Montagu and Lord Byron both used *firstly*.

- Let's be clear that *firstly* is a word. H.W. Fowler decisively dismissed the whole controversy about it, calling it "one of the harmless pedantries." But there may be reasons not to use it.

- With respect to *firstly*, Strunk and White prefer the numbers without the *–ly*: *first, second, third*. These are shorter. A more persuasive reason is that while *firstly*, *secondly*, and *thirdly* may sound OK, it starts to get awkward around *fifthly* and *sixthly*.

- Interestingly, a Google Books search shows *firstly* on the rise, but it is dwarfed by comparison with sentence-initial *First*. When in doubt, stick with *first*, but know that *firstly* is a word.

- The word *thusly* is another controversial case. This word was created in the 1800s, seemingly by humorists as a signal of uneducated usage. It has gotten picked up in more educated usage, with the meaning "in such a way." Here is an example from *Newsweek* (2009): "President Martin Van Buren described the economic crisis of 1837 in Britain and America thusly ...."

- But in 2002 usage survey, the AHD Usage Panel was given this sentence: "His letter to the editor ended thusly: 'It is time to stop fooling ourselves.'" Eighty-six percent of the panel rejected it, so *thusly* is an adverb to be wary of.

Questions to Consider

1. What kinds of words do you identify more with formal writing than with speech?

2. In your opinion, why do so many writers get confused about how to punctuate *however* when it occurs between clauses?

However to Use *However*

When a writer is struggling to get an idea onto the page, sometimes people will recommend, "Just say it out loud and then write that down" or "Just write it like you would say it." And I've been known to say this myself. That advice is fine as far as it gets you. It could help get that idea out of your head and onto the page, or hammered out onto your keyboard.

But in any formal register of writing, we should not write the way we speak. We're expected to use different vocabulary, and we're also expected to use different syntactic structures. For example, we're asked to use more subordination than we would in speech where we tend to use a lot of coordinators. In terms of different vocabulary, it's not just that in formal writing we often use more hifalutin words, that's more obvious, and it certainly is part of, for example, academic writing. We're using the jargon of whatever field we're writing in. There are also more subtle differences. And, in particular, what I want to talk about here is that we use different conjunctive adverbs in formal writing than we do in speech.

What do I mean here? To show you what I mean I'm going to tell you about some results from searches of the Corpus of Contemporary American English. As you may remember, this corpus has five registers in it. It has spoken, and then it has academic writing, newspapers, magazines, and fiction. This makes the corpus a really fun place to play to see how different words distribute across different kinds of writing, as well as how they distribute between speech and writing. First, I went in, and I searched for *therefore*. *Therefore* is far and away most common in academic writing. It occurs five times more often in academic writing than in magazines or spoken language. It occurs ten times more often in academic writing than in newspapers or fiction.

What happens if you search *thus*? Well, of course, I did that too. *Thus* is even more written. Again, it's most common in academic writing. It is more than 30 times more common in academic writing than in speech. In speech, we're much more likely to say something like *so* than we are to say *thus* or *therefore* or sometimes in speech we'll just use *and* to show a consequence. For example, we might say, "Rosie didn't get enough sleep the night before and she didn't do well on the final exam." There, the *and* is capturing consequence. As I said, in speech we tend to rely much more on coordinators like *and* than on conjunctive adverbs like *thus* and *therefore.*

What happens if you search *consequently?* Well, at this point, you can probably guess. *Consequently,* is 25 times more common in academic writing than in speech. Newspapers also don't use *consequently* very much. It's only about twice as common in newspapers as it is in speech. *Moreover,* 40 times more frequent in academic writing than speech.

Even less academic-y conjunctive adverbs or adverbials—because I'll talk about some phrases here too—even these are more common in written than spoken. For example, *in addition* is more than twice as common in newspapers and magazines than it is in speech, and then if you turn to academic writing, we seem to love *in addition.* It is more than seven times more common in academic writing than it is in speech. *Nonetheless* is four times more common in academic writing than speech. That said, *nonetheless* is more common in speech than *moreover, thus*, and some of the other ones I've talked about. There are, however, conjunctive adverbs that pattern the other way. For example, *anyway* is more common in speech, although it's also quite common in fiction where you're getting a lot of quoted speech. *Then* is more common in speech. So we do have some more colloquial conjunctive adverbs.

This seems like a good moment to back up and define a conjunctive adverb. Then we'll talk about the usage issues surrounding a few conjunctive adverbs such as *however, importantly*, in particular, *more important* versus *more importantly,* and *firstly.* The most basic definition of conjunctive adverbs is something like this. It's an adverb that conjoins two clauses. The clauses remain independent and they can even be separate sentences, or they can be put into the same sentence and conjoined by a semicolon.

Let's take this example from an article in *The Atlantic* from 2015. This uses the conjunctive adverb, *therefore*. "I feel depressed; therefore, my marriage is not working out." Now, we could turn that into two separate clauses and put a period in there instead of a semicolon. "I feel depressed. Therefore, my marriage is not working out." A conjunctive adverb is different from a coordinator because it can move. In the example I just gave you, the *therefore* was sitting right in between the two clauses, but it can move. Let me explain, and to do this, we're going to review a little bit of what we talked about with coordinators. A coordinator has to appear exactly between the two clauses, joining them from that medial position. If we take that same sentence from *The Atlantic* and put a coordinator in you can see it can't move. "I feel depressed, and my marriage is not working out." That *and* is stuck right there.

The conjunctive adverb, as I noted, can appear in the same place as *and*, but it can also move within the second clause. So here it is right in between: "I feel depressed; therefore, my marriage is not working out." But it could also be: "I feel depressed; my marriage, therefore, is not working out." Or we could move the *therefore* a little further down in this second clause: "I feel depressed. My marriage is, therefore, not working out." As we talked about, adverbs are relatively free when it comes to word order, and conjunctive adverbs follow that pattern, although sometimes we don't like them at the end of a clause. For example, I don't know how you'd feel about "I feel depressed; my marriage is not working out, therefore." You could do it, but it may not sound great to you.

Why do we get such a range of conjunctive adverbs in writing? There are real benefits to conjunctive adverbs that help us as writers. They can show with specificity how two clauses are connected with much more specificity than the more informal *and* and *but*. Here's some of the semantic work that these conjunctive adverbs can do. They can add to the previous utterance. This would be adverbs such as *furthermore*, *in addition*, *moreover*. The can express contrast: *notwithstanding, nevertheless, nonetheless, in contrast.* They can illustrate: *for example, for instance.* They can summarize: *in short, in sum.* Conjunctive adverbs can also show a sequence in time or in logic: *consequently, therefore, thus.* These adverbs can also emphasize, words like *certainly* and *indeed*.

Let's now turn to some usage issues with conjunctive adverbs, and we have to start with *however*. And why do we have to start with *however?* We have to start there given how many problems this causes writers. As a teacher of writing, I have to say I think I spend more time trying to help students understand how to punctuate *however* than I do on almost any other usage issue. *However* is one of the most common conjunctive adverbs in writing. In data from 2000–2009, in writing *however* is 2.5 times more common than *thus*, four times more common than *therefore*, and nine times more common than *nevertheless* When we write, we really like the word *however.*

Interestingly, though, *however* does look like it's on the decline overall in writing. This could be part of a bigger trend that linguists call colloquialization, which is that writing is becoming more like speech. In other words, it's becoming more informal. Now, that said, as I'm talking about in this lecture, there is still a pretty big gap between the way we speak and the way we write, but they might be getting a little bit closer. I've been doing a study of *however* with Lizzie Hutton, who's a graduate student at the University of Michigan. We were both interested in *however* given just how much students struggle with this issue of how to handle *however.* They often want to make *however* behave like *but* and just put a comma before it and let it act like a coordinator rather than putting a semicolon before it and putting a comma after it.

And it's not just students who are struggling with *however. The Harvard Review*, for instance, announced the following on its submissions web page: "Writers at all stages of their careers are invited to apply, however, we can only publish a very small fraction of the material we receive."

There's that *however* as a coordinator with commas on both sides. Usage guides would tell us that we need a semicolon here before the *however* because *however* is a conjunctive adverb, not a coordinator. They would say we need: "Writers at all stages of their careers are invited to apply; however, we can only publish a very small fraction of the material we receive."

Given this, Lizzie Hutton and I found ourselves asking: Can *however* be a coordinator? If enough people think it is, and treat it like it is, can it become one? Fundamentally, *however* continues to act like a conjunctive adverb because it can move around within the clause. That hurts our argument about whether or not it can become a coordinator. Let me give you an example of it moving around, "We can publish, however, only a very small fraction of the material we receive."

But we got curious about why so many writers want to punctuate *however* as if it were a coordinator. It can move around the sentence, yes. But does it tend to occur more often initially, which would make it look and act more like a coordinator? This research that we're doing is ongoing, but I wanted to tell you about it as an example of the kind of grammatical research that one can do about potential changes in the language. We used resources that I've been talking about in this course, the Corpus of Contemporary American English and the Corpus of Historical American English, which allows you to search written language from 1810 until 2009. Then we had to figure out how to search for *however* as a conjunctive adverb because we needed to rule out sentences like this one, "However you want to get there is fine with me." It's a perfectly fine sentence, but it's not the *however* we're after. As a result, what we searched for was "; *however*," and ". *However*," we also searched for ", *however*,".

We were surprised by what we found: clause-initial *however*—*however* right there at the beginning of the clause—has risen dramatically over the past 150 years. In other words, it has become more and more common to start a sentence with however. In fact, in the data from the Corpus of Contemporary American English, between 2010 and 2015, sentence-initial *however* becomes more common than *however* in the middle of the sentence of the sentence or clause. Why does that matter? Why were Lizzie and I so excited when we found that? As however becomes more and more common at the beginning of a sentence, it looks more like a coordinator. That could help explain why so many people treat *however* as a coordinator, and we're left with a question of whether we can accept that *however* might be working both as a conjunctive adverb and a coordinator. This research that we've been doing has been generating very interesting conversation with our colleagues as we try to sort through what the data tells—or tell—us.

Now, did you know that there is a history of prescription about not using however at the beginning of a sentence? I have to say this is not something that I was taught as a writer at any point in my writing career. But, here is William Strunk in the very first edition of *The Elements of Style,* published in 1918. He advises that *however,* "in the meaning nevertheless," is "not to come first in the sentence or clause." In the now classic 1959 version of this book, revised and expanded by E.B. White, this prescription is expanded a little bit. That edition says, "Avoid starting a sentence with *however* when the meaning is *nevertheless.* The word usually serves better when not in first position." Bryan Garner, in *Modern American Usage,* calls *however* at the beginning of a sentence or clause a "stylistic lapse."

These criticisms seem a little odd given how common sentence-initial *however* is, even in formal writing. Are editors editing this out? Clearly not.

What does the Usage Panel for *American Heritage Dictionary* have to say? This was just added to the 2015 ballot. The editors had not surveyed the panel about it before. Only 10 percent of the Usage Panel reported that they always follow the rule, another 30 percent said that they usually or sometimes follow the rule that you should not begin a sentence or clause with *however.* Sixty percent said that they rarely or never do so. And I have to say, as you now already know, I was part of that 60 percent. Clearly, this is a rule that is fading; I wouldn't call it a stylistic lapse.

As the restriction on clause-initial or sentence-initial *however* fades and we continue to use clause-initial *however* more frequently usage guides must now police the use of that semicolon before *however.* If we're going to use *however* to connect two clauses and have it start the second clause they want us to put that semicolon right before the however. This advice is all over the web and all over usage books, and I myself, as a teacher of English, I continue to enforce this rule. We all can and probably will potentially get judged based on our understanding of how to punctuate *however.*

I was very interested therefore to know what the Usage Panel had to say about the rules we follow about punctuating *however*. The editors of AHD added another question under *however* to see whether it or not it was acceptable to punctuate *however* as a coordinator. The sentence that they gave the Panel was this: "Main Street will be closed to traffic for the parade, however, the stores along it will remain open." Eighty-six percent of the Panel called this unacceptable. I was part of that eighty-six percent. When I did searches of edited writing it is very hard to find *however* punctuated with those two commas as a coordinator, and I said, right now, that's unacceptable. What I'm by is that struck that 14 percent of the Usage Panel said it was somewhat or completely acceptable. We'll keep tracking this to see what's going on with *however*.

Let's now turn to how you should introduce a sentence that you want to signal is more important than what precedes it. Should you say "More important, blah blah blah," or "More importantly, blah blah blah"? And clearly, whatever "blah blah blah" is is important. This came to my attention when a very well-known popular author's mother e-mailed me with a concern about how he started a sentence in his book. He started the sentence with "Even more strikingly," and she thought it should be "Even more striking." This got me digging because I hadn't really thought about this issue before. It turns out that the mother is using the form that is more common in writing, the linking adjective phrase "even more striking," but there aren't good grounds to criticize the conjunctive adverb choice.

Let's talk about this issue using *more importantly, more importantly* instead of *more striking, more strikingly* as the one with *important* that has gotten attention in usage guides. *Even more important* and *even more importantly* both express the writer's stance toward the assertion the writer believes that whatever they're about to say is more important. If we didn't have the *even more* there or just the *more*, we would want *importantly*. We wouldn't just put *important* comma and then just keep going, but should we say *more important* or *more importantly?* The *Merriam-Webster's Dictionary of English Usage* traces the debate over *more important* versus *more importantly* back to 1968 with some commentators condemning the adverbial phrase *more importantly,* and others, including William Safire, concluding that both were acceptable.

Why did this come up in the 1960s? I think it's because *more importantly* was just taking off as a conjunctive adverb. In Google Books, if you search Google books with the Ngram Viewer, you find that *more important* has been on the rise. It was on the rise for much of the 20th century and peaked in about the 1970s. *More importantly* rose dramatically between 1960 and 2000. And in 2000 it passed *more important* in Google Books. As commentators were noticing this new thing, as they were noticing that more and more people were using *more importantly* they became wary of this new construction. We're seeing exactly the same thing happen with *more notable* versus *more notably*. *More notably* is now more common than *more notable*. *More strikingly* is also on the rise, although here, *more striking* remains more common, which is probably why the mother who e-mailed me may have noticed the *more strikingly* and thought it was wrong. What we're seeing here I think is shifts in language taste and language style. It's about what phrasing we prefer at a given moment in time.

To conclude the lecture, I want to talk about a conjunctive adverb that some argue shouldn't even be a word. This would be *firstly*. Even though the word *firstly* was in the language at the time, it is not in Samuel Johnson's 1755 Dictionary. By the 19th century *firstly* was coming to be criticized openly. Now, H.W. Fowler, in his usage guide in the early 20th century, actually comes to the defense of *firstly*, and as part of his defense, he quotes some of the criticism. He quotes Thomas De Quincey, who wrote in 1847, and here I quote, "I detest your ridiculous and most pedantic neologism of firstly." Thomas Lounsbury wrote about the debate about *firstly* in *Harper's* in 1905. He quoted the English poet and writer Walter Savage Landor as saying "Firstly is not English," but Lounsbury also pointed out that letter writers such as Lady Mary Montagu and Lord Byron both used *firstly*.

It's interesting to think about why we're even debating the question of whether *firstly* is a word. We don't debate whether *secondly* is a word, or *thirdly* is a word. Those are totally fine. But for some reason, at some point, people latched onto *firstly* and said, "That one, we don't like," perhaps because it's the first in the row of *firstly, secondly, thirdly*, but it does show the ways in which our social judgments of words are idiosyncratic. That we will pick one word, in this case out of a lineup, and say that one's not a word, whereas the other ones in the sequence are OK. There's also the question of, for you, when does that sequence stop being OK? *Firstly, secondly, thirdly, fourthly*—that one's OK for me—*fifthly*, eh, *sixthly*. For me, by the time we get to *seventhly*, I'm really struggling. I don't like it anymore. I need to be doing sixth, seventh.

Given this discussion of *firstly* are you wondering if *thusly* is OK? According to the AHD Usage Panel, not so much. The word *thusly* was created in the 1800s, and it looks like it was created primarily by humorists as a signal of uneducated usage, in other words, they were putting it into the speech of people they were trying to characterize in particular ways. From there, *thusly* got picked up in more educated usage—beware of the words you create, you never know what's going to happen to them—and it got picked up with the meaning "in such a way." *Thusly* is still in the language, meaning that. Here is an example from *Newsweek* from 2009, "President Martin Van Buren described the economic crisis of 1837 in Britain and America thusly…" In other words, he described it in "such a way."

So there's *thusly* in *Newsweek*. What happened when *thusly* was given to the AHD Usage Panel? It was on the survey in 2002 and the Panel was given the following sentence: "His letter to the editor ended thusly: 'It is time to stop fooling ourselves.'" Eighty-eight percent of the Panel rejected it. Eighty-eight percent rejected *thusly* used this way. Given that, I would say that this is an adverb to be wary of.

How did you like that preposition at the end of my sentence? I'm going to claim it was a conscious choice, as the next two lectures are all about prepositions, including a whole lecture devoted to the idea that you shouldn't end a sentence with a preposition.

Lecture
17

Squirrels and Prepositions

This lecture is all about prepositions. We'll start by unpacking the concern about *different than* versus *different from*, touching on the idiomatic nature of prepositions in English. Then we'll take a step back to nail down just what prepositions are. From there, we'll cover issues like *between* versus *among* and *toward* versus *towards*. Then we'll end by looking at a fascinating change with the word *because*, along with why new prepositions are rare.

Different From or Than?

- One question on prepositions is: Is *different than* or *different from* correct? A common sentiment is that the adjective *different* does not set up a comparison on a scale the way that *more than* or *less than* do, so *than* is inappropriate. With *different*, we are distinguishing one thing *from* another thing.

- But the argument that because "X differs from Y," it should be *different from* isn't completely persuasive either: Prepositions don't hold across parts of speech. We sympathize *with* others but express sympathy *for* them.

- One fundamental issue at play here is that prepositions in English are not a totally rational bunch of words; instead, they are highly idiomatic. Why is it *due to* instead of *due by*? Why is it *in addition* instead of *on addition*?

- *Different than* initially came under criticism long ago. Robert Baker in *Reflections on the English Language* (1770) called *different*

The advice that prepositions cover "everything a squirrel can do with respect to a tree" runs into trouble with sentences like, "The squirrel was until the tree."

than "not English." This didn't pick up steam until the end of the 19th century, when *different than* came to be widely critiqued.

- It remains a construction many editors in the U.S. will correct toward *different from*, but not all the time: Since the mid-20th century, people have been opting for *different than* when it is followed by a clause, not a noun phrase.

- For example, take this sentence: "Social norms for Generation Xers are different than they were for Millennials." We can't use *from* here, because it would create: "Social norms for Generation Xers are different from they were for Millennials."

- *Different from* is still often seen as the most formal and standard in written American English, but there is nothing wrong with *different than*, and it is the standard alternative when there is a clause following the adjective *different*.

Changing Attitudes

- The way we deal with the word *sympathy* shows that attitudes about which preposition is the correct one change over time. We now say "sympathize with" but "feel sympathy for."

- But in the 19th century, essayist Thomas De Quincy called *sympathy for* a "monstrous barbarism." Prepositions may be little words, but people care about them.

Defining Prepositions

- Prepositions are notoriously hard to define and yet English grammar is highly dependent on them. A very common definition from Margaret Shertzer in *The Elements of Grammar* is this: "A preposition is a connecting word that shows the relation of a noun or pronoun to some other word in a sentence."

- Strunk and White define a preposition as "A word that relates its object (a noun, pronoun, or *–ing* verb form) to another word in the sentence."

- *The Riverside Handbook* puts it this way: "Prepositions show relationships between words, often relationships over time and space." They're always followed by a noun phrase (noun, pronoun, or gerund) and show relationships.

- One grammar guide tells us that a preposition isn't a preposition unless it has that related noun or pronoun as its object. This is the standard way of looking at prepositions, and you'll find it in pretty much every dictionary and every grammar book except one: Rodney Huddleston and Geoff Pullum's *Cambridge Grammar of the English Language*.

- As noted, prepositions often show relationships in terms of time (examples: *before*, *after*) and location (examples: *over*, *through*, *inside*). They can also show comparison and other distinctions, for example, *unlike*, *except*, and *excluding*. And they can focus our attention (example: *regarding*) or set up opposition (example: *versus*).

- Prepositions can also do grammatical work similar to the work that inflectional endings carry; for example, we have the possessive *of*: "The name of the ship." This brings up an interesting usage issue: double possessives.

  □ Is it "a friend of Kate's" or "a friend of Kate"? It seems much more colloquial to say "a friend of Kate's," but it is doubly marked, so is it wrong?

  □ Some would relegate it to informal contexts, but you can find it in more formal ones. And there are a few double possessives that are mandatory, for example, "a friend of mine" instead of a "friend of me."

- Interestingly, some single possessive alternatives are problematic and not all double possessives are idiomatic. As an example of the former, we can't say, "a bicycle of Kate" to indicate possession. As an example of the latter, we have double possessives that don't sound right: We can say "the name of the ship" but not "the name of the ship's."

Between, Among, Toward, and Towards

- Let's now turn to two other usage issues: *between* vs. *among*, and *toward* vs. *towards*. The rule about when to use *between* and when to use *among* can seem straightforward: Use *between* for two things and *among* for three or more things.

- But here's another way to think about it: Use *between* when talking about two things, and *between* or *among* when talking about three or more things depending on whether you're talking about them individually, or in terms of relationships in pairs (*between*), or whether you are talking about all the things and their relationship collectively.

- According to this principle, you could say, "I am choosing between the salmon, tuna, and swordfish for dinner." That works if you're looking at each fish individually. You need to know that style guides don't consistently disagree with this.

- Although etymologically, *between* goes back to mean "by two," it has been used for more than two things since Old English. According to the blog of the Oxford dictionaries, it should be, "A treaty was drawn up between France, Germany, Italy, and Greece," but, "There was agreement among members of NATO."

- Strunk and White are on the same page: Usually when there are more than two, we should use *among*, but when it is about individual relationships, we should use *between*.

- Several commentators on this question point out the difference between "Anne ran among the cars" and "Anne ran between the cars." The first suggests Anne weaving in and out; the second has Anne running with lines of cars on both sides.

- Regarding *toward* and *towards*: The bottom line here is that both are standard. *Towards* is more British and *toward* more American.

Because Prepositions

- Throughout this lecture, we've covered changes in preposition usage, but we haven't covered making new prepositions—and that's because it almost never happens. Historically, occasionally a borrowing such as *during* came in from Old French. Every once in a while, a participle will become a preposition (e.g., *considering*).

- In this context, linguists are very interested in what is happening with *because*, and they have been debating how to describe this new or expanded usage. Here's an example: "I can't diet because chocolate." It can also occur with adjective and interjections: "because tired" and "because argh."

- Can a preposition do that? Geoff Pullum says yes, but the linguist blogger Gretchen McCulloch says no. Pullum says that *because* has always been a preposition, rather than a subordinating conjunction. He argues that we need to recognize that prepositions can be followed by nouns, clauses, prepositional phrases, or nothing.

- *Because* has traditionally taken a clause or a prepositional phrase with *of*: "because of the cold." It is now expanding to take nouns and pronouns, and possibly adjectives as well.

Suggested Reading

Curzan, *Fixing English*.
Fogarty, *Grammar Girl: Quick and Dirty Tips*, http://www.quickanddirtytips.com/grammar-girl.
Yagoda, *When You Catch an Adjective, Kill It*.

Questions to Consider

1. Prepositions are notoriously idiomatic (e.g., *due to* not *due by*; *in addition* not *on addition*). Come up with two examples of expressions with prepositions where it is difficult to explain the logic.

2. Did you learn that *between* should be used for two items and *among* for three or more items? If so, try to imagine instances where you would want to use *between* for three or more items.

Squirrels and Prepositions

It is always interesting to me what language pet peeves jump to mind when people meet me and find out what I do. Last fall, I was at a tailgate for a football game at the University of Michigan, and I met an alumna who was a retired teacher. And we talked about what I did at the university, and she then said, "Oh, you know what always gets to me is people who say 'different than' instead of 'different from.'"

I was struck that this is the pet peeve that first jumped to mind for this former teacher. That said, I have a colleague in my department at the University of Michigan who has very strong feelings that it should be "different from," not "different than." At the same time, I have several other colleagues in the department who don't have strong feelings at all about whether it should be "different from" or "different than." I haven't yet surveyed everyone in the department yet.

This conversation I've been having about "different from" and "different than" with my colleagues reminds me of what students are navigating as they move among or between—we'll come back that—classes where professors have different usage issues that they notice. It's especially hard for students if professors have policies about, for example, losing X number of points for two or three grammatical errors per page. As this course has been making abundantly clear, people who know and people who care a lot about grammar do not all agree on what is an error, or a stylistic lapse, or an ill-advised choice—whether those people are writing usage guides, or serving on the American Heritage Dictionary Usage Panel, or editing academic journals or newspapers. In the case we're talking about here, students are navigating the choice between two prepositions, "from" and "than," and students will have routinely heard both "different from" and "different than" in spoken American English

This lecture is all about prepositions, and let's start by unpacking the concern about "different than." What I hear most often is that the adjective different does not set up a comparison on a scale the way that something like "more than" or "less than" does, so "than" is inappropriate. With "different," we are distinguishing one thing from another thing. In addition, we say that "X differs from Y," so we should say "X is different from Y," not "X is different than Y."

Of course, one could make the argument that difference is a form of comparison; we have to compare things to see that they're different. But I understand the point—that it is not a comparison on a continuum the way that more and less work. The argument that "because X differs from Y," means that it should be "X is different from Y" isn't completely persuasive to me. Prepositions don't necessarily hold across parts of speech. For example, we sympathize with others but express sympathy for others. One fundamental issue at play here is that prepositions in English are not a totally rational bunch of words; instead, they are highly idiomatic. Think about this: Why is it "due to?" Why isn't it "due by?" I think you could argue that would make just as much sense. Why is it "in addition" instead of "on addition," or "by addition," or "through addition?"

In any case, let's return to "different from" versus "different than." First, we need to add to the mix "different to," which is widely used in British English and, again, highlights how idiomatic usage is with prepositions. "Different to" is the oldest of the three; it goes back to the 16th century. "Different than" goes back to the 17th century. And "different from" appears about the same time. All three appear to have been in standard usage.

When did "different than" start to get criticized? It looks like it starts with Robert Baker in Reflections on the English Language, published in 1770. He calls "different than" not English. This criticism is not widely picked up until the end of the 19th century, and then "different than" comes to be widely critiqued. It remains a construction that many editors in the U.S. will correct toward "different from," but not all the time. Since the mid-20th century, people have been opting for different than when it is followed by a clause rather than a noun phrase. I would guess you do too, and let me show you what I mean.

Let's look at examples to show when you might want to use different than rather than different from, depending on whether you have a clause or a noun phrase. Let's start with a noun phrase. Take this sentence: "Millennials aren't all that different from GenXers." This could also be "than." "Millennials aren't all that different than GenXers," but that's the one that gets criticized. But now let's look at it with a clause: "Social norms for GenXers are different than they were for Millennials." "Are different than they were for millennials." We don't want to use "from" here. This, I think, doesn't sound right: "Social norms for GenXers are different from they were for Millennials." The only way to use "from here" is to do a somewhat awkward rewrite to get a noun phrase after "from." We could say "Social norms for GenXers are different from the way they were for Millennials." Or, "Social norms for GenXers are different from how they were for Millennials."

In sum, "different from," "different than," "different to" can all be considered within the realm of standard, especially if we look at speech. And all have been used by well-known authors for several centuries. "Different from" is still often seen as the most formal and perhaps the most standard in written American English, but there's nothing wrong with "different than," and it is the standard alternative when there's a clause following it instead of a noun phrase. I recognize that you may have been looking for more definitive advice about what is right and wrong with "different from" versus "different than," but I just can't responsibly give it to you. You will run into editors who care about this one and editors who don't care about this one. And if educated usage is your guide, you will find a mixed bag; you'll find both "different from" and "different than" even when you have a noun phrase after it. Rather than feel frustrated by the fact that there isn't a clear-cut right or wrong answer here, perhaps this is a place where we can all enjoy the flexibility that is sometimes allowed within the formal standard.

Before we go any further, I want to note another example that shows that attitudes about which preposition is the correct one change over time. We now say "sympathize with someone," but "feel sympathy for someone."

That is now totally standard. And while we can say "feel sympathy with someone," it is much more common to say "fell sympathy for someone." It might surprise you to know that in the 19th century, the essayist Thomas De Quincy called "sympathy for" to feel sympathy for someone a monstrous barbarism. Prepositions may be little words, but let it not be said that people do not care about their prepositions.

This seems like an apt moment to step back and define prepositions more specifically than "little words," and I realize it may not be reassuring for me to say that I don't have a very good definition of what a preposition is—and it's not just me. Prepositions are notoriously hard to define and yet English grammar, at this point, is highly dependent on them.

For those of you who remember *Grammar Rock*, there is the song "Busy Prepositions" It compares prepositions with busy bees and ants because they're such an important part in the language. The song goes on in the chorus to list the busiest of the prepositions: "Of, on, to, with, in, from / By, for, at, over, across."

Many years ago when I was teaching prepositions in a class on grammar, and I was asking the students what definitions they had learned, one student gave me this definition that he had learned from a teacher in seventh grade: "A preposition is everything a squirrel can do with respect to a tree." I love that. It accounts for prepositions such as up, down, in, around, toward, to, into, over, under, behind, at, beside, near. The squirrel is doing all those things with respect to the tree. But, it doesn't account for some other prepositions, like since, or including, during, unlike, until. Although the sentence "The squirrel was until the tree" is kind of a wonderful sentence, that poor squirrel.

Here is a very common definition of a preposition; I've taken this from Margaret Shertzer's, *The Elements of Grammar*—and here, I'll quote— "A preposition is a connecting word that shows the relation of a noun or pronoun to some other word in a sentence." So she says, "noun or pronoun;" it probably would be more accurate to say the relationship of a noun phrase to other words in the sentence. Here's Strunk and White in the fourth edition of Elements of Style: and they say a preposition is "A word that relates its object—a noun, pronoun, or -ing verb form—to another word in the sentence." You're getting the theme here; this is about relationships between nouns or noun-like things and something else in the sentence. Here's the Riverside Handbook: "Prepositions show relationships between words, often relationships over time and space." So, prepositions—here's one thing we can say—are always followed by a noun phrase, be that a noun, pronoun, gerund; and they show relationships. One grammar guide tells us a preposition isn't a preposition unless it has that related noun or pronoun as its object.

This is the standard way of looking at prepositions—that they require a noun phrase after them. And you'll find it in pretty much every dictionary and every grammar book except for one. This would be Rodney Huddleston and Geoff Pullum's *Cambridge Grammar of the English Language*. This is a magisterial work. It is a descriptive grammar that runs hundreds and hundreds of pages as they try to capture what we actually do in English grammar. And they're also trying to help us rethink some of our terminology. They trouble this definition of a preposition and the distinction between prepositions and conjunctions. We'll come back to this at the end of the lecture.

As noted, prepositions often show relationships in terms of time and location. Let me show you some examples. Prepositions that show relationships in time—this would be things like "before today," "after midnight," "since 1980," "during the Cold War," "at 3:00." All those little prepositions are helping us understand where we are in relation to time. They can also help us know where we are in relation to location—"over the river," "through the woods," "inside the house," "beneath the stairs." Prepositions also can show comparison and other distinctions; for example, "unlike Harry Potter," "except that one," "excluding money." They also can focus our attention; for example, "regarding this situation." Or they set up oppositions—think about a preposition like "versus." Prepositions can also do grammatical work similar to the work that inflectional endings carry, or at least that inflectional endings historically carried. Here's one example: we have the possessive "of" in English, and we also have that possessive final S, as in "Anne's." In English, we can show possession; therefore, through that final S or through "of"—which means we can say, "John's book," or "the name of the ship."

Now here is an interesting usage issue: double possessives. In some ways, these double possessives should be criticized, but they're not. Is it "a friend of Kate's" or "a friend of Kate?" For me, it is much more colloquial to say "a friend of Kate's," but it is doubly marked; you have the "of" and you have the possessive S. So is it wrong? Some would relegate these double possessives to informal contexts, but you can find them in more formal ones. And there are a few double possessives that are mandatory. For example, "a friend of mine," where you have "of" and you have the possessive pronoun "mine." But you wouldn't say, "a friend of me." So when the object of "of" is a personal pronoun, you're going to get a double possessive.

Interestingly, some single possessive alternatives are problematic, and not all double possessives are idiomatic. Here's an instance where the single possessive doesn't sound right. Let's imagine that we're talking about Kate's bicycle instead of Kate's friend. As you recall, we could say "a friend of Kate's" or "a friend of Kate." But while we can say "a bicycle of Kate's," I think most of us cannot say "a bicycle of Kate." On the flip side, we have double possessives that don't sound right. We can say "the name of the ship" but not "the name of the ship's."

There's a detailed treatment of this issue of double possessive by Grammar Girl, whose name is Mignon Fogarty, and she has a blog—a website called Grammar Girl. And it's a really nice blog; it really strives to provide relatively balanced grammar advice with some historical perspective. The blog post on double possessives describes a general rule that the object must be human in order to take a double possessive, which would explain why we wouldn't say "the name of the ship's." Grammar Girl then gives the example that we can't say "a friend of the museum's." But, in fact, if you search actual usage—and you may already be thinking this—you can find examples of "a friend of the museum's." I don't know if that's because museum is representing a set of people or somehow the museum is personified there. So it is generally a solid rule about when we can and can't get double possessives—that what comes after the "of" is to be human, but being the creative speakers that we are, there are also exceptions like "a friend of the museum's."

As I mentioned before, prepositions are highly idiomatic, as anyone who has taught or learned English as a second or foreign language can tell you. And I know this from having taught English as a second language myself. My students would ask, "When is it a story 'about' versus a story 'of?'" And I really had no good explanation. And then we could add to the mix that if we do a feature story, it's a feature on something. While we're at it, why is it "on purpose," but "by accident?" And here, I do want to note that things are changing, which you would know if you talk with teenagers or younger children who now, more often than not, do things "on accident." Well, it may not be fair to say more often than not, but certainly, a lot of them are now doing things on accident that is coming into the language. And I would guess that in the long run, if we take the long view, on accident will win. My brother-in-law, in response to this, is now threatening to say "by purpose."

Let's now turn to two other usage issues: "between" versus "among," and "toward" versus "towards." Then we'll end by looking at a fascinating change with the word "because." The rule about when to use "between" and when to use "among" can seem straightforward—use "between" for two things and "among" for three or more things. Let's imagine you're at a restaurant for dinner. You're perusing the menu in the older sense of that term—you're reading it carefully. You narrow it down, and you are now choosing between salmon and tuna for dinner. Or let's imagine that you're having trouble narrowing it down, in which case you are choosing among the many entrees on the menu. But you know by now that when I say a rule seems straightforward that all odds are that I'm then going to say that it isn't.

Here's another way to think about this rule about "between" and "among:" use "between" when we are talking about two things, and then you can use "between" or "among" when talking about three or more things. Whether you want to use "between" or "among" with three or more things depends on whether you're talking about those things individually; or in terms of their relationship in pairs, in which case you would use "between;" or whether you are talking about all of the things and their relationship collectively, in which case you would use "among." According to this principle, I could say that "I am choosing between the salmon, tuna, and swordfish for dinner." I'm looking at each of those individually

If you're thinking, "But that's wrong. That's not the way I learned it," you need to know that style guides won't consistently back you on this. And although etymologically "between" goes back to "by two," it has been used for more than two things since Old English.

On the *Oxford Dictionaries* blog, they talk about the way in which, according to them, we should say, "A treaty was drawn up between France, Germany, Italy, and Greece" because we're talking about the individual relationships there. But we would say, "There was agreement among the members of NATO." Strunk and White, in *The Elements of Style*, are on the same page. They note that usually when there are more than two, we should use "among." But when it is about individual relationships, use "between." Bryan Garner in *Modern American Usage* reminds us that "between" is the only word we have to describe the relationship of a thing or person to many other things severally and individually

Then several commentators on this question point out the difference between "Anne ran among the cars" and "Anne ran between the cars." "Anne ran among the cars" suggests me weaving in and out of the cars, whereas "Anne ran between the cars" suggests perhaps two lines of cars and I'm running down the middle. While we're at it, let me just say that I now read "amongst" in a lot of student papers. Bryan Garner says that "amongst" is now old-fashioned and even pretentious, but I would keep your eye on this one. There is something afoot with "amongst."

I also now see a lot of "towards" in student writing in addition to "toward." The bottom line here is that both are standard. "Towards" with an S is more British, and "toward" without an S is more American. Someone once told me to remember it by thinking that the Brits like to make the word longer; which is actually not a very helpful way to remember it, and yet I do. When I searched Google Books with the Ngram Viewer to see what was going on here, what I found was an upswing in "toward" in British English; and since 2000, an upswing in "towards"—the British form—in American English. So perhaps, at some point, we'll meet in the middle. Right now, you really can't go wrong with either one.

Throughout this lecture, I've been talking about changes in preposition usage—and perhaps form, such as "toward" and "towards"—but I haven't talked about making new prepositions, and that's because we almost never do. Prepositions are a closed class; they don't tend to admit new members. Now, of course, historically we have occasionally had borrowings of prepositions; such as "during," which came into English from Old French. And every once in a while, a participle will become a preposition, such as "considering." "Than" was—T-H-A-N—was historically a conjunction and now can also be used as a preposition, although not all grammarians agree on that one.

In this context, linguists are very interested in what is happening with "because," and they have been debating how to describe this new or expanded usage of "because." This would be the "because" that we see in something like "because science," or "because the Internet." Here's one of my favorite examples: "I can't diet because chocolate." Or students will say to me, "I'm stressed because exams."

Now maybe you're thinking, "I can't use because that way," and I have to say I can't really use because that way. I know it's out there, and I can do it now as a joke, but it's not really part of my grammar. I need a full clause after "because," not just a noun phrase. And it can be more than a noun phrase; this new use of "because" can also occur with adjectives and with interjections. For example, "because tired," "because argh." Can a preposition do that? Geoff Pullum says yes; the linguist blogger Gretchen McCulloch says no. Here are Pullum's examples to show that a preposition can do this with an adjective, or an interjection, or an adverb: He says, look at "I've moved on from frustrated," which sounds perfectly grammatical to me. He also gives us this example: "There is no way to do this except cautiously." Now one could argue that you have ellipsis here; that you're just leaving out the rest of the clause; but colloquially, at least, we can follow a preposition with adjectives and adverbs, as well as interjections.

Pullum is actually making a bigger argument here. He says that "because" has always been a preposition rather than a subordinating conjunction or a subordinator, and that we need to recognize that prepositions can be followed by noun phrases, by clauses, by prepositional phrases, or by nothing. He then looks at "because" and says, "'Because' has traditionally been followed by a clause or by a prepositional phrase that starts with 'of.'" For example, "because of the cold." Pullum then interprets what we're now seeing with "because" as an expansion of its function—that it can now take on noun phrases, and pronouns, and maybe adjectives. I recognize that this distinction of how to think about "because" as a subordinator or a preposition gets a little technical, but I appreciate that within the field of linguistics, linguists continue to debate what is the correct terminology to capture the most appropriate categories to describe English grammar most accurately.

Members of the American Dialect Society, which is an academic society to which I belong, were so interested in what is happening with "because" that we voted "because" plus noun as the word of the year for 2013. Now, we've been voting on the word of the year for about 25 years now. We vote every year in January, at our annual meeting, and this is a gathering of— it used to be fairly small, maybe about 60—now you get several hundred people in the room, and we consider new words of that year. Now, these could be words that are completely new, or they could be words that are newly prominent to a given year. In the past, we have voted for—for example—"Y2K" as the word of the year for 1999. "Chad" was the word of the year in 2000. Other words of the year include "bailout," "subprime," "app," "hashtag." For the year 2015, it was "singular they," in particular as it is used as the term of choice for individuals who identify outside the male/ female binary.

In 2013, it was "because" plus noun. Now, this choice was a little hard to explain to the press that we left our vote, and the press said, "What's the word of the year?" And we said, "Because." And they looked at us like "What kind of word of the year is that? That's not new." But what we were trying to capture here is that we were interested in this new use of "because"—"because" plus noun. It took a little explaining, but they were very interesting conversations to have. And we voted for it as the word of the year because when you think about it, it really is a historical oddity for "because" to become a preposition or to expand its prepositional reach. Given that, it seemed like a great choice as the word of the year. And I want to note here that it beat out "slash." "Slash" was the runner-up as a new coordinator. 2013 gave us some very interesting choices to think about as what should be the word of the year, and I was struck that we had two new function words competing for the title.

We're finished with this lecture, but we're not finished with prepositions. In the next lecture, we'll turn to probably the best-known rule about prepositions: don't end a sentence with one. Or, prepositions are words you shouldn't end sentences with.

Stranded Prepositions

An old joke about prepositions goes like this: A freshman on Harvard campus asks a senior, "Excuse me, can you tell me where the library is at?" The senior replies haughtily, "At Harvard, we do not end a sentence with a preposition." The first-year student tries again: "Can you tell me where the library is at, jerk?" The rule about not ending a sentence with a preposition is widely known. We're going to spend this entire lecture on it because it is so well known and widely enforced, and yet there is confusion about when it should apply and whether it is a worthwhile rule to follow at all.

The Joke

- Let's start with what is going on in the joke. The question "Where is the library at?" ends in a preposition, but concern about this construction is not really about the preposition. It's more about the redundancy of "Where … at." The *at* is not stranded.

- This sentence, however, has a stranded preposition: "Which library are we meeting at?" The preposition gets stranded when the noun moves up to the front of the clause. There are two times when that fronting happens: wh-questions and relative clauses.

- Wh-questions involve interrogative pronouns: *who*, *what*, *where*, *when*, *why*, and *how*. That interrogative pronoun gets put at the front of the question, no matter what function it plays in the sentence: "What did you eat for dinner?"

- If the interrogative pronoun is the object of a preposition, it can still front, with or without the preposition. Let's look at an example, first with the question in a form where the interrogative pronoun is still positioned as the object of the preposition: "You cooked dinner for whom?" can become "Whom did you cook dinner for?"

- Both of these are completely grammatical in English in the descriptive sense; the question is whether we find it more pleasing to front the preposition too. The term in linguistics for this is pied-piping, which we covered in Lecture 7.

- The same kind of fronting happens in relative clauses with *which*. For example: "That is the house that I was telling you about" can also be "That is the house about which I was telling you." Both of these sentences are fully grammatical, although the second one sounds very formal.

The Rule's Origins

- We know that there is a rule that we shouldn't strand a preposition at the end of a sentence. Where does that rule come from? John Dryden (who also proposed a language academy in the 1660s) is usually cited as the first to notice and disparage the stranded preposition.

  - In 1672 he picked out for critique the writing of Ben Jonson. Here's the line from Jonson: "The bodies that those souls were frighted from."

  - Dryden commented: "The Preposition in the end of the sentence; a common fault with him, and which I have but lately observ'd in my own writings." He subsequently not only avoided stranded prepositions in his own prose but went back and revised earlier work that contained stranded prepositions.

- Interestingly, if we go back to Ben Jonson's 1640 grammar, we see that he very descriptively notes that prepositions "follow sometimes the Nounes they are coupled with." Joseph Priestley says very much the same thing in 1761, in his important grammar *Rudiments of English Grammar.*

Prepositions generally precede their substantives; as *He went to London*: but sometimes a verb more elegantly parts them; as *This is the thing* with which *I am pleased*; or *This is the thing* which *I am pleased* with.

- So in 1761, Priestly is allowing for stylistic variation, saying that sometimes it is more elegant to strand the preposition. But Priestley's view lost to Bishop Lowth's opinion on the construction, written down and disseminated in *English Grammar* of 1762:

> The Preposition is often separated from the Relative which it governs, and joined to the Verb at the end of the Sentence, or of some member of it: as, "Horace is an author, *whom* I am much delighted *with*." "The world is too well bred to shock authors with a truth, *which* generally their booksellers are the first that inform them *of*." [Pope, Preface to his Poems] This is an Idiom, which our language is strongly inclined to; it prevails in common conversation, and suits very well with the familiar style in writing; but the placing of a Preposition before the Relative is more graceful, as well as more perspicuous, and agrees much better with the solemn and elevated Style.

- Notice that it is not yet a rule per se. Lowth first playfully strands a preposition in the sentence "This is an Idiom, which our language is strongly inclined to." He then opines that it is more graceful, solemn, and elevated to pied-pipe the preposition.

- From what we can tell, this opinion started to influence the usage of authors, even as some grammarians argued that sometimes the language was better served by stranding the preposition at the end of the sentence. The final nail that secured this rule is probably that it got picked up in Lindley Murray's best-selling grammar of 1795.

- Over time, the prescription became less about what was elegant and more about what was "bad usage." But in the 1920s, H.W. Fowler, in *A Dictionary of Modern English Usage*, tried to make the conversation again about elegance rather than about hard-and-fast rules:

> If it were not presumptuous, after that, to offer advice, the advice would be this: Follow no arbitrary rule, but remember that there are often two or more possible arrangements between which a choice should be consciously made.

■ You'll notice that Fowler actually chooses to pied-pipe a preposition in that last sentence ("two or more possible arrangements between which a choice should be consciously made"). That was a good choice over "two or more possible arrangements which a choice should be consciously made between."

■ Fowler is giving us very good advice: Make stylistic choices and enjoy the freedom in English grammar that allows us to do so.

■ The third and fourth editions of Strunk and White's guide advise that it's about having a good ear:

> Years ago, students were warned not to end a sentence with a preposition; time, of course, has softened that rigid decree. Not only is the preposition acceptable at the end, sometimes it is more effective in that spot than anywhere else. "A clawhammer, not an ax, was the tool he murdered her with." This is preferable to "A claw hammer, not an ax, was the tool with which he murdered her." Why? Because it sounds more violent, more like murder. A matter of ear.

■ But Microsoft Word's grammar checker can't be that flexible. When the box pops up, it advises: "Although a preposition at the end of a sentence may be used informally, consider deleting or repositioning the preposition for a more formal or traditional tone." This gives some flexibility, but it suggests that it is somehow wrong in formal writing.

Churchill

- There is a story out there that Winston Churchill rejected the "do not end a sentence with a preposition" rule. The story goes that Churchill said something like, "That is a silly rule up with which I will no put."

- Ben Zimmer, executive editor of *Vocabulary.com* and columnist for *The Wall Street Journal*, has done some digging, though, and we don't have evidence that Churchill said this. The first instance of the quote is in *The Strand Magazine* in 1942. Churchill contributed to the magazine, but here's the quote, per the *Wall Street Journal*:

  > When a memorandum passed round a certain Government department, one young pedant scribbled a postscript drawing attention to the fact that the sentence ended with a preposition, which caused the original writer to circulate another memorandum complaining that the anonymous postscript was "offensive impertinence, up with which I will not put."

After recapping a situation, a newsperson might utter the informal-sounding sentence, "That's where we're at."

- In 1948, Sir Ernest Gowers wrote in *Plain Words*: "It is said that Mr. Winston Churchill once made this marginal comment against a sentence that clumsily avoided a prepositional ending: 'This is the sort of English up with which I will not put.'" Zimmer has found it in multiple newspapers.

- What makes the supposed Churchill quote funny is that he is playing with a phrasal verb, not a prepositional phrase. A phrasal verb is a two- or three-part verb with a main verb and one or two participles; *call up* and *put up with* are examples.

- These verbs don't like to have the particle fronted because it doesn't work like a preposition: "With that I will not put up" and "Up with that I will not put" are clunky. "That is something I will not put up with" works.

- Remember that some of the words that look like prepositions at the end of sentences are not functioning as prepositions. Follow your judgment about when it works well—even elegantly—to strand a preposition.

Suggested Reading

Lowth, *A Short Introduction to English Grammar.*
Yáñez-Bouza, "To End or Not to End a Sentence with a Preposition."
Zimmer, "A Misattribution No Longer To Be Put Up With."

Questions to Consider

1. In what contexts might it sound better to strand the preposition (e.g., "That was the decision for which we were waiting" versus "That was the decision we were waiting for")?

2. Imagine you are listening to live radio coverage of a hurricane. The reporter has some information about the damage but is awaiting more information. She says, "That's where we're at right now." Would you consider that standard usage? Why or why not?

Stranded Prepositions

There's a joke about prepositions out there that people tell me every few months, given that they know I appreciate a good grammar joke. It goes like this: A first-year student is on Harvard's campus and asks a senior, "Excuse me, can you tell me where the library's at?" The senior replies haughtily, "At Harvard, we do not end a sentence with a preposition." The first-year student tries again, "Can you tell me where the library's at, jerk?" And that's the tame version of the joke. I actually usually hear the joke with a less tame insult there at the end of the question.

The rule in question here is about not ending a sentence with a preposition, and it is one of the most widely known rules. It comes up whenever I ask students about the rules that they have learned in high school, along with the rule not to split an infinitive and not to use the first-person pronoun "I" in formal writing. We're going to spend this entire lecture talking about this rule because it is so well-known and so widely enforced. And yet, there's confusion about when it should apply and whether it's a worthwhile rule to follow at all.

Let's start with what's going on in the joke. The question, "Where's the library at?" ends in a preposition, but the concern about this construction is not really about the preposition. I think the concern is about the redundancy of "where" plus "at." So in that way, it is about the preposition, but it's not about whether it's stranded, it's about whether it's redundant with the where. And the "at" in "Where's it at?" isn't stranded, it's just extra. Now we could reword the question to get a stranded preposition, if we reworded the question this way: "Which library are we meeting at?" That would be stranded.

I call it a stranded preposition, and let me explain what I mean here. In the last lecture, we talked about how a prepositional phrase is preposition plus noun phrase. The preposition gets stranded when the noun phrase moves up to the front of the clause. For example, "Which library are we meeting at?" If you undo that, you would get "We are meeting at which library?" There are two times that prepositions can get stranded at the end—this kind of fronting can happen: It can happen in what we call wh- questions and in relative clauses.

Let's start with those wh- questions. Wh- questions involve the interrogative pronouns who, what, where, when, why, and how. You can see why we call them wh- questions, except for the how, which we just sort of tack on—but who, what, where, when, why. Now, these interrogative pronouns get put at the front of the question, no matter what function the interrogative pronoun plays in the sentence or in the question. If the interrogative pronoun is the subject, it's already going to be up there in the front—"Who made dinner?" It's the subject, already there in the front. But if it's in object position, it still needs to move up to the front.

Let's look at a question with an object relative pronoun—and I'm going to start by leaving it in object position—"You ate what for dinner?" And we can do that, especially if we're trying to be emphatic. But the generic form of the question would be "What did you eat for dinner?" where the "what" gets fronted—moved up to the front of the question. So, if the interrogative pronoun is the object of a preposition, it still fronts, with or without the preposition.

Let's look at an example, first with the question in a form where the interrogative pronoun is still positioned as the object of the preposition— "You cooked dinner for whom?" Now let's front the object of the preposition, "Whom did you cook dinner for?" Or, as we've already talked about, perhaps "Who did you cook dinner for?"—if you would rather use a "who" there. Now, we could also front the preposition with the interrogative pronoun and get, "For whom did you cook dinner?" Both of those questions—"Who or whom did you cook dinner for?" and "For whom did you cook dinner?"—are completely grammatical in English in the descriptive sense. The question is whether we find it more pleasing to front the preposition, too. As you know, the term in linguistics for this kind of fronting of the preposition is pied piping, where the preposition follows its pronoun up to the front of the sentence. We talked about that in Lecture 7 when we were talking about relative clauses.

Speaking of relative clauses, that same kind of fronting happens in those relative clauses with "which." For example, let's take this sentence: "That is the house that I was telling you about." Here we see the relative pronoun "that" has gotten fronted, and the "about" is still there. Let me undo that sentence and get the relative pronoun back into its position as the object of the preposition. "That is the house." And now here comes the relative clause: "I was telling you about that house." Then the "that" gets fronted— "That is the house that I was telling you about."

Let's imagine now that we also want to front the preposition "about." We would get, "That is the house about which I was telling you." Both of these sentences are also fully grammatical, although I will admit that the second—"the house about which I was telling you"—sounds very formal to me. That "about which" is formal. I have to say, if I use an "about which," it feels like one of those moments that could make me sound a little English professory, and sounding like an English professor isn't always great for my social life. Now, as I'm noting here, there is a difference between speech and writing, and we might be more likely to pied-pipe that preposition to bring it up to get "about which" in writing and more likely to strand it in speech.

A quick reminder here of something I mentioned in Lecture 7 when we were talking about relative clauses: you may have noticed that something else odd happened in that example sentence about the house. In the relative clause, we had "that I was telling you about." And then when we fronted the "about," it turned into "about which I was telling you," not "about that I was telling you." This is just one of those things about English that when the relative pronoun "that" gets fronted to appear after the preposition, it turns into "which."

OK, so we've clarified when a preposition might get stranded, and we know that there's a rule out there that we shouldn't strand it at the end of a sentence or the end of a question. Where did that rule come from? It looks like to answer that question, we need to talk about John Dryden. It's amazing to think that one person could be responsible for such a long-standing grammatical tradition. And it may well not be true that we can pin this on John Dryden, but it makes for a good story. John Dryden, who also proposed a language academy in the 1660s—he wanted an academy to control this language, to keep our grammar in order—he's usually cited as the first to notice and to disparage the stranded preposition.

In 1672, he picked out for critique the writing of Ben Jonson. And I love it when we do this; that we pick out another writer, and then we say, "Look at what they're doing. They shouldn't be doing that." Here's the line from Jonson that Dryden was concerned about: "The bodies that those souls were frighted from"—"frighted from." Dryden commented, "The preposition in the end of the sentence; a common fault with him, and which I have but lately observed in my own writings." Dryden subsequently not only avoided stranded prepositions in his own prose, but went back and revised earlier work that contained stranded prepositions so that his earlier work wouldn't have those prepositions.

Interestingly, if we go back to Ben Jonson's 1640 grammar—and yes, Ben Jonson did write a grammar; not everyone knows that—we see that Jonson very descriptively notes this about prepositions: He says that they "follow sometimes the Nounes that they are coupled with." And note how cleverly he does exactly that right there, that he strands a preposition "the Nounes they are coupled with." So the noun is coming before the preposition instead of after. He could have said: "the Nounes with which they are coupled," but he chose not to.

Joseph Priestley, in his grammar, says very much the same thing. And as you may recall, his grammar was published in 1761; it's called *The Rudiments of English Grammar*. And here's what he writes: "Prepositions generally precede their substantives; as in 'He went to London.' But sometimes a verb more elegantly parts them; as 'This is the thing with which I am pleased;' or 'This is the thing which I am pleased with.'"

So in 1761, Priestly is allowing for stylistic variation, saying that sometimes it's more elegant to strand the preposition. But Priestley's view lost to Bishop Lowth's opinion on the construction, which was written down and disseminated in his English grammar published 1762. I'm going to read the whole thing because it's important to hear how Bishop Lowth explains what has now become a rule. So here's Lowth: "The preposition is often separated from the relative which it governs, and joined to the verb at the end of the sentence, or of some member of it as"—and here he quotes—"'Horace is an author, whom I am much delighted with.'" And here's another quote he puts in: "The world is too well bred to shock authors with a truth, which generally their booksellers are the first that inform them of." And he said that's from Pope; *Preface to his Poems*. And here Lowth continues:

> This is an Idiom, which our language is strongly inclined to; it prevails in common conversation, and suits very well with the familiar style in writing; but the placing of a preposition before the relative is more graceful, as well as more perspicuous, and agrees much better with the solemn and elevated Style.

Notice that it is not yet a rule per se. Lowth first playfully strands a preposition himself, and it has to have been intentional. You may have heard it; he writes: "This is an Idiom, which our language is strongly inclined to." It's brilliant that as he talks about what our language likes to do in terms of stranding prepositions, he strands one himself. He then opines that it is more graceful, solemn, and elevated to pied-pipe the preposition. And I get the sense that he's talking about in writing; that it's more elegant and graceful in writing—and perhaps maybe in very formal speech.

From what we can tell, this opinion started to influence the usage of authors, even as some grammarians argued that sometimes the language was better served by stranding that preposition at the end of the sentence. The final nail that secured this rule in the English grammatical tradition is probably that the rule got picked up in Lindley Murray's best-selling grammar of 1795. Murray copied Lowth's words—and he really did copy them, which was fairly common in these grammars. He copied Lowth's words, except that he unstranded Lowth's preposition in "which our language is strongly inclined to." And instead he wrote "this is an Idiom to which our language is inclined." And I have to say, I read that and I think, "Where is Murray's sense of humor? Didn't he get wat Lowth was up to?"

Over time, the prescription about not stranding the preposition at the end became less about what was elegant and more about what was bad usage. In fact, there's even evidence of grammarians arguing that the natural construction in English is to pied-pipe the preposition, which is striking to me that they're arguing that "to which" or "about whom" is the natural construction. In that scenario, the stranded preposition somehow becomes unnatural, which as you now know is clearly not where we started. In these early grammars, the grammarians were noting that this is an idiom that our language is inclined to.

By end of the 18th century, we find rules that state "Never close a sentence with a preposition;" and many people still believe this, or have been taught it in school. But if you look at style guides today, you'll see that the tide may be turning on this one.

You might be surprised to learn that as far back as the 1920s H. W. Fowler, in *A Dictionary of Modern English Usage*, tried to make the conversation, again, about elegance rather than about a hard-and-fast rule about correctness. Here is Fowler, and I'm going to quote him at length here because I think this passage is wonderful and wise.

Here's Fowler:

> It was once a cherished superstition that prepositions must be kept true to their name and placed before the word they govern in spite of the incurable English instinct for putting them late. The idea that—and here he quotes—'A sentence ending in a preposition is an inelegant sentence' represents what used to be a very general belief, and it is not yet dead. The fact is that the remarkable freedom enjoyed by English in putting its prepositions late and omitting its relatives is an important element in the flexibility of the language.

The legitimacy of the prepositional ending in literary English must be uncompromisingly maintained; in respect of elegance or inelegance, every example must be judged not by an arbitrary rule, but on its own merits, according to the impression it makes on the feeling of educated English readers. If it were not presumptuous, after that, to offer advice, the advice would be this: Follow no arbitrary rule, but remember that there are often two or more possible arrangements between which a choice should be consciously made.

So, there we have Fowler talking about the rule about stranded prepositions. You'll notice that Fowler actually chooses to pied-pipe a preposition in that last sentence. He writes: "two or more possible arrangements between which a choice should be consciously made"—"between which." And I think that that was a good stylistic choice for Fowler. The other option would have been: "two or more possible arrangements which a choice should be consciously made between." That is really not particularly stylistically graceful, and Fowler opted to pied-pipe his preposition. Fowler is giving us very wise advice here: make stylistic choices and enjoy the freedom in English grammar that allows us to do so

Strunk and White, in the third and fourth edition of *Elements of Style*, give us similar advice. They say it's about having a good ear. They go on to say,

Years ago, students were warned not to end a sentence with a preposition; time, of course, has softened that rigid decree. Not only is the preposition acceptable at the end, sometimes it is more effective in that spot than anywhere else—and here, they provide an example—'A claw hammer, not an ax, was the tool he murdered her with.' This is preferable to 'A claw hammer, not an ax, was the tool with which he murdered her.' Why? Because it sounds more violent, more like murder. A matter of ear.

I love that these usage guides are giving us this kind of flexibility to trust our ear about what we're trying to achieve in a sentence. But the Microsoft Word Grammar Checker understandably has trouble determining when that stranded preposition is an effective stranded preposition and when it's not. And as a result, it identifies most of them—it doesn't catch all of them, but most of them. The grammar checker can't be that flexible. When the box pops up next to a stranded preposition, what it says is: "Although a preposition at the end of a sentence may be used informally, consider deleting or repositioning the preposition for a more formal or traditional tone." So, it's providing some flexibility, but it suggests that it is somehow wrong in formal writing to strand the preposition. And I'm struck by the wording of "if you want a more traditional tone." But we now know that in terms of tradition, there's a long tradition of actually accepting the stranded preposition as effective sometimes.

There's a story out there that Winston Churchill rejected the "do not end a sentence with a preposition" rule. The story goes that Churchill said, "That is a silly rule up with which I will no put." Or he said, "That is the sort of bloody nonsense up with which I will not put." Or he said, "This is the type of arrant pedantry up with which I will not put." Or, "This is the sort of English up with which I will not put." Or, "nonsense up with which I will not put." You can tell there are a lot of versions of the story.

Ben Zimmer, executive editor of *vocabulary.com* and a language columnist for the *Wall Street Journal*, has done some digging to find out if Winston Churchill, though actually said this, and it turns out that we don't have evidence that he actually did. The first instance of the quote is in *The Strand Magazine* in 1942. Churchill contributed to *The Strand*, but the quote in *The Strand* actually sites as its source *The Wall Street Journal*.

So, here's the quote in *The Strand*—the citation of *The Wall Street Journal*, 1942:

> When a memorandum passed round a certain government department, one young pedant scribbled a postscript drawing attention to the fact that the sentence ended with a preposition, which caused the original writer to circulate another memorandum complaining that the anonymous postscript was "offensive impertinence, up with which I will not put."

So the original shows up in *The Wall Street Journal* in 1942. By 1948, Sir Ernest Gowers wrote in Plain Words: "It is said that Mr. Winston Churchill once made this marginal comment against a sentence that clumsily avoided a prepositional ending: 'This is the sort of English up with which I will not put.'" So we can see six years later, Churchill's getting credit. And Zimmer has found that in multiple newspapers, clearly it was being said that Churchill had said this.

What makes the supposed Churchill quote funny is that he's playing with a phrasal verb, not a prepositional phrase. As we talked about earlier in the course, a phrasal verb is a two- or three-part verb with a main verb and a particle, or sometimes two—something like "call up" or "put up with." These verbs don't like to have the particle fronted because the particle doesn't work like a preposition. So, it doesn't work to say something like: "With that I will not put up," or "Up with that I will not put." Instead we say, "That is something I will not put up with." This is true for other phrasal verbs. For example, we wouldn't say, "Up I called him" and "Out I asked him;" they're not prepositions. "I called him up." "I asked him out." So remember that some of the words that look like prepositions at the end of sentences are not functioning as prepositions, and follow your judgment about when it works well, and even elegantly, to strand a preposition.

As I bring this lecture to a close, let's take stock of where we're at now. And I very deliberately just used "where we're at now," and perhaps you noticed. Because I want to come full circle back to the beginning of the lecture and talk about the stigma on the question "Where is X at?"—"Where is the library at?"

The phrase "where we're at now" seems to work a little bit differently from the question "Where's it at?" Bryan Garner, in *Modern American Usage*, calls "Where's it at?" uneducated, and it certainly feels informal. But Mark Liberman, in a very interesting post on *Language Log*, shows how this expression—"where we're at"—appears on National Public Radio, CNN, Larry King. In other words, it appears in the speech of lots of highly educated speakers, as well as in sports interviews and sometimes in writing.

For example, here is someone talking about China: "And that's where we're at right now, this very fluid and precarious situation." "That's where we're at right now." Would you notice if you heard that on NPR or CNN? Now, why does this happen, that we get "where we're at"? It's about whether or not we contract. Let's step back and think about this. "That's where we are" as opposed to "that's where we're at." You see two phenomena interacting here. First, we like to contract. So if we have something like "we are" in speech, we often like to contract to "we're." But once we contract "we are" to "we're," then we have to do something different syntactically; we need something else there at the end of the sentence. If we say, "That's where we're now," it doesn't sound so good; we tend to say, "That's where we're at now."

I'm not recommending scattering this phrase "That's where we're at" throughout your formal writing, but I am saying that it does appear in more formal places—including an educated speech—and we may not even notice.

This whole lecture has been about stranded prepositions, and I like the description of stranded to capture the preposition left out there at the end of the clause by itself. And as I've tried to capture in this lecture, that stranding can be very idiomatic; it's not inherently a bad thing.

In the next lecture, we'll turn to dangling rather than stranding. We'll turn to dangling grammatical elements; specifically we'll talk about dangling modifiers and get in some chuckles, I think, as we contemplate the images that some of these dangling modifiers can create.

The Dangers of Danglers

If we heard the sentence, "Clinging to the side of the aquarium, Mary saw a starfish," we would probably assume it was the starfish clinging to the side of the aquarium. But if we look closely at the structure of the sentence, the participial phrase "Clinging to the side of the aquarium" modifies Mary. This falls under the assumption that participles and other modifiers sit next to what they modify. To correct it, we'd switch to, "Clinging to the side of the aquarium, the starfish stared at Mary," or "Mary saw the starfish clinging to the side of the aquarium." This issue seems straightforward enough, but there are some twists, so this lecture explores "danglers" (as Bryan Garner calls them) in depth.

Terminology

- Many of us have learned terms like *dangling modifiers* or *dangling participles*. Participles are subcategory of modifiers and often the issue. Here's a dangler with a past participle: "Parked behind a row of tall bushes, the speeding teenagers didn't see the cop until it was too late."

- We're interested in the participles that are acting adjectivally. In addition to present and past participles, the modifier could also be a prepositional phrase: "As a teacher of writing, my students often tell me about traumatic experiences they have had with grammar in high school."

- When it comes to danglers, there can be a useful distinction between dangling modifiers versus misplaced/wrongly attached modifiers.

  - Misplaced/wrongly attached modifiers happen when the noun that the participle is supposed to modify is there in the sentence, just not next to the modifier: "Plummeting from the sky, Cindy watched the punted football drop right in between her outstretched hands."

  - Dangling modifiers are dangling because there is no noun in the sentence for them to modify: "Glancing through the document, the typos jumped off the page."

- There are some danglers that have become accepted in more formal writing. With these, the participle has come to be accepted as a preposition or disguised conjunction. An example: "Considering the danger, she is lucky to have gotten out alive." (She's not considering the danger—we are.) Such participial phrases are now understood to function adverbially, modifying the whole sentence.

Ends of Sentences

- All our examples have had the participial phrase at the beginning of the sentence. Garner points out that editors are often more lenient about these phrases at the end of sentences. His example: "Sarah stepped to the door, looking for her friend."

- It is hard to call this unacceptable—it's very clear Sarah is doing both actions. Garner calls it a *coordinating participle*, as it implies that this verb happened next: "Sarah stepped to the door and looked for her friend."

- Another example: "My colleague wrote me an email after our meeting, asking if he had unintentionally insulted me by joking about marathon runners." As you can see, danglers are not a totally cut and dried issue.

- Does our grammar, in the descriptive sense, allow participial phrases (and other modifiers) to be separated from the noun? Clearly, the answer is yes. As Garner notes, we are more forgiving when the participial phrase is at the end of the sentence.

- We remain stricter when it is at the beginning, and there are good reasons to avoid ambiguity in writing—but it's not certain that these sentences with danglers are mostly ungrammatical. There's a key difference between speech and writing here. These sentences are usually easy to parse in speech—we go with logic. In writing, we need to be more careful because we cannot clarify ambiguity caused by a dangler.

Present but Ambiguous

- A modifier can technically be in the right place and still be ambiguous in a way that merits rewriting. Here's an example from the New Jersey Administrative Code:

    Property owners and occupants of dwellings suffering damage from squirrel, raccoon, opossum, skunk, weasel, woodchuck, gray fox, red fox and coyote, or their agents designated in writing, may control these animals by lawful procedures at any time subject to State law and local ordinances.

■ The ambiguity: Are we talking about all these animals or their agents designated in writing? When you look closely at this sentence, though, the phrase "or their agents designated in writing" is not dangling or misplaced. There is a legitimate reading of the sentence where it stands as an alternative to "property owners and occupants of dwellings suffering damage." Yet this sentence desperately needs an editor.

■ The length of the prepositional phrase "from squirrel, raccoon, ... and coyote" stretches readers' working memory capacity, loading a lot of information in between the subject noun phrase ("property owners and occupants of dwellings") and the appositive phrase ("or their agents designated in writing").

■ There are some other potential issues. For example, the *and* between the red fox and the coyote, along with the omission of an Oxford comma after *red fox*, potentially raise the question of whether all these critters need to be working in cahoots for the regulation to apply, whether it is only the red fox and coyote who are working together, or whether all of the animals can be independent, free-agent damage doers. Lawyers think about these kinds of things. In addition, the *their* in "or their agents" is ambiguous, even if grammatically unproblematic.

■ Here we see why written language, and especially legal language, can require a high level of attention to modifiers and commas.

Absolute Constructions

■ One construction can look like a dangling participle, but it is instead something called an *absolute construction*. One of the very common ones is, "*Weather permitting*, the race will start at 8:00 am." The whole phrase functions adverbially to say, "If the weather permits."

- These will often have a noun and participle. It could be a present participle, as in "this being the case" or "the sun having risen." Or it could be a past participle: "all things considered."

- *Being that* has been controversial among grammarians: When is it OK because it is in an absolute construction, and when it is not OK because it means *because* or *since*? Here it is as an absolute construction: "The review criticized the book for taking a more philosophical than empirical approach, the implication being that the author strayed too far from the data."

- Now take the example, "Being that it's a holiday, I let the kids sleep late." Seventy-one percent of the AHD Usage Panel rejected it as unacceptable. And a full 83 percent rejected this one: "Being that he has never attended law school, it's strange that he's giving legal advice." Clearly, *being that* meaning *because* or *since* is not held in high regard right now, at least in more formal contexts.

- Let's return for a moment to absolute constructions with *being that*. One emerging pattern in student writing is the *being that* absolute construction becoming its own sentence.

- Ryan McCarty has been looking into this and has found it in published writing too, although it is criticized. Here's an example from a 2009 issue of the *Journal of Instructional Psychology*:

    There are a plethora of reasons to be given for the importance of the social studies. A major reason being that threats to humanity exist if nations continually spend excessive amounts of money on the military as well as plan attacks against each other.

- Clearly we have a fragment here. We could replace *being* with *is* and correct the issue. In speech it's not an issue: We wouldn't be able to hear whether this was a new sentence or an em-dash, and in the latter case it would be completely fine.

- In writing, absolute constructions (when they are not fragments) have their benefits. They can be a nice way to vary one's sentence structure: "The sun having risen, we jumped into the lake" versus "The sun rose and we jumped into the lake." Just beware of making them their own sentence in formal writing.

Questions to Consider

1. Consider this sentence: "Reviewing the grades at the end of the term, it became clear that the curve needed to be adjusted." Would you correct this sentence if you had your editor hat on? Why or why not?

2. Consider this sentence: "Being that it's a holiday, I let the kids sleep late." Do you have any concerns about the grammar?

I don't remember that many grammar lessons from junior high school, but for whatever reason, one sentence from the lesson about dangling and misplaced modifiers has stuck with me ever since junior high school. Here's the sentence, "Clinging to the side of the aquarium, Mary saw the starfish."

Poor Mary. It's exhausting to have to cling to the side of an aquarium that way. Now, of course, if we heard this sentence, we would probably assume that it was the starfish clinging to the side of the aquarium, not Mary. But if you look closely at the structure of the sentence, the participial phrase "clinging to the side of the aquarium" modifies Mary.

Why? How do we know it modifies Mary? Well, the assumption is that participles and other modifiers sit next to whatever it is that they modify. So to correct that sentence, it would need to be something more like, "Clinging to the side of the aquarium, the starfish stared at Mary," or, "Mary saw the starfish clinging to the side of the aquarium."

The issue seems straightforward enough, but there are some twists, so I'm going to devote this entire lecture to danglers, which is what Bryan Garner calls them in *Modern American Usage*.

Many of these danglers, are deemed unacceptable if not ungrammatical, and we'll return to that description. And yet, some of them are acceptable, which I will explain.

Let's start by talking about terminology. You may have learned these as dangling modifiers or dangling participles. Participles are a subcategory of modifiers, and the participles are often the issue. These could be present participles—those participles ending in -ing such as: clinging, in, "clinging to the side of the aquarium. Or they could be past participles with a final -ed or -en. Here's an example with a past participle—an example of a dangler. So listen carefully, and you'll catch the dangler: "Parked behind a row of tall bushes, the speeding teenagers didn't see the cop until it was too late."

Now, that sentence actually doesn't make sense if you take the dangler seriously—that parked behind the tall bushes, the speeding teenagers didn't see the cop. Well, it wasn't the speeding teenagers who were hiding behind the bushes. It was the cop who was hiding behind the bushes. So we would need to have, "Hiding behind the tall bushes, the cop caught the speeding teenagers."

We are interested here in the participles that are acting adjectivally. Let me pause here for a moment to talk about those –ing forms that are acting like nouns instead. These are called gerunds, and I know someone who claims that you can't say you know English grammar unless you can identify a gerund. So let's clarify between participles that are acting adjectivally and those -ing forms that are acting like nouns or like gerunds. You can identify a gerund by looking to see if the –ing form is functioning like a noun or like a noun phrase in the sentence.

Here's a straightforward example, "Morgan dislikes running." You know that that running there is acting like a noun because you got a structure: Morgan dislikes running. You expect a noun phrase right after dislikes. You've got running—so there you have a gerund. You can also get a full gerund phrase. Let's go back to our example with clinging. Let's imagine I say, "Clinging to the side of an aquarium is exhausting." There you can see the entire phrase, "Clinging to the side of an aquarium" is functioning as the subject like a noun phrase and then you get, "is exhausting." Clinging to the side of an aquarium is exhausting.

Now, back to the modifiers that can be danglers. In addition to the present and past participles, you can also have modifiers that are prepositional phrases. Here's a sentence with a dangler that is a prepositional phrase, "As a teacher of writing, my students often tell me about traumatic experiences they have had with grammar in high school." Did you catch the dangler?

As a teacher of writing, my students often tell me... Well, of course, in that sentence the first person "I" is the teacher of writing, so if you'd want to get rid of the dangler, you'd have, "As a teacher of writing, I often hear from students about their traumatic experiences with grammar in high school."

When it comes to danglers, there can be a useful distinction between dangling modifiers or dangling participles and misplaced or wrongly attached modifiers or participles. And were going to focus largely on participles as a subset of those modifiers. Now some people will use dangling participle to cover all of these, but I find the distinction useful.

Let's start with misplaced or wrongly attached modifiers or participles. These happen when the noun that the participle is supposed to modify is there in the sentence, just not next to the modifier. We saw this in the sentence with the starfish and clinging to the side of the aquarium and the cop, who is in the sentence, just not next to the participle hiding. These kinds of sentences can be really funny and let me show you what I mean.

Plummeting from the sky, Cindy watched the punted football drop right in between her outstretched hands. Clearly, Cindy was not plummeting from the sky. It was the punted football that was dropping from the sky, but it's kind of a wonderful image.

Let's look at another one, "Turning over the log with some trepidation, the spiders scurried out and made little Steven shriek." If you take this literally, assuming that the participle is modifying the noun next it—it is the spiders that turn over the log with some trepidation. Those are clearly very strong spiders.

Let's now turn to dangling modifiers, if we go with this distinction between dangling modifiers and misplaced modifiers. Dangling modifiers are dangling because there's no noun in the sentence for them to modify. So they're dangling out there without a noun or noun phrase.

Examples will help here, "Glancing through the document, the typos jumped off the page." Well, clearly the typos weren't dancing through the document—the narrator is glancing through the document. But the narrator is nowhere to be found in that sentence.

Let me give you another example, "Walking through the arboretum with my boyfriend on a beautiful April day, the birds sang uproariously, celebrating the arrival of spring." This sentence would suggest that these birds, who are singing uproariously, are walking through the arboretum with this person's boyfriend. Which, while possible, actually seems quite unlikely. It seems much likely that the narrator of this sentence is walking with the boyfriend, not the birds.

Sometimes these danglers happen, where the narrator is understood, because we have an existential "it." A sentence like this can sound very colloquial.

Let me show you what I mean, "Without knowing his name, it was difficult to introduce him." Without knowing his name, it was difficult to introduce him. Now, clearly again, we have the narrator for whom this is a difficult situation. The narrator isn't sure how to introduce this person because the narrator doesn't know their name. But the narrator's not in the sentence. We just have, "It was difficult."

Here's another example, "Reviewing the grades at the end of the term, it became clear that the curve needed to be adjusted." Once again, it's the narrator who's reviewing the grades. But reviewing the grades at the end of the term, it was clear. You can see how that existential "it" is creating a dangler.

Those last one or two sentences may feel almost okay to you or perhaps completely okay to you, and there's good reason for that. There are some danglers that have become accepted in more formal writing, and with these, the participle has come to be accepted as a preposition or what some would call a disguised conjunction.

Here's some examples of these participles that are no longer considered dangling, "Considering the danger, she is lucky to have gotten out alive." Considering the danger, she is lucky. Now, she is not the one who's considering the danger—we're all considering the danger collectively. And as we consider the danger, we all believe that she is lucky to have gotten out alive. But that "considering" is now considered by many a disguised conjunction.

Here's another one, "Even taking all these factors into account, a team cannot win without strong defense." Once again, it's all of us who are taking these factors into account, not the team who's taking these factors into account.

These participial phrases in the last two sentences are now understood to function adverbially, modifying the whole sentence with an understood "we" who are considering or taking factors into account. In that way, these participial phrases function like sentence adverbs, which we've talked about before. Sentences like, "Mercifully, or now for many of us—hopefully."

Which participles can do this—can act like disguised conjunctions and function adverbially. These would be participles such as: according, assuming, concerning, considering, given, judging, regarding, owing to, speaking. And let me give you a couple of examples with "speaking."

Roughly speaking a new edition is published every ten to twenty years. "Roughly speaking a new edition," well, the new edition isn't speaking at all. It's all of us roughly speaking or saying, or the narrator roughly speaking is saying, "A new edition is published every ten to twenty years.

Or, here's a very colloquial one, "Speaking of politics, what is going on with this election?" Speaking of politics, what...? Who's speaking of politics? We're speaking of politics. As I said, you can feel how colloquial that kind of sentence is.

H. W. Fowler, in his usage guide, raised the interesting question of when this kind of participle becomes accepted as a disguised conjunction or a preposition. How would we know? Here's the example that he provides to raise the question, "Referring to your letter, you do not state...," blah, blah, blah.

Well, the person who says the sentence is the person who's referring to the letter. It's not you—it's your letter. So in theory, maybe it needs to be,

"Referring to your letter, I find that you do not state…" But is "referring to your letter" now functioning adverbially—is referring now one of those disguised conjunctions—so that we can say it's not dangling. It's just sitting there like considering the danger—referring to your letter.

How would I answer that? Well, what I did was go to the *Corpus of Contemporary American English*. I looked in the Academic subsection to see what's going on in academic prose. And I search for those initial "referring to" participial phrases. What I found is that almost all if those initial "referring to" phrases have the relevant noun right after the phrase. For example, "Referring to X, the author argues…"

So there you're seeing, "Referring to X, the author…" It's the author referring to X. But, when I was in the *Corpus*, I did find exceptions. For example, "Referring to Figure 2, the presence of the safety provisions shifts the demand curve up." Well, the safety provisions are not what is referring to Figure 2, the author of the article is referring to Figure 2 or asking all of us, as readers, to refer to Figure 2. That would suggest that that "referring to" there is functioning like a disguised conjunction.

So right now, usage suggests, if I take my search seriously, that "referring to" remains a modifier as opposed to a disguised conjunction—at least editors are treating it that way.

But it's not confusing to say, "Referring to Figure 2, the data suggest…" If I were asked on the usage ballot whether or not it was acceptable to use "referring to" as a disguised conjunction, I would not say that it was unacceptable. I would probably vote somewhat acceptable because you can find the examples there in edited prose, but you find more examples where "referring to" is being treated as a modifier with a modifying noun right after it.

All our examples have had the participial phrase at the beginning of the sentence. Brian Garner in *Modern American Usage* points out that editors are often more lenient about these phrases at the end of sentences. Here's his example, "Sarah stepped to the door, looking for her friend."

It's hard to call this unacceptable. It's very clear that Sarah is doing both actions. Garner calls these kinds of participles coordinating participles because they imply that the verb happened next. In other words, "Sarah stepped to the door and looked for her friend."

Here's another example, "My colleague wrote an e-mail to me after our meeting, asking if he had unintentionally insulted me by joking about marathon runners." Again, you can see "sent me an e-mail and asked." It's doing that kind of coordinating work. But technically in the sentence, "asking" is after "our meeting." He sent me the e-mail after our meeting, asking…

As I said, danglers are not a totally cut and dried issue. And I'm struck by a line in Brian Garner's usage guide in which he writes, "Most danglers are ungrammatical." What he means is that somehow if a participial phrase at the beginning of the sentence is not followed by the noun it is supposed to modify, the sentence is ungrammatical.

But let's think again about the sentence, "Without knowing his name, it was difficult to introduce him." Is that ungrammatical to you?

With a sentence like that, do we understand the sentence? Does our grammar, in the descriptive sense, allow participial phrases and other modifiers to be separated from the noun or to even exist without the noun they modify?

Clearly the answer is yes. And as Garner notes, we are more forgiving when the participial phrase is at the end of the sentence. We remain stricter when it is at the beginning of a sentence, and as I've said, there are good reasons to avoid ambiguity in writing—that you aren't there to clarify, and so you want to make sure people know that Mary's not clinging to the side of the aquarium, and the speeding teenagers aren't hiding behind the tall row of bushes. But, I'm reluctant to say that these sentences with danglers are mostly ungrammatical—that doesn't feel right to our experience with these sentences.

There's a key difference here between speech and writing. These sentences are usually easy to parse in speech. We go with logic. We go with what's what. We know that it's the starfish clinging to the side of the aquarium and that Cindy is not plummeting from the sky—it's the football. As I said, in writing, we need to be more careful because we can't be there to clarify if the ambiguity comes up, and we want to make sure that our readers understand exactly what we mean.

So should you be careful about this in writing? Yes. When you edit more formal writing, check those modifiers that start sentences to see what comes right after the modifier, remembering that some –ing modifiers like considering and regarding are now considered exceptions.

Speaking of editing... Did you catch what I just did there? I want to point out that ambiguity around modifiers doesn't have to be about a dangling modifier. The modifier can technically be in the right place and still be ambiguous in a way that merits rewriting. This issue hit my radar in a very funny way—in legal writing, where writers are supposed to be so careful about exactly this kind of thing. And this story is good enough that I just had to share it.

My sister, who's a lawyer, sent me a provision from the New Jersey Administrative Code. She and her husband were trying to deal with the squirrels in the attic, and so she had checked the regulation.

The relevant regulation is N.J.A.C., the New Jersey Administrative code, 7.25–5.21, which is titled—and I've left out the Latin names for the animals in the title. But here's the title: Squirrel, raccoon, opossum, skunk, weasel, woodchuck, coyote, gray fox and red fox damage. I'm going to read you the first provision. See if you can spot the ambiguity given how this sentence is phrased:

> Property owners and occupants of dwellings suffering damage
> from squirrel, raccoon, opossum, skunk, weasel, woodchuck, gray

fox, red fox and coyote, or their agents designated in writing, may control these animals by lawful procedures at any time subject to State law and local ordinances.

Did you spot it? If you did, how can you not giggle? I started picturing a woodchuck with a little notarized affidavit. After all, we're talking about all these animals or their agents designated in writing.

My first reaction was that there must be a misplaced modifier here, which allows any or all of these critters to have agents designated in writing. Mary and the starfish jumped to mind.

When you look closely at this sentence, though, the phrase "or their agents designated in writing" is not dangling or misplaced. There is a legitimate reading of the sentence where it stands as an alternative to "property owners and occupants of dwellings suffering damage." Yet this sentence desperately needs an editor. Let's read it through again.

"Property owners and occupants of dwellings," okay so there's the subject. And now we're going to get a modifier of those dwellings, "suffering damage from squirrel, raccoon, opossum, skunk, weasel, woodchuck, gray fox, and red fox and coyote." So again, that's a modifying –ing phrase, describing the dwellings that may have suffered damage from this wide range of critters. We can now continue with the sentence, "or their agents designated in writing." Now this refers back to the property owners or occupants who are in the damaged dwellings, but it's been a while since we saw that subject, which is why we may think it's the critters who have the agents designated in writing. And then we go on with the sentence and have, may control these animal."

The length of the prepositional phrase "from squirrel, raccoon…" blah, blah, blah, "…and coyote," stretches readers' working memory dangerously far, loading a lot of information in between the subject noun phrase, the "property owners and occupants of dwellings" and the appositive phrase, "or their agents designated in writing." You can't blame us for wanting to attach the agents to the critters.

They're some other potential issues. For example, the And between the red fox and the coyote and the omission of an Oxford comma after red fox in the list of animals also potentially raise questions of whether all these critters need to be working in cahoots for the regulation to apply, whether it is only the red fox and the coyote who are working together, or whether all of the animals can be independent, free-agent damage doers. Lawyers think about these kinds of things. In addition, the "their" in "or their agents" is ambiguous, even if grammatically unproblematic. My sister the attorney explained the kinds of questions that lawyers could raise in a legal context in response to this passage. She sent me a wonderful e-mail.

She writes, "For example, suppose a coyote wished to transfer its right to chew through the insulation, including, but not limited to, associated electrical wiring, to a field mouse by means of a limited durable power of attorney. Would the coyote need to get the permission of each other animal in order for that power of attorney to be effective? Similarly, what if a squirrel, having no present use for such, wished to assign its interest in improperly locked garbage cans to a raccoon and a black bear by means of a general agency agreement? Could the squirrel assign its interest separate and apart from the interests of the others, or can specific rights and interests only be assigned collectively? It's a mess."

A mess indeed. Here we see why written language, and especially legal language, can require a level of attention to modifiers and commas unlike more informal writing—and certainly more than speech. With legal documents, we cannot get away with, "but that's not what I meant."

I want to close this lecture by talking briefly about a construction that can look like a dangling participle, but it is instead what is called an absolute construction. Here's a very common one, "Weather permitting, the race will start at 8 am." Weather permitting—the whole phrase, in this case, "weather permitting," functions adverbially. It functions like, "if the weather permits."

These absolute constructions will often have a noun and a participle—we saw it there with, "weather permitting." It could be a present participle. Here are a few other examples. "This being the case," again, we see the noun, This—or in this case, a pronoun—plus the participle, Being. Or here's another one, "The sun having risen, we jumped into the lake." Or it could have an absolute construction with a past participle. For example, "all things considered."

"Being that" has been controversial among grammarians. When is it okay because it is in an absolute construction, and when it is not okay because it means Because or Since? Here it is in an absolute construction, "The review criticized the book for taking a more philosophical than empirical approach, the implication being that the author strayed too far from the data." There we see "the implication being that" in an absolute construction. Compare that to this sentence, "Being that the condo development was just built, it does not appear on most maps." There the "being that" means Because. Because the condo development was just built...

What do you think of this sentence? "Being that it's a holiday, I let the kids sleep late." Does that sound okay to you? Seventy-one percent of the *American Heritage Dictionary* Usage Panel rejected that sentence as somewhat or completely unacceptable.

What about this sentence? "Being that he has never attended law school, it's strange that he's giving legal advice." Eighty-three percent of the Panel rejected that one. Clearly, "being that" meaning Because or Since is not held in high regard right now, at least in these more formal contexts.

Let's return for a moment to the absolute construction with "being that." One thing my colleagues and I are seeing in student writing is the "being that" absolute construction becoming its own sentence.

Ryan McCarty, who's pursuing his Ph.D at Michigan, has been looking into this, and he's found these absolute constructions with "being that" as their own sentence in published writing too—although it is criticized. Here's an example from 2009 in an issue of the *Journal of Instructional Psychology*. It reads:

> There are a plethora of reasons to be given for the importance of social studies. A major reason being that threats to humanity exist

if nations continually spend excessive amounts of money on the military as well as plan attacks against each other.

Clearly we have a fragment here with Being. We could put in an Is instead and correct the issue. In speech, we'd never notice because no one would do what I did which is say, "period" to indicate that the first sentence had ended. Instead we could imagine that there was a dash or even a comma so that the "being that" phrase was part of the sentence.

In writing, absolute constructions when they are not fragments have their benefits. They can be a nice way to vary one's sentence structure, "The sun having risen, we jumped into the lake," versus "The sun rose and we jumped into the lake." Just beware of making those absolute constructions into their own sentence in formal writing.

This last example highlights the question of how we package information we want to present. How do we package it grammatically? In an absolute construction such as: "the sun having risen," or in an independent clause, "The sun rose." Or do we want that idea at the end of the sentence? "We jumped into the lake after the sun rose." What would help us decide which version of the sentence works best in a passage of writing? We can answer that.

In the next lecture, we'll discuss in more detail how we can structure information in sentences and paragraphs to avoid what is colloquially known as choppiness.

Navigating the Choppy Paragraph

It's time to put together a lot of the grammatical pieces we've been talking about into the bigger picture of how we present information in our writing. This lecture will provide a few fundamental pieces of advice about how to help your readers follow your ideas by helping your readers follow you from sentence to sentence. You're going to see some real payoff for understanding how sentences work in terms of subjects and predicates, conjunctive adverbs and relative clauses, and the like. There are some wonderfully concrete ways that you can help make your prose clearer.

Flow versus Choppiness

■ *Flow* is not a very useful word to describe writing, although we use it all the time. The opposite is *choppy*. But what are we saying with *choppy*? Somehow we're having trouble seeing connections between sentences. Somehow our expectations as readers are not being met. We're reading along and expecting one thing and we get something else, and so our head metaphorically jerks up.

■ This raises the key questions: How can you know what your readers are expecting? And how can you help them navigate your prose?

■ One answer is using conjunctive adverbs or adverb phrases. Conjunctive adverbs are words like *therefore*, *nonetheless*, and *consequently*; and adverb phrases include *in addition* and *in sum*. These help us understand how one sentence is connected to the next.

- That said, there is a more fundamental principle at work in terms of how we can present information sentence to sentence in a way that makes sense to readers. It is often called the *known-new contract* or *given-new contract*.

- Here's the fundamental idea: As readers, we expect information we know to precede new information. Grammatically, known information will be in the subject position and new information in the predicate. Or, known information will be an introductory phrase, perhaps an adverbial like *given that*.

- Examples from real writing will help here. Here's a very straightforward one from *Boys in the Boat* by Daniel James Brown: "Since early in the eighteenth century, the London watermen had also made a sport of racing their dories in impromptu competitions. They were rough-and-tumble events." The first sentence introduces the impromptu competitions in the predicate. The second sentence then tells us about the competitions.

- Now let's look at a longer passage, this one from *The Immortal Life of Henrietta Lacks* by Rebecca Skloot. Here we're going to look at five consecutive sentences as context: HeLa cells are the cells that were derived from cervical cancer cells extracted from Henrietta Lacks in 1951—they were the first human cells grown in a lab that were "immortal".

> Researchers had long believed that human cells contained forty-eight chromosomes, the threads of DNA inside cells that contain all of our genetic information. But chromosomes clumped together, making it impossible to get an accurate count. Then, in 1953, a geneticist in Texas accidentally mixed the wrong liquid with HeLa and a few other cells, and it turned out to be a fortunate mistake. The chromosomes inside the cells swelled and spread out, and for the first time, scientists could see each of them clearly. The accidental discovery was the first of several developments that would allow two

researchers from Spain and Sweden to discover that normal human cells have forty-six chromosomes.

- Let's now unpack how the information is presented in these five sentences:

  □ First sentence: Researchers believed there were 48 chromosomes in human cells; the chromosomes contain genetic information.

  □ Second sentence: But the chromosomes clumped together, so they were hard to count. (Chromosomes have been introduced and explained in the first sentence, and now we learn something new.)

  □ Third sentence: "Then, in 1953," prepares us to meet a geneticist, who accidentally mixes the wrong liquid in with some cells.

  □ Fourth sentence: We were just talking about the cells and their chromosomes, so we're prepared to learn something new about them: They swelled and spread out.

  □ Fifth sentence: This sentence sums up what we've just been talking about and then tells us the implications of that accidental discovery: Two researchers from Spain and Sweden discovered that normal human cells have only 46 chromosomes.

- The passage is easy to follow, in part because our expectations are met as we go in terms of how information will be presented to us. We don't have to work too hard as readers in terms of how the information is structured, so we can focus on the story the sentences are telling.

A Detailed Example

- As an example of choppiness, let's take these sentences, modified from an article in *The Atlantic* called "To Remember a Lecture Better, Take Notes by Hand."

  A new study—conducted by Mueller and Oppenheimer—finds that people remember lectures better when they've taken handwritten notes, rather than typed ones. Adolescents these days suffer from short attention spans. The educational system must respond to new technologies. Perhaps it is time to bring back the pencil.

- This passage is choppy because it's been rewritten to make it choppy. It jumps from a study to adolescents to educational reform. Here's what the real article does:

  A new study—conducted by Mueller and Oppenheimer—finds that people remember lectures better when they've taken handwritten notes, rather than typed ones. What's more,

knowing how and why typed notes can be bad doesn't seem to improve their quality. Even if you warn laptop-notetakers ahead of time, it doesn't make a difference. For some tasks, it seems, handwriting's just better.

- The first sentence introduces the study and overall topic. The second sentence picks up the idea of typed notes (which was introduced in the predicate of the first sentence). The third sentence is still on this topic, introducing laptop-notetakers.

- The next paragraph in the article then brings in the question of education. It starts by referring back to the study (known information) and then introduces the new idea that this is relevant to education: "The study comes at a ripe time for questions about laptop use in class. Educators still debate whether to allow students to bring their laptops into the classroom."

- The second sentence here can then go from class to educators and use that to introduce the question of whether students should be allowed to use laptops in class.

Three Basic Patterns

- Three templates exist for helping readers along. These will seem very basic, but that is because they are boiled-down maps; these three templates sometimes underlie very long, complex, and beautiful sentences.

- The first template is the constant template (i.e., we're keeping the subject constant). An example: "The study shows that taking notes by hand helps students retain more information. The study further suggests that even when you tell laptop notetakers not to take notes verbatim, they still struggle to take effective notes." The subject is literally repeated.

- The second template is the derived template. The subject leads to one thing, and then a derivation of the subject leads to another. An example: "The time demands on student-athletes can be intense. For example, voluntary practices may not always feel voluntary."

- The third template is the chained template. One thing leads to another, which leads to another, which leads to another. Here's an invented sentence to go with the earlier *Boys in the Boat* example:

  > Since early in the eighteenth century, the London watermen had also made a sport of racing their dories in impromptu competitions. They were rough-and-tumble events. This informal exuberance could lead to heated debates about cheating and who had actually won.

- That example moves progressively: Competitions gets picked up in the second sentence and we learn they were rough-and-tumble events. Then, the third sentence captures that rough-and-tumbleness in the subject and tells us more about that.

- Chaining can work well, but be careful because it means your paragraph can end fairly far away from where it started.

Scientific Writing

- With this information about the known-new contract in our pocket, let's turn to a few principles proposed by George Gopen and Judith Swan in a wonderful article called "The Science of Scientific Writing."

- Their premise is that scientific writing doesn't need to be as hard to understand as it often is—it is as much or more about the prose than about the complexity of the concepts themselves. As they write, "complexity of thought need not lead to impenetrability of expression."

- Gopen and Swan reiterate fundamental principles about known/new information: Put in stress position the new information, which is usually in the predicate. Place the person/thing whose "story" the sentence is telling in topic position. (This can be a reason to use the passive.) Place old information in the topic position to link back and contextualize forward. In general, provide context for the reader before asking the reader to consider new things.

- It is a very humanizing article as it takes apart scientific writing. For example, they quote this passage:

    > Large earthquakes along a given fault segment do not occur at random intervals because it takes time to accumulate the strain energy for the rupture. The rates at which tectonic plates move and accumulate strain at their boundaries are approximately uniform. Therefore, in first approximation, one may expect that large ruptures of the same fault segment will occur at approximately constant time intervals. If subsequent mainshocks have different amounts of slip across fault, then the recurrence time may vary, and the basic idea of periodic mainshocks must be modified. For great plate boundary ruptures the length and slip often vary by a factor of 2. Along the southern segment of the San Andreas fault the recurrence interval is 145 years with variation of several decades.

- They conclude: "This is the kind of passage that in subtle ways can make readers feel badly about themselves." Each sentence in isolation is fine. But look at how the topics jump around: large earthquakes, rates at which tectonic plates move, one ("one may expect"), subsequent mainshocks, great plate boundary ruptures, and the southern segment of the San Andreas fault.

- The theme—recurrence intervals—is there but not usefully in the topic position. There is lots of great information here, but the reader has to work very hard to follow along. Technical material can be presented more clearly, and that should be our goal as writers.

Closing Advice
- One other good piece of advice: Beware of putting too much information in between the subject and the verb. This happens

with modifiers on the subject's noun phrase. An example: "The study, which looked at what happens when people take notes with laptops (with or without access to the Internet) versus when they take notes by hand, found that people with pencils retained more of the information." Our brains have trouble holding the sentence open waiting for the verb.

■ Finally, when is a sentence too long? When there are too many pieces of information that need stress or emphasis. In other words, look at whether you're trying to introduce a lot of new information in one sentence. If you are, revise. Readers will find new information more easily if it is in its own sentence, in the "new information" position.

Suggested Reading

Atkinson, *Scientific Discourse in Sociohistorical Context.*
Gopen and Swan, "The Science of Scientific Writing."

Questions to Consider

1. How would you explain what it means that a piece of writing is choppy?

2. How can the complexity of our ideas interfere with the clarity of our prose?

Navigating the Choppy Paragraph

It's time to put together a lot of the grammatical pieces we've been talking about into the bigger picture of how we present information in our writing. In this lecture, I will provide a few fundamental pieces of advice about how to help your readers follow your ideas by helping your readers follow you from sentence to sentence. We're going to see some real payoff for understanding how sentences work in terms of subjects and predicates, conjunctive adverbs, relative clauses, and the like. There are some wonderfully concrete ways that you can help make your prose clearer and make it "flow" through your syntactic choices.

Now, there's a reason I said, "flow." Flow is not actually a very useful word to describe writing, although we use it all the time. I have a colleague at Michigan who says, "Rivers flow, writing does not flow." What does flow mean—that the verb comes right after the subject? Well, of course, the verb comes right after the subject. We're trying to capture something about how sentences relate to sentences.

The opposite is that your writing is choppy, and I have to admit that I'm guilty of saying this to students about writing. But a student, when told that their writing is choppy asks, "How do I fix choppy writing," which is a completely fair question.

In this lecture, we'll address exactly that choppiness question, "How do you make your writing less choppy?" In order to do this, we'll need to talk about where we place the weight in the sentence. And here I'm talking about weight in the sense of content, where are we introducing a lot of new information and weight in the sense of the sheer number of words in different elements of a sentence. What helps readers to follow along as we write? What helps them process the information that we are presenting?

With that question, let's return to choppy. What are we saying? Somehow, as a reader, if we're experiencing writing as choppy, we're having trouble seeing connections between sentences. Somehow, our expectations as readers are not being met. We're reading along and expecting one thing and then we get something else, and so our head metaphorically jerks up. "What? Why is that right there? Where is this passage going?" This raises the key question: How can you know, as a writer, what your readers are expecting? And how can you help them navigate your prose? I am going to give you some very specific answers to those questions.

One answer is about how you use conjunctive adverbs or adverb phrases, which we discussed in an earlier lecture. Conjunctive adverbs are words like therefore, nonetheless, consequently and phrases like in addition or in sum. These adverbs help us, as readers, understand how one sentence is connected to the next. As writers, they can help us prepare our readers for what is coming. That said, just to use a conjunctive adverbial, you know right now that I'm about to provide a counter or a caveat because I just said, "that said." That said, there is a more fundamental principle at work in terms of how we can present information sentence to sentence in a way that makes sense to readers. It is often called the known-new contract or given-new contract. What I love about this concept is that it is not rocket science—it is actually very intuitive. And it can be completely revelatory about what is not working in a passage of writing.

Here's the fundamental idea. As readers, we expect the information we know to precede new information. Grammatically, how that works, is that known information will appear in subject position and new information will appear in the predicate. Or known information will be in an introductory phrase—an adverbial, for example—such as "given that."

As an aside here, you can see the way this known-new or given-new contract plays out in tables in publications in English and other languages that read from left to right. As readers, as I just talked to you about, we tend to expect the context or information we know in the subject, which in an English sentence is to the left and new information to the right. In tables, you will often see context or old information in left-hand columns and information to pay attention to in right-hand columns. It's something to think about when you design your own tables.

Let's now return to how the known-new contract plays out in prose. Examples from real writing will help here. Let's start with a straightforward example from the book *Boys in the Boat* by Daniel James Brown. This passage is just two sentences, and we're going to look at how the information is structured within these two sentences. Here we go: "Since early in the eighteenth century, the London watermen had also made a sport of racing their dories in impromptu competitions. They were rough-and-tumble events."

Let's now look at how the information is structured. The first sentence introduces the impromptu competitions in the predicate. The second sentence then tells us about those competitions using the They that refers back to the competitions. The competitions are now known information, and they get picked up in the second sentence in known position. And then we learn something new about them in the predicate of the second sentence.

Let's now look at a longer passage, this one from the book *The Immortal Life of Henrietta Lacks* by Rebecca Skloot. Here we're going to look at five consecutive sentences. And as context for this passage, let me just note that HeLa cells are the cells that were derived from cervical cancer cells extracted from Henrietta Lacks in 1951. They were the first human cells grown in a lab that were immortal.

Here's the passage, and again, this is five sentences:

Researchers had long believed that human cells contained 48 chromosomes, the threads of DNA inside cells that contain all our genetic information. But chromosomes clumped together, making it impossible to get an accurate count. Then, in 1953, a geneticist in Texas accidentally mixed the wrong liquid with HeLa and a few other cells, and it turned out to be a fortunate mistake. The chromosomes inside the cells swelled and spread out, and for the first time, scientists could see each of them clearly. The accidental discovery was the first of several developments that would allow the researchers—two researchers—from Spain and Sweden to discover that normal human cells have 46 chromosomes.

Okay, let's now unpack how the information is presented in these five sentences. The first sentence, "Researchers believed there were 48 chromosomes in human cells." All right. So now we've set the context.

The second sentence, "But chromosomes clumped together..." We, as readers, are prepared to be talking about chromosomes, which have been introduced and explained in the first sentence—and now we learn something new about them. They clump together so they can't be counted accurately.

Moving on to the third sentence, "Then, in 1953." That Then prepares us for the introduction of new information right there, and we're going to get that new information in subject position—but we're ready. This geneticist in Texas, who appears out of nowhere, but we're prepared because we had that Then. So we're not actually surprised to see the geneticist, who accidentally mixes the wrong liquid in with some cells.

Now the fourth sentence, "The chromosomes inside the cells..." Well, we were just talking about those cells and their chromosomes, so we're prepared to learn something new about them—they swelled and spread out.

Now the fifth sentence, "This accidental discovery was..." The "this accidental discovery," sums up what we've just been talking about and then tells us the implications of that accidental discovery—that two researchers from Spain and Sweden discovered that normal human cells have only 46 chromosomes.

To sum up, the passage is easy follow, in part because our expectations are met as we go in terms of how each sentence presents the information. We don't have to work too hard as readers in terms of how the information is structured, so we can focus on the story that the sentences are telling.

What I'm trying to capture is this—each sentence creates expectations for what's going to come next. As readers, we don't read with a completely open mind—equally happy to see whatever the author is going to talk about next. As we read, we make predictions, and we can be thrown when our predictions or expectations for what's going to come next are not met.

Let me show you what I mean. Let's take these sentences from an article in *The Atlantic* called "To Remember a Lecture Better, Take Notes by Hand." It was published in May of 2014. This is passage is four sentences long:

> A new study—conducted by Mueller and Oppenheimer—finds that people remember lectures better when they've taken handwritten notes, rather than typed ones. Adolescents these days suffer from short attention spans. The educational system must respond to new technologies. Perhaps it is time to bring back the pencil.

All right. Let's step back and look at that passage. Things are jumping around here. Handwritten notes are introduced in the first sentence. Adolescents and short attention spans come in the next sentence. Then we get educational reforms due to new technologies, and then at the very end we go back to handwritten notes.

Okay, it's time for me to be honest. This passage is choppy because I rewrote it to make it choppy. Let's look at what I did and then what the real article does.

Let's take the first sentence, which is real. This one is actually in the article. "A new study—conducted by Mueller and Oppenheimer—finds that people remember lectures better when they've taken handwritten notes, rather than typed ones." Where do you, as a reader, expect the passage to go next?

I would guess that you're thinking about possibilities such as handwriting. We're going to talk more about handwriting. Or we're going to talk more about typing. Or we're going to talk about more details from this particular study.

Where did we go instead? Well, the next sentence was about adolescents and their attention spans. It's clearly related, but nothing in this second sentence actually picks up information in the first sentence to make it given information in the second sentence.

So the second sentence is, "Adolescents these days suffer from short attention spans." Now what are the expectations for the next sentence? Perhaps what causes these short attention spans or the effects of them.

What actually follows? This sentence, "The educational system must respond to new technologies." We're smart readers, and we'll try to connect dots. Okay, so we were just talking about attention span, so maybe that is linked to the new technologies. But the sentence actually starts with educational reform, and new technologies is not actually linked to the attention spans explicitly. We can make it work, but readers are having to do a lot of work here. The passage introduces information and then seems not to follow through because things don't get clearly picked up in the next sentence of the passage. As a result, the passage feels choppy and not fully satisfying.

What does the actual article do? Okay, here's the actual passage from the article. What you're going to see is much better than my version.

> A new study—conducted by Mueller and Oppenheimer—finds that people remember lectures better when they've taken handwritten notes, rather than typed ones. What's more, knowing how and why typed notes can be bad doesn't seem to improve their quality. Even if you warn laptop-notetakers ahead of time, it doesn't make a difference. For some tasks, it seems, handwriting's just better.

Let's unpack the actual passage. The second sentence picks up the idea of typed notes, which was introduced in the predicate of the first sentence. The third sentence is still on this topic. It's talking about laptop-notetakers. This passage, therefore, will not feel choppy to us because we have information getting picked up from sentence to sentence as given information, and then we're learning new things about it.

The next paragraph in the article then brings in the question of education. Let's look at how it starts by referring back to the study. The study is now known information in article and then introduces the new idea that this is relevant to education. Here's the passage: "The study comes at a ripe time for questions about laptop use in class. Educators still debate whether to allow students to bring their laptops into the classroom."

The second sentence in this passage can then go from class, because we talked about introducing technology in the class, to educators and the fact that they're debating this use and introduce the question of whether students should be allowed to use laptops in class. Again, the passage is taking information we've been given, carrying it over into the next sentence, and then using that to introduce new topics and questions.

What we're doing here—what I'm doing with these passages—is mapping how information is presented in terms of the structure or the grammar of the sentences. It is a usefully concrete way to understand how our written content is being packaged and how that might or might not work well for our readers.

Here's more good news. There are some basic templates for what readers find helpful in terms of how we package information. I'm going to introduce these useful patterns for adhering to the known-new contract over the next few minutes. These will seem very basic, but that is because it's a boiled-down map or template. These templates can actually underlie very long, complex, and beautiful sentences sometimes. And it's not that we always have to map out information across sentences according to one of these templates, but I can tell you that it is helpful to think about these if you're wrestling with your own writing—or if you're trying to help someone else with their writing that feels choppy.

I can tell you as a teacher, it is so much better than just telling a student, "This feels choppy," and sending them off to fix it on their own. Instead we sit and we map out how the information is working, and they can suddenly see why, as a reader, my head might do that metaphorical jerk up where I think, "Wait. Why did that sentence come right there?"

So here are three general methods for following the known-new contract. The first is what we're going to call constant. What this means is that we're keeping the subject constant as we go from sentence to sentence. Let's imagine the subject is A. So we have A is the subject, and we said B about A. In other words, B is the predicate. So we have A—we say B about A. In the second sentence, we keep A as the subject, and now we say C about A. In the third sentence, we keep A as the subject, and now we say D about A.

Here's an example, "The study shows that taking notes by hand helps students retain more information. The study further suggests that even when you tell laptop-notetakers not to take notes verbatim, they still struggle to take effective notes." You'll see there that the subject is literally repeated. It's the study in both instances.

Here's another example of this constant pattern that's in some a bit more sophisticated in the way it holds the subject constant. Here we go: "Richard Grant White held strong opinions about what constituted correct language. The 19th-century grammarian singled out for critique verbs liked donate, leave, and state."

You can see what I did there. I kept the subject constant—I had, "Richard Grand White." But in the second sentence, I referred to him as the 19th-century grammarian—so using a synonymous phrase, but keeping the subject constant.

The second pattern is what we're going to call derived. In this pattern, let's again imagine our first sentence is AB. A is the subject. B is the predicate that introduces new information about A. In the second sentence, I then have a subset of A, and I say C about a subset of A. You can see why we call it derived. In the second sentence the subject is a subset of the subject of the first sentence.

Here's an example, "The time demands on student-athletes can be intense. For example, voluntary practices may not always feel voluntary." There we're seeing the first sentence has time demands as the subject. The second sentence has voluntary practices as the subject. Voluntary practices are one of the time demands that student-athletes face.

The third model or pattern that you can follow here is called chained. Again, for the first sentence, let's imagine A to B. A is the subject; B is the predicate. Now the second sentence picks up B, makes it the subject, and then tells us C about B. The third sentence picks up C from the predicate of the second sentence, makes it the subject of the third sentence, and then we learn D about C. So you get A to B, B to C, C to D.

Here we can go back to the *Boys in the Boat* example, and I'm going to add my own third sentence just to make the example change. Daniel James Brown is not in any way responsible for the third sentence.

Since early in the eighteenth century, the London watermen had also made a sport of racing their dories in impromptu competitions. They were rough-and-tumble events. This informal exuberance could lead to heated debates about cheating and who had actually won.

You can see how this passage moves progressively. The competitions that are introduced in the predicate of the first sentence gets picked up in second sentence and become the subject, "They were rough-and-tumble events." Then the third sentence captures that rough-and-tumbleness in the subject "this informal exuberance" and tells us something about that informal exuberance.

Chaining can work well, but I have to warn you here to be careful because it can mean that your paragraph can end fairly far away from where it started because you've been chaining from A to B, B to C, C to D, D to E and now we start at A, and we're at E. Of course, what happens in most actual prose is a combination of these different patterns where two sentences are chained and then the next sentence involves holding the subject constant, and so on.

With this information about the known-new contract in our pocket, it seems like a good time to turn to a few principles proposed by George Gopen and Judith Swan in a terrific article called "The Science of Scientific Writing." You can see how Gopen and Swan are building on what we've just been talking about in their subtitle to the article. Here's the subtitle, "If the reader is to grasp what the writer means, the writer must understand what the reader needs." As you can see they're talking about our expectations as readers for how information will be structured.

The premise of the article is that scientific writing doesn't need to be as hard to understand as it often is—it is as much or more about the prose than about the complexity of the concepts themselves. As Gopen and

Swan write, "Complexity of thought need not lead to impenetrability of expression." I love this quote. I think it's something that perhaps should be framed on all of our walls, or we should post it above our computer screen as we write. Complexity of thought need not lead to impenetrability of expression.

Gopen and Swan reiterate some fundamental principles about known-new information. For example, put in stress position the new information, and stress position is usually the predicate. Place the person or thing whose story the sentence is telling in topic position. This, as we've talked about, can be a reason to use the passive voice to get the thing you're telling the story about up into subject position. Gopen and Swan note that you should place old information in topic position to link backwards and to contextualize forwards. In general, they say provide context for the reader before asking the reader to consider new things.

It is a very humanizing article as it takes apart scientific writing. For example, they quote the following long passage. And I'm going to quote it in full because it is worth seeing what they're talking about in terms of the impenetrability of scientific writing sometimes. So here we go:

> Large earthquakes along a given fault segment do not occur at random intervals because it takes time to accumulate the strain energy for the rupture. The rates at which tectonic plates move and accumulate strain at their boundaries are approximately uniform. Therefore, in first approximation, one may expect that large ruptures of the same fault segment will occur at approximately constant time intervals. If subsequent mainshocks have different amounts of slip across fault, then the recurrence time may vary, and the basic idea of periodic mainshocks must be modified. For great plate boundary ruptures the length and slip often vary by a factor of 2. Along the southern segment of the San Andreas fault the recurrence interval is 145 years with variation of several decades.

Gopen and Swan conclude, after quoting this lengthy paragraph, "This is the kind of passage that in subtle ways can make readers feel badly about themselves." I love that because maybe you were feeling bad about yourself as you listened to that paragraph and thought, "I'm not sure I'm following." And if you're thinking that Gopen and Swan could have said that it makes readers feel bad about themselves instead of feel badly about themselves—you know that you're right.

Now, each sentence in this passage of scientific writing in isolation is fine. It's not too long. It uses the appropriate vocabulary.

But look at how the topics jump around when we map them out, which Gopen and Swan do. The first sentence we start with large earthquakes Then, in the next sentence, the subject is "the rates at which tectonic plates move." Third sentence we get one as the subject in, "one may expect." Next sentence, we get subsequent mainshocks. Next sentence, great plate boundary ruptures. Then we get in the next sentence the southern segment of San Andreas fault.

As you can see when I map it out that way, we are often getting new information in the given information spot. In other words, we're getting new information in subject position.

The theme of the paragraph—which seems to be recurrence intervals—is there, but not usefully in topic position. There's lots of great information in this passage, but the reader has to work very hard to follow along. Technical material can be presented more clearly, and I have to say, I think that should be all of our goal as writers.

One other good piece of advice is beware of putting too much information in between the subject and the verb. So don't put too much information between the subject and the verb. You think, "I would never do that." Well, this can happen. It can happen when we get modifiers on the subject noun phrase—particularly long relative clauses.

Let me give you an example, "The study, which looked at what happens when people take notes with laptops, with or without access to the Internet, versus when they take notes by hand, found that people with pencils retained more of the information."

Okay, we can make it through that sentence, but our brains have trouble holding the sentence open long enough to wait for the verb. We had, "the study," then we got a lot of information about the study in terms of what it studied with laptops, whether people could have access to the Internet, and then, finally, we got "found" and learned what the study found. It's very hard to hold onto to the subject, take in all this other information, and then say, "Oh right—here's the verb." So be careful about putting too much information in there between the noun phrase and the subject and the verb.

And finally, when is a sentence too long? Gopen and Swan provide one answer to that. They say, "When there are too many pieces of information that need stress or emphasis. That can be more than one sentence can handle.

In other words, look at whether you're trying to introduce a lot of new information in one sentence. If you are, it's probably worth revising. Readers will find the new information—they'll find it more easily—if it's in its own sentence in the new information position. And you want readers to be able to identify and pay attention to the new information that you're presenting.

We've been focused intensively here on writing, and I'm going to switch gears in the next lecture to focus on the grammar of speech. As part of that, we'll look at some of the fundamental differences between how we present information in speech and on the page.

In formal writing, we don't use Well, and we tend to minimize the So's. But these words do useful work in speech. They serve as traffic signals to help our listeners know what's coming, much like the kinds of written strategies that we've been talking about in this lecture.

What Part of Speech is *Um?*

Lecture 21

The grammar of conversation can be quite different from the grammar of formal writing. And when we study grammar, we often pull our sentences from literature or academic writing or newspapers in order to understand their structure. But the rules we learn from examples like that often don't translate to how conversations work. In this lecture, we'll talk about some fundamental differences between speech and writing, and then how discourse markers function.

Speech Patterns

- It's surprising how often we speak in incomplete sentences and run-ons, and how many other little words there are in there: *um*, *well*, *like*, *you know*, *I mean*, and *yeah*. Obviously this is less true of very formal speech—especially if it is scripted.

- Below is an example of classroom talk, from a teacher in a high school English classroom, talking about Hero and Claudio from Shakespeare's *Much Ado About Nothing*:

  > Right I mean she—OK so she's still dead but she didn't betray him, and if he didn't feel so bad, he didn't feel so bad about her being dead when she betrayed him but now, now when the h— like, when it's his honor, right, i— when he's at fault now he's like oh I feel really bad about her being dead, actually, thought about it a little bit more. Right?

- We see here false starts: "she—OK so she's still dead" and "now when the h— like, when it's his honor." There are effects of real-time processing: The speaker often starts with one grammatical structure and then needs to do something different. We also can see how hard it is to find sentence breaks sometimes in spoken language. The above example is potentially all one sentence.

- When the teacher quotes speech, she puts in a speech discourse marker. Quoting Claudio, she says, "now he's like oh I feel really bad about her being dead." The *oh* is like an opening quotation mark (because we don't get quotation marks when we speak).

- This bit of real speech, because it is a monologue, is actually pretty orderly compared with conversation where people are interrupting each other, taking over the conversational floor, or even just back-channeling. People might also be simultaneously watching TV or texting, or having more than one conversation at once.

The Grammar of Conversation

- Genuine conversation can look chaotic, but it has a grammar of its own. Of course, spoken utterances are filled with nouns, verbs, adjectives, and adverbs, as well as prepositions, pronouns, determiners, and the like. And we obey all the rules we have talked about for creating descriptively grammatical utterances (except when we make false starts or get tangled up in our syntax because we change course in the middle of an utterance).

- We might not, though, follow some of the rules that govern stylistic niceties such as distinguishing *who/whom*, avoiding "equally as important," or catching a "There's three reasons for this." Speech is also filled with words like *um* and *well*—and for younger speakers, lots and lots of *like*.

Involved and Informational Discourse

- To talk about some differences in the grammar of conversation and writing, it is useful to focus on the distinction between involved discourse and informational discourse, as described by linguistics expert Doug Biber.

- The purpose of involved discourse is to build relationships. This is the type of discourse most associated with classroom settings. It involves lots of first- and second-person pronouns. Discourse markers (like *well* and *um*) are frequent. There is a heavy reliance on *to be*. Contractions are also frequent.

- Informational discourse is used to deliver information. This type of discourse packs a lot of information into nouns rather than letting full clauses carry the weight (e.g., "when the company started" becomes "at the company's founding"). Information discourse is also characterized by longer words and attributive adjectives.

- The notion of a *high type/token ratio* captures the much higher rate of variation in word choice in more formal writing. Each word is a type, and each token is a time it appears in the discourse. In writing, we often use a word only once or twice because we've learned to avoid repetition. But in speech, we repeat a lot because this is actually helpful for the people processing in real time.

- The differences captured by the distinction between involved and informational discourse align to some extent with the different processing demands of speaking and writing.

  - In speech, we benefit from repetition and coordination when processing in real time. In writing, we can go back and look again at a more complex syntactic structure.

  - This is part of why listening to someone read a speech, especially, if it wasn't written to be read aloud, can be hard to follow. Speech can also tolerate more ambiguity, which is part of what makes writing hard.

Discourse Markers

- Discourse markers are the little words at the margins (the beginning and end) that help organize discourse and manage listeners' expectations. People sometimes want to talk about them as meaningless, but in fact they do a lot of work for us in conversation. They don't carry meaning the way a noun does, but they are meaningful for us as speakers and listeners.

■ Discourse markers include words such as *so*, *now*, *well*, *uh*, *um*, *oh*, *and*, *but*, and *like*, and lexicalized phrases such as *you know* and *I mean*. They are optional, but can be very helpful as long as we don't overuse them.

■ Discourse markers are not just the disfluencies that people often think they are. Certainly they are sometimes fillers (like *um*), but even that serves a purpose: holding the floor. Discourse markers also do two other important things:

   □ They can be like signposts in a conversation. They can signal to listeners how to understand an utterance in relation to the utterances that precede and follow it.

   □ They can help the listener understand the utterance in the context of the relationship being negotiated between the speaker and the listener.

■ Think about the grammatical choices we make in terms of how to phrase a request, depending on who we're talking to: "Save that seat for me" versus "Could you please save that seat for me?" versus "I'm sorry to bother you, but is there any way you could save that seat for me?" Discourse markers help with this; for example, we can signal ending a turn: "I'm not sure what I think about that, so …."

■ Let's look at five specific discourse markers to see how they work.

   1. *So* shows effects or logical consequences. It can also introduce summaries or rephrasings: "So, the main point here is…." And in an extended narrative, it can introduce different parts of the story: "So I get to the building …."

2. *Now* can signal a topic shift (like a paragraph marker): "Now, let's talk about how determiners differ from adjectives." Like *so*, it can also flag that something important is coming: "Now, this raises a fundamental question ...."

3. *Well*, according to work by Andreas Jucker at the University of Zurich, can also introduce a new topic, but one of its most interesting functions is prefacing a dispreferred response: "Well, I can see what you're saying, but ...."

4. *Um* functions in much the same way as *well*.

5. *Oh* does a surprising amount of work. One function is indicating surprise; for example, consider: "Thank you" versus "Oh, thank you." *Oh* can also preface a suddenly remembered question: "Oh, did you ask about when the road will reopen?" It can also help if we need to repair: "Oh, it is on Liberty Street, not Washington."

When someone wants to signal the end of their turn, they might end a sentence with "I mean..." and trail off.

- Look at two more phrases that help us navigate relationships with our listeners.

  1. *You know* (or *y'know*): This can conclude an argument or trail off at the end of a turn. It can also introduce a story. Importantly, the phrase can establish solidarity with an audience. Here's an example from an interview of Ken Wheaton (editor of *Advertising Age*) on CBS This Morning in 2015: "We'll pretend to like PBS but we really want to go, you know, go home and watch junk on TV."

  2. *I mean* can signal an upcoming adjustment: "I would never do that. I mean, I'm not saying that I wouldn't think about it." It can also help minimize the authority of the speaker, which speakers often choose to do to make their audience feel more equal. Compare "I think that would work" with "I mean, I think that would work."

And, Like

- *And* is both a conjunction and a discourse marker depending on what it is doing. Here is *and* as a discourse marker in a conversation between two people:

  □ Person 1: "I started watching the new season of *Frankie and Grace* last night."

  □ Person 2: "And is it good?"

- *And* is building from one utterance to the next, to suggest a connection.

- *Like*, too, can be a discourse marker. It can be a filler, or it can be a focuser: "It was, like, awesome."

- Some younger speakers use it a lot, which can be distracting. That's true of any discourse marker. If you're concerned that you're overusing *like* or any other discourse marker, awareness is the first step. A countermeasure: Record yourself.

Suggested Reading

Biber, Conrad, Reppen, and Byrd, "Speaking and Writing in the University."

Dailey-O'Cain, "The Sociolinguistic Distribution of and Attitudes toward Focuser 'Like' and Quotative 'Like.'"

D'Arcy, "*Like* and Language Ideology."

Schiffrin, *Discourse Markers*.

Vuolo, "So...."

Questions to Consider

1. What are some of the problems with the advice "Just write it like you would say it?"

2. You may have noticed that when people are being interviewed on television or radio, they may sometimes (or often) start their answers with *So*. What work do you think *So* might be doing in this context?

Lecture 21 Transcript

What Part of Speech is *Um*?

I cannot emphasize strongly enough how different the grammar of conversation can be from the grammar of formal writing. And when we study grammar, we often pull our sentences from literature or from academic writing or from newspapers in order to understand their structure. When I teach my course on the structure of English, I often use an assignment where I send students out with their phones to record real-life conversations and then to transcribe them. I teach them the conventions where we transcribe every pause, every bit of laughter, every false start; then we analyze what is happening in those real-life conversations. Students often can't believe how often we speak in incomplete sentences as well as in run-ons, how often we start a sentence one way and then shift halfway and go somewhere else, as well as how many other little words there are in there: um, well, like, you know, I mean, yeah.

Obviously, this is less true of very formal speech—especially if it is scripted. Right now, I'm on my best linguistic behavior. Now, I have the advantage that I've had time to think about what I want to say ahead of time, and I can slow down a little because I know you 're not going to interrupt me. I'm also being careful. This means that I will have fewer false starts, but I will have some. Because this speech that I'm doing right now is also more planned, and you and I can't really interact right now, there are also fewer discourse markers like *well* and *um*, but there are some.

What we know from studies is that in classroom contexts where everyone is in the same room and can interact, formal classroom speech patterns more like informal conversation than it does like a lecture. This is true even if someone is lecturing, as long as they are not completely reading from a prepared speech. Let me show you an example of real classroom talk, from a teacher in a high school English classroom, talking about Hero and Claudio from Shakespeare's *Much Ado About Nothing*. Here's the teacher:

> Right I mean she– OK so she's still dead, but she didn't betray him, and if he didn't feel so bad, he didn't feel so bad about her being dead when she betrayed him but now, now when the h– like, when it's his honor, right, i– when he's at fault now he's like oh I feel really bad about her being dead, actually, thought about it a little bit more. Right?

We see here, in real classroom talk, false starts such as "she– OK so she's still dead," and "now when the h– like, when it's his honor." We also see the effects of real-time processing. For example, when we start with one grammatical structure and then need to do something different because we realize that our sentence is somehow now taking a new turn. We can also see how it's hard to find sentence breaks sometimes in spoken language. That entire passage could potentially be one big long sentence. Then there are all the discourse markers like "OK, like, oh" and "right." What about *right?* I have to say; I think that this is maybe a teaching thing. I hear it in other contexts too, but I'm aware that I do it as a teacher, that as I'm talking, particularly if I'm taking a longer turn, I will intersperse these *rights* as I go. It seems to be a way to signal, without stopping, signal my desire for students to be following along. So I'm talking, and I say, "right?" And then I just keep going. Someone pointed out to me that it also can feel sometimes perhaps a little bit coercive. It forces people into implicit agreement if they don't interrupt you after you say *right*. Or it forces them to interrupt you regularly if they want to make it clear that they disagree with you.

One other thing I like about this excerpt is that when the teacher quotes speech in it, she puts in a speech discourse marker. When she's quoting Claudio, she says, "now he's like oh I feel really bad about her being dead,"

the *oh* is something we often do when we actually start talking, and she puts it into Claudio's spoken discourse. "Claudio was like, 'oh.'" One of the reasons to do this is that, of course, in speech, we don't get quotation marks. She needs to signal that Claudio has started talking. We have the *like,* and then we get the *oh* to signal that what he's saying has now started. The teacher also uses that quotative *like.* She says, "Claudio was like." The *like,* as a quotative, usefully blurs direct and indirect speech. We don't know if Claudio actually · said what she quotes him as saying, or whether it's indirect speech, he said something like what she quotes him as saying. The quotative *like* also usefully blurs the distinction between speech and thought. Perhaps Claudio just thought that. He thought, "oh I feel really bad." Quotative *like* can be really very useful, and it is a quotative that many of us are using at this point.

This bit of real speech, because it is a monolog, is actually pretty orderly compared with conversation where people are interrupting each other and taking over the conversational floor from each other or even just back-channeling. Back-channeling is what we do as speakers when we're talking with other speakers and want to show them that we're following along or listening. This can be gestures like nodding your head or smiling, but it often can take the form of those little listening noises that we make. Things like "uh-huh, uh-huh, yeah," that's what linguist call back-channeling, and when you record real life conversation you'll often get a lot of simultaneous speech because some speakers are back-channeling. In real life conversation, people might also simultaneously be watching television, or texting, or having more than one conversation at once. Real conversation does not look like a movie script. Now, I myself grew up in a home of interrupters. We believe that if you already know what someone's going to say you might as well interrupt and help them finish so that you can just keep going. We see this as highly cooperative behavior, but I've come to learn that not everyone sees it this way, and I try to be a little better behaved when I'm talking with people and reduce the amount of simultaneous talk.

All in all, when we look at genuine conversation, it can look a bit chaotic, but spoken conversation has a grammar of its own. Of course, spoken utterances are filled with nouns, verbs, adjectives, and adverbs, as well as prepositions, pronouns, determiners, and all the other parts of speech that we've discussed. And we obey all the rules we've talked about for creating descriptively grammatical utterances except for when we make false starts or get tangled up in our syntax because we change course in the middle of an utterance—it can happen..

We might not, though, in speech, follow some of the rules that govern some of the stylistic niceties that we've talked about in this course such as distinguishing *who* and *whom*, avoiding *equally as important,* or catching a *There's* three reasons for that. But speech is also filled with words like *um* and *well*, and, for younger speakers, with lots and lots of *likes*. In this lecture, we'll talk about some of these fundamental differences between speech and writing, and then how those little discourse markers like *well* and *um* work.

To talk about some of these differences in the grammar of conversation and the grammar of writing, particularly formal writing, it's useful to focus on the distinction between involved and informational discourse. This distinction between involved and informational discourse comes from Doug Biber, who's a linguist at Northern Arizona University. This difference captures a difference in terms of the grammar and how we present content. And this difference stems from fundamental differences in purpose. For spoken language, Biber points out; we are very focused on building relationships a lot of the time, and this is the involved discourse pattern. In written language, we can often be more focused on the purpose of delivering information, and this is where we get the informational discourse. Biber has shown that even classroom discourse tends to pattern more like involved discourse, that it's about the relationships that teachers and students are building, it's not in any way just about the delivery of information.

Let me describe to you some of the features of involved discourse. This is the kind of discourse that we see a lot in spoken language. You get a lot of first and second person pronouns *I, we,* and *you.* That's unsurprising in terms of conversation. You also get a lot of demonstratives this would be things like *this* and *that.* We do a lot of pointing in conversation with or without specific nouns after it. That we'll talk about *this means,* or *that over there.* Involved discourse also shows a heavy reliance on *to be* versus what we've talked about already in this course about powerful, varied writing where you'd see a wider range of verbs. Spoken involved discourse also relies on hedges, things like *kind of, maybe, sort of.* In addition, we tend to get intensifiers or emphatics, words like *very, really, so, super.* Spoken involved discourse tends to use a lot of present tense and contractions. Then you get those discourse markers as we've talked about: *well, um, so, now.* Spoken discourse also gives you these coordinated structures where we get clauses connected by *and, or, but, so.* You also will see a good amount of the subordinator *because.*

In contrast, let's turn to informational discourse. Informational discourse, and again this characterizes more formal writing, packs a lot of information into nouns rather than letting full clauses carry the weight. Let me show you what I mean. In spoken language, we might say something like "when the company started." In more formal written language we might say, "at the company's founding." Here's another example, in spoken language we might say, "how we did it was," in written discourse we might say, "the process was," or "the procedure was." You can see how that information is getting condensed into just a noun phrase. This process of nominalization where we turn a verb or an adjective into a noun or a whole clause into a noun often removes agents and removes active verbs. It can be a very efficient way of transmitting a good amount of information in a short, dense way, but it can also result in very content-heavy nouns that become abstract as they lose the agents doing the actions. I do want to say that this can be something to check in your own writing, especially when you're trying to talk about complex ideas. See if you've gotten all the information packed into abstract nouns and lost the agents.

Informational discourse is also characterized by longer words, and by attributive adjectives. These are the adjectives that sit right before the noun in the noun phrase, and this is related to this idea that we're packing a lot of information into the noun phrase in informational discourse. You also get what is called a high type/token ratio. Let me explain what I mean. What this really captures is that you have a much higher rate of variation in word choice in more formal writing. Here's what we mean by the high type/token ratio. Each word is a type, and each token is a time that that word appears in the discourse. So let's imagine I'm writing and I use the noun *exuberance,* and I use it only once in the essay I'm writing. Well, that gives me a 1/1 ratio, which is very high. But let's imagine the verb *to be* in a passage of spoken discourse. One verb, *to be,* I use it 312 times. Well, that would be a low type to token ratio. In writing, we often use a word only once or twice because we've learned to avoid repetition. In speech, we repeat a lot because this is actually helpful for the people when they're processing in real time to hear the same nouns and verbs and other words come up again and again.

The difference captured by the distinction between involved and informational discourse aligns to some extent with the demands of speaking and writing. In speech, we benefit from repetition and from coordination when we're processing in real time. In writing, we can go back, and we can look again at a more complex syntactic structure, and we can parse it again if we didn't get it the first time. I have to say; this difference is part of why it can be difficult to listen to someone reading a speech, especially if they haven't written that speech to be read aloud, it can be hard to follow. Speech, as we've talked about in this course, can also tolerate much more ambiguity than writing. This is because in speech we're typically there, we can see on someone's face if they aren't following or if we've said something that's confused them, and we can correct. The fact that written language cannot tolerate ambiguity this way is part of what makes writing really hard.

So those are all differences in grammatical structure as well as some differences in word choice. One of biggest differences you'll notice between speech and writing is the presence of discourse markers, like *so*. When students transcribe for the assignment that I give them in class they often tend to leave these discourse markers out the first pass they make through the transcription. I think what's happening here is that, as speakers and listeners, we've trained ourselves not to hear these little discourse markers as words, as content, so we learn to ignore them. When students go back the second time, and they try to transcribe everything carefully they'll catch all those *ums, wells, sos, yeahs.*

Discourse markers are these little words often at the margins of the discourse, at the beginning of an utterance, at the end of an utterance that help us organize the discourse and manage listeners' expectations. You will see sometimes they happen in the middle, but often they're happening at the margins. People sometimes want to talk about them as meaningless, but in fact, they do a lot of work for us in conversation. They don't carry meaning the way a noun carries meaning, but they are meaningful for us as speakers and listeners. As we've talked about, these include words such as *so, now, well, uh, um, oh, and, but,* and *like,* as well as lexicalized phrases—phrases that have come to function as a unit—such as *you know,* and *I mean.*

These discourse markers are optional in the sense that they're not required to transmit the content of the utterance. There isn't a distinction in content between "here's the main point" and "now, here's the main point." But these discourse markers can be very helpful, as I'll show you. When they become less helpful is when any one of us overuse a particular discourse marker, at which point that discourse marker can get distracting, and then it can't do it's subtle work within the conversation. From the beginning, I want to emphasize that these little words are not just disfluencies the way that people often think they are. Certainly, sometimes they are fillers, they're a way to hold onto the floor, but that in and of itself is a purpose. If I'm not done speaking, and I want to make sure that you know that I'm not done speaking, then I need to make some noise. So I'm talking and then I say, "Uh…" and then I keep talking, and you didn't interrupt.

First discourse markers can be like signposts in a conversation, the equivalent of "U-turn ahead," or "I'm coming to a stop." They can signal to listeners how to understand an utterance in relation to the utterances that precede and follow it. We sometimes call this information management. How the information is building, contradicting what came before, or repairing what came before—that might be the U-turn. Discourse markers can also recognize old information as somehow newly relevant, or that we're winding down here, or perhaps we're revving up to tell a story

The second thing that discourse markers can do is help the listener understand the utterance in the context of the relationship being negotiated between the speaker and the listener. Am I as the speaker trying to connect with you? Am I trying to mitigate the effects of a not very nice thing that I'm about to say to you? Maybe I'm minimizing my own authority. Discourse markers can help me do that.

This last point reminds us how much negotiation happens in conversation: both negotiation of the floor—whose turn is it to talk—and negotiation of our relationships with other people, even our closest friends. Think about the grammatical choices we make in terms of how to phrase a request, and the ways in which this is a negotiation because it depends on who we're talking to. I might say, "Save that seat for me" or I might say, "Could you please save that seat for me?" Or if I want to be super polite "I'm so sorry to bother you, but is there any way you could save that seat for me?" All of those involve a different negotiation with this person about saving this seat.

We are always trying not to step on other people's feet, or on their toes, in terms of politeness and just in terms of just the logistics of talk. When is it our turn to take the floor? Discourse markers can help with this. For example, we can signal that we're ending a turn. Think about "I'm not sure what I think about that, so..." and now you know that I'm done. Or "I'm not sure what I think about that, I mean..." and again I'm signaling to you that I'm finished speaking. Let's look at five specific discourse markers to see how they work. We'll start with *so* given that it is becoming a peeve for some, given how common it is. For example, listeners are writing into National Public Radio about how often people use *so* to start answers in interviews.

The discourse marker *so* can do a few different things. It can show the effects or logical consequences both within one person's turn or from turn to turn to show that what I'm saying is a logical consequence of what you just said. *So* can introduce summaries or rephrasings; "So, the main point here is...." Within an extended narrative or story *so* can also indicate parts of the story. I think about it as the equivalent of paragraph breaks. Here's a story, "So while I was driving over here..." blah blah blah. "So I get to the building..." blah blah blah. "So there I am in the elevator..." blah blah blah. You can see, it's narrating those different little episodes within the story. Then let's imagine that you interrupt and then I need to recommence the story because you've interrupted and I recommence by saying, "So we were in the elevator...."

You may have noticed that *so* is on the rise, that you are hearing it a lot. It was featured on a 2012 episode of *Lexicon Valley,* which is a really great podcast on *Slate,* and in this podcast, they did with interviews with Geoff Raymond at UC Santa Barbara and Galina Bolden at Rutgers. As I noted, many people have noticed that *so* often happens in response to an interview question. Bolden, in her research, argues that the *so* used in this way is what she calls an other-centered way to begin. In other words, you asked something and when I say *so* it suggests that you've asked me that I was thinking about, and I have a response for you because I care about you, and I've been thinking about this. If I ask a question, and I use *so* at the beginning, it can also make the question seem like my question is a logical consequence of seeing you. *So* can also be a way to trail off, it passes the conclusion of whatever I just said back to you. Here's the conversational floor. Stand-alone *so* can be a way to prompt action by another person in a conversation. You just say, "So." And then it's their turn.

Now, let's turn to *now*. *Now* can signal a topic shift like I did right there. I hear myself do it a lot when I'm teaching. I will say, "Now, let's think how determiners differ from adjectives." What I'm saying is that we're now turning to a new topic. But *now* and *so* can also flag that something important is coming—a main point or key a question. For example, "Now, this raises a fundamental question…" these are sometimes called attention getters in speech, and you think about how helpful they are. Let's just imagine that you're in a meeting where you just happen to be multitasking, and you may realize that you're listening to those little attention getters to know when you need to tune in more closely to what's happening.

Let's look at *well*. There's been some terrific work on *well* done by Andreas Jucker at the University of Zurich. He notes that *well* can also introduce a new topic, but here's one of its most interesting functions: *well* can preface what linguists call a dispreferred response. A dispreferred response is one that expresses disagreement or is in some way face-threatening; it's saying something that the other person doesn't really want to hear. Let's imagine a conversation in which person A says, "People really trust her." And then person B says, "Well.…" You know that person B is about to contradict person A, or say something that means, "I'm not sure if everybody trusts her." Here's another example. Someone asks, "Can you join us for dinner tonight?" And you say, "Well.…" We know you're about to say no. That's your dispreferred response. Here's one other example, "Well, I can see what you're saying, but…" and the *well* signals that that *but* is coming, that I'm about to say something that doesn't completely agree with you. The discourse marker *um* can do the same thing

The discourse marker *oh* does a surprising amount of work in conversation, and one of its functions is to indicate surprise. You might be surprised how often we want to indicate surprise. Consider getting a compliment. You could say, "Thank you," or you could say, "Oh, thank you." The second makes it seem like you weren't expecting that compliment, you were a little surprised by it. *Oh* could preface a suddenly remembered question "Oh, did you ask about when the road will reopen?" Or if you remind me of something, I might say "Oh, that's right." *Oh* can also preface a question or a statement with wrong information. I need to repair what you said, and I say, "Oh, it wasn't that." Or perhaps I need to repair something I said. I say, "Oh, it's on Liberty Street, not Washington."

Let's now look at two more discourse markers that are phrases that help us navigate relationships with our listeners. One is *you know*. *You know* can conclude an argument. For example, "that's just the way I see it, you know?" Or it can be the way we trail off at the end of a turn "because I couldn't figure it out. You know...." You know it's your turn. *You know* can be a way that we introduce a story "You know when I was a kid..." and off I go. But importantly, one of the things *you know* can do is establish solidarity with an audience. Here's an example from an interview of Ken Wheaton, who's the editor of "Advertising Age" on CBS *This Morning* in 2015. He says, "We'll pretend to like PBS, but we really want to go, you know, go home and watch junk on TV." And that *you know* is saying, "you know, you in the audience, you agree with me, you know what I'm saying." *You know* can seem like it's inviting participation or at least asking for a back-channel. That's a moment for you to nod because you know, or perhaps inviting it's inviting disagreement, but it's inviting you to participate. It's difficult if you overuse *you know* because if you're saying, "you know," all the time and the person says, "Wait a minute, I don't know," or if they just get distracted by all those *you knows*.

The phrase *I mean* can signal that there's an upcoming adjustment in the conversation. I need to repair or adjust. For example, I say, "I would never do that. I mean, I'm not saying that I wouldn't think about it." You can see what the *I mean* does there. The other thing that *I mean* can do is help minimize the authority of the speaker, which speakers, at least sometimes, choose to do to make their audience feel more equal. Think about the difference between "I think that would work," versus "I mean, I think that would work." The *I mean* adjusts a little bit, gives a little more space to you as we have this conversation. *I mean* can also signal a turn-taking moment. It's another way that we can trail off at the end of a turn "I think that would work. I mean…" I'm signaling signal some hesitation; now you can come into the conversation.

So, what part of speech is *um?* It's a discourse marker, and linguists often call discourse markers a lexical class all by themselves. The word *and* as we know can be a coordinator. It can also be a discourse marker depending on what it's doing in a conversation. For example, when it's connecting two utterances by different speakers it can be a discourse marker. Here we have a conversation between person one and person two. Person one says, "I started watching the new season of 'Frankie and Grace' last night." Person 2: "And is it good?" That *and* is a discourse marker that says my question connects directly to what you just said. *And* is building from one utterance to the next.

Now, you will notice that I haven't talked about *like* here, and it too can be a discourse marker. It can also be a filler, and it can be a focuser. It's focuser in something like, "It was like awesome." Some younger speakers use *like* a lot, which can be distracting. As we've noticed, this is true of any discourse marker. Here's one student from that class about Shakespeare's *Much Ado About Nothing*, still talking about Hero and Claudio. The student:

> Well I think, in rebuttal I think that, um, I think he thinks that he loves her, like I honestly think that he thinks that he's in love with her, but I think that like, like, like I agree with you, like he is like a jerkface and he like only cares about his honor, but I think that he like, he himself like legitimately thinks that he like loves this girl.

That's a lot of *like*. *Like* can signal youth, that's one of the things it can do. This student will, in the long run, benefit from growing out of using this many *likes*, and that student probably will grow out of it. Awareness is the first step. One piece of advice that I give to students who are trying to ween themselves from *like* is to record themselves. When you hear how many *likes* you have in your own speech, it can help you start to monitor for those.

So, with that, I will conclude this lecture, feeling enormously self-conscious about every discourse marker that I have used for the past half an hour and I know that you will now be primed to listen for in future lectures, no matter what new topic I'm talking about. And our new topic is going to return to the written language: we're going to talk about punctuation.

I've mentioned Oxford commas a few times in previous lectures, and I have kept saying, just wait. We'll we're there. Now we get to dive into commas and semicolons and their other punctuation friends or accomplices like the colon and the all-purpose dash.

Lecture 22

Duck, Duck, Comma, and Duck

In both American English and British English, according to a study in 1987 by linguist Charles Meyer, the comma and the period are neck-in-neck for the most common punctuation mark (40–45 percent each), with comma winning by a nose. In terms of which punctuation marks people are most confused about, the comma, the semicolon, and apostrophe are at the top of the list, with the dash not far behind. We'll focus on the comma, semicolon, colon, and dash in this lecture: the punctuation marks that structure the sentence.

Early Punctuation

- Punctuation is a key part of how we organize language on the page. Sentences end with periods, question marks, or exclamation points. They do not end with commas, colons, semicolons, or dashes. Slashes now have a very little role to play other than in things like *and/or*, but that has not always been the case.

- The earliest manuscripts in Roman antiquity typically did not have punctuation; readers often were familiar with the texts, and this way scribes did not prejudice the reading. The earliest punctuation marks that were added to texts were guides to phrasing.

- It is a modern notion that punctuation should align with grammatical structure as opposed to spoken phrasing (and not everyone agrees on this). For English, the printing press started to stabilize punctuation after it was introduced in 1476, but there was lots of variation in the Renaissance.

- The following example shows a few of the differences in punctuation. It's a couple of lines from a story, "How the Witch Served a Fellow in an Alehouse," which was published in 1606 in a pamphlet called *The Most Cruell and Bloody Murder*. Here is the passage: "At last the witch got so much time to cal to him, Doest thou heare good friend (quoth she?) What sayst thou ill face (quoth he?)"

- The dialogue is framed by "quoth she/he" in parentheses. You'll notice that the question mark is in the "wrong place": in the parenthetical as opposed to at the end of the question. Then there is no period after "(quoth she?)" or "(quote he?)" to end the sentence.

- The rise of prescriptive grammars in the 18th century started to set down stricter standards for how punctuation should and shouldn't be used—but if you read 18th and 19th century texts, you'll still see punctuation used in ways we wouldn't see as standard now.

- Often that is because there is more punctuation than we're now accustomed to. Let's consider the first sentence of Jane Austen's *Pride and Prejudice*: "It is a truth universally acknowledged, that a single man in possession of a good fortune, must be in want of a wife." We now wouldn't have either of those commas, especially the second one.

Modern Rules: Commas

- The 20th century witnessed some reigning in of punctuation. We'll focus on the modern rules for the rest of this lecture. Let's start with rules about commas.

- Commas are designed to mark or set off phrases or groups of words shorter than a sentence. There are a few set rules for how to use commas and then some variation.

- Here are five times when commas are now recommended if not required:

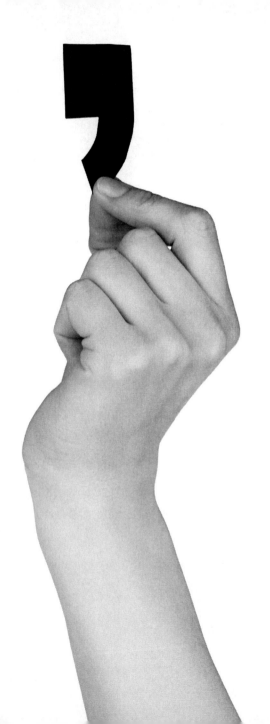

1. Between two full clauses coordinated by a coordinator like *or, and,* or *but*: "He played tennis for four hours yesterday, and his back and arm muscles are letting him know about that today."

2. Commas around a non-restrictive clause. This is how we show it is nonrestrictive and it does correspond to a pause in speech. As an example: "Paul's sister, who is an attorney in NYC, paid him a surprise visit." Here Paul has just one sister. But let's imagine Paul has more than one. Then we'd have: "Paul's sister who is an attorney in NYC paid him a surprise visit."

3. Commas around any kind of parenthetical phrase: "The U.S. Constitution, as discussed earlier, outlines ...."

4. Commas after introductory subordinate clauses: "After the mayor met with citizens from the neighborhood, she approved a zoning change that would allow a high-rise hotel."

5. Commas in a list between items: "nouns, verbs, and adverbs" or "nouns, verbs and adverbs."

- That last category raises the question of the Oxford comma, which occurs after the penultimate item. With attempts to streamline or minimize punctuation in the 20th century, the Oxford comma was taken out in some style guides. Today, it's typically a question of "house style" or personal style.

- People can have strikingly strong feelings about the Oxford comma. Some argue it should be required because otherwise there can be ambiguity.

Commas, Consistency, and Aesthetics

- The question of consistency comes up with constructions where a comma is variable, in particular with introductory adverbials. Most everyone wants a comma if the adverbial gets long: "In addition to higher pay for all employees, ..." The word *however* always requires commas around it.

- Part of each of our decisions about commas is going to depend on whether we prefer lightly or more heavily punctuated text. The difference between "Hi Eileen" and "Hi, Eileen" is really about aesthetics, not correctness.

- But for all this, there is one thing a comma cannot do: connect two clauses without a coordinator—at least according to most style guides for formal English. This is the comma splice. An example: "Erica was the queen of the prom, she dazzled everyone."

Modern Rules: Semicolons

- Many people have strong feelings about the semicolon. Some, like Kurt Vonnegut and George Orwell, think it should never be used. Others, like Charles Dickens and David Crystal, find it nuanced and sophisticated.

- The 18th century witnessed the explosion of the semicolon. Lindley Murray described it as the punctuation mark that divided a compound sentence into two or more parts, "not so closely connected as those which are separated by a comma, nor yet so little depend on each other, as those which are distinguished by a colon."

- There was some heavy use of semi-colons in 20th century. For instance, take these lines from Evelyn Waugh's 1945 novel *Brideshead Revisited*:

> "I have been here before," I said; I had been there before; first with Sebastian more than twenty years ago on a cloudless day in June, when the ditches were white with fool's parsley and meadowsweet and the air heavy with all the scents of summer; it was a day of peculiar splendour such as our climate affords once or twice a year, when leaf and flower and bird and sun-lit stone and shadow seem all to proclaim

the glory of God; and though I had been there so often, in so many moods, it was to that first visit that my heart returned on this, my latest.

■ Today, semicolons have two main uses:

1. Joining two independent clauses that have a close semantic relationship. There could be no conjunctive adverb or something like *nevertheless*, or *thus*, or *put differently*. The semicolon shows readers these ideas are tightly linked.

2. In a list where items are long and have punctuation within them. For example: "I went to Vegas with my friend Auden, who had never been to Vegas; my sister, who loves Vegas in a way I don't understand; and my mom, who just wanted to spend time with us."

Modern Rules: Colons

■ The colon, when introduced at the end of the 16th century, was used to mark a pause longer than a comma or semicolon but shorter than a period.

■ One apt description of the colon is that it urges the reader forward, foreshadowing that what is to come is going to explain or exemplify what you have just read. Colons are now used before lists, examples, definitions, or other explanatory material.

■ The colon and semicolon barely figure in the written English of texting: Their formality makes them a bad choice rhetorically and aesthetically. But they do serve an important role in the non-emoji smiley and winking faces: :) and ;).

Modern Rules: Dashes

■ Now we turn to the dash. Can one misuse the dash? Yes, but it's hard. Overuse is more common. The dash can serve the same function as a comma, semi-colon, or colon, but with a different, less formal connotation. It often suggests an interruption or a new thought/afterthought.

- Here's a nice example of dash usage from an article by Marko Dragojevic and Howard Giles published in *Human Communication Research* in 2016: "Two experiments examined the effects of processing fluency—that is, the ease with which speech is processed—on language attitudes toward native- and foreign-accented speech."

- Sometimes no other punctuation mark will quite do the trick. One instance is with an introductory list followed by a clause to explain: "X, Y, Z—all these help explain ...."

- Another instance is with an added phrase (not a clause) that wouldn't do well with a comma. Here's an example from George Eliot's *Middlemarch*: "He had done nothing exceptional in marrying—nothing but what society sanctions, and considers an occasion for wreaths and bouquets."

Formal and Informal Writing

- As we think about punctuation in formal writing, remember Bishop Lowth in the 18th century: "The doctrine of punctuation must needs be very imperfect: few precise rules can be given, which will hold without exception in all cases; but much must be left to the judgement and taste of the writer"

- There are guidelines, but the very creativity of human language and of good prose will require some flexibility and some application of good sense to punctuation. Also recognize that punctuation in different registers will function differently.

- There is a sense out there that texting is ruining our sense of punctuation. But that isn't necessarily the case—it's more that the rules of punctuation in texting need to do something different.

- Think about early punctuation, which tried to capture oral delivery. In texting, punctuation is used to try to capture tone, facial expression, and other parts of context.

- Emoticons and emoji do this work, as do shorthands like *jk*, and *lol*. And punctuation marks have been repurposed: The exclamation mark shows agreement but not necessarily lots of enthusiasm unless there are several. The period is serious if not angry. The ellipsis is skeptical or invites a response. And the unmarked/generic punctuation choice is no punctuation at all.

Suggested Reading

Crystal, *Txting*.
———, *Making A Point*.
Parkes, *Pause and Effect*.
Truss, 2003. *Eats, Shoots & Leaves*.

Questions to Consider

1. What do you see as the relationship between punctuation marks like commas, periods, semicolons, colons, and dashes and the spoken language?

2. Do you like the Oxford comma or find it unnecessary? Make your case.

Lecture 22 Transcript

Duck, Duck, Comma, and Duck

W hat is the most common punctuation mark? Let me give you a moment to think about that. What is the most common punctuation mark? What is your guess? I would be willing to bet that none of you guessed the semi-colon or the exclamation point, and you'd be right.

And probably, you didn't guess the question mark either, right? In both American English and British English, according to a 1987 study by the linguist Charles Meyer at UMass-Boston, the comma and the period are neck-in-neck for most common punctuation mark; both of them sitting at 40–45 percent of punctuation overall, with comma winning by a nose—or by the length of an ellipsis, so to speak. Then, in terms of frequency, it goes the dash at 2–3 percent, the semi-colon at 1.5–2 percent, then the question mark, the colon, and finally the exclamation mark. Are you surprised that the semi-colon is more common than the question mark? I was.

In terms of which punctuation marks people are most confused about, I think the comma, the semi-colon, and then the apostrophe—which you'll see wasn't in that list, but we'll talk about it—those three are at the top of the list of the punctuation marks people are confused about. Perhaps also the dash, which can feel a bit like a free-for-all. We'll focus on the comma, the semi-colon, the colon, and the dash in this lecture—the punctuation marks that structure the sentence. We'll spend the entire next lecture on the apostrophe.

Punctuation is a key part of how we organize language on the page. Sentences end with periods, questions end with question marks, and exclamations end with exclamation points. Sentences do not end with commas, they do not end with colons or semi-colons, and they do not end with dashes. Slashes now have very little role to play other than in things like "and/or," but that has not always been the case.

Let me provide a brief history on punctuating sentences in the West. The earliest manuscripts in Roman antiquity typically did not have punctuation. Readers were often already familiar with texts, and this way the scribes felt they weren't prejudicing the reading by inserting their own punctuation to indicate how they thought a sentence or passage should be read. The earliest punctuation marks that were added to texts were guides to phrasing. And what I'm talking about here is taken in part from a great book by Malcolm Parkes called *Pause and Effect: An Introduction to the History of Punctuation in the West.*

It is a modern notion that punctuation should align with grammatical structure as opposed to spoken phrasing. As I said, that's how punctuation first came in; was to capture how we should say a text aloud. And to this day, not everyone agrees about what the relationship between spoken phrasing and punctuation should be. For English, the printing press started to stabilize punctuation after it was introduced in 1476. But you continue to see lots of variation in punctuation in the Renaissance, including between what was called the virgule—which we would now call a slash—and the comma. The virgule and the comma could be used interchangeably; the comma starts to take over in about 16th century.

Just to show you a few of the differences between punctuation in the Renaissance and today, let me share a couple of lines from a story called "How the Witch Served a Fellow in an Alehouse." This story was published in 1606 in a pamphlet called *The Most Cruell and Bloody Murder.* This pamphlet was the kind of popular publication in the 17th century that catered to the same human interests that sells tabloid magazines today. Here's the passage from this story: "At last the witch got so much time to cal to him, Doest thou heare good friend (quoth she?) What sayst thou ill face (quoth he?)"

So the dialogue here between the witch and the man is framed by "quoth she" and "quoth he," which is put into parentheses. There are no quotation marks; we just have to figure out from context "she calls" and then we get what she calls without quotation marks. And you'll notice that in those parentheses with the "quoth he" and "quoth she" the question mark is put in what is now the wrong place; it's in the parenthetical "quoth she?" as opposed to at the end of the question that she actually asked. Then there's no period after "quoth she" or "quoth he" to mark the end of the sentence.

It's the rise of prescriptive grammars in the 18th century that starts to set down stricter standards for how punctuation should and shouldn't be used. But if you read 18th- and 19th-century texts, you'll still see punctuation used in ways you wouldn't see as standard now. And often that is because there is more punctuation than we're now accustomed to. Let's consider the first sentence of Jane Austen's Pride and Prejudice: "It is a truth universally acknowledged, that a single man in possession of a good fortune, must be in want of a wife." That's a lot of commas for a not very long sentence. We now wouldn't have either of the commas in that sentence, and in some ways, especially the second comma that comes between "that a single man in possession of a good fortune, must be in want of a wife." And we would not put a comma in between that subject noun phrase and the verb.

The 20th century witnessed some reigning in of punctuation so that we were getting less of it, and we'll focus on the modern rules here. Let's start with the rules about commas and then we'll move onto semi-colons and to colons.

Commas are designed to mark or set off phrases or groups of words shorter than a sentence, and this is the etymology of "comma" in ancient Greek rhetoric. There are a few set rules for how to use commas at this point, and then there's some variation. And at the end of this discussion, we'll talk about what the comma splice is—the dreaded comma splice.

There are five times when the comma is now recommended, if not required. First, the comma is recommended between two full clauses coordinated by a coordinator like "and," "or," or "but." For example, "He played tennis for four hours yesterday, and his back and arm muscles are letting him know about that today." But you wouldn't put a comma if the second clause is not a full clause but instead is just a verb phrase referring back to the same subject. In other words, you wouldn't get a comma if the sentence read "He played tennis for four hours yesterday and won two of three matches"—no comma. Why? Because we're told not to separate the subject and the predicate with a comma unless there's intervening material such as non-restrictive relative clause.

Number two, commas around non-restrictive relative clauses. These commas are how we show in writing that it's non-restrictive, and it does correspond to a pause in speech. For example, "Paul's sister, who is an attorney in New York City, paid him a surprise visit." Here, Paul has just one sister and we're mentioning that she lives in New York City. But let's imagine that Paul has more than one sister, and we're specifying which sister it is—no commas. "Paul's sister who is an attorney in New York City paid him a surprise visit."

In some ways, the third rule for commas is very similar to the second. So third, we should have commas around any kind of parenthetical phrase. For example, "The U.S. Constitution, as discussed earlier, outlines…." "As discussed earlier" is a parenthetical.

The fourth time that we're told to use a comma: We should use commas after introductory subordinate clauses. Here's an example: "After the mayor met with citizens from the neighborhood, she approved a zoning change that would allow a high-rise hotel." There's some debate about whether a comma should or shouldn't separate a subordinate clause like that if it comes after the main clause. So, let's take that sentence and rearrange it— "The mayor approved a zoning change that would allow a high-rise hotel after the mayor met with citizens from the neighborhood." Should you have a comma before the "after the mayor?" People debate it. I would probably say no; I tend to be a bit more of a minimalist when it comes to commas, but some people like the comma there.

The fifth time that commas are recommended for us: We should have commas in a list between items. For example, "nouns, verbs, and adverbs" or "nouns, verbs and adverbs." As you can tell, what I've just said raises the question of the Oxford comma. This is the comma, sometimes called the serial comma, after the penultimate item in a list. It's called the Oxford comma because Oxford University Press has been following this rule to put a comma after the penultimate item since 1893. It's in some ways a holdover from the heavy punctuation of the 18th and 19th centuries.

With attempts to streamline or minimize punctuation in 20th century, the Oxford comma was taken out in some style guides, but not all. Now in terms of whether or not you would use an Oxford comma, it's typically a question of house style or personal style.

One of the things that I've noticed is that people can have strikingly strong feelings about the Oxford comma, myself included. I really like the Oxford comma, and I tend to use the Oxford comma. Now, some people argue that the Oxford comma should be required because otherwise there can be ambiguity in the sentence—and there is a funny cartoon that's been circulating on the internet to capture the problem, or the potential problem, with leaving out the comma. This cartoon starts with a drawing of JFK, Stalin, and two female strippers with this sentence: "We invited the strippers, JFK, and Stalin." Then beneath that, it has a picture with JFK and Stalin dressed as strippers with the sentence: "We invited the strippers, JFK and Stalin."

It's clever, and yes, the Oxford comma helps here to disambiguate whether you have four people, or whether you only have two and somehow JFK and Stalin had become strippers. But I have to say you actually have to work quite hard to create a list where it is ambiguous based on whether or not the Oxford comma is there. Think about the list I started with—nouns, verbs, and adverbs—there's no ambiguity; it doesn't matter whether I use the Oxford comma or not.

My own view on this—you know that I like the Oxford comma and I tend to use it. As an editor, if there is no house style, I just tend to insist on consistency. If you're going to use the Oxford comma, always use the Oxford comma. If you're not going to use the Oxford comma, then don't use it. I do realize that I can sometimes put perhaps too high a priority on consistency; I'm not sure that all readers would notice if sometimes there was an Oxford comma and sometimes there wasn't. But some of you might be the kind of reader who would notice, and I don't want to distract you. So let's either always use the Oxford comma or always not use it.

The question of consistency comes up with constructions where the comma is variable, like whether or not you can use an Oxford comma. And this can come up particularly with introductory adverbials. It often depends on how long that introductory adverbial is. Let me show you what I mean. Let's imagine the sentence: "Suddenly the peace treaty seemed untenable." Would you put a comma after "suddenly?" Most people probably wouldn't; it's just a one word adverb or adverbial. You could also have something like: "In addition the data were hand-checked for accuracy." Would you put a comma after "in addition?" There you're going to see a lot of variations. Some people would and would say, "I'm trying to capture the pause—"in addition;" some people would not.

Then most people would put a comma if the adverbial starts to get longer than that. For example, "In addition to higher pay for all employees..." because now we don't just have "in addition," we've got "in addition to higher pay for all employees." And we separate that out from whatever's coming next.

As we've already talked about, the adverbial "however" has its own rules for how we need to deal with commas. If it's coming in the middle of a clause, say we'll get commas on both sides; if it's coming at the beginning of a clause, it will get a comma right after it.

Part of each of our decisions about commas is going to depend on whether we prefer lightly or more heavily punctuated text. There are the aesthetics of the page to consider. I'm having an ongoing discussion with one of my colleagues about whether in email it would be "Hi Eileen" with no comma, or "Hi, Eileen." I argue for the no comma because "Hi Eileen," for me, is a greeting similar to "Dear Eileen." But she argues for "Hi, Eileen" because that's what you would do if you were writing dialogue in, say, a short story. In the end, it's really about aesthetics, not correctness on that one.

But for all this, there is one thing a comma cannot do: It cannot connect two clauses without a coordinator—at least according to most style guides for formal English. When a comma does this, when it connects two clauses with no coordinator, his is what we call a comma splice. It's called a comma splice because we're using splice in the sense of to fuse together; we're splicing those two clauses together, and the comma is trying to splice them together all by itself. The comma can do many things, buy we say it can't do that; it needs a coordinator. It was possible to use comma splices in formal edited standard prose before the 20th century, but now we're told we're not allowed to use comma splices unless, of course, you're licensed to do it because of your stature as a writer. This is one of those you're allowed to break the rule if you know it and if other people think you know the rule.

Now speaking of aesthetics, many people have strong feelings about the semi-colon. There are those who think the semi-colon should never be used; for example, Kurt Vonnegut, George Orwell. The semi-colon has been called ugly, odious, girly, useless. But then, the semi-colon has some big fans. Ben Jonson was a fan, as was Charles Dickens. David Crystal, the linguist, also quite likes the semi-colon. People sometimes call it nuanced and sophisticated.

The 18th century witnessed the explosion of the semi-colon. Lindley Murray described it as the punctuation mark that divided a compound sentence into two or more parts. And here's the way he described it: "not so closely connected as those which are separated by a comma, nor yet so little depend on each other, as those which are distinguished by a colon."

And you can still find some quite heavy use of semi-colons in the first half of the 20th century. You'll often see cited Evelyn Waugh's 1945 novel *Brideshead Revisited* for its—well, let's just call it heavy use of semi-colons, including these lines:

> "I have been here before," I said; I had been there before; first with Sebastian more than 20 years ago on a cloudless day in June, when the ditches were white with fool's parsley and meadowsweet and the air heavy with all the scents of summer; it was a day of peculiar splendour such as our climate affords once or twice a year, when leaf and flower and bird and sun-lit stone and shadow seem all to proclaim the glory of God; and though I had been there

so often, in so many moods, it was to that first visit that my heart returned on this, my latest.

Now that's a lot of semi-colons. At this point, semi-colons have two main uses. The first is that they join two independent clauses that have a close semantic relationship. There could be no conjunctive adverb along with the semi-colon, or there could be a conjunctive adverb like "nevertheless," or "thus" or "put differently." Now that semi-colon is trying to show us as readers that the ideas in those two independent clauses are tightly linked—more tightly linked than they are if we put a period in between. At one point, one of my students described the semi-colon as "a California stop"—a period is a real stop sign, a semi-colon is when you're at a stop sign and you do that rolling stop as you go into the next clause.

The second time we're told to use a semi-colon is in a list where the items are long, and perhaps where those items in the list already have punctuation within them. Here's an example: "I went to Vegas with my friend Auden, who had never been to Vegas; my sister, who loves Vegas in a way I don't understand; and my mother, who just wanted to spend time with us." So you can see the semi-colon is usefully separating out the items in that list. And those are the main uses of the semi-colon, whether you're a fan of the semi-colon or not.

The colon, when it was introduced at end of 16th century, was used to mark a pause that was longer than a comma or a semi-colon but shorter than a period. As I said, punctuation when it first came in was about how to read a text aloud. I love the description of the colon as somehow urging us as a reader forward; that it's foreshadowing what is to come.

One of the things the colon can do is tell us that what's coming is going to explain what we've already read, or it's going to exemplify what we've already read. We now typically use the colon before lists, before examples, before definitions or other kinds of explanatory material.

The colon and the semi-colon barely figure in the written English of texting—their formality, I think, makes them a bad choice both rhetorically and aesthetically for those who are frequent texters—but they do serve an important role in the smiley and winky face.

And now the dash. Can one misuse the dash? I think the answer has to be yes, but it's hard to do. Now what one can definitely do is overuse the dash. And I have to say I see this as an editor as well as as a teacher that I will read a paragraph that has, say, four dashes in it because people just start using it instead of semi-colons or colons and that can get distracting.

The dash can serve the same function as a comma, a semi-colon, or a colon; but sometimes with a different, less formal connotation. The dash may suggest that this is an interruption, or a new thought, or perhaps an afterthought. The dash can also set off an explanation. Here's a nice example from an article in the journal of *Human Communication Research* that was published in 2016: "Two experiments examined the effects of processing fluency—that is, the ease with which speech is processed—on language attitudes toward native- and foreign-accented speech." So you see there that the dash is separating out the explanation of the term.

But sometimes no other punctuation mark will quite do the trick, you actually need a dash. For example, let's imagine you have an introductory list and that's followed by a clause; you'll often see a dash there, especially if that list is long—you have X, Y, and Z; and X, Y, and Z are all sort of long items. And then you get a dash and say, "all these help explain…" A dash can also help you add a phrase, not a clause, that wouldn't do well with a comma. Here's an example from George Eliot's *Middlemarch*: "He had done nothing exceptional in marrying—nothing but what society sanctions, and considers an occasion for wreaths and bouquets." That dash there, I think, does better than a comma.

As we think about punctuation in formal writing, I think we do well to remember Bishop Lowth in 18th century who wrote: "The doctrine of punctuation must needs be very imperfect. Few precise rules can be given, which will hold without exception in all cases; but much must be left to the judgement and taste of the writer." I think that's great advice. There are guidelines, but the very creativity of human language and of good prose will require some flexibility and some application of good sense to punctuation.

And then we need to recognize that punctuation will differ in different registers. There is a sense out there that in texting, no one knows how to use punctuation, or perhaps that texting is ruining our sense of punctuation. And I want to finish this lecture by talking about what I think is happening in terms of punctuation and texting. This idea that texting is the wild west of punctuation and young people don't care about how punctuation works; that idea, I think, is not true.

In my experience working with undergraduates, what's actually happening is that the rules of punctuation in texting are different than the rules we follow in formal edited prose. In texting, punctuation needs to do something different, and there are rules. One of the things that I do in class sometimes is I ask each student to bring in 10 rules of texting etiquette, at least 5 of which need to involve punctuation. As a class, we compile those rules into a shared etiquette guide for texting. And what all of us are struck by is how much shared knowledge there is about how to use punctuation when you're texting, and what punctuation marks mean.

Think about early punctuation, which was used to capture oral delivery. Now, in texting, punctuation is being used to capture tone, to capture facial expression, and other parts of context. This is one of the real problems with texting is that we're having a conversation often in almost real-time, these texts are going back and forth very quickly, but we're often missing the context we would have in spoken conversation. I can't see whether you're smiling. I don't know if you're laughing. And as we know, without that context, texting can go really wrong. For this reason, texters are adapting punctuation and other elements of text to try to help capture tone, facial expression, and the like.

So emoticons and emoji help do some of this work. That smiley face says, "I'm just joking right now," or "I'm smiling." The emoji where you can have the laughing so hard, I'm crying is a way to capture context. Also, these abbreviations like "jk" for "just kidding," "haha" to show I'm laughing, or "lol" which started meaning "laughing out loud." It's now weakened and often now, undergraduates tell me, that they will put it at the end of the text much like just kidding. It's a way to say I'm not being serious about whatever I just said.

Some punctuation marks have then been repurposed to help capture tone. And I like that verb "repurposed" because it suggests that there is nothing chaotic about what's happening with punctuation on texting. An exclamation mark is to show agreement, but not necessarily lots of enthusiasm unless there are several. So "Yes!" is just a happy yes. The period has become serious, if not a little bit angry. The ellipsis is skeptical, or perhaps it invites a response. If I put an ellipsis at the end, it's a way to do some turn taking in text and say now it's your turn to text. The unmarked/generic punctuation and texting at this point is no punctuation.

Let me show you what I mean with a few different texts around "OK." Let's imagine one text that is "okay," no punctuation. Then let's imagine one that is "okay." And one that is "okay..."—and my students tell me that it's dot, dot, dot; not ellipsis. Are those three OKs feeling all the same to you? When I show those three OKs to a room of undergraduates, they say, "Oh, those are completely different." The first "okay," no punctuation, is neutral— like, "OK." The "okay" with a period, that one is angry. That's "OK, but I'm not happy about it." And the "okay..." is very skeptical. In tone, that would be something like "OK, but I'm not happy." And they tell me that if you absolutely want to end a relationship, you just write "k.," that's it.

Students tell me stories about passing around a phone to edit a message before sending it out to decide, "Should that be two exclamation marks or three?" Or passing around a phone when a text comes in to decide what that punctuation means in the text they just received. What I'm trying to say here is that this is not chaos, and young people who are on text a lot do care about punctuation; they're just using punctuation in a different way.

Punctuation can do lots of different things in different registers. I think it's important for us to remember that its function is to help us create meaningful, less ambiguous prose in writing. Let's keep that in mind as we think about our attachment to any one rule we've learned about punctuation. Punctuation can and will adapt to our needs in different contexts. And right now, one of those contexts is texting.

Speaking of punctuation on the move, let me transition to the next lecture, which is about apostrophes. This punctuation mark just won't sit still. And yet, we can be quite judgmental of people when they get those apostrophes wrong.

Lecture
23 Its/It's Confusing

The apostrophe is perhaps the most unstable punctuation mark in English. Yet we will sometimes judge others severely based on how they use the apostrophe: poking fun at grocers' apostrophes in *apple's* or deciding not to go on a date with someone because their online profile misuses *its/it's*. Many of the rules for apostrophes are extremely idiosyncratic, as we'll see in this lecture. We'll also learn about how contractions work, the deal with plurals, and what the future holds for apostrophes.

The Apostrophe's History

- The word *apostrophe* is a French borrowing, coming into English in the 16th century. It has historically been used for contractions, and eventually it expanded to possessives (both nouns and pronouns) and plurals.

- It was then reigned in as part of standardization. Now the apostrophe is used for possessives of nouns and contractions (and a few plurals, just to make things confusing). It is this double use of the apostrophe for possessive and contractions that makes *its/it's* tricky, as we'll discuss.

Contractions and Possessives

- Contractions are largely straightforward: When two words are smashed together, letters and/or sounds get left out, and the apostrophe represents that. *Cannot* becomes *can't*; *do not* becomes *don't*; *I am* becomes *I'm*.

- We can also use the apostrophe to show that we have left off a letter or sound at the beginning or end of words: *'tis, runnin'*.

- Possessives in English are now marked with a final *s*, both in the singular and plural, and the only thing that distinguishes them is where the apostrophe goes. In the singular to make the possessive, take the noun and add –'*s*. For instance, *cat* becomes *cat's*.

- It is understandable that we want to extend the pattern to pronouns, but pronouns work differently. The first-person singular doesn't use –'*s* at all: The possessive is *my* or *mine*. For all others, there's a change of form in possessive, and then we add –*s* for pronouns: *you* becomes *yours*; *we* becomes *ours*.

- *It* is the only pronoun that stays the same in the possessive and adds –*s* (becoming *its*), so it is no wonder that speakers are more inclined to want to use an apostrophe. *It* acts more like a noun than a pronoun in how it makes the possessive. Before you judge someone's *its/it's* error, pause and consider what judgment you're about to make.

- Now let's deal with the nouns where the possessive gets tricky: nouns that end in –*s*. Do you add another –*s* with an apostrophe or just an apostrophe?

- Some style guides say to let pronunciation guide your choice: If there is an added syllable in the possessive, add another –*s* to represent the new syllable; if not, just add an apostrophe.

- But other style guides, including Strunk and White's, advise that we should always make the possessive of singular nouns by adding –'*s*. That is, always except for a selection of ancient proper names ending in –*us*, –*es* or –*is*. They cite Jesus, Moses, and Isis (the goddess.) According to them, it is always Moses' and Jesus'— or you can take the escape hatch and go with "the laws of Moses."

- Other guides only mention Moses and Jesus, but not always other ancient figures. Bryan Garner also defers to this tradition, making an exception (to use just the final apostrophe) for classical names like Jesus and Aristophanes, along with names of companies and countries like General Motors and the United States. Most people would prefer the look of "General Motors' reputation" over "General Motors's reputation."

- We often get out of the possessive issue with the United States because we use it as a noun modifier; for instance, we might say "The United States economy" or "the U.S. military." Or we can rephrase with an *of*-construction: "the president of the U.S." But in the end, most people prefer the aesthetics of *United States'* over *United States's*.

- Then we have plural nouns that end in *–s*. Let's imagine that there is a family with the last name Jones. This family has one car, and we want to refer to that car. Is it the *Jones' car* or the *Joneses' car*? Most guides say *Joneses'*. An escape hatch would be the *Jones family's car*.

- Two other issues come up with the possessive. One we already talked about in the lecture on prepositions: the double possessive in "a friend of Kate's."

- The other issue: How does the apostrophe distribute when there are two owners? Let's imagine two people, Kate and Dean. Together, Kate and Dean own two cars. Should we talk about "Kate and Dean's cars" or "Kate's and Dean's cars?" In other words, does the apostrophe distribute through the conjoined phrase that describes the owners ("Kate and Dean") or can you have just one apostrophe that encompasses the whole thing?

- Arguably, there is a distinction in meaning. If "Kate and Dean" is a unit (for instance, they're married) and together they own the car, then let's use just one apostrophe: "Kate and Dean's car." Then we can use two apostrophes to show that there are two cars, which Kate and Dean own independently: "Kate's and Dean's cars."

Plurals

- We're sometimes allowed to use the apostrophe to mark plurals, specifically with numbers and letters. As an example regarding decades, *1960s* and *1960's* both appear, depending on the source. It's more common to omit the apostrophe, but *The New York Times* still uses it.

- If we're talking about plural individual letters, we can say "three As" or "three A's." But lowercase letters require an apostrophe; this creates "three a's" rather than "three as."

- We use the apostrophe to create a plural when we are referring to multiple instances of a word. An example: "There are four *the*'s in the passage."

The Future of the Apostrophe

- What is the future of the apostrophe? It's hard to say, but we can speculate.

  - John Richards, a retired copy editor and reporter, in Boston, England has founded the Apostrophe Protection Society.

  - There is also the *Kill the Apostrophe* website, which calls them redundant, wasteful, and snobbish.

- The apostrophe probably will not die entirely (although a couple of linguists have suggested this). It is likely that its use will diminish.

- One factor is the increasing use of noun modifiers in English such that nouns appearing before other nouns are assumed to modify the noun afterwards, often through possession. Take, for example, "the book's cover" versus "the book cover." This leads to an overall reduction in the possessive marker *–s*.

- Some nonstandard dialects of English already do zero possession with expressions. For example, the lyrics of Beyonce's 2016 song "Formation" include features of African American English throughout, including the zero possessive "I like my baby hair" (a defense of her daughter wearing her hair in an afro).

- The history of English is the history of the loss of inflectional endings, and it is not surprising to see the possessive –s drop in varieties of English.

- We're also seeing the loss of the apostrophe, while the –s remains, in some street signs and names of well-known geographical spots. In the U.K., the Birmingham City Council banned apostrophes from street signs in 2009. Cambridge did the same for any new street names in 2014, but then quickly reversed the decision after a public uproar.

- The U.S. Board on Geographic Names has a policy of removing apostrophes from titles proposed for towns, mountains, caves, and so on. Examples include Pikes Peak (which lost its apostrophe in 1891) and Harpers Ferry. Exceptions include Martha's Vineyard (which got it back in 1933), Clark's Mountain (apostrophe granted in 2002), and Ike's Point (apostrophe granted in 1944).

- People have experimented with apostrophes before. George Bernard Shaw used apostrophes in contractions only when there would be ambiguity without them (for instance, *I'll* versus *Ill*). He explained, "There is not the faintest reason for persisting in the ugly and silly trick of peppering pages with these uncouth bacilli."

- We probably overestimate the ambiguity that would happen without apostrophes. People say *she'll* will be *shell* and *he'll* will become *hell*. In context, though, sentences like "Shell be here at 9:00" probably would not be ambiguous if we were used to seeing *Shell* this way.

- But there is concern that if we aren't careful, chaos will reign in the written language. John Richards posed the sentence: "Residents' refuse to be placed in bins." If you remove the apostrophe, it becomes: "Residents refuse to be placed in bins." The lack of apostrophe creates ambiguity. But such sentences are hard to find or construct. This isn't to say we should get rid of apostrophes; rather, we should just keep our concerns about ambiguity in check.

- It's good to know the rules about when and where to use apostrophes, and adhere to them in formal and many informal contexts. Judgment is rampant. But in terms of how we judge others, we should exercise some caution. Many brilliant writers are not great proofers, and almost everyone gets mixed up at least sometimes on *its/it's*.

- We still read and celebrate historical texts that used the apostrophe very differently, with less consistency than we insist on today. And even in that consistency, as we have talked about in this lecture, there are lots of exceptions and idiosyncrasies regarding "standard" use of the apostrophe.

Suggested Reading

Crystal, *Making A Point*.
Truss, *Eats, Shoots & Leaves*.

Questions to Consider

1. Should the possessive form be *Bill Gates'* or *Bill Gates's*? What about *boss'* or *boss's*? Should we be consistent in how we handle the possessive for all nouns that end in −*s*?

2. Why shouldn't we use an apostrophe in possessive pronouns and write *your's*, *our's*, *her's*, *their's*, and *it's*?

Its/It's Confusing

I think there is an idea out there that there was a moment in the history of the English language, say the mid-19th century or so, but everyone has a different date in mind. There was this moment when English speakers and writers all agreed on how to use an apostrophe. And then, it's been all downhill since then. I'm here to tell you that from what I can tell as a historian of the English language, there has never been such a moment.

The apostrophe is perhaps the most unstable punctuation mark in English, and it has long been unstable. Yet, we will sometimes judge others severely based on how they use the apostrophe—joking at grocers apostrophes in like apple's—apostrophe -s—or deciding not to go on a date with someone because their online profile misuses its no apostrophe versus it's with an apostrophe.

I'm not going to say that I don't notice apostrophes that are missing or have gone astray from standard conventions, but I work hard to keep any conclusions I might draw in check. I know, if I'm honest about it, how many times I've caught a wrong it's, with an apostrophe, in an e-mail before I sent it. I have to think about whether it is masters degree—not apostrophe or master's degree—apostrophe -s. And when I learned more about the rules for apostrophes, I realized how idiosyncratic some of them are, as we'll talk about in this lecture. For example, the Moses/Jesus exception? I'm being serious—stay tuned…

The word apostrophe is a French borrowing, coming into English in 16th century. Etymologically it comes from the Greek for "turning away or elision."

The apostrophe has historically been used for contractions—there you see that elision meaning. For example, the older contraction on't—O N apostrophe T for "on it." As well as refus'd,—R E F U S apostrophe –D which was used to indicate that that would only be two syllables instead of refuse -ed, which was one of the possible pronunciations. So the apostrophe started being used for contractions and then it, perhaps because it was just so useful, it expanded to start to be used for possessives. And this was in earlier eras both possessives of nouns and possessives of pronoun. So you'll find her's, H E R apostrophe S; theirs, T H E I R apostrophe S; and it's, IT apostrophe S. Yes, that is a historical form.

The apostrophe was also expanded to include plurals. Yes, plurals—historically the apostrophe has been used that way in English. The apostrophe was then reigned in as part of the standardization of punctuation. At this point, the apostrophe is used for possessives of nouns, as wells as contractions, and then a few plurals still just to make things confusing—and we'll talk more about that. It is this double use of the apostrophe for possessive and for contractions that makes it's/its, with and without an apostrophe tricky, as we'll discuss.

Let's start with contractions. Contractions are largely straightforward. What happens is we take two words and we smush them together—smush being the technical term for this process—and then letters or sounds get left out. The apostrophe represents those letters or sounds that have been omitted. So cannot becomes can't. Do not becomes don't. I am becomes I'm. You are becomes you're, it is becomes it's. Fine.

We can also use the apostrophe to show that we've left off a letter or a sound at the beginning or the end of a word. We see this in something like 'til—apostrophe T I L—if people want to show they've shortened until.

We also see that to capture the pronunciation runnin' instead of running—R U N N I N apostrophe. Now, as a linguist, I do have to note that we often think that apostrophe in runnin' is to capture the fact that we've dropped the –g. If you listen to runnin' and running, you will hear that almost all English speakers have dropped the -g. It's the difference between the sound "n"—runnin' and –ing—running. But we use the apostrophe in runnin' to capture that difference in pronunciation. As I said, the use of apostrophes for contractions or omitted sounds and letters is pretty straightforward.

Possessives in English are now marked with a final –s, both in the singular and the plural—and the only thing that distinguishes singular from the plural is where the apostrophe goes.

In the singular, the apostrophe was put in there to represent the omission of the -e from the historical possessive, final –es. That –e got lost and the apostrophe was put in to represent that loss. So here we're seeing that –s is an old inflectional ending that has come down—we lost the vowel, but we kept the –s. The –s apostrophe for the plural did not settle down until the 19th century.

Now, I know this is basic, but as long as we're here, let's just do this as part of the review in terms of how singulars make the possessive. You take the noun—you add an apostrophe –s. So cat becomes cat's—apostrophe –s; my mother—my mother's apostrophe –s; the moons—the moon's apostrophe –s; it—it's apostrophe –s. No. No. We don't get to do that with "it."

It is understandable that we want to extend this pattern with the singular noun and apostrophe –s to pronouns. And that's part of why I was playing right there, by putting all those nouns with apostrophe –s, and then just putting the It at the end to show how understandable it is that we want to do that. But pronouns work differently.

In the first person-singular, we don't actually get an –s at all to make the possessive. We have I, as the nominative form and then My or Mine for the determiner or the stand-alone pronoun—no –s.

With all the others, we see the change of form, and then we get the –s for the pronoun. For example you have you or you have your or yours—the determiner and the stand-alone pronoun. So you change the form and add the –s. We becomes our or ours—they, their or theirs. He/his and because it already ends in –s, it has the same form as the determiner or the pronoun, and then she becomes her or hers. We don't see confusion here about whether there should be an apostrophe because the pronoun is changing form as it becomes a possessive.

The pronoun It is the only personal pronoun that stays the same in the possessive and just adds –s its to create its—no apostrophe. So it's no wonder that speakers are more inclined to want to use an apostrophe with it's. It is acting more like a noun than like a pronoun in how it makes the possessive. It seems like it should be easy to remember that pronouns don't take the apostrophe to make possessive, but when you step back and think about it—it is understandable why people get mixed up on it's versus its. So, before you judge, and it's gone wrong, I would encourage you just to pause and consider what judgment you're about to make. I get e-mails from brilliant people from across the university who sometimes mix up their apostrophes—people for whom proofing e-mails or at least proofing e-mails at that moment, was not at the top of their priority list. And I realize, that I may have sent a few mixed up it's/its if I wasn't proofing carefully that day.

Now let's deal with the nouns where the possessive gets tricky—nouns that end with –s. Do you add another –s and have an apostrophe –s, or do you just put an apostrophe at the end of the word given that it already has a final –s?

This one gets me every time, and my aesthetics about it seem to change over time. For example, in one book that I published, I was writing about Lynne Truss and I was writing about Lynne Truss's book, *Eats, Shoots & Leaves*. In the first pass, I had Truss's, T R U S S apostrophe –S. And then, when I was going over the page proofs, I decided I didn't like the way that looked, and I went to T R U S S apostrophe. And then, after I sent off the proofs, I had some moment of panic—and I e-mailed the editor and said, "No, no. Please put the apostrophe –s back on.

Before I talk about what style guides say, let's see what your intuitions are about what looks right. Let's start with, "Charles' friend." Do you like, "Charles' friend?" C H A R L E S apostrophe? Or Charles's friend—with a final apostrophe –s at the end? I, myself, like the second.

Let's talk about Burns and a poem by Burns. Do you like, "Burns' poem?" B U R N S apostrophe? Or Burns's poem—apostrophe –s? Some part of me kind of wants the first one, and maybe to pronounce it, "Burns's poem." But the part of me that likes consistency goes for the second and says if I'm going to have Charles's—apostrophe –s; I'm going to have Burns's—apostrophe –s.

You'll notice that as I said those, I was running into a pronunciation issue as to whether that final –s in the possessive is pronounced. Is it Burns' poem, or is it Burns's poem. In other phrases, it's clear that the –s always would be pronounced, but with Burns one could argue it either way.

Here's one where the –s would always be pronounced, and again, let's see where you want that apostrophe. We're talking about a memo that was written by the boss. It's the boss' memo. Is that boss'—B O S S apostrophe? Or is that boss's—B O S S apostrophe –S. To me, that's clearly the second because the pronunciation of the extra syllable, and I want apostrophe –s.

Some style guides say to let pronunciation guide your choice: if there is an added syllable, add another –s and the apostrophe to represent the new syllable; if not, just add an apostrophe. But other style guides, including Strunk and White, advise that we should always make the possessive of singular nouns by adding apostrophe –s. Always except for a selection of ancient proper names ending in a final –us, –es or –is. Strunk and White cite Jesus, Moses, and Isis—the goddess—as exceptions. So it is always Moses'—M O S E S apostrophe, even if you say Moses is. And Jesus'—J E S U S apostrophe, or you can take the escape hatch and go with something like, "the laws of Moses."

Other guides only mention Moses and Jesus as the exception, but not always other ancient figures. Bryan Garner in *Modern American Usage*, in the end also defers to tradition on this one, making an exception—in other words the place where you just use the final apostrophe for classical names like Jesus and Aristophanes and names of companies and countries like General Motors and the United States.

I would guess many of you will like the look of company names and the United States better if they are exceptions to the rule and only take an apostrophe.

Let's start with General Motors', and we're talking about the reputation of General Motors. It's General Motors' reputation, and they're two choices here. That could be Motors'—M O T O R S apostrophe or General Motors's—M O T O R S apostrophe –S.

And maybe you're thinking, "I wouldn't say General Motors -es reputation. I would say, "General Motors' reputation," just want the –s apostrophe.

Or, let's look at the United States and the apostrophe issue. We're talking about the next president—the United States's next president or the United State's next president. Do you want states'——s apostrophe? Or states's apostrophe s? I would guess many of you would want states' with just an apostrophe.

Now we often get out of the possessive issue with the United States because we can use the United States as a noun modifier. In other words, we can just put the United States before the noun that it's modifying, and not use a possessive there. So, for example, you an get something like, "The U.S. economy," or, "The United States economy," with no apostrophe. Or the U.S. military. Or we can rephrase with an of-construction and say, "the president of the United States" and then we don't have to worry about the apostrophe at all.

Then there are these funny cases where a word ends with the sound /s/ but the spelling doesn't end in –s. Our rule about always adding –s to a singular noun, if you follow that rule, means that nouns ending in, for example, –x and pronounced with /s/ get a final –s.

Let's talk about Karl Marx. Now Karl Marx had ideas, which means we might want to talk about Marx's ideas, and we're told to do M A R X apostrophe S—Marx's ideas. Then in English you sometimes get French nouns that the spelling ends in a final –s, but that is not pronounced because French doesn't pronounce that final –s.

So, for example, you have Descartes—the spelling ends in –s. Now we want to talk about his philosophy—so we have Descartes's philosophy, which ends with –s apostrophe –s.

Think about the state of Illinois, which, of course, the spelling ends with an –s. We want to talk about the governor of Illinois or Illinois's governor—the pronunciation only has one –s. But the spelling has Illinois, ending in –s apostrophe –s.

Where did the Moses/Jesus exception come from? Style guides since the beginning of the 20th century cite tradition. Tim Green, at the University of Michigan, notes that the King James' version of Bible uses Jesus' with just the –s apostrophe, and that that was then picked up in other English Bibles. That may be the tradition that we're talking about.

If you're now wondering how famous an ancient and classical figure you need to be to merit the exception—that is a very fair question. Does Socrates get the exceptpion? Ignatius of Antioch? You may get to decide. And I have to say if that Socrates is a cat, the exception does not apply?

Then we have plural nouns that end in –s. This is a nightmare. Let's imagine that there is a family with the last name Jones. This family has one car, and we want to refer to that car. Is it the Jones'—J O N E S apostrophe of is it the Joneses' car—J O N E S E S apostrophe? Most guides will say it's Joneses'—the second one J O N E S E S apostrophe and they will say that if the Hastingses' family has a car… It's the Hastingses' car, again, put on that –es and the apostrophe. I, myself, much prefer taking the escape hatch here and saying, "The Jones family's car…"

Two other issues come up with the possessive. One we already talked about in the lecture on prepositions in terms of the double possessive. Something lie, "a friend of Kate's." The other is, "How does the apostrophe distribute when there are two owners?" Let's me show you what I mean. Let's imagine, Kate and Dean. Together, Kate and Dean own two cars. Should we talk about "Kate and Dean's cars" or "Kate's and Dean's cars"? In other words, does the apostrophe distribute through the conjoined phrase that describes the owners "Kate and Dean" or can you have just one apostrophe that encompasses the whole conjoined phrase, Kate and Dean?

Arguably, there is a distinction in meaning, depending on how you use the apostrophe. Let's imagine that "Kate and Dean" are a unit—they're married, they're siblings, they're roommates who share possessions and together they own a car. Then let's use just one apostrophe, "Kate and Dean's car." That way, we can use two apostrophes to show that there are two cars, which Kate and Dean own independently—Kate's and Dean's cars."

In case things weren't confusing enough, now let's add to the mix that sometimes we're allowed to use the apostrophe to mark plurals. And you're thinking, "No we can't..." But yes we can. Think about these examples with numbers and letters. The 1960s. I would guess you have certainly seen the 1960s both with just a final –s and with a final apostrophe –s. And perhaps you've written both of those. The apostrophe in 1960's is now more often omitted now, but the *New York Times* still uses the apostrophe.

Let's imagine something with letters. As a teacher, I say, "I gave three As." That could be capital A, small, lowercase –s, or it could be capital A apostrophe –s. Again, there we see that apostrophe being used for plurals. But let's imagine I am describing the spelling of "aardvark," which has three a's, and there I would be talking about lowercase a's. And you pretty much have to use an apostrophe in three a's there, because otherwise it becomes As.

As a linguist, I realize that there's another place I use the apostrophe to create plurals, and that's when I'm referring to words as words. And I want to multiple instances of a word. So I might say, for example, there are four the's in the passage, and I would have T H E apostrophe –s.

What is the future of the apostrophe? Well, of course, I actually have no idea, and I do know better than to predict the future. But let me speculate a little.

John Richards, a retired copy editor and reporter, in Boston, England has founded the Apostrophe Protection Society. He is trying to make sure that the apostrophe is stabilized and remains in use. There is also the Kill the Apostrophe website, which calls the apostrophe redundant, wasteful, and snobbish. The apostrophe, at least in early texting wasn't used that much, which could be a predictor for the demise of the apostrophe. But now that we have autocorrect, the apostrophe is back in texting. And I think that texting may not be as relevant to the future of the apostrophe.

Honestly, I don't think the apostrophe will die entirely although a couple of linguists have suggested that this might happen. But I do think that its use will probably diminish. One factor is the increasing use of noun modifiers in English such that nouns appearing before other nouns are assumed to modify the noun afterwards, often through possession, but without a possessive –s. So book's cover could also be book cover: the building's steps can be the building steps. This leads to an overall reduction in the possessive marker –s and the apostrophe that comes with it.

Is that true only with inanimates that are possessing the book cover—the building steps? No. For example, if we talking about students' experience, we could do students plural –s apostrophe experience. We could also talk about the student experience, where we create a singular student—and we just talk about the student experience in general with no possessive marker.

Some nonstandard dialects of English already do zero-possession when, so that you don't get a final –s to mark possession. To give you just one example, Beyonce's 2016 song "Formation" got a lot of attention as an unapologetic celebration of blackness, and Beyonce's lyrics include features of African American English throughout, including a zero possessive like "I like my baby hair," which is a defense of her daughter wearing her hair as an afro.

As we've talked about in this course, the history of English is the history of the loss of inflectional endings, and it's not surprising to see the possessive –s drop out in some varieties of English.

If you're thinking, we can't possibly make do without the possessive –s, just remember how many inflectional endings we've lost over time, and we're doing fine. And once the noun, the possessor, is always consistently before the noun that's being possessed, that possessive –s is doing some redundant work—which is how it can get lost in some varieties of English. So do we need that possessive ending? One could argue we don't need it. I know that that's a radical argument, but this is the perspective you get when you study the history of the language.

So that's the loss of the –s possessive ending in some circumstances and some varieties of English. Then we're seeing the loss of the apostrophe, while the –s remains, in some street signs and the names of well-known geographical spots.

The Birmingham City Council in the UK banned apostrophes from street signs in 2009. Cambridge in the UK did the same thing for any new street names in 2014, but then there was such a public uproar that they quickly reversed their decision.

The United States Board on Geographic Names has a policy of removing apostrophes from titles proposed for towns, mountains, caves, and the like. Pikes Peak lost apostrophe in 1891. Harpers Ferry also lost its apostrophe.

The Board allows for a few exceptions, and only a few, Martha's Vineyard got it's apostrophe back in 1933, Clark's Mountain has had its apostrophe since 2002, and Ike's Point in New Jersey since 1944.

People have experimented with apostrophes, especially getting rid of them before. George Bernard Shaw used apostrophes and contractions only when there would be amAbiguity without them. So he would use it in I'll because it could also be Ill. And he wrote, "There is not the faintest reason for persisting in the ugly and silly trick of peppering pages with these uncouth bacilli."

And we probably overestimate the ambiguity that would happen without apostrophes. That sure, if you wrote, She'll without and apostrophe it could be "shell." But most of the time, you would know form context it whether it is she'll or shell. For example, "She'll be here at 9:00." It would be odd to say,

'Shell be here at 9:00." if we were used to seeing "shell" written without the apostrophe [?] in a lot of places it wouldn't be ambiguous.

There is the concern, and I do understand it, that if we aren't careful about our apostrophes, chaos will reign in the written language. John Richards, who as you remember is trying to preserve the apostrophe, posed the sentence to capture the problem. "Residents' refuse to be placed in bins." So there you get residents' –s apostrophe and their refuse is to be placed in bins. If you remove the apostrophe from the sign it says, "Residents refuse to be placed in bins." Fair enough—I don't want to be place in a bin either.

It's a wonderful example of what could happen if you didn't have an apostrophe, and its ambiguity is clever. But, these sentences are hard to find or hard to construct. Again, it's rare we would get this kind of sentence without any context to know if we were talking about the residents' garbage or we're talking abut stubborn residents, who don't want to be put in the bins.

I'm not trying to say here that to say we should get rid of apostrophes. I'm simply trying to keep our concern about chaos that might ensue in check.

So where are we with the apostrophes? It's good to know the rules about when and where to use them and adhere to them in formal and many informal contexts because the fact is that judgment is rampant about apostrophe use.

But, in terms of how we judge others, I would recommend exercising some caution. Many brilliant writers are not great proofers and almost everyone gets mixed up at least sometimes on its/it's.

Do you really want to write someone off over an apostrophe? Now, I have one friend who says an emphatic "yes" to that question. She said, "I'm absolutely willing to write someone off over an apostrophe." But I do think about the fact that we still read and celebrate historical texts that used the apostrophe in very different ways and with less consistency than we insist on now in terms of where that apostrophe needs to be and where it needs not to be. And even within that consistency, as we have talked about in this lecture, there are lots of exceptions and idiosyncrasies to what is considered standard use of the apostrophe.

In the last lecture of the course, and how are we already at the last lecture of the course—but here are. In the last lecture, we'll step back and think more generally about what it can mean to have all of this grammatical knowledge at your disposal.

Trending Language

In this final lecture, we'll start by covering two tricky issues: the use of "based off of" and "advocate for," two evolutions that are currently controversial but may end up sticking. Then we'll move on to discuss what makes a rule a rule—as we've seen throughout this course, it's a murky issue. We'll close with some general advice on when you should and shouldn't correct someone, as well as a look at how you can make deliberate, effective choices as a writer.

Based Off What?

- In student writing, "based off of" has become very widely used (rather than "based on"). The Google Books Ngram Viewer reports that "based off of" has risen dramatically since 1980, including tripling in use between 2000 and 2008. But "based on" still outnumbered it 10,000 to 1 in 2008.

- It's not surprising that we're seeing "based off of" in students' writing. They are the movers and shakers of change, and it is a fairly colloquial feature that they may not know to edit out of their academic prose.

- Changes in grammar typically happen first in the spoken language, which can make new forms feel more informal. Why might speakers be shifting to "based off of?" There is no definite answer, but we can point to two factors:

□ Prepositions are notoriously idiomatic. You just have to learn them, and they don't always make sense. For example, why is it "as a result" and not "in a result" or "for a result"?

□ While "based on" makes sense as we build *on* the base that is there, we also can build *off* things (when we extend them). We also have "jumping-off points," so one could argue there is a logic to "based off of" as well.

■ Some folks don't like "off of" because they think it is redundant, which is a fair point. Interestingly, it's not a new redundancy. Being old doesn't make a construction good per se, but it does suggest that this is a redundancy that doesn't grate on speakers too much in the general scheme of things.

■ Here's an example from Shakespeare's *Henry VI*. Simpcox, when asked why he is lame, responds, "A fall off of a tree." This construction tends to be colloquial, but it will sometimes appear in more formal writing.

■ The bottom-line question: Is it OK to use "based off of" in formal/ professional writing? There is some informal censure of "based off of" out there. But there isn't a lot of formal prescription on "based off of" yet. In other words, the writers of style guides and usage manuals have not started paying attention to this new construction on the rise.

■ In sum, change is afoot. If usage guide writers continue to let it fly generally under the radar and don't clamp down on it as "wrong," then the change may happen fairly rapidly and "based off" will become more and more standard in formal contexts. But right now, writers use it with some risk of judgment.

Advocacy
■ Let's look at another tricky prepositional issue. Here are two sentences from a question on the AHD usage ballot:

- Sentence 1: The teacher advocated a new educational technique.

- Sentence 2: The teacher advocated for a new educational technique.

■ Sentence 2 makes some people grimace. But forty-five percent of the panel voted it as acceptable, so clearly opinions are split. The AHD editors as a result stayed conservative in their summary: "A careful writer" will use *advocate* transitively without *for*. A writer should only use *for* in a sentence like, "She advocates for former foster children" (where the beneficiary is present).

■ Notice that the AHD editors do not say "advocate for" is wrong. Rather, the goal is to make choices that are careful about context, audience, and expectations. And as part of our care, we should recognize that opinions as voiced by usage guide writers and entities like the Usage Panel will change over time.

Rules

■ Given all this, let's think again about what makes a grammar/usage rule a rule. As we've done throughout this course, we first need to distinguish the descriptive from the prescriptive.

- Descriptive rules are patterns that govern how we use the language to create grammatical utterances that others will understand; an example is the order in which determiners must occur.

- Prescriptive rules are created by real people, at specific moments in time, to try to manage the language, especially the written language. An example is consistency in the use of commas, which has the goal of minimizing distraction for readers.

■ In the end, we make choices based on the grammatical information we have at hand. This is empowering. It also reminds us that

English usage is a living thing, changing along as generations of speakers roll over.

Changes to Watch

■ What changes should you be watching? Predictions are dangerous, but here are some guesses as to what the future might hold:

1. New modals could emerge (in addition to *hafta* and *gonna*, we might also see *sposta*).

2. The demise of *whom* might be underway.

3. We could see growing acceptance of singular *they*.

4. An expansion of the perfect and the progressive could occur.

5. We might see the death of the subjunctive. But this is hard to know—the most remarkable thing is that it hasn't died yet. The subjunctive mood captures belief, intention, desire; and it states information contrary to the facts. It appears in sentences such as, "If I were grammar queen for a day." Many people don't know what it is, and yet some studies indicate that in American English its use is increasing in sentences like, "I demand that he study grammar joyfully."

6. Noun modifiers could increase. An example: "Great Courses lecture material."

7. *Slash* as a conjunction and because as a preposition might grow.

8. The use of *on accident* could increase; the same goes for *impactful*.

9. The quotative *like* will grow in frequency.

10. *Hone in* will fully replace *home in*.

- Regarding the last example: *Home in* showed up in the 1920s and took on the metaphorical meaning of *focus on* by 1950s. By the 1960s, *hone in on* also took on this meaning.

- Today, is *home in on* losing its status as the standard form? Research with Google Books shows *home in on* is still more common, but the gap has narrowed significantly.

Should We Correct?

- We should be very careful about how and when we alert other people to a usage issue. It can be a very powerful move, to stop and correct someone. It shows you're listening to how they are talking as much or more than what they are saying.

- Correction is one thing if you're a teacher reading a piece of formal writing. It's quite another if you're in a conversation. Correcting someone in a conversation can be very silencing. You can see this online when people correct other people's grammar as the ultimate weapon in an argument.

- Hopefully, we can embrace how much we care about language and use that caring for good. We can create beautiful prose—or clever prose or efficient prose or funny prose—in a variety of genres, being careful about how we use the language and being deliberate in our grammatical choices, without being unnecessarily overly fussy.

- Of course, we are going to notice things in language. We'll notice typos, and then we can decide what we want to make of them. We'll notice new grammatical developments and differences across regions and social groups—we can't control that.

- What we can control is what we think we know about that person based on that bit of grammar—or based on their accent, or a word choice that reflects what region they're from, or what social group they identify with. We can control what judgments we want to make.

- We can control any impulse we might have to go "grammando" when we hear something. Ask: Does that thought stay in our head or do we say it out loud? What is the goal? What is the context? Are we being helpful or hurtful? Are we sure we're right?

- Let's think of ourselves as caretakers of the language, tending it to allow it to do its work in powerful, effective ways. To be effective, language (both written and spoken) must respond to its audience and context, which requires some flexibility in what kind of grammar is preferred. And as we've talked about, there are many English grammars; the formal written standard is just one of them. To be effective, formal written language also benefits from consistency (so as not to distract readers) and from minimizing ambiguity.

- Language also needs to be creative; it needs to be allowed to surprise us and to adapt to the needs and desires of the speakers and writers who are both older and younger than we are. The next time you find yourself contemplating a grammatical construction that strikes your ear as not quite right if not downright wrong, imagine yourself being asked to judge its acceptability as if you were a member of the AHD Usage Panel.

■ This course has hopefully given you new tools and perspectives to approach that question, to think about what acceptability means in what context and how that may change over time. Key tools you can use include usage guides, the Google Books Ngram Viewer, the *Corpus of Contemporary American English*, and the *Corpus of Historical American English*.

■ With this knowledge and these tools, you can effectively be an advocate for what you see as the most effective language choices. Remember that whatever you choose—whether to embrace tradition or embrace change—you are following in the footsteps of many eloquent speakers and writers who precede us. To make those kinds of decisions about grammar more consciously and deliberately is what it means to harness the power of language.

Suggested Reading

Cassidy, Hall, et al., eds., *Dictionary of American Regional English*.
Leech, Hundt, Mair, and Smith, *Change in Contemporary English*.
Lippi-Green, Rosina. *English with an Accent*.
McWhorter, "A Matter of Fashion."

Questions to Consider

1. Now, at the end of this course, if you needed to decide if the phrasing *advocate for a proposal* is acceptable in formal writing, how would you go about answering the question?

2. What grammatical changes are you noticing in the English language you see and hear every day?

Lecture 24 | Trending Language
Transcript

As you can probably now imagine, given what I do for a living, I regularly get emails from friends and colleagues—and people I don't know—with questions and concerns about what is happening in, or to, the English language. I love this. If I hadn't noticed this bit of grammar before, now it is squarely on my radar, which I really appreciate. If it is something that I've thought about before, the person who e-mails me and I can geek out about this bit of grammar we both care about together. I hope that you will feel welcome to e-mail me about changes in usage that you are noticing too; this is how I try to stay "in the know."

Here's one example of an e-mail. It was near the end of the term, and one of my colleagues at the University of Michigan sent me this e-mail: "I'm losing my mind reading papers with the expression based off of, which has become very widely used rather than based on. What do you know about where it came from?"

Now, at the time I got the e-mail, I knew very little about *based off of,* although I had also noticed it in student writing, and you may have noticed it in writing too. I went to go learn more about this construction. How new is *based off of?* Where does it come from? Is it ever used in formal writing, and why or why not?

You now know where I went to learn more about *based off of.* I went to online databases, of course. First, I went to Google Books Ngram Viewer and searched for *based off of.* I discovered that it has risen dramatically since 1980, including tripling in use between 2000 and 2008. And the reason I have to stop at 2008 is because Google Books, the searchable database, only goes up to 2008 at the time of this taping. Now, before you decide that the tide has turned on *based off of* and it suddenly, because it's had this dramatic rise is standard use, search *based on*. *Based on* outnumbers *based off of* 10,000:1 in 2008.

Now, it's not surprising that we're seeing *based off of* in student writing. Students, if you're teaching undergraduates, are at the age where they are the movers and shakers of language change, as we've talked about before in this course. And *based off of* is a fairly colloquial feature that they may be bringing into use and may not realize is colloquial and know to edit it out of their academic prose. Change in grammar typically happens first in the spoken language, which can make it feel less formal, and that's why we may notice it when it first finds its way into writing.

Why might speakers be shifting to *based off of?* There's no definite answer here, but here are a couple of factors. As we've talked about before in this course, prepositions are notoriously idiomatic. You just have to learn them, and they don't always make sense. Why is it *as a result* and not *in a result* or *for a result?* It is, after all, *in conclusion*, and *for a reason*. And then sometimes the idiom just shifts, and we need to use a new preposition.

Second, while *based on* makes sense as we build on the base of something that's already there, we can also build off things, if you think about that. When we extend them, we build off them, and we do have *jumping off points,* so one could argue that there is a logic to *based off of* in addition to *based on*. Some folks don't like *off of* in *based off of* because they think it is redundant, which is, I have to say, a completely fair point.

Interestingly, *off of* is not a new redundancy. As we've seen many times in this course before, something we notice and we think, "Oh, that's new…" or not. It's been around for a while. Now, being old doesn't make a construction inherently good, but it does suggest that this is a redundancy that doesn't grate on all that many speakers at least too much in the general scheme of things. Here's an example of *off of* from Shakespeare's *Henry VI, Part II*, and it's Simpcox when he is asked why he is lame, and he responds, "A fall off of a tree." Now, *off of* tends to be colloquial, but it will sometimes appear in more formal writing. I went and searched in the Corpus of Contemporary American English, and I could find it in academic prose, for example, in medical writing where people are talking about something being "elevated off of the chest wall."

The bottom line, is it OK to use *based off of* in formal professional writing? There is some informal censure of *based off of* out there, and it's not just my colleague who wrote me. When I wrote a blog post about *based off of* for "Lingua Franca" for the *Chronicle of Higher Education,* the first commenter who wrote in response to my post wrote, "'Off of' makes me grind my teeth. 'Based off of' makes me want to puke."

That said; there isn't a lot of formal prescription on *based off of,* at least yet. In other words, the writers of style guides and usage manuals have not started paying attention to this new construction on the rise. It's not in Strunk and White's *The Elements of Style* or Bryan Garner's *Modern American Usage*; there is no usage note about *based off of* in the American Heritage Dictionary yet. In sum, change is afoot, and if usage guide writers continue to let it fly generally under the radar and don't clamp down on it as somehow wrong, then the change may happen fairly rapidly and *based off of* may become more and more standard in formal contexts. But right now, if you use *based off of,* you use it with some risk of judgment.

I hope at this point in the course, this kind of guidance about usage is feeling satisfying. I'm not saying *based off* or *based off of* is wrong; I'm saying that it's on the rise and may be judged right now. This way, we can make educated decisions about what form we want to use. I would avoid *based off* or *based off of* in formal writing right now, and I would alert students to the fact that others may not like that construction so that they can make informed choices. They may not want to irritate their readers if their readers are going to get irritated by *based off of.* But *based off of* is not something to judge anyone severely on or to lose your mind over, and I think it's worth watching to see if and when *based off of* speakers and writers become an ever larger percentage of writers, and perhaps at some point also of copyeditors.

Let's look at another tricky prepositional issue, as we reflect on this approach to grammar and usage that shows careful attention to language choices without categorically calling things incorrect.

Here are two sentences from a question on the AHD usage ballot, and this will bring us full circle back to lecture one when I introduced the whole idea of the usage ballot. I'm going to give you these two sentences, and you can see what you think. Sentence one: The teacher advocated a new educational technique. Are you OK with that sentence? I would guess that most, if not all of you are. I was, I voted completely acceptable, and the editors who made the ballot meant for that sentence to be completely standard. Here's sentence two: The teacher advocated for a new educational technique. Now, what do you think? Did that one get you? Maybe you're grimacing right now over that sentence. I polled a class of 80 undergraduates on sentence two, and they overwhelmingly had no issue with it. The question is whether you can *advocate for* something that you want to happen or something that you're trying to advance, or do you just *advocate that*. I went to Corpus of American Contemporary English and went to the academic section. And I could find *advocate for* plus the noun of what people were advocating. For example, "to advocate for continuation of funding" or "to advocate for action on a bewildering array of diseases." So when I voted on sentence two on the usage ballot, I voted acceptable, and 45 percent of the Panel was with me. Well, I guess I was in that 45 percent, so 44.5 percent of the Panel was with me. So clearly, when you see that 45 percent, you can see that the Panel is split on this right now, that some people don't mind it, some people still don't like *advocate for.*

The AHD editors, as a result of this split vote, stayed conservative in their summary. They wrote, and here I quote, "A careful writer will use advocate transitively without for;" that they would only use the *for* in a sentence like "She advocates for former foster children" where the foster children are the beneficiary, the people you're advocating for. As we've talked about the Panel is overall going to be fairly conservative, and that is helpful to know. It will keep you on the careful side of things if that's where you want to be. But notice that the AHD editors do not say that *advocate for* plus the noun of the thing that you want to have happen is wrong. It's about choices and choices that you are thinking through, that you're being careful about. And here I want to use careful in that sense of you're showing care, you're thinking them through, you're thinking about context, and audience, and expectations, and as part of our care, we should recognize that the opinions as voiced by usage guide writers and entities like the Usage Panel will change over time

Given all this, let's think again about what makes a grammar or usage rule a rule. As we've done throughout this course, we first distinguish the descriptive from the prescriptive. Descriptive rules are patterns that govern how we use the language to create grammatical utterances that others will understand. For example, the order in which determiners must occur, the insertion of do so that we ask "do you know?" not "know you?" The fact that we can and do strand prepositions because the language has that flexibility.

Prescriptive rules, as we've talked about throughout the course, are created by real people, at specific moments in time, to try to manage the language, especially the written language, and they can do some very useful things. One of the things that prescriptive rules can do is distinguish standard forms and constructions from nonstandard ones. This would be something like distinguishing *ain't* as nonstandard. But please do remember, it doesn't mean that there's something inherently wrong with *ain't*. It's distinguishing standard usage, which can be a shared and useful form of communication, from nonstandard. Some prescriptive rules aim to promote a particular kind of logic. This could be a rule such as "none of the books is" rather than "none of the books are." Some rules aim to maintain consistency, which can minimize distraction for readers, for example, the rules we talked about with commas where if someone's always using the Oxford coma that may minimize distraction for readers. Some of these prescriptive rules aim to minimize ambiguity in very useful ways. For example, think about those danglers, and if you don't have a dangling modifier, then you reduce the ambiguity for your reader, and because you can't be there to help your reader if they are confused, it's helpful to reduce the ambiguity.

Some of these prescriptive rules aim to create aesthetically pleasing prose. For example, not splitting an infinitive with a whole lot of words between the *to* and the verb or, for some people, not writing *equally as* because that redundancy is not aesthetically pleasing. Some prescriptive rules try to preserve distinctions that historically have been there, for example, the difference between who and whom. And some prescriptive rules try to create distinctions where those distinctions may never have been quite so clear. Think about the distinction *less* and *fewer*, as well as between *that* and *which*. Some prescriptive rules aim to advance equality in language and respect for other people's identities. Think here about singular *they* both for generic uses and for individuals who identify outside the male-female binary.

Categorizing rules this way is not meant, as I think you know now, to say that we shouldn't take these rules seriously or that we shouldn't follow them if we think that they are on solid footing. It is to say that we can think critically about what those rules are trying to do, and if we believe that that's a good idea. Now, I know, for example, that there is nothing wrong with *impact* as a verb, but I tend not to use it in formal writing right now because I don't want to distract or annoy people who care about *impact* as a verb. I also use singular *they* in a lot of my writing, but in a short university memo, where I can't put in a little footnote, right now I'll probably just use *he* or *she* and not get into it. I'm making choices based on context and on audience.

Did you catch what I did there? I said I'm making decisions *based on* context and audience. I could've said *based off of* context and audience, but I said *based on* both because that's more a part of my grammar and because I had a feeling that maybe some of you didn't like *based off of.* These are the kinds of informed decisions about grammar that I have in mind. I think it's empowering to think about grammar this way. It also reminds us that English usage is a living thing, changing along with the rollover of generations of speakers. When we think about grammar this way, it can make us more informed editors and better teachers, as well as savvier writers.

What changes in the language should you be watching? As I've said before, predictions about language change are dangerous, but here goes, and I'm not alone here, I'm drawing on work by other scholars who've also ventured into the land of prediction. First, watch those new modals in addition to *hafta*, and *gonna*, we have to emerging modals like *sposta*. Second, the demise of *whom*; as I've talked about *whom* has been on the decline for hundreds of years, and it will probably continue to decline. Third, the growing acceptance of singular they; as we've talked about, we're now seeing this move into more and more formal genres, and I think that that will continue. Fourth, the expansion of the perfect and the progressive; this is something that linguists have been watching, and we're starting to see the perfect where you might expect the past tense and an increasing use of the progressive aspect.

Fifth, the death of the subjunctive, OK, it's really hard to know whether we're going to have or witness the death of the subjunctive. People have been predicting the death of the subjunctive for over 100 years, and it just won't die. I think one of the most remarkable things about the subjunctive is that it hasn't died yet. The subjunctive mood captures belief, intention, demands, desire, as well as states contrary to the facts. It appears in sentences such as "If I were grammar queen for a day," which is clearly hypothetical, or "I insist that she wear the grammar crown." I insist *that she wear* rather than *she wears*, that *wear* is the subjunctive where we're seeing a demand. Or we could see the subjunctive in "I wish there were such a thing as a grammar queen and a grammar crown." *I wish there were,* this is my desire, but clearly it's not actually a reality. Many people don't know what the subjunctive is, aren't sure if English has a subjunctive, we still do have a subjunctive, and what's interesting is that some studies indicate that in American English the use of the subjunctive is actually increasing in sentences like "I demand that he study grammar joyfully." Stay tuned, watch that subjunctive, it isn't dead yet.

Other things to watch: watch for the increase in noun modifiers. For example, noun phrases like Teaching Company course lecture material. You'll notice there was no possessive in that string. Watch *slash* as a coordinator. Is it going to make it? And *because* as a preposition plus noun, *because* grammar. As I talked about, *on accident* seems to be coming into the language, and I think it might, in the long run, replace *by accident*. Much to my chagrin, *impactful* is making inroads into the language. I think I just have to give that one up. We've talked about quotative *like*. Quotative *like* might be here to stay as the way that many of us quote people in a story. He was *like,* she was *like,* that could be something someone said or that they thought. And here's one more to watch for, *hone in* will fully replace *home in.*

Let me tell you a funny story on this last one. I used to correct *hone in on* in student writing, and I would change it to *home in on*, and I will admit that I felt a little bit smug when I did it. I thought, "Ha ha, I know that this technically should be *home in*," and I would underline it and I'd write *home* above *hone,* and think, "I bet this student didn't know that." Now, historically I'm justified here, but I'm less justified in terms of current usage. *Home in* shows up in the 1920s and it has since taken on the metaphorical meaning of to focus on*,* to *home in* on something. That happened by the 1950s. By the 1960s, *hone in on* had taken on the same meaning. And you can imagine *hone*, meaning to sharpen, could come to take that meaning of focusing in on something.

Is *home in on* losing its status as the standard form or, at least, as the only standard form? This question was raised for me with this sentence that I read in a graduate student exam. Here's the sentence, "Or a tutor might home in on an argument which runs counter to the tutor's own beliefs." I was reading the sentence, and I thought, "Wow, *home in on* looks a little bit funny there." And the thing is, that I knew that the only reason that she had written *home in on* there was because I had underlined it in an earlier draft and written *home* over *hone*, which is what she'd written in the first draft. I went to look at Google Books with the Ngram Viewer, and what I discovered is that *home in on* is still more common, but the gap between *home in on* and *hone in on* has narrowed significantly. It raises the question for me of whether *home in* will eventually be replaced, and perhaps start to feel a little bit old-fashioned. And it was starting to look old-fashioned to me. It's why, in that graduate student paper, I noticed it because I thought, "Huh, that *home in on* is starting to look not quite right." The other possibility is that *hone in on* and *home in on* will continue to coexist as two standard forms being used synonymously. But I do wonder whether, at some point, writers will get criticized for using *home in on* instead of *hone in on.* In enforcing the rule, changing the *hone in on* to *home in on* was I being helpful or was I being persnickety? Was it like changing *nauseous* into *nauseated*, where there is this idea that nauseous means causing nausea, as in "The roller coaster was nauseous"? But for most of us, at this point, *nauseous* means *nauseated*, and I think it's being a little persnickety at this point to change *nauseous* into *nauseated*.

I tell this story to show that I still fall prey to enforcing distinctions that may not be fully justified. But I try to keep an open mind so that I will change my practices as needed. I've also learned to be very careful about how and when I alert other people to a usage issue. This is an extremely powerful move, to stop someone when they're talking and to go grammando on them. It can indicate to them that you're listening to how they are talking as much or more than to what they're saying. It's one thing if you're a teacher, and you're reading a piece of formal writing, and you're underlining things and writing a more standard usage above it. It's another thing if you're in conversation, anywhere. It can be a silencing move to stop someone and correct them, and we see this online when people are chatting or arguing online, and one of the most powerful moves you can make when you get really angry is to correct somebody else's grammar and to say, "You don't know what you're talking about. You don't even know how to use an apostrophe."

I remember a time in graduate school when I was talking to a friend of mine who used what linguists call a positive anymore. He said, "They sell shoes there anymore." And I said, "You're a positive anymore speaker!" At which point he looked like a deer caught in the headlights, and looked like he wanted to stop talking, which is exactly what he did. And I was, in fact, excited about what he just said, but he was struck by the fact that I called him out on the way he was using the language, not what he was saying. I also remember a story from my own schooling where I was in an English seminar, and I was saying the word rhetoric as rhetoric because I knew the word rhetorical and clearly hadn't heard rhetoric said out loud all that often. After class the professors were on the way out the door, just said to me "You know Anne, a lot of people say that 'rhetoric.'" It was the kindest correction, in private, not in front of other people.

What I hope we can do is embrace how much we care about language and use that caring for good. We can create beautiful prose—or clever prose or efficient prose or funny prose—in a variety of genres both formal and informal, being careful about how we use the language, being deliberate in our grammatical choices, without being unnecessarily or overly fussy.

Of course, we're going to notice things in language; that is my life. We'll notice typos, and then we can decide what we want to make of them. Was this just a quick e-mail, is this a sloppy proofreader, is this someone who didn't really care about the document, and do we want to draw conclusions from that, is this someone who's focusing their intellectual energies on other things and not on apostrophes. We'll also notice new grammatical developments in the language, and differences across regions and social groups. Of course, we'll notice these; we can't control that.

What we can control is what we think we know about that person based on that bit of grammar or based on their accent or a word choice that reflects what region they're from or what social group they identify with. And we can control what judgments we want to make based on that knowledge that we have. We can control any impulse we might have to go grammando when we hear something. Does that thought we had, that grammando-like thought, stay in our head or do we say it out loud? What is our goal? What is the context? Are we being helpful or hurtful? Are we sure we're right?

Let's think of ourselves as caretakers of the language, tending it to allow it to do its work in all its powerful, effective ways. To be effective, language both written and spoken must respond to its audience and context, which requires some flexibility in what kind of grammar is preferred. And as we've talked about, there are many English grammars; the formal written standard is just one of them.

To be effective formal written language benefits from consistency so as not to distract readers, and from minimizing ambiguity you're not there to clarify. And to be effective, language needs to be creative, to be allowed to surprise us and to adapt to the needs and desires of the speakers and writers who are both older and younger than we are. Next time you find yourself contemplating a grammatical construction that strikes your ear as not quite right if not downright wrong, imagine yourself being asked to judge its acceptability as if you were a member of the Usage Panel.

I hope this course has given you new tools and perspectives to approach that question, to think about what acceptability means in what context and how that may change over time. You've gained some key tools, for example, usage guides and an informed perspective on how you want to use those as a writer a speaker. You now can turn to Google Books and the Ngram Viewer and the Corpus of American Contemporary English and the Corpus of American Historical English to answer your questions about what's going on with grammar in different registers of the language.

With this knowledge and these tools, you can effectively be an advocate for—notice how I sidestepped the whole *advocate for* as a verb issue—you can be an advocate for what you see as the most effective language choices, be those more conservative or more playful, be those choices that stay within the boundaries of traditionally accepted usage or choices that exuberantly push the boundaries of accepted usage.

I hope you will remember that whatever you choose, be that to embrace tradition or to embrace change; you're following in the footsteps of many eloquent speakers and writers who precede us. In the end, to make those kinds of decisions about grammar more consciously and deliberately, with your descriptive and prescriptive grammatical ducks metaphorically lined up behind you, that, that is what it means to harness the power of language.

Thank you for spending these hours geeking out about grammar with me, sharing our peeves and our passions. May you split an infinitive when you need to. And strand a preposition when it sounds right. May you follow your gut and your heart about whether it should be *equally as important* or *equally important*. And may English grammar be one of your life's pleasures.

BIBLIOGRAPHY

The American Heritage Dictionary of the English Language. 5th ed. Boston; New York: Houghton Mifflin Harcourt, 2011.

The Associated Press Stylebook 2015. New York: The Associated Press, 2015. http:www.apstylebook.com.

Atkinson, Dwight. *Scientific Discourse in Sociohistorical Context*: The Philosophical Transactions of the Royal Society of London, *1675–1975*. Mahwah, NJ; London: Lawrence Erlbaum, 1999.

Bailey, Richard W. "Talking about Split Infinitives." *Michigan Today News-E* (June 2006). http://www.umich.edu/NewsE/06_06/words.html.

Balhorn, Mark. "The Epicene Pronoun in Contemporary Newspaper Prose." *American Speech* 84, no. 4 (2009): 391–413.

Baron, Dennis. *Grammar and Gender*. New Haven: Yale University Press, 1986.

Baugh, Albert C., and Thomas Cable. *A History of the English Language*. 5th ed. London: Routledge, 2002.

Biber, Douglas, Stig Johannson, Geoffrey Leech, Susan Conrad, and Edward Finegan. 1999. *Longman Grammar of Spoken and Written English*. Harlow: Pearson, 1999.

Biber, Douglas, Susan Conrad, Randi Reppen, and Pat Byrd. "Speaking and Writing in the University: A Multidimensional Comparison." *TESOL Quarterly* 36, no. 1 (2002): 9–48.

Bodine, Ann. "Androcentrism in Prescriptive Grammar: Singular 'They,' Sex-Indefinite 'He,' and 'He or She.'" *Language in Society* 4, no. 2 (1975): 129–146.

Chapman, Don. "The Eighteenth-century Grammarians as Language Experts." In *Grammars, Grammarians and Grammar-Writing in Eighteenth-Century England*, edited by Ingrid Tieken-Boon van Ostade, 21–36. Berlin; New York: Mouton de Gruyter, 2008.

Collins, Peter C. "*Get*-passives in English." *World Englishes* 15, no.1 (1996): 43–56.

Crawford, William J. "Verb Agreement and Disagreement: A Corpus Investigation of Concord Variation in Existential *There + Be* Constructions." *Journal of English Linguistics* 33, no.1 (2005): 35–61.

Crystal, David. *The Fight for English: How Language Pundits Ate, Shot, and Left*. Oxford: Oxford University Press, 2006.

———. *Making A Point: The Persnickety Story of English Punctuation*. New York: St. Martin's Press, 2015.

———. *The Stories of English*. New York: Overlook, 2004.

———. *Txting: The Gr8 Deb8*. Oxford: Oxford University Press, 2008.

Curzan, Anne. *Fixing English: Prescriptivism and Language History*. Cambridge: Cambridge University Press, 2014.

———. *Gender Shifts in the History of English*. Cambridge: Cambridge University Press, 2003.

Curzan, Anne and Michael Adams. *How English Works: A Linguistic Introduction*. 3rd ed. New York: Pearson Longman, 2012.

Dailey-O'Cain, Jennifer. "The Sociolinguistic Distribution of and Attitudes toward Focuser 'Like' and Quotative 'Like.'" *Journal of Sociolinguistics* 4, no. 1 (2000): 60–80.

D'Arcy, Alexandra. "Functional Partitioning and Possible Limits on Variability: A View of Adjective Comparison from the Vernacular." *Journal of English Linguistics* 43, no. 3 (2014): 218–244.

———. "*Like* and Language Ideology: Disentangling Fact from Fiction." *American Speech* 82, no. 4 (2007): 386–419.

Davies, Mark. *Corpus of Contemporary American English*. http://corpus.byu.edu/coca/.

———. *Corpus of Historical American* English. http://corpus.byu.edu/coha/.

———. TIME *Magazine Corpus*. http://corpus.byu.edu/time/.

Dictionary of American Regional English. Ed. Frederic G. Cassidy, Joan Houston Hall, and others. Cambridge, MA: Belknap Press of Harvard University Press, 1985–2011.

Finegan, Edward. "Usage." In *The Cambridge History of the English Language, Volume VI: English in North America*, edited by John Algeo, 358–421. Cambridge: Cambridge University Press, 2001.

Fleisher, Nicholas. "The Origin of Passive *Get*." *English Language and Linguistics* 10, no. 2 (2006): 225–252.

Fogarty, Mignon. *Grammar Girl: Quick and Dirty Tips*. http://www.quickanddirtytips.com/grammar-girl.

Fowler, H. W., and F. G. Fowler. 1906. *The King's English*. Oxford: Clarendon Press.

Fowler, H.W. *A Dictionary of Modern English Usage.* 2nd ed., revised by Sir Ernest Gowers. New York; Oxford: Oxford University Press, 1965 (reissued in 1996).

Garner, Bryan A. *A Dictionary of Modern American Usage.* New York; Oxford: Oxford University Press, 1998.

———. *Garner's Modern American Usage.* 3rd ed. Oxford: Oxford UP, 2009.

Gilman, E. Ward, ed. *Merriam-Webster's Dictionary of English Usage.* Springfield, MA: Merriam-Webster, 1994.

Google Books Ngram Viewer. https://books.google.com/ngrams.

Gopen, George D., and Judith A. Swan. "The Science of Scientific Writing." *American Scientist* 78, no. 6 (1990): 550–558.

Green, Lisa. *African American English: A Linguistic Introduction.* Cambridge: Cambridge University Press, 2002.

Greenbaum, Sidney. *Oxford English Grammar.* London: Oxford University Press, 1996.

Grossman, Ellie. *The Grammatically Correct Handbook.* New York: Hyperion, 1997.

Hartwell, Patrick. "Grammar, Grammars, and the Teaching of Grammar." *College English* 47, no. 2 (1985): 105–127.

Huddleston, Rodney, and Geoffrey K. Pullum. *The Cambridge Grammar of the English Language.* Cambridge: Cambridge University Press, 2002.

———. *A Student Introduction to English Grammar.* Cambridge: Cambridge University Press, 2005.

Language Log. http://languagelog.ldc.upenn.edu/nll/.

Leech, Geoffrey, Marianne Hundt, Christian Mair, and Nicholas Smith. 2009. *Change in Contemporary English: A Grammatical Study*. Cambridge: Cambridge University Press.

Lingua Franca: Language and Writing in Academe. http://chronicle.com/blogs/linguafranca/.

Lippi-Green, Rosina. *English with an Accent: Language, Ideology, and Discrimination in the United States*. 2nd ed. London; New York: Routledge, 2011.

Lowth, Robert. *A Short Introduction to English Grammar*. London, 1762.

Maddox, Maeve. "A Historic vs. An Historic." *Daily Writing Tips*. http://www.dailywritingtips.com/a-historic-vs-an-historic/.

McWhorter, John. 1998. *Word on the Street: Debunking the Myth of a "Pure" Standard English*. Cambridge, MA: Perseus, 1998.

———. "A Matter of Fashion." *The New York Times Opinionator* (July 9, 2012). http://opinionator.blogs.nytimes.com/2012/07/09/a-matter-of-fashion/.

Millward, C. M., and Mary Hayes. *A Biography of the English Language*. 3rd ed. Boston: Wadsworth, 2011.

Newman, Michael. *Epicene Pronouns: The Linguistics of Prescriptive Problem*. New York; London: Garland, 1997.

Nunberg, Geoffrey. The Decline of Grammar. *The Atlantic Monthly* (December 1983): 31–46.

O'Conner, Patricia, and Stewart Kellerman. "Grammarphobia: Grammar, Etymology, Usage, and More." http://www.grammarphobia.com/.

Oxford English Dictionary, online. 1989 (2nd ed.), 2007– (new ed.). Oxford University Press. http://www.oed.com.

Parkes, Malcolm B. *Pause and Effect: An Introduction to the History of Punctuation in the West.* Burlington: Ashgate, 1992.

Perales-Escudero, Moisés D. "To Split or To Not Split: The Split Infinitive Past and Present." *Journal of English Linguistics* 39, no. 4 (2011): 313–334.

Pinker, Steven. *The Sense of Style.* New York: Viking, 2014.

Pullum, Geoffrey K. " 50 Years of Stupid Grammar Advice." *The Chronicle of Higher Education* (April 17, 2009). http://chronicle.com/article/50-Years-of-Stupid-Grammar/25497.

Schiffrin, Deborah. *Discourse Markers.* Cambridge: Cambridge University Press, 1987.

Skinner, David. *The Story of Ain't: America, Its Language, and the Most Controversial Dictionary Ever Published.* New York: Harper, 2012.

Strunk, William, and E. B. White. *The Elements of Style.* 3rd ed. New York: Macmillan, 1979.

Swales, John. "Attended and Unattended 'This' in Academic Writing: A Long and Unfinished Story." ESP Malaysia 11 (2005): 1–15.

Tagliamonte, Sali, and Chris Roberts. "So Weird; So Cool; So Innovative: The Use of Intensifiers in the Television Series *Friends.*" *American Speech* 80, no. 3 (2005): 280–300.

Tieken-Boon van Ostade, Ingrid. 1982. "Double Negation and Eighteenth-Century English Grammars. *Neophilologus* 66, no. 2 (1982): 278–285.

———, Ingrid. 2011. *The Bishop's Grammar: Robert Lowth and the Rise of Prescriptivism.* Oxford: Oxford University Press, 2011.

Truss, Lynne. 2003. *Eats, Shoots & Leaves: The Zero Tolerance Approach to Punctuation.* New York: Gotham Books.

Vuolo, Mike. "Between You and I." *Lexicon Valley Podcast*. Episode No. 3. http://www.slate.com/articles/podcasts/lexicon_valley/2012/02/lexicon_valley_why_we_keep_saying_between_you_and_i_.html.

———. "So..." *Lexicon Valley Podcast*. Episode No. 7. http://www.slate.com/articles/podcasts/lexicon_valley/2012/04/lexicon_valley_beginning_and_ending_all_of_our_thoughts_with_so_.html.

Webster's Third New International Dictionary of the English Language. 1961. Ed. Philip Gove and others. Springfield, MA: G. and C. Merriam, 1961.

Williams, Joseph M. *Style: Ten Lessons in Clarity and Grace*. 8th ed. New York: Pearson Longman, 2008.

Yagoda, Ben. *When You Catch an Adjective, Kill It: The Parts of Speech, for Better and/or Worse*. New York: Broadway Books, 2007.

Yáñez-Bouza, Nuria. "To End or Not to End a Sentence with a Preposition: An 18th-century Debate." In *Perspectives on Prescriptivism*, edited by Joan C. Beal, Carmela Nocera, and Massimo Sturiale, 237-264, 2008. Bern: Peter Lang.

Zimmer, Ben. "A Misattribution No Longer To Be Put Up With." *Language Log* (December 12, 2004). http://itre.cis.upenn.edu/~myl/languagelog/archives/001715.html.

IMAGE CREDITS

NOTES

NOTES

NOTES

NOTES